Developing
Sybase®
Applications

SAMS
PUBLISHING

201 West 103rd Street
Indianapolis, Indiana 46290

To all of you
who have worked with me
on systems
in the past,
your intelligence, commit-
ment, and effort
have been an inspiration.

And to my sons,
Alexander and Tristan,
for your understanding
and patience
while Dad was away so
much
at work.

Copyright © 1995 by Sams Publishing

FIRST EDITION

International Standard Book Number: 0-672-30700-6

Library of Congress Catalog Card Number: 95-67644

98   97   96   95   4   3   2   1

Interpretation of the printing code: the rightmost double-digit number is the year of the book's printing; the rightmost single-digit, the number of the book's printing. For example, a printing code of 95-1 shows that the first printing of the book occurred in 1995.

Composed in AGaramond and MCPdigital by Macmillan Computer Publishing

Printed in the United States of America

Trademarks

Overview

Section 8   Auditing Your Sybase Applications

Contents

Section 2   Overview of the Client/Server Development Process

Section 3   Tools of Choice

Section 4   Application Concepts

Section 5 Design

Section 6   Implementation of the Design

Section 7   Client/Server Applications Development Support

Acknowledgments

Much to my surprise, I find that some people actually do read the acknowledgments. Although it's never possible to fully credit the contribution that any given person makes to a work such as this, there are a number of people who deserve special mention.

In no particular order, I would like to thank Bob Culmer, Rick Hess, and Chris Meggs for helping me to gain a fuller understanding of client/server development from the standpoint of a mainframe migration. I would also like to thank Zuhair Shlah, Brian Ellert, Grant Stanford, and Dave Novak for giving me the opportunity to work with one of the largest SQL Server implementations anywhere.

The Amoco Canada team, with whom I worked closely during the writing of this manuscript, were especially helpful and contributed to this book in myriad ways. I'd like to single out Kevin Butler for his encyclopedic grasp of indexing, query performance, and problem diagnosis. Then there is the notorious ZMEG 10, Mike Gallagher, who has a greater appetite for disk space than any other human in the hemisphere. And, most definitely Greg Berry, whose experienced and well-reasoned opinions on development techniques, among other topics, helped me to refine my own positions.

Deeply felt appreciation goes to the entire CausesDB team: Jannette Anderson, Sue Carter, John Daum, Marsh Duncanson, Dennis Kao, Joe Unelli, Rick Wattling, and Marie Worden. Without you, there would be no application.

Thanks to the many people who provided me with insight on the behavior and future of the many tools discussed in this book; and thanks to John Matthews for his assessment of Visual Basic. Rick Wattling deserves notice again for sharing his outlook and opinions about the direction of client/server in billion-dollar, global companies.

My editors as well deserve a note of thanks for keeping me focused and lucid. Dean Miller, Susan Christophersen, Kezia Endsley, and Chris Denny, take a bow.

Last but not least, to those of you who helped but who I've not had space to mention explicitly, thanks. You know who you are, and so do I.

About the Author

Daniel J. Worden has published, among other articles and systems-related topics, *Sybase Developer's Guide* (also from Sams), which has been recently translated into Chinese. He is on the faculty of Clark University as an Adjunct Professor for the Client/Server continuing education program. Mr. Worden is President and founder of Word N Systems, a client/server consulting and training firm that has provided seminars and systems expertise throughout North America since 1991. He first began architecting and implementing communications-based information systems in 1982 and has specialized in UNIX, PCs, and relational database technology since 1985.

Introduction

When it comes to client/server systems, keeping up with the Joneses is not only a good idea, it's essential. Everyone is getting into the act these days and new products, techniques, and discoveries abound. This book has been written for anyone who works, or is expecting to work, on a Sybase application development project.

Previously, when you said Sybase, you meant SQL Server. With the incorporatation of PowerBuilder and Watcom into the Sybase fold, developing Sybase applications means developing true GUI-based, client/server systems.

In the course of this book, you'll find every aspect of developing client/server systems covered.

Analysis and design techniques, modified to take advantage of client/server technology, are introduced, along with specific and practical recommendations for how to structure these phases for your project. The technology itself is reviewed, including explanations of various features and how they can be applied in a development setting. Also, specific products are used as examples of how to best take full advantage of the features offered in the Sybase architecture.

Drawing from the my own background as a designer and manager of client/server systems based on Sybase, I have tried to encapsulate all of the lessons learned from experience. This should prove helpful to those of you who are facing a new application development project in which the stakes are high and the time frames short. In fact, I talked extensively with dozens of developers who have lived through the learning curve and shared their observations and cautions throughout the book.

Anyone who has worked in a mainframe environment and who is now investigating the GUI, event-driven, relational, and distributed features inherent in client/server technology will benefit from reading this book. In the first section I specifically address the aspects of your background that are applicable to the new environment and I identify elements that are vastly different from the older mainframe model.

This book focuses on a high-level treatment of the design, development, and support aspects of building client/server systems using Sybase. The techniques and practices are relevant for any client/server technology, but all of the examples and case studies use Sybase and related technology.

Anyone looking a review of the SQL Server product with features and syntax should check out my first book, *Sybase Developer's Guide*. If you have already read it, hey, good to see you again!

Like the first book, the writing style for Developing Sybase Applications is meant to be somewhat entertaining as well as informative. I would be gratified to hear that some of the stuff actually made people laugh.

In any case, the responsibility for developing Sybase applications is not taken lightly and I think that this book can serve you well, not only in meeting that challenge, but in helping to make your development effort shine.

The sample applications provided on the CD with this book include source code for PowerBuilder 4.0 and Visual Basic 3.0. If you're developing with either of these tools, you should find some of the logic quite useful for your own purposes. Others will find the sample application to be an interesting example of what you can do with Sybase technology as it helps to illustrate the principles laid out in the book.

I'd like to thank you, the reader, for picking up this book, and I hope that it provides you with some useful insight or practical tips that can be applied to your Sybase applications now and in the future.

Daniel J. Worden

1

Prerequisites

Introduction to the Section

Frequently, people want to jump right into things and get on with it. Developing your first Sybase application may be no exception. Still, experience shows that it is important to make some preparations before getting underway.

Anyone who has ever bought some assembly required furniture can tell you that the first thing to do is check that you have all the screws, bolts, nails, tools, and instructions. This section will cover all the things that you need to have or should know before getting down to work on your first Sybase application.

False starts and new directions are endemic to client/server technology. By working through this section, and ensuring that you have all the necessary ingredients, you can get your Sybase application off on the right foot.

By the end of this section, you will have been introduced to the approach I take to developing client/server systems, the audience to which the book is geared, and the process of successfully applying Sybase and related technologies to your organizations strategies. The issues surrounding the selection of tools will also be explored to ensure that you have the right tools for the job. Finally, the specific Sybase project that this book undertakes will be explained.

Thanks for reading. I hope you find the book a practical and useful description of how Sybase can be used in developing successful client/server systems in your organization.

1.1

How to Use this Book

Like any tool, this book is designed to be read and used in a certain way. This is not to say that you won't find your own unique way to interpret and apply what you find here, but it's always best to state the objectives and define the terms used at the outset.

Before getting down to the business of developing Sybase applications, I will cover who this book is written for and some of the assumptions I have made in writing it.

Who this Book Is For

I would like to tell you that everyone should read this book, but I won't. This book is designed to lay down the concepts, detail the components, and explore the implications and issues of developing client/server applications in Sybase. It is intended primarily for people interested in the methods and techniques used in this process and will most benefit those who wish to avoid the mistakes made by pioneers and earlier adopters of the technology.

The key focus is at the technical manager or project leader level. Whatever role you play in your development effort, this book is intended for those who want to understand the Sybase development process.

Client/server programmers may appreciate seeing the broader scope of where their team project fits into the overall scheme of things or how the technology supports the larger objectives of the organization. Systems architects and planners will get a great deal of value from the discussions of how Sybase solutions should be integrated into an overall framework. Primarily, however, this book is oriented to those who are looking for ways to manage the introduction and integration of Sybase products into their organizations.

This book will be especially useful for people embarking on their first client/server implementation. I have assumed that you as a reader are familiar with the general process of building systems: analysis, planning, specifications, development, testing, and so on. However, this book does not require that you know the workings of a relational SQL database such as Sybase SQL Server.

The focus of *Developing Sybase Applications* is on the techniques and methods you can use to successfully identify a business problem that can be solved using client/server technology.

As you progress through the book, you'll find that *Developing Sybase Applications* addresses both the server side of development as well as the issues surrounding the integration of front-end GUI applications.

On the whole, my intent was to provide a complete end-to-end review of the systems development process with specific focus on using Sybase products. It should be highly relevant for experienced developers coming from traditional mainframe environments, or for single-user PC application developers.

Why You Should Read this Book

The biggest single benefit you will receive from reading this book is to gain an understanding of the Sybase development process. Like other areas of life, implementing client/server solutions is a jungle, and this book will serve as a map.

This book takes a slightly different tack than many systems books. It is about how the technology is used, rather than about the technology's features and functions. As you read it, you will begin to frame your thinking around how to apply those features directly to your organizations systems requirements.

You will gain the benefit of insight into other peoples mistakes and, more important, their successes in working with Sybase technology. You will have the opportunity not to reinvent the wheel, but to refine it and adapt it to meet the specific needs of your unique situation. Sybase technology is fundamentally about integration, and this book covers all the elements you need to pull together, as well as making practical suggestions for accomplishing this integration.

Relating the Book to Your Situation

There will be a consistent and recurring emphasis on how you can make the techniques covered in this book work for you in your organization. Necessarily, some of the descriptions are generic, but I then discuss various ways to adapt and apply that description to a specific situation. Of course, ultimately, it is entirely your responsibility to apply not only this book but all of the client/server technology with which you work to your requirements.

The good news is that the approach taken to the subject matter will first cover general principals, and then mitigating factors, and finally the implications of the various choices you can make. Sybase and associated technologies provide a wide range of potential combinations, each with a feature set, advantages, and trade-offs. Throughout this book you will be shown the advantages and disadvantages of a particular approach, and then see how it can be modified to change those pros and cons. Implementing Sybase solutions means facing a wide array of choices and integrating a fundamentally complex feature set.

There is rarely a right or a wrong way to go about applying the technology; it is merely a question of greater or lesser returns. The key is to orient your technology to meet your requirement, and this book addresses the specific questions that must be answered for you to accomplish this.

Author's Background

Of course, a book of this nature has to be the direct result of a particular individual's or group's experience. To help you gain a better appreciation of how this book has come to be, and the assumptions under which it has been written, you should probably have some idea of the writer's background (that's me).

On the other hand, this book is about you and your Sybase project, not about me, so I will keep it reasonably brief.

Experience with the Tools

I have worked with communications-based systems since 1982; specifically, I have been responsible for analyzing business requirements, designing systems solutions to meet them, acquiring and implementing the technology, and managing the systems people who are responsible for making it happen. In the mid-1980s, I became heavily involved in UNIX mini-computers, Novell, and relational databases. By the late 1980s I was convinced that Microsoft Windows had a future, and I have worked with Sybase SQL Server and Windows-based PCs since 1990. My consulting company was incorporated in 1991, and we have a solid core of experienced client/server developers, trainers, architects, and designers on staff.

As you might expect, to play so many roles—especially during the earlier part of my career—I worked with relatively small systems. Primarily, my systems were departmental or division-wide in scope. For the past couple of years I have been involved as an advisor to larger shops with scores of SQL Servers throughout their organizations and data volumes with tables measured in gigabytes and millions of rows.

All this has helped me gain an appreciation for all sides of the client/server architecture and application development process.

For those of you who prefer to qualify the people they find standing on soapboxes and spouting their professional opinions, I will also mention that my previous book on Sybase, *Sybase Developer's Guide* (also from Sams) has been well received. It has recently been translated into Chinese.

As well, I have been training and lecturing on client/server development in organizations and conferences throughout North America. The feedback from these sessions has helped me understand the wide range of backgrounds and challenges that you as readers face.

Tried in the Trenches

Well, enough about me. The main point of interest for you will probably be that the observations and suggestions made in this book are from an implementer's perspective. Although I have spent time writing and instructing on client/server systems, the bulk of my career has been spent as an Information Systems manager making the technology do something worthwhile. If that's your job, believe me, you have my sympathies!

The real key to success is to be practical, applicable, and relevant. The theoretical stuff is best left to those employed in ivory towers. All the material covered in this book has been tested in the field, and you gain the benefit of the results: good, bad, and indifferent.

A Dynamic Process

Even if some of what you find in these pages is the latest word in client/server development techniques, rest assured that it won't be the last word. This industry is enjoying (or enduring) some of the most rapid evolution of any discipline in the 20th century.

The half life for products is measured in months, not years, and dramatic new offerings and capabilities are brought out in an avalanche of innovation. Far from being mature, the client/server arena is just now beginning the maturation process, especially in regard to Sybase products. And the techniques you will find in this book are evolving just as rapidly.

There are those who would argue that client/server is not unique in its rapid-pace of development. Although this is true to an extent, client/server systems integrate virtually all of the other components of the systems world, causing its rate of change to be exponentially fed by the rapid change elsewhere in the industry.

Advances in hardware, software, development techniques, and problem-solving workarounds in a client/server system span the range of all systems and communications components on the market today. The key to staying on top of this change (or at least coping with it) is to communicate with others in the same boat.

As part of the communication process, I have been committed to sharing my experience with client/server technology generally and using Sybase products specifically. Other people and organizations have been quick to assimilate that experience and add their own hard-won observations. This feedback dynamic has resulted in a widely applicable client/server development methodology that you can use and adapt to help you successfully implement your first Sybase application.

One way that my company assists in this process is by publishing a newsletter, *Client/Server Technology Watch*. In it we take the down-and-in experiences of developers using Sybase, PowerBuilder, and other products and relay not only their real-life experience but, frequently, the how-to at the syntax level. There is contact information about us at the back of this book.

Specific Objectives

Now that you have an idea of the audience for this book and the background assumptions of the author, I would like to get down to the specific objectives this book must reach to be successful. Using these objectives, you can determine whether this is the right book for you at the right time, or whether you need to pursue a different line of investigation to meet your needs.

Objective One: Understanding the Development Methodology

Developing Sybase Applications addresses the need for new developers to have a methodology for developing systems in a client/server architecture incorporating the SQL Server database engine.

Any rapidly evolving technology should have a mechanism for describing what works and what doesn't. The biggest single problem with client/server technology (and Sybase is no exception) is the complexity that must be managed. As already stated, the problem is fundamentally one of integration. The number of specific considerations to be managed increases geometrically with the number of products and scope of the problem to be addressed.

A methodology is not a cookbook and it will not relieve you of the responsibility of actually preparing the ingredients yourself. At the same time, an effective methodology will describe the necessary steps and prepare you for the implications as you take each one.

Structured Systems Development Methodologies were developed primarily for big systems by the aircraft manufacturers in the 1960s. These were promoted as the key to business systems savings in the 70s, and the bloom came off the rose in the 1980s. Commercial offerings of these methodologies were characterized as cumbersome, rigid, and expensive.

Yet, organizations have still struggled to create a common systems development framework. A common definition of terms is vital in any enterprise involving more than one human, and systems development is no exception.

To assist in this, *Developing Sybase Applications* will propose a five-stage development cycle, designed specifically to address client/server projects. Also, you will be introduced to common products that perform functions ranging from application generation to automated testing and building help files. Taken together, this book will make sense of methods, products, and techniques for building effective Sybase applications.

With the unprecedented rate of change that were seeing in the client/server world, it's not reasonable to try to replace our existing legacy systems, aggressively adopt emerging technology, and risk our mission critical applications without some common understanding as to how this work is performed. This is the purpose of a systems development methodology, and this book will propose one that is open, flexible, and inexpensive.

Objective Two: Identifying Development Techniques Used by Sybase

There are many different ways to climb the client/server mountain, and even if the view from the top is the same, the problems posed by each route vary greatly. To discuss development techniques in a general sense might be a useful exercise, but in this book you will be brought back to the assumption that you are working with Sybase and SQL Server as a core technology.

As you read through this book, you should gain a sense of being involved in a typical Sybase project, one of the key characteristics of which is the number of other products involved.

Because Sybase has acquired Powersoft and, through that, Watcom, the range of Sybase products has been extended to windows-based tools and work group databases. The various options open to you as a systems designer and developer is covered.

Just as important, you will actually get to follow through the development of our sample application, using SQL Server, Watcom, PowerBuilder 4.0, and Visual Basic. The source code for the application is contained on the CD attached to the back of the book.

Throughout the book you will be treated to discussions of the features and benefits of products that work specifically with Sybase and SQL Server. ER-Win, for example, is a data modeling tool that connects to SQL Server and automatically creates database objects from the model. How and why to use these product families is covered in this book.

Objective Three: Incorporating Good Management Techniques

One absolutely critical factor in developing successful client/server applications is the level of management provided to the development effort. In fact, your chances of success are directly related to the quality of the project and business management practiced in your organization. Bad management, characterized by arbitrary deadlines and directions, lack of communication or positive feedback, and unrealistic demands and disregard for the people doing the work, will kill your project.

The interesting thing about dysfunctional management is that those who are exhibiting the behavior rarely recognize it for what it is. As such, they are in no position to modify their behavior and increase their chances for success. With this book, I hope to help transform bad management behaviors into effective ones. Okay, I'll grant you that this goal is not only unlikely but impossible. Well, would you settle for a book that identifies good management techniques as practiced in other client/server projects and raises red flags on behaviors with potentially deleterious effects? What seems to be lacking in many client/server methodologies is a recognition that humans are actually trying to implement these systems and follow these guidelines. Any endeavor with people involved is intrinsically flawed. The objective of this section is to provide useful, practical, and realistic advice for implementing successful Sybase solutions. To do that, you will need to see how the human factors can be identified and managed.

Of course, the idea that you the reader may be a management-level individual who has some less-than-perfect management techniques never occurred to me. What's more likely is that you work for someone like that and you will photocopy the relevant pages to give them to your manager before he drives everyone crazy and blows the project.

Specific management techniques range from how to select and manage user involvement to addressing the need for an external auditor to review your project. The emphasis is on first understanding the requirement, and then identifying an appropriate attitude, followed by recommended steps to take in planning and implementing your Sybase project.

Objective Four: Experiencing a Complete Development Process

Most people only really begin to understand something that they can actually see, touch, and taste. Although some of you will no doubt be able to immediately incorporate the somewhat abstract recommendations immediately into your development effort, many will not. To make this book as useful as possible, I have opted to include the development of a complete application as part of the text and ship the application along with the book.

I like this idea very much, partially because I develop Sybase systems for a living (and including the application makes the book a little easier to write), but more because it shows how the general observations about Sybase can be applied. Balancing the processing between the client and the server, for example, is one of the key considerations in the technical tuning of a Sybase application. It's extremely difficult to reduce these considerations to general rules that will be relevant for every application, server configuration, client platform in use, and network scheme.

However, by walking you through the development decision points and tradeoffs that I face when developing a specific Sybase application, it should be easier for you to identify the issues, and to relate that process back to your situation. This is a major concern for those of us involved in creating this book. We want you to get a lot of useful and valid information out of this publication, to retain it, and most important, to effectively apply your knowledge to your environment.

Objective Five: Adopting a How To Approach

As you might have noticed in the previous objectives, this book was designed to take a different slant on Sybase technology. It is focused on how to build applications and use the Sybase products, instead of describing feature by feature the products technological capabilities. True, we do want to ensure that the how to is applicable to Sybase, hence the name of the book. And we are providing you with an application that was developed using the toolset. However, the key consideration for this objective is that if you do not already know something about the technology, you may want to come back to this book after learning some of the basics.

This is not to imply that you have to know the Sybase products inside and out before you can get anything out of reading this. I just wanted to make it clear from the outset that this book employs a practical focus on how to use the technology and doesn't go into any great depth talking about how the products themselves work. For those of you who want an overview of the Sybase organization, product line, and feature set, you might want to read (or reread) *Sybase Developer's Guide*.

Enough sales promotion! By reading this book, you should gain a better understanding of how the technology is used and how implementation drives certain compromises and design decisions. The key objective for this book is to describe how you can get the business advantages needed from the client/server technology as you move through the design and implementation phases.

Summary

At this point, you should have a clear idea of the objectives and assumptions I held while writing this book. You should know to whom the book is directed, and you should have a sense of my background and experience, which directly affects its content and, no doubt, its relevance in certain situations.

Wherever possible, you will find recommendations that can be generally applied. This book is not intended to become easily dated with the next version of Sybase products introduced to the market. First and foremost, it is about using Sybase technology to build client/server systems.

I would also hope that it has been clearly stated that you and I are forming a partnership as you read this book. It is not my job to tell you what to do. There are too many unknowns for that advice to be either workable or valuable. I can, however, show you how other people and myself have successfully built systems with this technology in the past, and raise the key questions that would come up in a new development environment. With luck, reading this book will provide you with enough information to launch you on your own successful project.

1.2

What You Need to Get Started

Introduction

At this point, you should have determined that, yes, this approach to developing client/server systems can be of value to you and your organization. In this chapter, you will read about preconditions that should be satisfied before you can really begin the development process with any amount of confidence. Preparation is an important component to success in any endeavor, and the client/server graveyard is littered with the corpses of the careers of those who underestimated the difficulty involved. Because you are reading this book, I can assume that you have no intention of joining that number.

As you progress through this chapter you will see that there are a number of things that you already know, and they are significant. Of course, once your confidence has been built up, I will immediately move to all the things you don't know and need to know in order to succeed in developing Sybase applications, but that comes later in the chapter.

As an ancient Chinese general said, if you know yourself and know your opponent, you will win all of your battles. This chapter will take you through a checklist of skills you need, and by reading it you will be in a better position to value what you already know, to understand how your background can lead you into false assumptions about Sybase applications development, and to determine what training you still require.

Give Yourself Credit

One of the important values that I was taught while growing up was to give credit where credit is due. (I've tried explaining it to my bank manager, but some people are very resistant.) In any case, you should take the time to evaluate your own background and set of skills to appreciate your own value and the contribution you can make to your project.

Don't underestimate the value of experience. In many organizations, people are given the impression that they had better move to client/server technology or they will be out on the street. In some organizations this is probably true, but it is rather rude to say so. The first effect of presenting new technology in this way is to make people feel awkward and frequently stupid. You must take the time to identify what you already know and how this can be applied to a new system built with Sybase technology.

The Logical Mind

Right off the bat, experienced developers have an analytic outlook. Experience in reviewing problems and determining potential solutions is directly applicable to building systems regardless of the technology used. Interestingly (at least to me), this is not a quality shared by many people outside the technical area. Obviously, that includes many of our systems users. As systems people, we tend to think that the rest of the world sees things in a similiar fashion, but it doesn't. With Sybase technology, it's not only possible but desirable to include all the players involved with building and using the system. In many cases, this includes end users who don't necessarily have the same analytic skills or logical processes that you, as an experienced systems developer, have developed and honed.

Another attribute of systems people is a high degree of problem-solving abilities. This is not a characteristic shared by most, say, golf pros. Or, for that matter, users, whether they are in finance, sales marketing, or management. As a systems person, you are more likely to be able to use your logical mind to break problems down into constituent parts and work through various methodologies to solve them.

At this point I have probably demonstrated my complete ignorance of just how much perception, evaluation, and judgment is required of a good golfer. I hope this doesn't mislead you from the point; in general, systems people require and rely on their analytical abilities.

This is an especially critical skill when building client/server systems. Even if you do not have the first idea about client/server technology, this underlying ability will serve you well as you learn and gain experience.

Understand the Major Concepts First

I have met a number of individuals who consistently develop applications across multiple platforms. Windows, Mac, Motif, OS/2, NextStep, it doesn't seem to matter to them which; each has its strengths and weaknesses. The interesting thing about people who do this, or people who are good at picking up languages, is their focus on concepts first and syntax second. It seems that if you know what should be done, and you know how to go about doing it, actually framing the correct syntax becomes easier. In fact, people who move from one platform to another consistently use the wrong syntax until they get back into the groove, as it were (typing `dir` rather than `ls` to get a file listing on a UNIX system, for example, or vice versa). It's more annoying than anything else.

On the opposite end of the spectrum are people who choose to master a single technology. Whether that technology is as obscure as ADA or as common as Lotus 1-2-3, the world is filled with proponents of a particular expertise. The problem with such an orientation is that it makes it difficult for people to accept that they don't have to have mastery of an environment to the "magic words" level to be effective Sybase developers.

What is absolutely critical is to understand the conceptual framework, first for designing solutions and then for problem solving and optimization. Having a firm grasp of the key concepts allows you to move from one language or development environment to another without wasting much time.

Your experience gives you many of the concepts you need. Through other means, such as reading this book and other training, you will be in a better position to flesh out your concepts. This in turn will allow you to bring that framework to the specific tools that you have to work with when designing and implementing your Sybase application.

Know Your Environment

Consultants frequently move from one company to another, requiring them to quickly become familiar with new development environments and organizational cultures. Even when systems professionals become good at this process, they will still miss subtle but important things that are understood and taken for granted by people who have worked in the environment for some time. If you have many years invested with your organization, this understanding of the culture and the business can be a real strength when implementing client/server systems.

It's important, however, not to prejudge your environment. Too often, people refer to past failures or objections and let this drive their vision of what can be accomplished with any new system. On the other hand, someone coming fresh into the organization is unaware of what was tried and failed in the past, and may propose a similar solution. This new system may then succeed due to differences in timing, technology, or management commitment.

Let your understanding of the environment help you frame solutions, rather than provide you with reasons why any new efforts are doomed. By shaking yourself loose from the confines of the past, while maintaining your understanding of the organization's long-term goals and underlying culture, you can help position your new Sybase system for success.

Have Confidence in Learning Technology

You've done it before; you can do it again. As you prepare for your new client/server system, be sure to review the other major environments that you've learned to use in the past. If managing complexity is the single biggest problem with client/server systems, staying with the learning curve is a close second. There is a mountain of detail, on top of a broad base of new concepts that must be fully encompassed before you will feel comfortable with the technologies.

As an experienced systems person, you know which technologies you mastered in the past, and this should provide you with a source of confidence that you are competent to learn the new client/server concepts, architecture, and syntax.

Be Open to New Concepts

Unlearning restrictions from past systems is one of the key hurdles to be faced by those of you who are already familiar with more traditional technologies. When you were new to the work force—fresh-faced, bright-eyed, bushy-tailed, and so on—you were eager to learn. As time went on, if you are like most people, you came to have a certain vested interest in the skills already acquired. To move to the new tools, you need to adopt that attitude of a student, allowing yourself to absorb new systems concepts and capabilities. Constant change is a feature of the new client/server environment. To accommodate it, you must learn to learn.

As an experienced systems professional, you have an advantage over those who are just starting out, as the new technologies are built on many of the same concepts as older technologies. Indexes and logic loops, for example, work much the same way in a relational database as on more traditional mainframe systems. You will be able to reuse a great deal of that knowledge in the move to client/server.

The key here is that you applied yourself to the process of learning these things once, and you can feel confidence in your ability to acquire new skills and put them to work.

Moving Up from PCs

Having established that you can reuse your experience in systems, it's important to establish which area of systems your time has been spent on. The systems business is rather large, and client/server solutions invariably mean integrating diverse technologies.

You can assume that, regardless of how experienced you are in any one area of computing, when you move to client/server, you will be exposed to new things. Within the major computing environments, there are certain key concepts that need to be gained in the move to client/server. There are features of one's familiar environment that are kept as well. Over the next few pages, I will review the strengths and weaknesses of the PC components of a client/server system.

PC Developer Strengths

PCs allow and encourage a great degree of customization of individual users' systems and software. Necessarily, developers for PC environments are accustomed to thinking of individual choice as a key requirement for these systems. This translates into a willingness to accommodate users and provide them with a range of solutions and options. In turn, this is perceived as a high degree of service to the users, which can make or break a client/server project.

Personal computers also have a history of working with graphical user interfaces, input devices, and newer technologies such as CD-ROM drives and sound cards. When combined with color and high-resolution monitors, the net effect is an ability to create flexible, attractive, and highly stylized applications that appeal to end users. This is most definitely a strength of the PC world and one that developers familiar with this environment can cash in on.

Another key aspect of the PC architecture is the ability to do local processing. As a PC developer, you probably take for granted fast local disk and RAM with which to work. Again, this is not only a strength of the PC world, but one of the key drivers pushing organizations toward client/server architectures.

PC users and, frequently, PC developers, are used to seeing their particular machine as an extension of themselves. It's a tool to be used by a single individual who, when taking advantage of that tool, can perform multiple tasks, and leverage data and information management through PC applications. Ultimately, no matter how large a system is, it comes down to how well a single user can perform tasks. The benefits of a large installation are simply the benefits afforded to a single user multiplied by the number of people who use the system.

Systems people experienced with personal computers have no difficulty in adopting a single-user focus when designing and developing applications. It should be noted that, no matter what happens with the competing PC operating systems and user interfaces, the environment is here to stay. Sybase applications are more likely to require integration with personal computers than any other kind of system. On the basis of sheer numbers installed, PCs are a significant component in any client/server system. Those of you already familiar with this technology have a definite advantage in ways to present and support individual users.

PC Developer Weaknesses

Many of the experienced PC developers I have met tell me that they find it difficult to appreciate many of the systems features that mainframe programmers take for granted. The issues involved in managing multiple concurrent users is one example. For those of you who have in-depth Xbase experience, you may feel that you already have a good grasp of database issues. Most of the Clipper, dBASE, and FoxPro applications that I have seen, however, don't have to manage user populations greater than eight.

In any case, it's a fair observation to say that the personal computer development environment is focused almost exclusively on a single user. Many Sybase applications, on the other hand, must support literally dozens if not hundreds of user connections. This level of concurrency poses its own unique challenges which, as a PC developer, you may have to learn from the ground up.

Additionally, the PC environment has not been a strong platform for relational databases. This is not meant to disparage the single-user database packages with which many of you are familiar. Again, the feedback I have gotten from many of the PC developers is that they found the relational model and the need to design data integrity into the database to be new and challenging.

It should be noted that volume poses its own challenges. Have you ever tried to find a PC printer to replace a mainframe page printer capable of printing a page per second for hundreds of thousands of pages per month? The volume of transactions and data can be staggering when you move to a departmental, let alone enterprise-wide, Sybase application.

Databases measured in gigabytes, with tables containing millions of rows, are becoming standard operating procedure. Frequently, PC developers are not used to dealing with requirements of this size, and this is the area requiring the greatest attention and development when systems people with that background move to a Sybase development environment.

The cost of cycles on the mainframe is often underappreciated or misunderstood by PC developers who move into a client/server environment. Because many client/server applications integrate a number of technologies, including the mainframe, there are a great many options for determining on which platform the processing should be done. Mainframe processing is expensive, as well as being typically less flexible than that on a smaller platform. When moving to the new development environment, those of you with PC backgrounds may find it difficult to accept that organizations have paid so much for so little in the way of flexible data access and reporting.

Moving Down from the Mainframe

In many cases, it seems that these client/server projects, using Sybase or otherwise, are being initiated by management and are being led by people who don't understand or value the role the mainframe has played in organizational computing in the past. Personally, I believe it's a mistake to assume that there are no valuable lessons to be retained from the experience with big iron technology.

In conversations with mainframe developers and administrators, I have come to appreciate that many of the critical issues over which client/server projects struggle have already been resolved, albeit with different technology. In any case, if you are experienced with mainframe applications and are now in a position to move to client/server or to develop Sybase applications, there are a number of strengths and weaknesses of which you should be aware.

Mainframe Developer Strengths

If you want to find people with experience in developing and supporting global applications, where do you go? Certainly, the mainframe world includes any number of very large applications that have been deployed over a wide geographic area. As mentioned in the discussion about personal computer industry weaknesses, the same issues are strengths in the mainframe world. Extremely large data volumes, supporting large numbers of transactions conducted by a large user population, and widespread communications networks have been the mainstay of the mainframe. Personal computer applications, on the other hand, have been much more flexible and comfortable for any given user or operator.

Perhaps more important, the management techniques used to create and control large-scale applications evolved in the mainframe world. The relative effectiveness of large and small development teams, modeling techniques, structured development methodologies, and change and version control procedures are all old hat in the mainframe environment.

I'm not going to pretend that these techniques were invariably effective and well implemented. The problem with any large group is the tendency of bureaucracy to stifle creativity and initiative for the sake of consistency and control. At the same time, you should consider the alternatives. As Sybase moves into computing areas and requirements typically addressed by the mainframe, how much can the management techniques change? Are we truly working with an entirely new and radically different organizational computing model, or is it more like a replacement set of tools?

Let me answer that question for you. Sybase and related technologies can be used to integrate many applications, systems, and data that previously existed in isolation. However, the design and management techniques used to achieve this integration borrow heavily from mainframe experience. As the old guy said, if we have seen far, it is because we have stood on the shoulders of giants.

There are only so many ways of dealing with the process of organization. Any differences among the methods can be reduced to variations on a theme, usually balanced somewhere between the two poles of complete centralization and decentralization.

Those of you who have worked in the trenches and in architecting mainframe solutions will be pleased to hear that much of that experience is directly applicable to working with Sybase applications. For example, you are probably used to dealing with the need for unique keys on very large tables.

It's important to remember that you have a great deal to offer in spite of the differences in the toolsets and the way they work. PC developers will be used to tailoring their applications for the individual, whereas developers in mainframe environments have stressed the discipline required to successfully share large data volumes. Sybase solutions allow you to integrate both of these extremes in the same set of applications.

Mainframe Developer Weaknesses

So much for the good news. If you have been trained and experienced in developing mainframe applications and you are now expected to work with Sybase and client/server technology, wow, are you in for a shock. Client/server implementations are more like opening Pandora's box than anything you might have experienced in the past, and opening this box brings with it a great deal of what looks like anarchy and chaos.

The mainframe is not known for its flexibility. As Henry Ford used to say, "You can have one of my cars in any color you'd like—as long as it's black." This approach to service has taken root and flourished in many mainframe environments. That is not to say that, if you have worked in a mainframe shop, you were not committed to service or delivering the right information to the right people at the right time. I am asserting only that the tools themselves are restrictive in what they allow you to do. And, of course, human nature being what it is, people typically don't try to fight an uphill battle. After a while, you learn to accept that some things can't be done and you do without them.

After your organization opens the Pandora's box of client/server, a great many more things are possible. This means that some of you will need to relearn how to see things from a "can do" as opposed to a "can't be done" perspective. This is one of the things that management is pushing the client/server architecture to accomplish.

Another accomplishment is to reduce costs. In the past, it may have been possible to retrieve certain data and manipulate the results, but it was simply expensive to do so. There is a whole class of desirable things that people will do without if they cost too much money. This is another thing that integrating Sybase helps an organization address.

Arguably, the overall costs of client/server may not be less than the mainframe. But data access and report generation most certainly are. The cost equation is not necessarily something that affects you, but it is worth noting as a weakness of traditional systems.

Anarchy and Chaos versus Choice and Freedom

Don't you just love those black and white decisions without the annoying shades of gray? When working within a Sybase architecture, people frequently find that the range of potential solutions is much greater than they have experienced in the past. In fact, this range of choice may be so great that it verges on complete anarchy, with users doing exactly what they please with little in the way of consistency or standards.

Part of this is driven by the nature of the technology itself. With its commitment to openness and by providing access to third parties, the number of potential components that can be integrated into a Sybase system is staggering. Without some kind of organizational direction, this could result in a different set of tools for each user. From the sheer number of possible combinations and permutations, this looks like anarchy; and from a support or maintenance perspective, it is chaos.

On the other hand, it is most definitely the highest degree of freedom of choice for the users, which we are told is important. The business rationale says that nonsystems people should be able to access data with whichever tool they can use most effectively. Although there are any number of provisos and qualifications to this, it remains a fundamental reality. People have to use a system, any system, to gain the benefits of automation.

Working with a client/server system specifically based on Sybase products will provide these features and demonstrate the practical difficulties of the "come one, come all" approach. The true key to success is in splitting off the server side or back-end issues from client tools or front-end considerations. As you go through the development process in this book, the details and implications of this will be made clear.

From the standpoint of an experienced mainframe developer, you have no idea just how open these client/server systems are. At the same time, there are techniques that allow you to ensure some modicum of data integrity and systems security. Just be aware that the place to do this is not by restricting the software by which users access the data. In that way lies a great deal of conflict, and these days the users will win.

Making the Transition

Unfortunately, many organizations mishandle the change process when moving into client/server and developing corporate applications with Sybase. In spite of all we know about resistance to change and the need for buy-in and so on, many companies still make an announcement that the systems technologies are changing, and everyone will have to deal with it. Those who can't or won't will be shown the door.

I have spent a good deal of time training and talking with systems people who are in the process of the forced march from mainframe systems to client/server. There is, naturally, some bitterness, cynicism, and skepticism. Certainly, any remotely idealistic statement about what the technology can achieve or enable is greeted with a raised eyebrow, if not a derisive snort.

Well, if this describes you, sorry, but you have to get over it.

Seriously, there will be a shakeout of the people who can make the transition, and attitude will be a very important part of surviving the move. One of the reasons for spending so much time in this chapter on what you can offer from your mainframe experience is simply to help put the transition in perspective. Even if you are being pushed into the new computing model, it doesn't mean that you won't gain a great deal from adapting to the new way of doing things.

The trick is to assess your role on your own and then make a personal decision to adopt the new technologies. There is no substitute for personal commitment and by its nature only you can make that decision. Reading this book should help you with the process, however, if only by pointing out some of the obstacles and pitfalls already encountered by people in this position. Well, with that stated, let's get on with it.

Basic Training

The most daunting aspect of implementing a Sybase application is often the learning curve, so it stands to reason that training will be a critical factor in the success of the endeavor. Of course, training can take any number of forms from the old standbys of classroom instruction to the "mentoring" services offered by consulting firms. It's important to have a firm grasp of the basic underlying concepts and skills on which Sybase applications are built and implemented.

As part of the prerequisites you should meet before leaping into your first application development with Sybase, you should analyze your training needs. This section will cover what developers, architects, or technical managers should have under their belts before getting their hands on the technology. From the coverage earlier in this chapter on the differences between a mainframe and a PC developer mentality or background, you will, of course, want to tailor your training programs accordingly. What shouldn't be in doubt is that training is required.

Training Methods

Everyone's first preference is to fly to an exotic location, stay at a five-star hotel, and take a six-hour-a-day training session presented by the most experienced and interesting people in the field. Nice work if you can get it, but these days any such rewards are lavished on executives and owners, if anyone gets them at all. This doesn't mean that there aren't equally effective and, in some cases, much less expensive ways of acquiring client/server training.

Periodicals

By reading this book you are adopting one such method. It makes sense to read everything you can get your hands on about your new technology and application area in which you will be involved. Periodicals are also a traditionally useful means of keeping abreast of events. Of course, there is always the problem of identifying a book that will prove useful to you, and the proliferation of magazines and journals poses some problems in terms of selecting the right materials and not wasting time sorting the wheat from the chaff.

Newer technologies and services can also be highly effective. If you are a subscriber or have access to a copy of Computer Select, online copies of dozens of computer trade magazines can be searched for keywords. This lets you focus on the body of work published over the past year, sorted and filtered according to your exact needs at the time.

Online Information

The biggest problems with published materials is that they are written to sell and are not interactive. You can't easily ask for clarification on a particularly obscure point, and magazine articles are necessarily short. Speaking of clarification, feel free to ask about any particular point raised in this book, but please, don't call my 800 number unless you have a support agreement <grin>. Really, I do appreciate comments, so if you care to drop me a line, try 71664,2623 on CompuServe or `djworden@wordn.com` on the Internet if my address gets set up this month as planned.

If you want to actually discourse with people who are working with the gear itself, you can always sign up for CompuServe or a local bulletin board. The Sybase forum in CompuServe frequently posts powerpoint presentations from Sybase courses and conventions. You can download these and flip through them at your leisure. Conversely, you can post questions and digest the feedback of the online community. Tools such as the Navigator utility from CompuServe allows you to specify regular topics and search for new messages or files related to those areas. The Internet supports similar "info rooting" with utilities such as Archie, which, like Navigator, searches Internet nodes for particular topics.

These are good supplements but poor substitutes for the personal training experience bolstered with hands-on exercises.

User Groups

Conferences and user groups are also frequently worthwhile; however, you should be careful to ensure that the speakers are not just consultants telling you how wonderful client/server is, but rather sharing hard-won experience in practical applications of the technology. User groups are often overly political organizations, with any number of people looking to see and be seen rather than actually promoting a better understanding of specific tools and products.

Which brings us back to what you can do: evaluate courses based on their contents and the experience of the instructors. If at all possible, make sure that there is a practical component to the course and, most important, don't take a course on a technology you can't work with when you get back to your place. Time spent on technical training that is not immediately reinforced by working with that technology is wasted money and effort. You will forget what was covered, and retention is the key to getting the value for your training investment.

Okay, so you know what you can do, and what to look for in a training program. Now I'll introduce the fundamentals that any Sybase development effort must have before the outcome has any likelihood of success. Of course, the rest of the book builds on these basic principles, but at this point I would like to at least touch on them.

An Overview of SQL Server

Sybase offers a course called "The Fast Track to SQL Server." Many other organizations also offer similar training. When you first know that you will be working with Sybase, or even before that, if you think there is a strong possibility that you or your group might be working with the technology, try to send someone to a course who will become familiar with the technology and how to integrate it.

In many situations, people have committed to developing client/server applications without having a clear understanding of the constituent parts. You may know, for example, that the client and the server are integrated across the network, but you may not have anyone on the team who understands how this is accomplished.

When you're first designing your Sybase solution, there are a number of design issues that can be handled in one of many ways. There are no right answers when trying to balance the workload across multiple processors, client and server alike, and networking provides its own constraints and features.

The key to success is to understand, at least conceptually, how this architecture works from the outset, so that the logical model or the application design will fit onto the physical platforms made up of clients, networks, and servers.

However, there is a preliminary step before this that you may find necessary to address, if only to ensure a uniform understanding of the technology across the members of your development team.

Understanding the Relational Model

For many developers, the concepts and features of a relational database are only somewhat clear—for example, the role of the entity relationship diagram, the difference between a logical datamodel and a physical datamodel, resolving many-to-many-relationships, and so on. Why you would want to include any of these concepts and features must also be explained.

There is enough experience now with developing relational systems to have a great deal of existing knowledge about relational database management systems and the techniques that have been developed to design and build such systems. Client/server generally revolves around a relational database, and because you are reading a book about developing Sybase applications, I think it's a pretty safe bet that you expect to be working with a relational database management system as well.

I will cover many of these issues throughout the book. If you have an extensive DB/2 background, never fear; the book won't include general conceptual stuff, but simply enough background to understand the specific features of Sybase as they relate to developing applications for the real world.

Those of you who have been PC developers, though, take note, because there is less similarity between any given RDBMS and Xbase than you think. Don't underestimate how much time, effort, and complexity are involved in the relational model. Nor will you be doing yourself any favors by skipping over this area in your training and research.

Good Sybase applications invariably incorporate a good grasp of how relational systems work. Key elements such as referential integrity (sorry, couldn't resist the pun), join strategies, and index considerations work much the same way from one RDBMS to another. Especially during the design phase, you should be aware of how the model works and what the trade-offs are. As you get more familiar with the specifics of the Sybase implementation, you will have other things to address.

Basic SQL

Hot on the heels of your relational model courses and training should follow your initial explorations with Structured Query Language. Again, the specifics of the Sybase implementation are not as important as having a solid working knowledge, or taking a refresher, in how SQL statements are constructed. SQL painters for any number of single-user tools are readily available, so even if your SQL Server has not arrived or been installed, you can still practice your SQL until you feel completely comfortable with it.

Keep in mind that SQL is really just a core set of commands for manipulating data. It is first and foremost a query language. It is the extensions to SQL provided for each specific database engine that provide features for data definition and allow you to create complex transactions. These are constructs that are best layered on top of a good grasp of the basic SQL syntax.

Again I have to make different recommendations depending on which group you identify with. Mainframe programmers, assuming that you already know something about SQL from DB/2, you may be ready to move right into Transact-SQL (T-SQL) and begin evaluating the Sybase syntax for transaction management. PC developers and those mainframers who do not have previous relational experience should start with SQL as a method of manipulating simple tables and obtaining desired results. This capability is at the core of any Sybase application, and it will give you a better appreciation for exactly what your more technical end users will be facing as you implement the system.

GUI Training

Whatever the target client environment for which you expect to be developing, you will need to have some personal experience with that tool. This applies no matter what role you will occupy in the project, including that of data modeler or systems architect. Everyone involved in the project should have the basic skills and terminology of the environment. As you progress through the application development process, this occurs naturally. It actually works for the best if you begin with this objective in mind.

Client/server systems generally, and Sybase applications specifically, work out when the entire team has some appreciation for the end-to-end elements of the client/server equation. Segregation and division of labor don't help the development process, and familiarity with the interface is just one part of the overall system.

Everyone should have at least a nodding acquaintance with each aspect and the role that it plays in pulling the application together.

There is another practical benefit from having some GUI experience when developing client/server applications: you become more productive.

I should probably take the time to mention that, if you are already sold on and familiar with a particular or even several GUI environments, it will be worthwhile to plow through this part of the chapter, if only to ensure that the other members of your team are up to speed as well, and so that you can quickly explain the benefits to them of doing so, if they are not.

Multitasking is rather difficult in a single-screen, terminal-based environment. Most organizations moving to Sybase are not that interested in terminals as a strategic client platform, anyway, but the point remains that you should use it to obtain the benefits for yourself.

Most of the third-party tools for developing and managing Sybase applications have either GUI components or offerings. Some of them would be impossible to use without understanding the graphical environment; modeling tools are not the least example of this.

So, if you're not already a confirmed user of some graphical environment, stop reading now and go out and get familiar with one. It doesn't matter which one. Like relational concepts and good design technique, the principles transcend specific implementations. A widget is a widget, meaning that a window scrollbar works the same way in Mac, UNIX, or Windows, and it's something you need to know.

Identifying What You Don't Know

Human resources circles have what is referred to as *training needs analysis*. The first time I saw this particular expression, I thought that it referred to a need to analyze training. More to the point, it means that you should analyze your training needs. This is especially true when developing Sybase applications.

A Little Knowledge

The traditional saying goes, "a little knowledge is a dangerous thing." And it most certainly is dangerous to the success of your client/server development effort. Of course, it's not quite as dangerous as having no idea at all that you should know something.

Well, no doubt you're ready for something a little less like a bad fortune cookie and more germane to your particular objectives.

The guiding principle is this: *Don't overestimate how ready you are or how much you know.* Impatience and a desire to get down to the nuts and bolts is a characteristic shared by many systems people. And it's one of the traits that has not been so endearing to applications users. Where client/server differs is simply in the vast number of potential contributors to the system. You can count on not knowing anything at all about certain processes, products, and techniques that will be absolutely vital to the success of your system.

In a way, this gets back to the learning curve. The more respect you have for the amount you have to learn, and the more preparation you put into learning it, the more likely you are to master it and move on. Keep in mind that nothing you learn will stay learned. Not so much because you don't have a good memory, but because in this fast-paced information age, new things are being thought up, new versions and products are being brought to market and new demands are being placed on organizations so that what you thought you knew becomes outdated. In cases such as this, thinking that you already know this stuff will make you more of a liability than an asset to your project and to your team.

Anyone who spends a good deal of time with children will tell you that an open mind makes for an effective learning experience. I hope I don't have to convince you that to succeed in developing client/server applications, you have to start learning and keep learning. This is not only a good thing, but it can be as fun, challenging, and as rewarding as it is demanding.

Summary

How many of you remember hearing about someone who got an education in the school of hard knocks? This may not make you feel better, but client/server is generally a hard-knocks experience. In fact, I have one client who, having worked with the technology since 1988, refers to the architecture exclusively as client/suffer.

When developing Sybase applications, experience is hard won and highly valuable. You should make every effort to acquire it early and keep it long. This last point is one that I will focus on in the course of the book. For the time being, the point is simply that you want it, you need it, and you should place a premium on it. Experience is most assuredly the best teacher when it comes to client/server systems.

This experience applies to much more than just the technology. Experience with the organizational culture, the politics, the management practices, and traditional applications can also be invaluable. Remember, you have to keep the existing systems working even while you're developing replacements. This has been a major problem for organizations that did not appreciate the body of knowledge and expertise that existed in the heads of their long-term systems employees.

1.3

Establishing the Business Strategy

Introduction

In this short chapter, I will review the process by which you can tie your Sybase applications into an overall strategy for your business. This will necessarily be a high-level and somewhat cursory treatment of the topic. Many good books, and in fact entire careers, are devoted to the issues surrounding management strategies. I am including this chapter only to emphasize how important the tie-in to strategy is to the success of the project and to tug a proverbial forelock to management direction.

As you proceed through the chapter, you will be introduced to strategic considerations more from the standpoint of identifying and applying strategy as opposed to laying down strategies for your organization.

The process of downsizing or organizational flattening that has been occurring over the past decade has resulted in many consequences, some good and some detrimental. In this chapter you will see how important it is to fit into your true corporate strategy and, more important, how to use your applications to communicate and further those strategies.

Establishing the Course

If you decide to interview the senior management responsible for the area in which you will be deploying and using your Sybase application, you will likely discover that there actually is a defined strategy for that particular business unit.

For those of you who enjoy working for companies with formalized and consistent management planning and communication of those plans throughout the organization, take heart. I won't be spending a lot of time on this topic. However, especially in North America, being kept up to date with changes in company direction or philosophy can be like the movements of an amoeba; you must flow into circumstances that tell you as you go, rather than have the knowledge communicated in advance. Communication of strategic plans is often strictly on a need-to-know basis.

For those of you who work in organizations of this nature, it's up to you to dig the information out of management; you will need it to protect your application from drastic shifts in requirements or perceived relevance to the company.

The three basic methods of establishing the corporate direction are quite simple:

1. Ask

   Even highly placed middle managers are hired and promoted for their ability to see parts, if not all, of the big picture. You can establish the specific management initiatives by interviewing or asking the line management responsible for your application area to determine the specific company strategies or initiatives they would like to see supported by technology. In some cases, this can raise the profile of the system with management and give you an opportunity to demonstrate that you, too, can see and incorporate the big picture.

2. Observe

As you attend meetings with your boss or, better yet, the boss's boss, identify key terms used in conversation. By identifying consistent themes in the managers' communication, you can sometimes sift through the rhetoric to see what issues worry them. Positioning your system to address a concern of your boss's boss is an excellent way to ensure that your application is seen as worth the investment in time and money.

3. Read

Obtain your organization's annual report. Even public service and smaller organizations do some form of periodic reporting to a group to which they feel accountable. By researching this material, you can identify not only the strategic direction for the company as a whole, but often pull out other significant points that can serve as terms of reference for your application—an articulated "constitution" for the application, if you like.

Typical Strategic Hot Buttons

Typically, organizations will focus on key strategic areas to help position the company or unit for optimum operation. These generally include areas noted in the following sections.

Quality

Not all organizations want to develop and provide the highest-quality alternatives. There is room in any market for mules as well as racehorses. You're never going to get an argument from top management by looking for ways to improve quality. However, by showing that your system will reduce defect rates, or affect quality of service in a tangible way, you can press an important button for many firms and help obtain management approval for the application. If quality is job one for your organization, you will want to have identified that fact from the beginning.

Customer Service

As with quality, customer service is one of those business mandates that just does not go out of style. A self-serve organization is not as likely to see it as crucial to business survival, whereas a company specializing in high-ticket items may see it as the prime directive. If this area is one considered of key importance within your company, you should identify specific ways in which your application will impact current levels of customer service.

This implies that you can quantify or in some way establish a baseline for customer service, which you will use to compare levels provided after the application has been implemented. However, this effort will pay off only if you have correctly identified customer service as a key corporate strategy to be supported in your organization.

Cost Reduction

In some cases, companies must slash costs to the bone in order to successfully compete on price. You may discover that your company is concerned with quality and customer service only to the extent that there must be acceptable levels to stay in business. Many industries have successful companies that focus on providing great value for the money. That is, the quality may not be the highest, but the product represents getting the most for the cost. If your organization needs operational costs cut as part of its corporate priorities, you had best get this firmly established at the beginning or you may find the costs of your technology being scrutinized.

Time to Market

Logistics are vital to organizations that move goods from one place to another. Suppliers of fresh produce are a great example. The quality of the goods, the level of service with which they are provided, and the cost of producing them are all secondary to getting them to the customer as quickly as possible.

For those of you who work for firms in the business of growing and shipping lettuce or eggs, you now have a likely business strategy for your system to support. Even for those of you whose firms do nothing of the kind, responsiveness to market demands and the ability to cut down on research and development time can be a highly valued trait.

As with the other general strategies, the key to success is to identify which is driving the business from the perspective of your senior management. By isolating management's key concerns, you can then invest the time to investigate exactly how your Sybase application will impact its pet priority.

The Value of Management Support

Once you have identified the key business strategies that your application will support, the next step is to ensure that your management team knows that your system will make a significant contribution to that strategy.

Look at the flip side: If your system does not actually have an impact on the issues that your clients perceive as most important, why would they bother to give it any time or attention? And when they understand that the system will also serve a strategic role as well as providing quantifiable operational services, they are more likely to support the endeavor.

Many methodologies stress the importance of obtaining a mandate from management, especially when your application is going to cause change. The key value in obtaining management support is that they will actually provide the resources should the budget get tight or stand firm with policies that help you during the course of systems implementation.

The members of the management team are much more likely to do this when the systems value has been explained to them in terms they understand and to which they relate. You are likely to accomplish only if you take the time at the beginning to identify the strategic directions and initiatives near and dear to the hearts of your executives.

The Strategic Difference

Strategies don't usually change over short periods of time. Only companies in the process of mergers, divestitures, or avoiding insolvency are typically motivated to thrash around the market looking for a strategy.

Generally, business strategies are marketing oriented. This orientation is not one much appreciated or considered natural for systems people. It is vital for you as a systems developer or architect, however, to understand the choices driving those who make the decisions. One of those decisions is likely to be how good or worthwhile that client/server project is!

In marketing terms, there are four *P*s that define what an organization must do to be successful. These are the following:

- Product
- Position
- Price
- Promotion

The representative initiatives described earlier in this chapter can relate to any or all of these items. Price, of course, is obvious. But promotion as an initiative is something more subtle. Take frequent flyer or frequent shopper programs. In these cases, the organization has translated a systems capability, that of tracking customers and transactions, and turned that into a customer service enhancement.

Positioning of various products can be affected by things such as "just-in-time" shipping or buying practices. Product research and market feedback can also be a strategic advantage provided by a system. All you have to do is identify exactly what buttons are likely to work for you in your organization.

Summary

As promised, this was indeed a short chapter. However, if you want to ensure that your Sybase application is a success, and that it is not put on the back burner or no one notices when it actually gets implemented, one key is to understand and align with your company's business strategies.

Realistically, that is the only way you can be sure to explain your system to management in terms they can understand and appreciate.

It is also important to note that management has the right to expect that people in the organization will bother to uncover what needs to be done, rather than wait to be told. This chapter should have given you a basis for investigation, or interpreting management directives you have already been given.

Unless you are at (or want to be) at the vice-president level, no one expects systems people to be proficient marketers and business managers. Even if you have no intentions of moving into management, however, it can only help you to understand your organization's strategies and look for ways to make your application support them.

In some cases, your Sybase application could form the basis for a new product, or provide a competitive edge over your organization's competitors. Frequently flyer and shopper programs are very popular methods of building and rewarding customer loyalty. Supermarkets can now sell profiles of their customers shopping habits to advertisers and product vendors. Both of these business practices are based on the ability to locate and manipulate information effectively in a strategic manner.

If you can find a way to use information systems technology to help your company in the marketplace, you will likely be rewarded. Your Sybase technology and skills can help you do just that.

1.4

Taking Inventory

Introduction

The first step in any systems development effort is to determine the "state of the nation." Whether you decide to integrate existing technology or replace it all wholesale, you must first establish what is out there.

In this chapter you will be taken through the process by which you determine the size of the challenge you face in designing and implementing your Sybase application. This process should be done as part of the analysis performed before a system is designed. Frequently, it's done as part of the justification for a new system and the associated expenditures.

The areas to be analyzed will be identified and you will see how to assess the existing situation to determine where financial savings can be obtained, how data may be hidden, or where sacred systems cows may sleep.

Each of these areas creates an opportunity for your system to succeed if the areas are understood, and poses potential obstacles or threats if they are not. As you will see from this chapter, the best way to minimize the difficulties you encounter in implementation is to thoroughly investigate the application area at the beginning.

Too often, systems people confuse analyzing user requirements with understanding the ins and outs of the environment they will be automating or upgrading. This chapter will cover the steps you should be taking at the very beginning of your project to ensure that you understand the real situation, instead of buying into a somewhat optimistic depiction of how a department, group, division, or organization functions. As the old French saying goes, "There are two reasons why someone does something. The reason a person will tell you and the real reason."

This chapter should familiarize you with methods that you can use to establish the real reason why things are done in your organization.

The Lay of the Land

For millennia, military thinkers have propounded the importance of understanding the terrain on which a battle was to be fought. Although implementing Sybase applications may be a good deal more constructive than a military campaign, there will be times when you feel you are in a combat zone. In fact, for years I have used that term to describe the critical first few weeks of cutting over to a new system. After all, no one really sees the myriad of critical details that have to be addressed as part of a systems migration until you actually try to implement the design. The "combat zone" is where change meets the status quo.

The Big Picture

Paraphrasing the second law of thermodynamics, everything is wearing down. This includes older hardware, software, the relevance of business practices—everything, in fact, that makes up an organization. The status quo is then the inertia of the existing situation and all that it contains.

The best way to ensure that your changes will take effect is to understand that status quo fully and completely.

Every working environment is made up of people, equipment, and procedures. These may incorporate technology or they may be manual. However, these three elements underly all the activities that go on in any given organization regardless of its mission or focus.

Your mission (should you choose to accept it) is to identify who does what with which. As well as to whom. The preliminary analysis should be done with one attitude firmly in mind. You are not there to change things (yet), you are simply there to find out what is being done, what is being used, and how it is being done.

Who to Talk to

In any organizational area you investigate, there are usually a number of key individuals with whom you will want check. The controller or financial manager accountable for the area is definitely someone to work with closely. They usually understand the function as it relates to the organization as a whole, and will be able to point to areas where the symptoms of bad systems are financial. If your system addresses these areas, the results are then measurable.

To address the units at the operational level, you should spend some time with each supervisor. While these people frequently do not appreciate why organization wide policies and procedures are effected, they can tell you how they affect their particular part of the world. Supervisors can give you a very specific list of deliverables for a smaller component of the organization.

Every individual working within an organization sees it differently. You might also keep in mind that from the perspective of the organization, each employee has a specific role and contribution to make. A thorough analysis of any existing situation will include at least random reviews of individual employees within the units being scrutinized prior to designing any new system.

You may not get any new information (though you might!), but at the very least you will have an opportunity to determine the attitude of the unit employees towards systems and change in general.

The Right Approach

I mention attitude because of its importance, not only to the area where new systems are to be applied but to the systems development process itself. As with any recommended set of steps, there will be people who can make it work and people who cannot. We have all seen people who faithfully follow the recipe printed on the side of the pancake box and still don't end up with anything edible. The key to making it work is the way you approach it, which is every bit as important as the steps you take.

During the investigation phase you just want to find out as much as you can. The proper attitude is one of sympathetic, nonjudgmental appraisal. I stress this because I am a judgmental person and it took me a few years to get the approach right.

You will find that implementation goes much more smoothly if your system will address the issues identified by the users from the beginning. The way to get them to identify these issues is to ask while you still have an open mind. Later, you can translate their description of the business and their requirements into systemspeak. But during this stage the key is to see the organization from the perspective of the other people working there.

Outcome and Results

The output of this investigation is typically a set of lists. You make lists of equipment, you have phone lists of people, lists of data, and lists of the steps the employees take in performing their duties. At some point you will want to translate these lists into flows and charts, if only to make confirmation of the data easier.

At a minimum, you should have lists which identify all hardware in use within the business unit, its function, value (financial) and any outstanding liabilities it represents, such as lease payments or support contracts.

This also applies to software. You should be able to identify all applications in use within the unit (whether the software is home grown or shrink wrapped), version numbers, and the status of any software support agreements.

You should document each employee, or, for large organizations, the number and type of positions, as well as include an assessment of their attitudes and requirements as they perceive them.

Evaluating Equipment

I have lumped all the hardware, software, peripherals, and other miscellaneous gear into this category. At this point, you don't have to care about sorting or organizing your findings too finely. What you want to do is ensure that you know about all of the stuff in use in the area in which you will be launching your Sybase application.

Many really large firms don't have good records of the equipment purchased and put in place over the years. In fact, the larger the company and the longer it has been in business, the less likely it will be that your clients even know about some of this stuff. Your inventory may be the first time in years that the existence of this equipment is made known.

I had one client who maintained that the company had so much gear in use throughout even one plant that, by the time it had been inventoried, new stuff would have made its way into the organization, unbeknownst to the people keeping track. That's not really a good reason for not doing this exercise. You need to know about all of the subsystems in use in your application area in order to identify the consequences of automating any given function. That is one of the key benefits to going to all this work.

Another benefit is the opportunity to identify monetary savings. Older pieces of equipment may have leases or support contracts associated with them. If your application will make any of that equipment obsolete, you may be able to use the savings to demonstrate a quantifiable benefit for the application.

It's very dangerous, however, to identify that you will save money by replacing gear unless you really know what function it serves and unless the users will cooperate with the change, allowing you to actually pull the plug on the obsolete equipment. The time to identify this is before you start designing and developing your client/server application. It's a preliminary step that is dangerous to ignore.

Summary

In this chapter you were introduced to the concept of taking inventory as it relates to designing and implementing new Sybase systems. You should have gained a sense that the individuals and their attitudes are just as important as thoroughly cataloging all of the hardware and software maintained within the unit.

When you're first investigating a unit that is to be automated or retooled, you are presented with both an opportunity and a risk. This chapter should have shown you the value of setting aside time to perform these interviews and walkthroughs as an initial development step. The opportunity is to form relationships that will last through the entire development process.

The risk is that you never get a second chance to make a first impression. If someone is assigned to review the existing situation, and in the process the users are alienated, you could find yourself fighting an uphill battle through each of the successive steps.

1.5

Selecting a Toolset

Introduction

Arguably, selecting a toolset is not a prerequisite but a natural progression to the identification of systems requirements. Throughout this chapter and the remainder of the book, you will find a strong emphasis on the idea that all systems tools, including Sybase, must fit a requirement. Successful Sybase applications are never tools in search of an application, but rather the solution of a real business problem using technology.

That may be all well and good, but why deal with selecting a toolset as part of the prerequisites? First, most of you already have selected tools, or have had tools selected for you. The purpose of this chapter is to asses the tools selection process itself in order to identify the steps necessary for ensuring that your client/server toolset is appropriate.

In this chapter you will be exposed to some of the considerations underlying the selection of any systems tools, especially before you have a complete definition of the users' requirements or the business problem to be solved.

Many systems are technology driven. Certainly, when you face choices involving emerging technology, you will want to have some idea of what you can make the technology do in your setting, rather than rely on vendors' claims or consultants' assertions. Therefore, you must be prepared to evaluate the technology as a separate issue.

This is the issue that I will address in this chapter. By the time you have finished reading through it, you should have a clear idea of the considerations to balance when identifying tools to use in building your Sybase application.

Humans — The Tool Users

We tend to think of our species as tool makers. I remember a film shown in my seventh grade science class that referred to "Man the Tool Maker." I wanted to update the label to reflect the more politically correct characterization of our species as Human.

Our facility for tools and the ability to think abstractly characterize the key differences between us and the other denizens of the planet. The real physical attainments of our history, however, are not the tools that were invented, but rather the use to which those tools were put. Relative to Sybase as a tool, I would like to stress that your use of it is far and away more important than the features the vendor designed into the product when it was made.

Throughout this book, you'll be exposed to the assumption that applied technology is at the core of a successful Sybase application. If this were not the case, it would simply be sufficient to acquire the right tool and success would be axiomatic. The horror stories and bad investments in client/server technology clearly demonstrate that this is not the case.

The opposite view is that there is some value in technology for technology's sake. This is not so black and white an issue. There is indeed some value to be obtained in reviewing and experimenting with technology without having a concrete purpose in mind for it. However, for that experience to be truly useful, it must turn out to be more widely applicable than merely the experiment itself.

At some point, the expertise gained in experimentation must be applied to a real problem and the value derived from solving that problem. The trick is to find a balance between the technology and its application.

Learning by Doing

The real reason for acquiring any emerging technology or toolset without a practical goal in mind is simply to look it over. Once you have some hands-on familiarity with anything, it's much easier to predict its applicability and estimate the amount of time required for implementation. For many of you, however, the time and expense involved in this approach is a luxury that your organization may not be able to afford.

For those of you in that position, you may find that you have to recommend a toolset with which you will be expected to build functioning, flexible client/server systems without truly understanding the workings or the restrictions inherent in the technology. As you proceed through this chapter, you will find several recommendations for ways to limit your risk in this area while taking the minimum amount of time to identify appropriate tools and restricting the expense.

Even those of you who already have several Sybase applications under your belt will benefit from reviewing this material. One of the facts of life in this era is that nothing is static and tools change on an almost weekly basis. Even though you may have had experience with a tool during one version, new releases and/or competitive products may make that tool obsolete. You may find yourself feeling that you are continually starting from scratch. At the beginning of any new Sybase project, you should take the time to review the market and your existing tools to determine whether they still fit as well as they did at the beginning of other projects.

Tools, Directions, and Trends

In the past several years there has been tremendous pressure to provide GUI-based applications on the desktop. This pressure for flexible, pretty client interfaces combined with the economic sense of downsizing to increasingly powerful servers and more pervasive networks has made client/server applications a natural migration for many organizations.

It would not be sensible to imagine that this will be the last radical shift in our toolset for the foreseeable future. In fact, there are many emerging trends that will directly affect us. Advances in communications technologies, increasing bandwidths allowing remote connectivity, 32-bit operating systems on the desktop, products allowing the integration of data stores in a single, enterprise-wide architecture, and object-oriented programming are all transforming our toolsets and systems options.

Years ago, people delayed acquiring tools because they felt that the rapid obsolescence made it possible to wait until a clear path emerged. Increasingly, people are recognizing that they need to master certain skills as soon as possible, not the least of which is determining which technology will turn out to provide the greatest degree of short-term functionality and long-term dividends from the investment in learning.

I have been saying for years that rapid change is here today and here to stay. The challenge at this point is to learn how to appraise tools, put them to work, and replace them with new tools when the time is right.

Later in the book, I'll address the emergence of new tools such as object orientation and increased communications bandwidth through ATM (Asynchronous Transfer Mode) and other protocols/products. These products generate a great deal of interest in the systems community and have tremendous potential to impact client/server architectures. Also, tools for cross-platform development, gateways, and middleware represent significant new technologies. However, the true key to their ultimate success is applicability and usefulness.

To that end, I will now describe an approach to assessing tools for your organization.

Organizational Culture and Philosophy

The first thing to understand is the general preference of your organization when considering tools. Some shops prefer to build systems themselves, so they look for the best development tools. Other companies would rather buy turnkey or off-the-shelf products, relying on external vendors to support and maintain the products.

There really is no one right way (or, for that matter, two or three) to design and implement client/server systems. Ultimately, whatever approach you take must yield a functional, applicable system that provides value to the organization. How you arrive at that is a secondary process.

The Role of the Vendor

The traditional method of acquiring tools was to determine which vendor represented the best integrated set of products. This was known as the One-Vendor Solution and everyone pretty much acknowledges that, these days, no one vendor does it all, let alone well.

This hardly means, however, that people are forced to acquire components from different vendors at all times. Many vendors are working together to provide compatible sets of tools, resulting in a total suite from a handful of allied vendors. At the other end of the spectrum, an organization might decide to opt for the "best of breed" approach. This label is taken from awards presented at dog shows, which is ironic when you consider the performance of some of these tools.

In any case, some IS organizations want to provide their staffs with the best performing tools on the market, independent of how well they work together. In these cases, the organizations opt to provide all of the integration themselves.

There is little difference in the trade-offs between these two approaches and the arguments offered when evaluating options for PC desktop tools for single users. A single suite of products from one vendor provides easier maintenance, tighter integration, and support.

On the other hand, there are always weaker products contained within the suite. To get the best possible product for text processing, spreadsheets, presentations, and communications, the PC must be loaded with products from many vendors. Getting these products to peacefully coexist can be a major headache, though the boost in features and performance may be worth it.

Your challenge is to understand where your organization's preferences lie and to work with those.

Expected Life of the Tool

There is a great degree of difference in the useful life of many of the tools. Earlier in this chapter I indicated that you needed to pay very close attention to new releases and competitive products that come onto the market. Although this is certainly true of desktop suites and application generators such as PowerBuilder and SQL Windows, it is less true of database engines and server operating systems.

In fact, there is less risk in opting early for experimental tools where the application is confined and the value can be obtained over a short period of time. Systems monitoring tools, for example, can be experimented with and disposed of with limited risk.

Say that you have a discrete project with its own servers, data, application software, and benefits case. You could install any given monitoring tool. Because the tool provides a support function, even a bad tool doesn't necessarily impact the project or the benefits case. As long as the system works, the monitoring tool doesn't have to perform. On the flip side, if the monitoring tool is the only aspect of the project that works, you may ditch the other technology and keep the monitor. Either way, the monitoring technology is not such a risk and you can take the opportunity to experiment with various options.

The cost of the products may be only in the thousands of dollars and the number of users limited to key systems specialists. Trying to select a standard database engine and then changing your mind will affect many more people and generally cost a great deal more money, unless the decision to change is made before rolling out the product or converting large volumes of existing data.

The following list sorts products into the two types:

Short-Term Life with *High Exchangeability*	*Long-Term Life with* *Low Exchangeability*
Contact managers	Operating systems
Desktop productivity tools	Database engines
Windowing environments	Communications networks
Application generators	Gateways
Design tools	Class libraries

Performance Monitoring Tools

Many of you may be surprised that I rank windowing environments and end-user programs in the short-term category. Certainly, many users will resist changing to a new set of tools once they have mastered one, but overall, the significance of changing tools on that side of the client/server equation is much less than on the other.

The sunk costs in infrastructure are significant and require many years to pay back. *Sunk costs* is an accounting term that refers to expenditures that have already been made, or *sunk*, by the organization. In this case, sunk costs refer to investments already made in systems technology.

Looking at the radical development of PC GUIs and the relentless delivery of newer, more powerful chipsets, you can see that even in the past 10 years, the desktop tools have changed radically. The tools used to design and generate chips and other systems components have changed as well, along with the desktop products. This means that it is necessary to write off investments in systems technology over a very short lifecycle.

New product offerings such as Windows 95 and OS/2 Warp demonstrate that user interfaces and desktop capabilities will be changing, no matter how much retraining and reconfiguring has to be done. This presupposes that these products offer capabilities attractive enough that users would rather switch than fight, and that IS organizations adopt and support these new offerings.

The point is that you must be aware not only of your organization's philosophy and tradition when it comes to tools, but you should review the expected lifetime of the product types in question to ensure that the appropriate weight is given in the evaluation process.

The Evaluation Process

The first step in the process is to become aware of the alternatives. This research is typically handled through continual reading of industry trade magazines, attending product demonstrations and conferences, and even using such tools as CD-ROM libraries for searches and posting questions on electronic bulletin boards. No doubt you are already quite familiar with the process.

Of course, even for the most preliminary review of potential tools, you must have a general idea of the requirements your organization has for the products. When it comes to selecting tools, suitability to task is everything.

Most tools, however, were designed with a certain set of requirements in mind. Sybase SQL Server, for example, was always intended to be a high-performance, transaction-oriented relational database engine. Even if you're just beginning the process of identifying your requirements, you can make every effort to determine where potential tools shine and relate that to your requirements once they are better defined.

Looking at the specific features of Sybase SQL Server, as shown in Table 1.5.1, you can see how they will provide benefits in applications that play to those strengths.

Table 1.5.1. Features and benefits of Sybase SQL Server.

Feature	*Benefit*
Multithreaded architecture	Performance remains consistent as users added
Online transaction processing support	Handles large volume of short transactions
Application Programming Interface	Allows easy interconnection of third-party applications
Scaleable	Easily moves from small- to large-scale systems
Integrates with Replication Server	Allows guaranteed synchronization of data on multiple servers across a wide area network
Integrates with OmniSQL Gateway	Allows integration of SQL Servers with other vendors' databases

At this point, most people reduce their choices to a decision matrix. This is a useful exercise because it tends to reduce some of the natural but unconscious bias you might have concerning one vendor or another. It makes communicating the decision making process to others that much easier, as well, and often more defensible.

The matrix should include a listing of each attribute or feature desired and whether each product being considered has addressed that feature. Naturally, it's somewhat easier to manage such a list if the features are expressed in binary terms (for instance, "Supports ODBC connectivity, Y/N").

Additionally, you should include allowances for such things as local support by the vendor, especially if you expect to roll out the tools beyond major centers. Last, you will need to factor in such nonquantifiable elements as how much the vendor wants to sell you the product. This is especially important if you plan to do any leading-edge work and will be relying on the vendor for high levels of technical support or problem solving.

The feature sets of two different vendors' tools can present a choice amounting to six of one, half dozen of the other. In such a case, it always makes more sense to go with the vendor who is most motivated by your success. This generally translates into backing the underdog so that your organization can be used by that vendor as a reference or success story. If you are an early adopter, or will be working with larger-than-normal volumes of transactions or data, these requirements should factor heavily in your decision-making process.

Managing Vendors and Users' Expectations

If at all possible, you should shortlist your potential suppliers and arrange a no-obligation, hands-on trial period. If the vendor is confident that the product will meet your requirements, it should have no qualms about letting you have a loaner. On the other hand, if the vendor is unwilling to provide even that level of service before the sale is made, how much help can you reasonably expect after the check clears the bank?

Another benefit to arranging hands-on internal trials is the ability to get your own people to provide feedback about their impressions before the decision is made. Yes, we all know that involvement translates into buy-in and, without that commitment, experimental projects often fail. The internal trial and review is a practical method of obtaining that buy-in.

One of my clients went so far as to put price tags and a catalog of pros and cons for each of the major brands of PCs they were thinking of standardizing on. After several weeks of review by IS staff and user departments, the completed comment sheets indicated a clear preference for one vendor.

Interestingly, problems with those units did not give rise to the usual complaints about the systems support people. There were as many problems as were found with the previous type of machines, but because staff members had been preconditioned to those weaknesses, they took them in stride instead of blaming the group that selected them. This approach works as well for software and development tools.

Remember, too, that the vendors who lose the sale are continually selling to your organization. This may be highly impersonal, such as TV and magazine advertisements, or it might consist of follow-up visits in which a salesperson looks for opportunities to "twist the knife" and exploit any problems or weaknesses in the toolset that was selected.

Users, whether end users or systems staff, will see the tools that got away as bigger, better, faster, and just plain more attractive than the realities of the tools they have been given. This has as much to do with human nature and the "grass is greener" syndrome as anything else. Anything you can do to encourage their expectations to stay in touch with reality will pay dividends as you work through the implementation process.

Platform Tradeoffs

You may be interested in seeing a sample review of the three major platforms on which Sybase SQL Server runs. From this you can take away more of an approach to how such a review could be structured, rather than the accuracy of the data itself. Remember, these vendors excel at leapfrogging with each other from one version to the next, and yesterday's drawback can be tomorrow's competitive edge. Table 1.5.2 shows some of the key features in each of the major UNIX platform vendor offerings.

Table 1.5.2. Platform feature comparisons.

Platforms:	IBM AIX	HP HP-UX	Sun Solaris
Features:			
Logical Volumes	Yes	Yes	No
First Tier Sybase Platform	Yes	Yes	Yes
Multiprocessors (SMP)Support	No	Yes	Yes
Built-in UPS	No	Yes	No
UNIX System V	Yes	No	Yes
Included C Compiler	Yes	Yes	No

Each of the three vendors provides systems that do different things well. Hewlett-Packard has long been known for its rigorous and exacting quality standards. Sun is an innovative software company. IBM has a tremendous marketing and support history. These are very difficult things to measure objectively, however.

For your site, you should not only identify the characteristics that are the most important for your applications, but provide a 1 to 10 weighting before performing the review. This way, you can take a simple statement of fact, such as that HP provides built-in, uninterruptible power supplies with all its servers, and determine just how important this feature is in an overall context. Add up the scores and you will have your technical product ratings!

Please use the preceding matrix only as an example for your own investigations. Although I believe that the foregoing statements are true, they may not be accurate for the products you're reviewing as of your particular stardate.

Summary

Even without delving into the specific features and attributes of any given tool or set of tools, you can see from this chapter that there are a number of assumptions that must be defined and tested. It's critical that you understand your environment, evaluate market trends and directions, and involve as many of your people as you can before making critical decisions about the tools to be used in building your Sybase application.

If you are not in a position of making these decisions, or perhaps were not even involved in the selection process, it's a good idea for you to investigate the thinking that went into selecting the tools that you do have to use.

Not the least reason is that you will have a better idea yourself about what the company expects you to accomplish with tools beyond the straightforward development of a system. The best tools will allow you not only to develop any given application, but will also provide the organization with a more strategic benefit. Developers tend to see tools in light of the application on which they are working, rather than in light of the value they provide to the organization or team as a whole.

The other important consideration is to understand the costs of shifting tools. In some cases, you may be able to make a case for moving to another product or vendor. In other cases, it may be a better idea to simply find a new place to work.

In any case, this chapter should have given you a better idea of the process that an organization undergoes when evaluating new tools. As you proceed though the book, you will see how this general review and somewhat ambiguous set of expectations translates into very specific features and implications as you select your own set of tools and develop a representative application.

1.6

Applying the Concepts

Introduction

This chapter ties together all of the ideas presented in this first section and demonstrates a practical example of how they can be applied. Identifying prerequisites is much like ensuring that you have easy access to your spare tire and jack before beginning a long drive. In some cases, you hope not to need to use them, but if the need does arise, you cannot afford the time to get organized.

In any case, this chapter introduces you to the concepts underlying the specific application that forms the practical basis for this book. The people who have been working with me on developing this application call it CausesDB because the database is built out of all the charities and worthy causes anyone might review when trying to determine whether to support the aims of a particular charity.

If you have no interest in worthy causes, don't worry; the idea is simply to show how to apply the techniques and methods outlined in the book. These techniques will work on any project, regardless of the nature of the data or users' requirements for massaging it.

On the other hand, anyone who is interested in the volunteer work performed by various organizations will get two benefits from this sample application. Not only will you see how to build an application with Sybase, but you will also be able to review the characteristics and objectives of many charitable organizations. Who knows? Perhaps by using the application, you will identify an organization whose cause you would like to support with time and money.

The Theory in Practice

It's always easier to discuss anything in general terms rather than bring it down to the level of specifics. Of course, the more general a discussion, the less likely you are to be able to do anything with the ideas that are being discussed. In this chapter, I introduce the CausesDB project and its objectives and requirements, as well as review the strategy for the project and identify the toolset we use to build the application. I use the term "we" advisedly here. This application is the result of the efforts of a team of individuals, performing the same functions and in the same roles that you would see in Sybase projects of your own. Their efforts are greatly appreciated and they have been acknowledged by name at the beginning of this book.

An important criterion underlying our approach to the application was that it had to represent the kind of projects any of you might be called on to implement. For this reason, I wanted to avoid using an overly specific business application such as a personnel database or, as is provided with the SQL Server product itself, the pubs database or a bookstore application.

Instead, in the book you will see how each of the design methods and topics can be applied to the building of a database containing comparison and marketing data for publicly funded charities.

The application will allow you to browse through the data to identify which, if any, of the causes appeal to your particular preferences. At the same time, you can also review the financial statistics of different charitable organizations to allow you to choose organizations you might be interested in supporting. This will allow you to determine whether there is a smaller, lesser known group with whose aims and objectives you might sympathize.

CausesDB as an application reflects the requirements of a typical Decision Support System (DSS). The underlying concept is that data needs to be accessed, filtered, and sorted in an ad-hoc fashion. Increasingly, Sybase is being used in this fashion as opposed to On-line Transaction Processing (OLTP) applications.

As we proceed with the development effort, you will see how Sybase SQL Server can be used in association with other Sybase products such as Watcom and PowerBuilder 4.0. Additionally, you will see how Sybase continues to maintain an open environment to allow interconnection of products such as Visual Basic through ODBC.

The Strategy

I work with a group of people who provide consulting services for building client/server applications using graphical front ends and Sybase or Oracle databases for the back end. As part of this book, I wanted to be able to share with you the approaches and methods we have been using to design and develop these systems successfully. As indicated previously, the idea from the beginning was to reinforce the concepts with a specific application that you could then reverse engineer to better understand how to build these systems.

This put me in a peculiar position. As a writer, I wanted to be able to select and develop the most widely applicable example of a client/server project using Sybase tools. On the other hand, it's not good business to give away the store. So, to meet both of these requirements, the strategy for the application was to address the same features and functions as any decision support system while dealing with a noncompetitive application area: charities.

For those of you who would have been able to use a Human Resources system or a Customer Management system, please feel free to contact me and I'll arrange to provide you a quote for professional services. For everyone else, I am confident that, as we go through the process of building the CausesDB application, you will gain an appreciation for all of the decision points and trade-offs that must be accommodated when building Sybase applications.

It will then be up to you to apply the process to the requirements of your particular organization and applications.

User Requirements

The primary group of people to review this application is you, the readers. As long as the application provides sufficient detail to allow you to see how we constructed the application, it should be useful as a learning and reinforcement tool.

At the same time, someone has to actually use the application, and this drives the structure and feature set to be implemented. On one level, I intended from the beginning that you would not only be observing how the application was built, but would use the application, hands-on, as well. For those of you who are more interested in what's under the hood, we are providing the source code for the application. If you see an interesting feature or function while executing the application, you can review the code to see how we did it.

Another important user group is the charitable organizations themselves. As some of you will already know, government funding for charities has been steadily reduced over the past decade or more. This places greater pressure on these organizations to acquire private sources of funds to continue their operations.

Private individuals, as a result, have been increasingly exposed to a barrage of requests for funding. People I have talked with have expressed some irritation at continually being asked for money. This is not to say that they are unwilling to lend some assistance. Rather, most people don't enjoy being bombarded with so many apparently equally worthy causes. It tends to make one callous and resistant to any message at all.

Many of the charitable organizations are aware of this irritation and donor resistance as well. They have begun sponsoring the idea that all of us should decided to back a single or small set of charities and lend our support to them. CausesDB was intended to support that process and to address the question: "How do I choose?"

If you want to find information on the biggest private companies, you can research the Fortune 500. However, obtaining information on charitable organizations is more difficult. Certainly, there is no shortage of advertising for your volunteer time or charitable donations. But comparison data is not readily available. This is exactly what we will be addressing in our CausesDB application.

The key purpose of the charitable organizations application is for potential supporters to discover key attributes of the cause and be able to easily donate funds or identify a contact for information. This is another important service provided by the CausesDB application.

Taking Stock

The first hurdle is to identify who is out there. Like the prerequisite of inventorying your own organization to determine where the data is stored and which systems are using what equipment, it was necessary for us to review the charities "market." Naturally, the first thing to avoid was any duplication of effort in assembling a database of charitable organizations and causes.

As you might expect, we discovered that not only was there no database of this nature, but that the idea had a tremendous appeal to a great many of the organizations we approached.

It was also interesting that not all of the institutions expressed interest. On occasion, the response was a polite acknowledgment of the concept but no real willingness to invest any effort or participate in any way.

We noticed that this attitude tended to come from the larger, more established organizations with highly organized funding drives and donor lists, but we had no information to back up our assessment. This would have to wait until CausesDB was actually completed.

The bottom line, however, was that most organizations were understaffed, underfunded, and very enthusiastic about anything that would get their message across to people interested in the topic area.

Like any project, however, an inventory is not just about determining who will use a potential application or data source. There are very pragmatic concerns that must be determined and that will dictate important systems elements such as the toolset and approach to implementation.

To establish the user requirements from the standpoint of the charitable institutions, we sent letters to registered charities, using a listing obtained from a reference book at a public library.

The letter indicated the objectives of CausesDB, much as they have been laid out here, and asked for expressions of interest.

From the faxes, phone calls, and letters we received in response, we decided that we had to develop a list of core users. The role of these people would be to assist us in determining the real requirements of non-profit organizations and to evaluate the suitability of our application as it was developed. The major point here for those of you just beginning your development exercise is that we made every effort to expose ourselves to people who would willingly participate in the work during each phase.

This is a critical deliverable to fall out of your inventory of your market, whether it is the largest or most visible 500 charities, or simply the department, division, or organization in which you work. The key is to identify who you can work with. This is a prerequisite to developing successful applications using Sybase in a client/server architecture.

Selecting a Toolset

From the discussion of user requirements, you should be able to see how the choice of development tools is driven. Because we established that you the reader are really the most important constituent, it made sense that we would choose Sybase as the development environment. (That was supposed to be funny.) Okay, to be honest, the only reason we chose Sybase was because we already had a title for the book. (You're not going to buy that one, either?) Actually, in this case our choice of tools was driven by the systems that the charities already had in place. As you might expect, this primarily consisted of Windows-based personal computers and an odd assortment of Apple Macintoshes. Not surprisingly, UNIX workstations did not figure highly in the list of preferred technologies.

In your situation, you'll find also that the choice of technologies is often driven by existing investments in technology and expertise. The key to successful development is to find a way to incorporate and take advantage of this investment, rather than to force a radical shift to a new platform. As discussed in Chapter 1.5, "Selecting a Toolset," there are occasions when it makes perfect sense to do just that. Given that we were hoping to attract the participation of an independent group, however, being restrictive in the client technologies did not make a great deal of sense.

This situation, however, does have an additional advantage from your point of view. Because there is a great variety of client workstations in place within charitable organizations—and this is most certainly true as well for you readers as a group—we determined that we needed to demonstrate our application on a variety of client platforms.

We knew that the data itself had to be stored within a Sybase SQL Server. This is not much different for those of you who are implementing your applications using key technologies that have been set as corporate standards. Sometimes you end up working with certain tools "just cuz."

In the case of CausesDB, we decided that we needed a tool that would be provided by a third party, because openness is a distinctive feature of working with Sybase, and we wanted something that would be multiplatform. As our organization had been granted involvement in the Powersoft HeadStart program, PowerBuilder version 4.0 was a perfect choice.

At the same time, we wanted to put as much emphasis as possible on developing Sybase applications, and that does not necessarily mean simply for the back end. To achieve this, we decided to provide you with a blow-by-blow description of how we developed CausesDB in both PowerBuilder 4.0 and in the Sybase Build Momentum product.

By using two separate tools, we thought we could best show how Sybase applications can be built taking advantage of server side utilities and services while allowing maximum access to client applications from multiple vendors. Of course, we wanted simultaneously to be able to compare and contrast the features of PB 4.0 and Build Momentum when both were attempting to address the same set of requirements.

The choice of PowerBuilder 4.0 also meant that we could release a version of the database in a stand-alone format, incorporating the Watcom database engine that is included with the Powersoft product. Because off-site development is a frequent requirement in many development projects, I wanted to cover some of the issues involved in developing an application that would port data from a stand-alone, third-party PC database to a multiuser corporate Sybase database.

The final reason for choosing PowerBuilder and Build Momentum for the development of the CausesDB application was our in-house experience. As I mentioned earlier, a Sybase project usually requires a number of people to be involved, and this application was no different. My team of developers and systems designers included people with a background and training in both products, and this meant that we had the opportunity to push the tools to their limits in certain areas. After reviewing who had time to assist me in this project, we developed a training plan for the developers to ensure that they had an opportunity to build on their experience with developing GUI applications in a Sybase environment.

From the first interviews with the charities and discussions about the design of the application, I knew that we would need to provide more than simply a database of facts and figures. To make the project more interesting technically, as well as to ensure that the finished application would hold a user's attention, I decided that CausesDB had to include the facility to retrieve and display any advertising used by the organization to get its message across.

From the organization's standpoint, this provided an opportunity to use a new medium (PC based CD-ROM) to distribute advertising. On the technical side, it meant that you would be taken through the process by which Sybase can be used to store and manipulate binary large objects (BLOBs). These BLOBs include representative .WAV, .TIF, and .AVI files that contain sound, still pictures, and video captures, respectively, of advertisements used by the organizations to get the attention of potential donors.

Also from the technical perspective, the inclusion of this requirement meant that you would see how PowerBuilder 4.0 and Build Momentum could be used to incorporate multimedia capabilities into an application using Sybase as the back end.

By evaluating the requirements of all of our users, assessing the technology available to us and our current levels of expertise, the choice of PowerBuilder 4.0, Build Momentum, and Sybase as the toolset seemed a logical one.

Summary

You should now have an overview of the application that will serve as the example for all of the development techniques covered in this book. I hope that, besides being a functional exercise, the application itself has some merit.

In this chapter I detailed the process of addressing the prerequisites for developing a client/server application. The first and most important point was to find the client. In this case, you are the first client and the charitable institutions are the secondary client.

Next, you saw how we assessed the existing situation to determine where we fit into the overall scheme of things. As it turns out, this was a unique approach and we did not duplicate any existing efforts.

The review of the strategy and its application to the project was also an important preliminary step, without which it would be difficult to create a truly useful application. Finally, I identified the resources and approach to be used in developing the application.

These have been covered in the most general terms because they are prerequisites or preliminary steps. As you continue through the book, you will see how the client/server design and development process becomes increasingly more detailed and focused, allowing the creation of a working application that meets the needs identified in this chapter.

From this specific example of how a potential project is assessed, you should have a clearer idea of the practical application for the concepts described in this section.

2

Overview of the Client/Server Development Process

Introduction to the Section

Developing Sybase applications implicitly means developing client/server applications. Of course, it's possible to develop traditional host/slave applications complete with character-based interfaces and dumb terminals, but I seriously doubt that that is the reason you're reading this book. To understand how to best take advantage of Sybase, you should first understand how developing for a client/server architecture differs from more traditional development efforts.

Of equal benefit is understanding the similarities between the two development paradigms. (I had promised a friend of mine never to use that term, so I guess now I owe him a beer.) As indicated in Chapter 1.2, there are a number of useful techniques that you should incorporate into your client/server systems, whether your experience is as a mainframe programmer or a PC systems developer.

In this section you will be taken through the step-by-step approach that will be used to develop our sample application. Included is a description of the major components of a client/server systems development lifecycle and the specific steps that make up each one.

The objective of this section is to provide a comprehensive, high-level overview of all the steps that must be performed when you are developing a working, maintainable application under a client/server architecture using Sybase.

The development lifecycle and methodology represented in this section has been used by a number of the consultants in my firm for more than a decade in a wide variety of application areas and with a diverse assortment of tools. The only thing that was consistent in each case was that the process yielded a working system that provided real benefit in the eyes of the users.

You may be interested in knowing the specific kinds of environments in which this development process was used successfully. For the private sector, we have used the methodology to develop the following:

- Order entry and back office administration systems for financial services companies
- Data gathering, statistical analysis, and reporting applications for an international management consulting firm
- All nonfinancial applications, including customer, order, manufacturing, and sales systems for a cable manufacturing firm

For public sector organizations, we have developed systems using the methodology for the following branches and state controlled corporations:

- A patient record tracking and reporting system in a specialized health care setting
- PC software and hardware support as well as migration of mainframe data to departmental LANs

Sybase was not used in all of these cases, but either the elements or the entire systems development methodology described in this book were incorporated. I hope you will find this experience applicable and that you will use it to develop successful Sybase applications of your own.

2.1

The C/S Development Process

Introduction

In this chapter you will exposed to the five major elements of client/server systems. You also will be provided with a complete list of activities that must be performed as part of each element. Further, each of the activities will be described to allow you to understand what must be done and the ultimate outcome of each of the development processes. Taken together, this framework organizes all the work that is usually performed as part of a major systems development effort using Sybase and related products.

In this chapter I focus more on the processes and data than on the technology or tools that you can use for assistance. Whether you opt for specialized software tools or work with standard systems products and adapt the methodology, this chapter will help you learn what must be done to succeed in your development effort.

The objective of this chapter is to provide a brief description of the development process as a whole. Specific examples of the techniques you can use to accomplish these things will be provided in Chapter 2.3. For now, the intent is to provide a high-level description of the life of any given client/server project, including your Sybase application.

Client/Server Development Lifecycle

There are five major elements in the lifecycle of any client/server application. These are shown in Figure 2.1.1.

FIGURE 2.1.1.
The five-step client/server systems lifecycle.

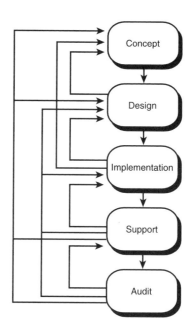

Someone once pointed out to me that all of these lifecycle diagrams look alike. However, I believe that this overview provides the cleanest and most complete coverage of systems developed using client/server technology. Of course, this process can be applied to more than just client/server projects, but it's especially useful in the context of emerging technologies. Descriptions follow for each stage in the lifecycle.

Concept

This is the complete description of the project at a high level. It is essentially a sketch of what the application will do and the role it will play. The business proposal that justifies expenditures on a system is part of the conceptual level. In this way, management and the users can determine whether a system is worth the investment in time, effort, and money without necessarily understanding exactly how the system will be built.

Design

The design differs from the conceptual stage primarily in the degree of detail. Whereas the concept identifies the systems elements at the highest level, the design must incorporate sufficiently detailed specifications to allow the system to be built. Elements of the design stage include building data and process models as well as data flow and entity relationship diagrams. The design process also includes a detailed work plan with task assignment and delivery dates.

Implementation

To gain the desired results from a system, the design must be put into effect. This is where the techniques for managing change become the critical success factor, because no one ever identifies all the work to be done as part of the design process. Implementation is most definitely a process that must be managed carefully and effectively if you are to gain the benefits expected from your Sybase application.

Support

This distinct area occurs throughout the life of the project, with the greatest impact during the implementation process. Support includes such activities as training, help desk, troubleshooting, upgrades, enhancements and performance tuning after the application has been accepted by its users.

Audit

All projects should be audited to determine whether the expectations set out in the feasibility study were fulfilled. The audit process will also identify where the project can be enhanced as part of the continuing life of the application. In some cases, the audit will recommend new objectives for a new project to meet requirements that were beyond the scope of your Sybase application. In either case, it's a key component in the success of any client/server application development effort, especially if your organization is to retain and communicate the lessons learned during your project.

As mentioned earlier in this chapter, many people have reviewed this model and reacted with a ho-hum, who cares attitude. Certainly, I don't believe there is anything radical about it; however, I have found that it provides a useful and widely applicable model to allow you to begin organizing the myriad tasks that must be performed as part of any Sybase development.

The Waterfall versus the Iterative Model

The introduction of client/server tools such as Sybase has not eliminated the need to manage the development process. Iterative development is not some magic bullet that eliminates the need to perform systems development steps that have been used for years in the mainframe world.

The differences are more subtle than that, and, frankly, that makes them more difficult. What on the surface appears similar can be likened to hoary old practices without looking underneath for what makes them effective.

In the past, systems development models have called for the completion of one phase, with identified outputs from that phase, which form the input for the next phase. This "waterfall" model (see Figure 2.1.2) clearly depicted the lifecycle of a system from the initial requirements through the design phase and then coding, testing, user acceptance, and maintenance. One of the key attributes of these models was a freezing of analysis, specifications, or code at various times to ensure that a particular stage was actually completed, instead of it turning into some never-ending hamster wheel of activity without achievement.

The iterative method assumes that you learn more about the application as you go along. This is a very different assumption than the older approach. It's simply not effective to study a business unit until you feel that you know everything about it and then go away and design an application. The key to the new approach is to analyze, design, and develop as part of a linked process that allows the application under development to reflect changes in the business when and as they happen. This necessarily requires a more flexible design and development methodology than the more traditional, structured approaches.

I want to take a minute at this point to stress something to those of you who have been developing single-user PC applications, while at the same time reassure those of you who have been traditional mainframe developers. The old guys knew a thing or two about building systems. A person coming from a PC background tends to think that flexibility and user preferences are paramount. However, that bias can bring a development effort to a screeching, grinding halt when the data volumes move up into the gigabytes and the number of concurrent users number in the hundreds and possibly thousands. Volume has its own demands and the mainframe world has been addressing these, however imperfectly, for a few decades. Client/server systems are here to enhance those capabilities, not replace them.

FIGURE 2.1.2.
A typical waterfall development model.

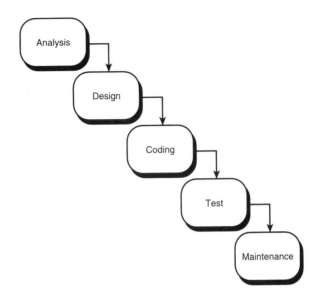

That being stated, it's important to recognize that there must be a balance between the client- and server-side considerations. One of the issues I address throughout this book is the balance that should exist between client and server capabilities.

In the next chapter you will be taken through specific recommendations for creating Sybase applications under a rapid, iterative methodology. Here, I simply want to organize the work into discrete phases to help you see what work must be performed at what time, as well as providing a description of the appropriate degree of detail. When taking the iterative approach to client/server systems development, the five steps are organized more in this fashion.

Figure 2.1.3 shows how the iterative model encompasses each stage and builds on work performed in previous stages and iterations.

FIGURE 2.1.3.
Iterative development model for client/server applications.

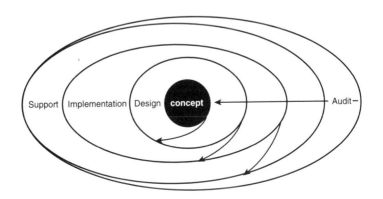

The Client/Server Systems Concept

There are a number of deliverables that you must meet before you can say that you have fully defined your application at the conceptual level. These include:

■ To prepare and present the business case

■ To secure executive sponsorship

■ To describe the user requirements

■ To determine the application platform and toolset

Each of these has its own underpinning deliverables that also must be addressed.

As one of the prerequisites, you should already have addressed the business strategies your system will support. This is the key to writing a winning business case. Keep in mind that not only must you go through the process of writing and presenting the business case, but also that it must explain the system in business terms, rather than technological terms. At the same time, you must already have identified sufficient user requirements for the system to address so that the executives can see the system as practical and worthwhile. Naturally, you must already have some idea what tools you wish to use, because this will form the basis for the budget you need to allocate in the business case.

Minimize the Tactical Techie Details

Successful client/server proposals describe the functionality of the system at the highest level of abstraction and work their way down to the details. I don't mean that these proposals start off with an executive summary. I am saying that a winning business case clearly identifies at the beginning of the proposal what strategic initiatives the system will support, and then it moves into how the user requirements for systems services will be met by the application. This forms a description of how the technology will be applied at the strategic and business function level. With this kind of applied systems technology, you should have less difficulty finding an executive willing to sponsor and support your system. Without this kind of clear description of the business and strategic benefits, why would any executive be willing to take the risk of the project failing?

If you don't have the credibility with your management for them to believe that you will successfully implement the system, you're probably wasting your time. The business case is not the place to design the system. As far as the technology goes, you should merely take your best guess at how much gear, training, and outside expertise you'll need, and then double the estimated cost. If the savings you can generate with your application will not cover that level of expense, chances are that you should be looking elsewhere to apply your client/server technology.

With these elements in place, look at what you have already. First, you have a clear description of where the systems will be aimed and who they will support, as well as a description of the technology to be used and estimates for the cost. All in all, this forms a conceptual description of a Sybase application.

Designing Your Sybase Application

Now we can assume that you have secured approval for your project and you have identified that Sybase and a number of other tools will be used to develop the application. The first thing you do is *not* to run out and place an order for tools and toys. This is where you design your system.

Securing User Backing

In every organization I have ever visited, systems people give lip service to the idea that applications must be designed with user involvement. Frequently, however, they then proceed to design their systems without real and significant user involvement.

There is no magic formula for determining how much user time must be allocated to an application during its development, but a reasonable barometer is whether the users feel they are involved. Requiring too much of their time is equally detrimental to their acceptance of the system. The bottom line is whether they would tell an objective observer that they have been involved in the process. And the best place to start involving them is at the beginning.

During the conceptual stage, you will have identified the application area and general user requirements. As well as having an executive sponsor, you should have contacts and supporters within the user groups who will be affected by implementing the new system. The last thing you want to do is catch them by surprise with a big announcement that their new system has been approved. This is virtually guaranteed to put them on the defensive and your application on the wrong foot.

Timing of User Involvement

In practice, your business case has a much greater likelihood of being approved with strong user support from the outset. Naturally, this support will have the most credibility with your decision makers if the user support comes from the management level. But to really bind the user community to your systems project from the beginning, you should start the design process with the lower-level folks *before* your system is approved.

This accomplishes several things. First, it gives you something to do while you await approval. Frequently, systems people simply sit on their hands waiting and wondering whether their project proposal will be given the go ahead. In fact, this is an excellent opportunity to get started on the design process, for which there is never enough time anyway.

Second, it dramatically increases user commitment to the development process. Users are no less subject to the "us and them" phenomenon than anyone else. By designing the system with them while you wait to determine whether you will actually be given the systems resources to implement, they will pick up the anticipation of your systems people and begin hoping that the approval is granted. This obviously helps to get them on-side for the development process once management gives the nod to the project.

Last, if the funding is not allocated or is postponed, the worst that happens is that you better understand the area to be automated. This is not a down side, in as much as you can find stronger justification for your business case or even alternative means of achieving some efficiencies without applying systems technology. Remember, there has to be some business purpose to any systems effort, and if your project is not approved, you can still make improvements in the business unit and your systems design efforts will have yielded a desirable dividend.

Structuring Your Design Effort

Now that you know when to begin the design process, the next important step is structuring the design team and its approach. Good design is the result of a managed process and never occurs by accident. Left to their own devices, systems people will almost always skip over the part where they talk to other nontechnical staff about the system and go right into doing the work itself. By structuring the design effort and clearly stating expectations, you can avoid this.

The key steps to be performed as part of this structure include:

- Preparing a project plan
- Defining roles and responsibilities
- Establishing reporting structure
- Appointing project team members
- Identifying user champions
- Training in technologies concepts
- Developing a business process model
- Developing a data model
- Performing hands-on technology training
- Providing development application specifications
- Providing a development prototype

As part of the systems concept, you will have identified key milestones and delivery dates. As you structure the design process, you'll have a better idea of exactly what steps must be performed and when they must be completed in order to meet the milestones presented to management as part of the systems proposal.

Establishing a Reporting Structure

If you did not identify how progress would be reported and managed as part of your systems concept, you must do so at this point. Most organizations have a steering committee or some other mechanism for coordinating projects that cross departmental or divisional lines. Identifying who and how frequently the design and development team(s) will be accountable to must be defined no later than this point, along with what progress they will be expected to achieve by which points.

These clearly stated expectations should be represented in a project plan that is shared with all of the members of the team involved in doing the work.

Training in a Technology's Concepts

Now, this is where the line between the new techniques and the traditional approach gets blurry. Of course, systems people have been putting together systems plans complete with GANTT and PERT charts. And, of course, systems have missed their delivery dates and had to have the deadlines pushed back. This is made even worse when you're dealing with new technologies that you do not really understand yet. How do you estimate how long it will take to develop a system when you have to first learn the tools with which you expect to develop said system?

To begin with, it's important to budget time to learn. Second, ensure that everyone is scheduled to learn at the same time and that the result of their training will be tangible, reusable products that are directly relevant to the system to be built.

By focusing on in-house training, for example, you have an opportunity for developers to work with users in creating disposable examples of how the technology can be used in your organization. Instead of using canned examples and irrelevant tutorials, you can incorporate your design findings into samples that can be reviewed by systems people and the users as well. Certainly you should expect these samples to be rather feeble attempts to show what the technology can do, but the important thing is to get people used to the fact that applications will grow and change in front of them. By presenting examples of functions and feature set fragments for user review right from the beginning, you can start the adoption and transfer process immediately. However, this kind of effort should be scheduled to take place after the documentation of the business and data models.

If your group is new to the relational model as well as to the specific client/server technology with which you'll build your system, it's an excellent idea to schedule concepts training prior to the design effort. Concepts training incorporates abstract (as opposed to hands-on) review of all the major elements of a technology and identifies the implications and benefits of using that technology.

A general introduction to GUIs, for example, would identify the various widgets and objects to be found in a typical graphical environment and describe the benefits of using the technology, such as multitasking and flexible access to data. This is especially beneficial to developers who are migrating from character-based applications and who may be somewhat intimidated by the need to learn a complex set of new technologies and techniques.

Identifying User Champions

During the initial investigation phase, you should have gained some insight into which members of the business units were most motivated and interested in participating in the systems design and development process. Once these people have been identified, you need to make every effort to get them officially assigned to your project team.

In some cases, this can be made more difficult by the existence of unions or other organizations that aren't necessarily interested in having the new system proceed. I have even heard of cases in which user involvement was assigned by the union on the basis of seniority, or some basis other than interest, willingness, and qualifications. If your organization presents challenges such as these, consider creating temporary management-level positions for which interested people can apply.

Even if your organization is not unionized, you may find that a technique such as this is one way to ensure that the user department actually provides a team member with sufficient time to dedicate to the project team. All too frequently, user champions are provided to the team with instructions to keep on top of their regular workload as well. This is not a realistic expectation. The most effective user champions not only understand their business unit and its operation, but are in a position to invest significant time in transferring that understanding to the application design and development team while learning about the systems technologies as well.

Once you have assembled your team and assigned responsibilities, you are finally in a position to get down to work.

Modeling the Business Process

A great deal of discussion has been generated in recent years over the term *business process reengineering*. Of course, this term implies that business procedures were ever engineered to begin with, a premise that does not bear up under scrutiny in many organizations. Most business units have instituted practices and procedures piecemeal, each individually growing up to address some requirement or change in the unit's function. To assume that you can simply reengineer these processes is an assumption fraught with complications.

The first order of business is to understand the existing procedures, systems, and data. In Section 1, you were taken through a discussion of prerequisites, and I identified the need to determine which technology was in use throughout the business unit. During the design phase, you take this to a greater degree of detail, and inventory the data along with the procedures for moving it around.

This happens best when treated as a two-step process, though the same groups of users will provide you with the information needed, and they will frequently see the processes and data as tightly integrated. From a documentation perspective, it's easier to start documenting the business flows first, and then model the data used. This requires a certain degree of discipline on the part of your project design leader, as users typically do not have a concise and clear view of exactly how their business unit functions.

In fact, your design effort may be the first time they have a set of leveled diagrams that show how they conduct business. If you do your design correctly, they will begin to adopt the diagrams as a means of explaining their jobs to nonsystems people, such as new hires in their unit.

In any case, you'll want two separate design documents, the business process model and the data model. In the documentation of each of these models there should be two distinct sections: documentation of the current situation and proposed changes to the models. This is how you document business process reengineering. First, reverse engineer the processes in place, then review the model to determine where improvements can be made. Once the changes have been documented, they can be presented to various users for critical review and refinement.

Developing a Data Model

Once you know how work is performed within the business unit, division, or even within the enterprise as a whole (now there is a documentation challenge!), you can then associate data with each of the processes. Meeting with typically the same group of users who assisted in the modeling process, you review the approved process model and determine which data is captured, used, and modified at each step. The idea is to ensure that you have completely inventoried all of the data used within the unit. After you're confident that you have it all, you review the proposed changes to the process to ensure that any new information has also been identified.

From the complete listing of data elements, you are then in a position to manipulate the data into data flow diagrams and entity relationship diagrams.

In various courses I have taught on this process, there have been sometimes heated discussions between members of the class on the merits of this approach. At one point, I was accused of living in the 1970s, which was when many of the documentation techniques for data flow diagramming were developed. Interestingly, the ensuing discussion yielded agreement in the class that, although many of these techniques may be traditional, they are still valid.

More importantly, doing things the old way is much better than not performing this work at all. All the hype over object modeling can't take away from the effectiveness of documenting a complete map of all data within an application area and how it is moved from point A to point B.

I find that using a white board and bubble diagrams is the simplest, cheapest and most effective means of doing this, but you should feel free to use whatever techniques work for you. Just be sure that you take the time to do it. There is no substitute for understanding what data is used and how it is used. This is especially true if you expect to be working with an Order Processing application, when many different people work on the same data, each adding to or modifying it as part of their activities. Sybase projects involving work flow automation are doomed without clearly understood data flow models.

Making the Data Model Relational

The entity relationship diagram of all data to be used in your application is an integral part of designing a relational system. Few people would try to implement a database application without one. However, you should not confuse your general user population with ER diagrams.

Typically, only your most technically sophisticated users will be involved in the development of ER diagrams, because some users won't understand the concepts of one-to-one and one-to-many relationships, nor should it be necessary for them to understand. When determining which users are best suited to assisting you with this part of the modeling exercise, try asking yourself whether they will be using SQL as part of their activities. If not, leave them out of it; but if a user will be writing his or her own queries, that user should be involved in the ER modeling process, or at least be given every opportunity to review it.

Typically, the ER diagram is of more use to developers and administrators than to end users. You should avoid the temptation to develop an ER model in place of documents clearly depicting the flow of data from a business perspective. The two serve very different functions and should be treated as distinct entities (bad pun alert).

Hands-On Training

Everyone knows that, with training, if you don't use it, you lose it. This is especially true of any kind of syntactic-level, hands-on training. If you have not received your software or gear yet, don't waste your time on training. As pointed out earlier in the chapter, that time is better spent in the design and documentation process.

Eventually, you will get some technology on site, however, and you can expect that this will immediately receive number one priority status in the minds of your development team. Even though you're not yet ready to develop your system, the best thing to do next is to give the team the opportunity to play with their new toys.

In-house training is the best way to ensure a highly customized and relevant skills transfer session. Better yet, have the training conducted by someone from outside who not only performs the training but is also responsible for leading your people in the development of the application. That way, they are motivated to provide the most applicable training they can in the shortest possible time.

In any case, in-house training is not always feasible. You can still benefit from sending people out for technical training and then allowing them time to apply what they have learned when they get back to the office. Don't make the mistake of assuming that they will come back from training ready to develop.

After being inundated with new concepts, syntax, and techniques most people need at least a month to experiment and reinforce the training and are only then in a position to begin applying what they have learned.

Developing Application Specifications

There are few, if any, widely understood and endorsed standards for client/server application specifications. Because you are judged on the quality of the application, not the specifications, the specifications are often treated as secondary. On the other hand, it's less likely that you will successfully develop a system without specifications or a blueprint, so perhaps they should not be considered secondary or ancillary.

Well, that is all well and good, but what purpose do these specifications serve? In a nutshell, the specifications provide the complete list of services to be provided by the application.

If the user requirements form the question, the specifications provide the answer. I have seen other developers try to represent application specifications in the form of menus or dialog boxes. I think it's more effective, however, to start with a list of functions and describe them in writing.

For example, the Add New Customer function allows you to create a new customer and enter demographic and contact data.

Once you have the list of functions, you can begin organizing them into menu bars, dialog boxes, and screen forms. These applications specifications give you a place to begin prototyping, which is the first thing the users and management will accept as real progress toward building a working system.

The Prototyping Process

This has to be one of the most misunderstood elements of building client/server applications. Half the time, I see organizations working on prototypes that they believe can be quickly moved into production. In this systems development methodology, the prototyping effort is part of the design process and not part of implementation.

Of course, once again this is a blurry line in the iterative process. If a prototype helps prepare the users for the new system and provides a straw man for them to criticize weak features while reviewing the development proceeds, certainly it can be seen as an implementation aid.

The real value of a prototype, however, is found when you can throw it away. This may be a somewhat provocative remark, but follow through the reasoning. The prototype is the first reflection of the systems features through a development by people unfamiliar with a tool. It is fundamentally unfair and unreasonable to expect that this effort will be good enough to move up into a production system.

Instead, it makes more sense that the prototype will provide a clear example of what the system will do for the users, while giving the design team time to experiment with how to get the technology to do it.

The client/server development process is hard enough without expecting people to come immediately up to speed with new tools. You should remember that if you put into production the first few attempts at working with a new technology, the application will haunt you forever.

By assuring your development team members that you will actually throw away the prototype and let them start from scratch, you free them to experiment more readily and see what they can make the technology do. Let's face it, if they actually develop something worth keeping, you will be the first to know that they want to keep it.

The key to success with the prototyping process is not to see throwing it out and starting fresh as reinventing the wheel. The prototype is a living reflection of the design, and often the guts of the application were never incorporated into the prototype. If 80 percent of the systems functions take 20 percent of the time, the prototype is the place to demonstrate that functionality.

Avoid the temptation to address the myriad of exceptions and validations as part of the prototype. Once you know what your users want, and they have endorsed your prototype, you are then prepared to move into implementation with the development of a new system, using technology you are familiar with to address requirements you understand.

The Implementation Process

In the waterfall process of systems development, implementation is getting the job done right the first time. In the iterative process, it is getting the job done over and over. In either case, implementation is where the rubber meets the road, the acid test, the proof of the pudding (don't you just hate clichés?).

As I mentioned in an earlier passage, I tend to think of implementation as the combat zone.

This Is Not an Implementation Model that Works

In many systems development lifecycles, there is a testing phase prior to implementation. I believe implementation is really one cycle of testing, modification, and retesting until finally the product is deemed acceptable enough to be a production release.

Perhaps this makes me a cynic, but I have seen many implementations fail because the onus was on the systems delivery people to ensure that they had coded something that could be released to the user without further change. To me this is like the sculptor who toils away in the studio, crafting and carving a masterpiece, and then finally unveiling it with a dramatic flourish, breathlessly anticipating the audience reaction.

A much more effective approach is to understand that there will be last-minute changes, unforeseen implications, and complete reversals of business functions and priorities. The trick is to prepare for this process and meet it head on, rather than complain bitterly that you were not given enough time, that they changed the specifications, that no one had told you about this requirement, and so on.

Not that these complaints are unjustified, but that they are to be expected, and you have an opportunity with the newer client/server tools to fold these expectations into your software development process.

I once heard an interview with Frank Lloyd Wright on the radio. He said something like, there is nothing more beautiful than a plan. By definition, it's perfect. It contains everything you can imagine and meets every eventuality you've foreseen. He went on to point out that when you try to build according to the plan, you discover just how many things you forgot to plan for. This is every bit as true for client/server development projects as it is for building works of art that masquerade as houses (sorry, Frank).

I mention both the sculptor and the architect for good reason. Both are craftspeople, employing a combination of art and science to create something tangible. In this, your Sybase application is no different. However, a system is a living, changing entity and must accommodate and adapt to the people who use it. You should be careful to avoid too much artistic temperament or pride in your "creation." A truly successful client/server application belongs to the people who use it, not those who design and develop it.

Implementation Steps

Okay, the lecture is over. There are several key steps that must be addressed as part of any successful implementation.

- Developing a change plan
- Ensuring frequent reviews
- Focusing on rapid changes
- Identifying future changes
- Setting the user acceptance date

These are the critical components to a successful implementation.

Developing a Change Plan

A change plan is a written document that clearly identifies all of the obstacles to change and provides several methods for overcoming them. This can be as simple as an outline that delineates each potential hurdle that you must overcome as part of the change management process and alternatives to beat them.

Ensuring Frequent Reviews

Schedule frequent reviews to allow users a forum for expressing their frustration and identifying the obstacles they face. Criticism is always hard for anyone to accept, constructive or otherwise, but I have seen otherwise-doomed projects succeed because the development team accepted every critical comment without reacting defensively, and then went out and made each of the changes demanded as quickly as possible.

Focusing on Rapid Changes

No one will criticize forever if they realize that you are working very hard to give them what they ask for. Even if some of the changes are too large to be made quickly, you can provide your users with an avalanche of little ones. This will provide a higher level of confidence to the users in the idea that they will not be stuck with the system as it is initially delivered. When they come to understand how quickly modifications can be made, they will become a little more relaxed in the way they present their critique (though you shouldn't expect miracles; after all, they are still users).

Identifying Future Changes

Changes that can't be made at once or that fall outside a reasonable effort to accommodate must still be acknowledged. While you're busy implementing the dozens of little changes, you can post future enhancements to be provided in future versions. This is also a polite way of saying no.

Setting the User Acceptance Date

Set and stick to a firm acceptance date. Give your systems people as much time as you can to make changes, but make sure that the ultimate "go/no go" decision is in the hands of the users, and provide a deadline by which the verdict will come in. If the system can't be made to work, or if confidence is simply so low that success is impossible, you do yourself and everyone else a favor by setting a date to throw in the towel.

On a more positive note, by setting a deadline, you allow everyone to focus on the frenetic pace up to a particular point and then, ultimately, the decision is made: the systems stays or it goes. If accepted, the pace will likely become less hectic, though changes will no doubt continue to be requested and made.

By adopting these tactics, you can use implementation as a method to successfully graft the new system into the business unit, while identifying and fixing all the shortcomings in the design that were not clearly understood until it was time to make it work.

Support

Some would treat training as a support service, especially in a model that does not require all of its aspects to be contained within the same time frame. More traditional forms of support for implementation and continuing operation of the application include the following:

> Telephone support
> Online help
> Documentation
> Tutoring and mentoring
> Troubleshooting
> New version releases

The support services provided for an internally developed application are typically not as sophisticated as those offered by shrink-wrapped application vendors. Still, they should serve as the model of the kinds of support services your group should provide, if only because users are becoming more sophisticated. As they get more experience with good packages and the kind of support offered by third-party vendors, their expectations of you will also increase.

You have no doubt heard that executives want systems to be considered a service that treats internal users as customers. Well, support is one of the key areas on which you will be judged.

Telephone Support

Telephone support can range from a formal help desk with 1-800 service to a more casual information center request line. As part of your client/server systems development effort, you should plan, budget for, and implement a support model that at least identifies how these services will be provided, how they will be communicated, and how their usage will be measured and monitored.

Online Help

Online help has been made significantly easier with the advent of help engines such as Visual Help, RoboHelp, and Doc 2 Help. There really is no excuse for any software developer not to include at least some basic level of hypertext help in the client-side applications they develop.

Tutoring and Mentoring

Tutoring and mentoring sound impressive, but it really comes down to being willing to sit with someone who is having trouble and work through the application with them. This is especially vital during implementation, and interestingly, the most effective people are often users, not systems people. Identify this as a user role and see whether you can get people to willingly volunteer for the responsibility. It can be an amazingly effective means of transferring skills.

Documentation

E-mail or printed newsletters can also address the kinds of tips and techniques that should be shared over a wider area. Forget dismissing this as cute or some kind of political game. If you provide relevant, valuable tips, people will read and appreciate your newsletter regardless of its format or level of sophistication in terms of graphics or writing style.

Troubleshooters

External troubleshooters can provide you with heavy-hitting expertise for problems you just can't seem to solve. More important, by selectively bringing in outside expertise, you communicate that you take the users seriously and that you are willing to spend the money or effort necessary to get the job done. You don't have to do this often, but it pays to do it when necessary.

New Version Releases

Last, new versions are a form of support. Once the product has been designed, developed, and implemented, it needs to adapt and grow. At that point, it's not so much a new system as a maturation of the initial set of intentions or objectives for the application. New versions and bug fixes then become part of the support process.

Audit

Ah, the old report card. Many people are afraid of being measured, worrying that they will be found wanting. This attitude has no place in the development of a professional and successful Sybase application. If you believe that you can do a good job and make the technology work for your organization, you must be willing to stand up and be counted.

The purpose behind the report is to determine how well the actual delivery of the system met with the functions and features promised in the original business case. The ultimate point behind the audit is to keep you honest and to identify where the system development process broke down to allow others to improve on your efforts in the future.

To truly be effective, a project or application audit must incorporate several elements. It must be the following:

■ Objectively administered

- Planned from the beginning
- Used to identify weaknesses and strengths
- Used to confirm actual performance against the plan

These are the key elements of an audit under this iterative development model. In reality, the audit is not iterative; it marks the end of one cycle and may call for the beginning of another.

By planning for an audit, you ensure that your project will at some point end, freeing you to move on to other things (within your organization, one hopes). The idea behind planning for the audit from the beginning is to ensure that all the people involved recognize that their efforts will be monitored and reported. Certainly, a call for an audit can only help your case when you first look for approval from management. But it can also be a means of enforcing quality control during the development process. When compromises are suggested, everyone can consider whether they are things that would stand up to an independent audit.

This point is quite significant. To have any credibility in the rest of your organization, the audit must be performed by someone with nothing to gain. In larger shops, an internal audit department offers these "services," though not usually on a voluntary basis. In smaller shops, you might consider having an outside consulting firm hired to perform the audit and submit the report to management.

Summary

Well, there you have it, a complete client/server development lifecycle. From this chapter you should have a much better sense of how a Sybase project can be approached from beginning to end. You should also have a much clearer idea of all of the steps that must be taken and the order to take them.

Of course, it's quite possible to develop successful Sybase applications without adhering to this model. However, the purpose of this chapter is to familiarize you with the development process as a whole. To effectively apply this process, there are a number of techniques to be used, and these will form much of the substance of the rest of this book.

This methodology is not theoretical nor academic. It is inherently a practical approach to systems development, intended to provide the appropriate degree of emphasis where you need to pay attention and omitting or glossing over any practices that are irrelevant or don't significantly advance the likelihood of success for your particular project.

Those of you who have worked with structured methodologies in the past will recognize a great deal of the material covered in this chapter. I hope you can also see where the emphasis of this approach departs from more traditional development models and allows for the unique strengths of Sybase and related tools in building client/server systems.

2.2

Unique Features of the Sybase Environment

Introduction

Up to now, most of my comments have been somewhat general and apply to any product that falls into the client/server category. In this chapter you will find a focus on the differences between the traditional development environment and using Sybase tools, including the SQL Server engine.

This section is still intended to be at a higher level and, in keeping with this level of detail, I will not be delving too deeply into the Sybase architecture and feature set. This is covered more in Chapter 3.1, "SQL Server from Sybase," and in a lot more detail in *Sybase Developer's Guide.* In any case, even a cursory treatment of this environment will show you several key differences in how the tools are used compared to more traditional development efforts.

By the end of this chapter you should know the unique features of the Sybase environment (hence the chapter's title), but more important, you should have a solid sense of the opportunities and challenges these features present when it comes to designing and developing functional applications.

The Open Environment

In Chapter 1.5, "Selecting a Toolset," I discussed the range of choices you face when selecting a toolset. One of the poles of that range was to opt for a collection of highly open, best-of-breed tools. Sybase has definitely chosen to position its product at this end of the street.

To clarify the terms, open systems as they apply to Sybase are characterized by several key attributes:

- ■ Scalability
- ■ Interoperability
- ■ Third-party connectivity

Each of these attributes makes it possible to use Sybase products in new ways. The following sections describe these attributes.

Scalability

Sybase has been designed to allow you to start small and grow your application as required. This is especially useful if you intend to build a cheap prototype in order to secure user commitment before spending the big dollars on developing a large-scale system for a much wider roll out.

When you consider using the scalable aspect as part of your development approach, it should be much clearer why prototyping is really part of the design process rather than the first step in implementation. Your management is much less likely to confuse a system capable of supporting eight users with a system intended to support 250 concurrent user connections.

Should you design your applications in this manner, you should keep firmly in mind that, once you have identified the features and functions of the system, you will need to overhaul your design to work properly in the larger volume setting. Scalability does not mean that you can design for a small group of users and then roll out your applications across the enterprise without modification. Many larger Sybase shops have discovered that volume creates its own problems, and your design must allow for modifications that support the intended size of the target system.

At a high level, this summarizes the implications of Sybase scalability when designing and developing client/server applications.

Interoperability

Sybase has always been a multiplatform product with virtually identical operations on each system on which it runs. This has several interesting implications from an architectural and developers' perspective. First, it also provides you with the opportunity to start small and grow.

Although most organizations have some experience with client/server systems at this point, not everyone has been prepared to make the leap into, say, UNIX-based servers. If you're in a position of having to prove the value of the technology while at the same time developing a working application that will be used to determine that value, you may not want to bite off a new operating system at the same time.

This is where the interoperability feature provides several advantages because you can acquire the database engine for a smaller environment with which you already have experience, such as OS/2, and develop a sample or prototype application under that environment.

Once the users have an opportunity to play with the system and validate your approach, your plan may call for a further investment in a more powerful underlying server platform. Before any of you OS/2 fans go nuts over this statement, let's acknowledge that no one is using PC-based applications to support hundreds of users connected concurrently, processing hundreds of transactions per second, and manipulating volumes of data measured in gigabytes. Actually, let me retract that. I don't know of anyone successfully doing this; if you are, drop me a line on CompuServe. I would like to chat with you about it.

Exceptions aside, most organizations that begin using PC-based platforms for their initial Sybase application development migrate those applications to a UNIX environment at some point. The key here is not that UNIX is a wonderful environment (it might be more accurately described as a cruel hoax), but that once you have invested time and effort into developing Sybase applications for one environment, you are not locked into that environment. Your database structures, objects, and applications can all be moved quite transparently to run on a SQL Server of the same version on a different platform.

I put the proviso of the same version on because, like most software products, Sybase is not necessarily downwardly compatible, especially with applications that include the enhanced features of System 10. However, if all you change is the host platform, your migration to a different platform should be relatively painless.

The Advantages of Flexible Platforms

A second major advantage or opportunity presented by this interoperability is the facility to roll out your applications on a variety of server platforms. In one of my professional incarnations, I worked as an IS manager for a consulting company with offices around the globe. One of the key reasons for moving to Sybase for corporate client/server applications was the capability to release the data and database processing on Novell and OS/2.

Smaller offices in countries such as Venezuela, Mexico, and Spain had already gained some degree of expertise with these environments. They could support applications that ran on those platforms but would not have been able to deal with the complexities of a UNIX environment. It should go without saying that this was the experience of my company and not any sort of blanket statement that UNIX is not supported in these countries (but I'll state it anyway).

Third-Party Connectivity

This is my personal favorite because it really opens Pandora's box. On the features and functions side, Sybase has long been a leader in providing access to its database engine to any application programmer who wanted to write programs using the Sybase-provided API.

As a matter of policy, Sybase made a point of providing an inexpensive way to incorporate database calls into a program through its Open Client DB-Library. By making this available for C, COBOL, and a bunch of other languages, Sybase made it easy for third-party developers to link to the SQL Server engine and manipulate Sybase data. Because these libraries are cheap and the executables can be distributed without runtime fees, the approach caught on. The net result was a plethora of applications that were Sybase SQL Server aware.

There is a pretty significant implication here, in that not only can you use these features to develop your own client applications that are tightly integrated with Sybase databases, but you can choose to buy any number of packages to meet your users' requirements.

As mentioned at the beginning of the chapter, the loose federation of a wide variety of packages means that you have an incredible number of application alternatives to choose from. You not only do not have to reinvent the wheel, but you have any number of wheels to choose from.

This freedom of choice provides one of the key differences and major problems in the Sybase environment, that of multiple versions and compatibility. As you become more familiar with the Lego-like approach of the Sybase building blocks, you appreciate the facility to snap in and out pieces to meet changing needs without having to start from scratch. However, you should keep in mind that these products are all developed and supplied from very different sources. Each version change or upgrade can be the source of problems and bugs.

The client/server architecture is not mature and client/server systems are typically unstable. Not only does much of the technology (not Sybase specifically, but all of it) not work as advertised, it especially does not work together as advertised. Well, it does, but there are problems. With flexibility comes complexity and with that complexity comes instability. What starts off as an elegant architecture can transmogrify into an implementation and support nightmare.

The Pace of Change

Sybase applications frequently incorporate multiple server platforms and varied third-party client-side applications, and are integrated with other independent providers of services such as communications software. As you can appreciate, this translates into a rather rapid rate of change in the feature set and capabilities of the architecture as a whole. Because you have been working with systems technology for some time, I don't have to tell you that we are working in a world of unparalleled turmoil. But what does bear pointing out is that the typical Sybase application integrates and attempts to harness these forces into a cohesive whole.

A change to any one component of your client/server system can result in an unexpected and undesired side effect pretty much anywhere in the chain. Things that used to work yesterday stop working tomorrow, and it takes a great deal of investigation and analysis to get to the bottom of it. This is a necessary function of combining so many independent products that have never been tested together in quite the configuration you have implemented in your organization. I suggest that you rigorously document the stacks that work for you, and when you experiment with new configurations, first be prepared to fall back to a known working set, and second, isolate changes to a test environment.

In my training courses, I often like to point out that managing the change process in a client/server environment is like log rolling down an avalanche. Not only do you have to keep moving, but the ground under you is moving as well. And if you stop, well, it will just roll over on top of you.

Summary

You should now begin to have an appreciation for how some of the features designed into the Sybase architecture will affect your design and development approach. Certainly, easily integrating multiple applications from different vendors is a relatively new capability. And it makes sense that this will force changes in the systems development process.

I hope you are starting to feel just a little nervous. A healthy respect for the problems you will face when working with this technology is likely to help you more accurately estimate how long it will take to deliver and prepare you for the inevitable frustrations of implementation. And that is what this book is about: helping you identify what you need to do to successfully develop your Sybase application.

One of the common characteristics I have noticed in systems people who have successfully implemented applications using this technology is an acceptance, however reluctant, of its immaturity. For those of you who are coming from the mainframe world, this environment will frequently look like anarchy. Any of you who are upsizing from the PC world may well discover that the multiuser, multiplatform, and volume issues soon create their own problems.

The point of this particular chapter was to sensitize you to some of the specific considerations of the Sybase architecture, without getting into the technology itself. The other main objective was to point out that all these wonderful features have a downside, while at the same time letting you know that other people have seen the same dark side and still been able to overcome the difficulties inherent in the architecture.

2.3

Development Tools and Techniques

Introduction

In the first chapter of this section, I introduced an iterative, five-step lifecycle or model for developing client/server applications using Sybase. At various times within that model, I referred to techniques for eliciting user requirements, documenting and diagramming your findings, and managing the development process.

In this chapter you will be taken on a tour of some of the more common techniques for obtaining this information, as well as be provided with descriptions of tools that can be used to help you build your Sybase application. The objective will be to ensure that you are at least acquainted with the various management techniques and commonly available software tools that are offered as part and parcel of this rather new client/server world.

Those of you who have worked through DB/2 implementations on the mainframe will find much of the material and approaches familiar. On the other hand, there are some significant differences. One of the major distinctions is found in the vastly lower price of the tools, where the features and functions of the client/server approach borrow heavily on the experiences of the mainframe world.

In any case, no matter how familiar you are with developing relational applications in general, this chapter should provide a useful review as well as an up-to-date coverage of some of the more popular tools used in conjunction with Sybase products.

Joint Application Development (JAD)

When I first started designing and developing systems in the early 1980s, I did not realize that there was a way to build systems other than in conjunction with the users. More recently, I have discovered that people, especially in larger systems shops, have become exasperated with all these client/server consultants enthusiastically endorsing techniques such as JAD that have been used for years in the mainframe world.

First, I'll define our terms. *Joint Application Development* entails a structured process for meeting with users and systems people to elicit systems requirements and design applications to meet those requirements. You can breathe a sigh of relief; I have no intention of providing a tutorial on running a JAD session as part of this book.

I do, however, want to make mention of where I have seen most of these sessions fail. There is nothing magical about the structure of one of these meetings, and there are plenty of good books around to give you the details if you need them. What is magical is the process when it works. Effective JAD sessions result from a feeling in each of the participants of mutual regard and trust. Cynical, skeptical people may have valuable observations about what should or should not be done, but they do not make good team players and they bring everyone else down. To really make a JAD session worthwhile, you need to carefully select the participants and you absolutely must manage the meeting.

Throwing a bunch of users into a room and asking them questions is not going to make it. To really get to the heart of the matter, you must first convince them that your really want to work with them, that you care about their problems, and that you will do something about them. Given the history that most systems shops have, this means starting from a deficit position.

Rapid Application Development (RAD)

This is another way of saying, ready or not, here it comes. Okay, maybe that is a little cynical and unfair, but no doubt some of you have seen some of this approach toward RAD, too. As the sign in the restaurant says, good food takes time to prepare, and this applies equally well to systems.

At the same time, shorter development times are a reality. Management will no longer look at three-year development plans; they want results—not now but *right now.* The only way to accommodate this is to scale the systems down into smaller more manageable pieces and deliver those.

The rapid part of the new systems development models is achieved by leveraging systems technology into the design process. Just as manufacturers of integrated circuits are realizing tremendous productivity gains by using technology to design technology, client/server software developers must use the same approach.

Successful rapid application development occurs when you effectively combine the techniques and tools for a single application. Your JAD session sets the parameters for the application and begins the process of relationship building within the development team. The prototyping process allows you to translate the talk into a practical example of what the system can look like and allows changes to be made quickly, which in turn encourages the users to play with what different systems services would allow them to do. By incorporating various documentation tools and application generators into your development process, you can save time in making modifications. This is where the rapid part comes from. In most cases people are grappling with what the new systems technology can do for them, so it's not about how long it takes to define the system, it's about how long it takes to make the changes as you get to understand the process better. Another critical element is the ability to take full advantage of what already exists and to effectively address any leftover notions from past efforts.

Inheritance and resuability are not just attributes of the object-oriented programming paradigm (that word again!). They are quite practical and inexpensive means of saving time on your design and development efforts. This saved time translates into rapid development without cutting corners, which is the other way to decrease the turn-around time.

Reusable analysis consists of researching and validating reports and documents describing the objectives and functions of the application area to be automated. Even at this basic level, the temptation is to start from scratch, rather than obtain copies of older reports and determine what, if anything, still applies. The larger your organization, the more likely that someone at some time prepared a document reviewing the same business unit that your application is to address. As with all obstacles to reusablilty, the trick is to determine what exists and where it is located. Then you can determine how much of it still applies.

Ironically, inheritance can work in a cultural or psychological sense. If people have tried and failed in a particular business unit or with a particular technology, you will inherit that preconception. One critical factor is to identify and understand what must be inherited in terms of attitudes, data, legacy procedures, and systems as well as to take advantage of any relevant work done elsewhere. By doing this homework, you can set the stage for a successful Rapid Application Development effort.

Rapid Iterative Prototyping (RIP)

Whenever people talk about the new client/server development methods, several common themes emerge. Certainly, there is user involvement. However, this is not just in the analysis and requirements definition activities, but in the development effort itself. Technical users are just as likely to provide screens and logic as they are to make wishful lists of features and functions. The new technologies actively encourage users to take a hands-on position in the development process.

Still, it works best if users are not forced to do everything themselves, but can sit side by side and let a trained professional go to work. That the systems professional might have received his or her training in the new tools only last week is not important. What is important is that users and developers sit down together and work through a definition of what the system is to accomplish. This definition takes the form of a prototype, complete with screens and basic functions.

It can be useful to consider the example of a police sketch artist. How effective would this approach be if it were not iterative? No, the nose was a little longer. The eyes a little wider. When performing the iterative prototyping process, you need to focus on obtaining that feedback and making the modifications as quickly as possible. This allows the user to see the end product unfold and gives them confidence that the technology can be made to do whatever it is they decide needs to be done.

The prototyping process is often a creative one. As soon as people truly understand that the system will be developed according to their specifications, and that they can rapidly change those specs, the next step is for them to start thinking about what is possible. Users begin to play "what if" with their requirements, the changes reflected in the prototype, and the business implications debated among the business unit members.

The most effective role for a systems person to play here is a quiet one. The most effective advocates will come from within the business unit itself. Once you have demonstrated that you can in fact accommodate their requirements, and they trust you to do that, don't blow it by shooting your mouth off (always a temptation for me). Let them work through the issues and tell you what it is they really need. Your job is just to build it.

Business Process Reengineering

Applying the term engineering for what passes as systems practice is a generous interpretation of the word, at best. The harshest possible description is that engineering is a deliberate misnomer, designed to imply that the systems development process is far more scientific and proven than it deserves.

Of course, there are systems people and organizations that have done an outstanding job in supporting their organizations. At the same time, if North America can invest one trillion dollars over a decade in office systems and release on the order of a 2 percent productivity gain over that period, engineering is hardly the term to apply to that process.

But, as with most of the terms and practices used in client/server development, just because process engineering is improperly done in other organizations does not mean that your efforts have to fail. In fact, the best way to increase your chances for success is to learn from the mistakes of others.

During the chapter on inventorying the existing situation, I pointed out that the existing procedures and business practices also had to be identified and documented. This forms the baseline for your business process reengineering exercise.

The key to success in this effort is to apply systems thinking and capability to the underlying methods and procedures by which a given business unit operates. This is the complete opposite to being technology driven. Instead, you must find a way for technology to be incorporated and accepted by the people who operate the business unit.

There are a few approaches that will maximize your chances of success at this:

- Use their terminology
- Allow experimentation
- Focus on relevant measures
- Ensure that systems provide feedback

The first thing to remember when approaching a business unit to which you wish to apply systems technology is that it's up to you to communicate with them, not the other way around. As systems people, we tend to forget how intimidating the three-letter acronyms and jargon are to end users. Instead of teaching them systems, make sure that you understand their terminology and use it whenever possible as you describe the new systems approach.

Experimentation is the only way that people can determine the actual capabilities of a technology. At the heart of successful business process reengineering is that moment when a member of a business unit identifies for his or her colleagues a new way for things to be done as a result of understanding systems technology. Put in more business jargon terms, this occurs when technology is an enabler, not a driver of change.

Most process reengineering fails when the systems people try to do the work that properly belongs to the users. Unless you have extremely committed line management, you will not be able to force systems-designed changes onto a business unit, and, even if you do, the members generally find a way to subvert the process. Allowing them to experiment as a planned activity will allow you to ensure that the users themselves have an opportunity to understand the technology and look for ways to apply it.

As you proceed to reengineer your business, you need to identify the quantifiable measures by which the business unit determines performance norms. In manufacturing, you can quite easily identify these benchmarks. Defects per thousand units produced, for example. In administrative units, where a great deal of this client/server technology is applied, finding these measures is not so easy.

In any case, ask the supervisors and first-line managers what measures they use. Typically, these are people who need some method of tracking throughput and unit performance (whether to justify their own jobs or as part of the management process), and it is always better to incorporate existing measures are already established and accepted, as opposed to installing new ones. However, if the business unit you are automating does not have clearly understood and applicable measures, it may fall to you to determine what those measures should be and to sell the business unit on tracking performance with them.

You can determine the success of your system only if you have some way of comparing performance, as it relates to the business unit in which the system was applied.

This is one way of providing feedback to the users of the system. However, feedback may be nonquantifiable as well. For example, customer satisfaction is a "touchy feely" kind of thing (Do you like us? Do you really like us?). At the same time, especially when a customer has to deal with technology, this kind of feedback can be invaluable.

More to the point of business engineering (or reengineering if you have a process to do over), there should be no steps or activities in which a user interfaces to the system without getting some immediate and applicable feedback as to why that step was necessary. In the more bureaucratic eras, paper pushers would fill out forms and forward them to faceless individuals who did they knew not what with them. If you design and implement a system or business procedure like this, you will find people simply refusing to cooperate. Empowered individuals need to know why they are doing something, and when it comes to a system, that means you have to provide immediate feedback.

The engineering aspect of all of this means simply that it is designed, documented, reviewed, and approved prior to implementation. This is more a question of management discipline that anything else. If you are intending to use an engineering approach to business process modeling, be aware that you will need tools to document and keep the model up to date. Any other approach, although it still may yield valid results in the end, is more voodoo than engineering.

Computer Assisted Software Engineering (CASE)

The last of the most commonly employed buzzwords in our industry that I'd like to address at this time is CASE. CASE comes in two flavors: uppercase and lowercase. Uppercase refers to the higher-level modeling tools, whereas lowercase is generally used to describe code generators that are tied to the higher-level models.

Because I'm not a CASE wizard, I have had to rely on a few key resources to keep me abreast of CASE trends. I have a legitimate (his mother and father were married when he was born) CASE expert on staff and he has some interesting things to say about CASE tools in particular. For example, he says that CASE, like artificial intelligence, was oversold in its infancy.

Yes, it provides benefits to those organizations that use it, but it's hardly the be all and end all of systems development techniques.

In fact, the thing to remember about CASE is that it is merely a means to an end. You must have a clearly defined objective and benefits statement for your project, and CASE can assist you in realizing those benefits. It's hardly a panacea and most definitely not a magic bullet.

The biggest problem with CASE tools is that they are really only useful when integrated into both a methodology and other products capable of generating applications. This, of course, was the original intent of computer assisted software engineering; that you would develop models and requirements, and out would pop useful applications.

From my point of view, ER-Win is a CASE tool, which, when used in conjunction with PowerBuilder and SQL Server, can be highly effective at documenting, specifying, and building Sybase applications.

Summary

There are a great many movements afoot that may (or may not) be the greatest thing since sliced bread. It's not possible to divorce the technology from the discipline and methodology that surrounds and incorporates it. It's up to you to review the latest techniques and technology to determine which offers the greatest potential benefit to your application given your unique requirements.

Unquestionably, the move to client/server systems has generated a great number of new and innovative systems development techniques. In this chapter, I have tried to review the ones I personally consider the most significant, and made various pronouncements on them. I urge you to apply a similar judgment to the recommendations you encounter, including the ones I have made in this book.

Remember, ultimately, it is utility that determines the value of any tool, technique, methodology, or practice. This is especially true in the rather new world of building client/server systems.

2.4

The Learning Curve

Introduction

In various places throughout this book you will find references to the complexity of client/server and the pace of change in the systems industry generally. Because you are reading this book, I assume that you feel that you have a number of things to learn about client/server and about Sybase in particular.

This chapter will outline the nature of the learning curve as it applies to developing applications in a Sybase environment. Specifically, the learning curve as it relates to first introduction to mastery of the product suite is quite steep. By reading this chapter, at the very least you will get a sense of commiseration in the fact that life can be miserable on the leading edge, and that there is reason to believe that there is something you can do to minimize the shock.

More practically, I will make some recommendations for methods to shorten the learning curve and to ensure that your hard-won lessons are squeezed for every bit of value you can gain. After all, it's not that bright to make the same mistake more than once, even though we can all point to instances where we have seen it. (Usually practiced by someone else.)

The principle of abstraction is very important in several places in this book, but nowhere is it more important than when approaching the details you must learn to successfully develop a Sybase application. To help you understand how to apply this principle, I will draw on examples from clients and employers to illustrate the point.

So, hang in there and remember that although you may have nothing to fear but fear itself, a healthy respect for it can be prudent.

Learning Rule Number One: New Things Are Scary

Let's start off by acknowledging a truism: human beings are typically apprehensive about new things. Sure, we all have met people who seem fearless. They go new places, eat strange foods, sleep with all manner of flora and fauna, and so on. They just jump into new situations with enthusiasm and abandon. I have known people like this, and when it comes down to it, they are not always quite as comfortable as they seem. They just like that feeling.

Corollary: Fear Can Be Exhilarating

That feeling is excitement. Even things that are not so new, like going 60 m.p.h. down a snow-covered mountain, are both exciting and scary. At least that's what they tell me. Personally, with the mountain, I can't see the attraction. After all, it's scary. More important, it's expensive. So you see, developing client/server applications is a lot like skiing: scary and expensive.

Learning Rule Number Two: Good Judgment Comes from Experience

You can attend lectures, seminars, and training courses for months, go home and watch a self-paced video, read all kinds of technical books written by weird consultants, and still not truly internalize the points covered until you work through them yourself.

This is one of the reasons that professional training courses augment lectures with labs and workshops. They actually work to reinforce the point. Still, you can develop an absolutely trick, cool, neat, keen and otherwise hip application using the pubs database and end up creating a monster back at your ranch. Directly relevant experience is the key to understanding how to efficiently approach anything. Of course, then it's like a teenager's first job: you can't get experience without the opportunity and you can't get the opportunity without the experience.

> Corollary: Experience Comes from Bad Judgment

It seems that no one has failures, they have "experiences." At least I have seen failed projects described as tremendous learning experiences for everyone involved. And this brings me to the key point. People need permission to fail if they are going to experiment successfully. When approaching any new technology, experimentation is going to yield both successes and failures, but in either case you will gain experience. The key is to ensure that you receive full value for that experience and that may not be in the form of a successful conclusion of the experiment. Tip: Start small and work up to the mission-critical stuff.

Learning Rule Number Three: Necessity is the Mother of Invention

This time-honored bromide points out that people often reach breakthroughs when the point of need is greatest. Pressure can bring out the most creative, imaginative, and resourceful aspects of some people. If there's a will, there's a way. (I've got a million of 'em.) In any event, you get the point; when it comes to client/server applications, if you absolutely have to get it figured out, chances are that you'll find a way to do that.

> Corollary: Necessity is the Mother of All Deadlines

Pressure tactics are tough to endure and it doesn't really matter if that pressure is self-induced or externally applied. Also, not everyone bears up well in a crisis. If you can do anything about it, you should make sure that your first forays into a new technology aren't high-pressure, high-stakes situations that mean your career is over if you fail (see corollary to rule number two).

Learning Rule Number Four: Remember the Zen Master

There is a story about a systems professional who sought to gain enlightenment from a Zen Master. After traveling to the Far East, he at last sat down to have tea with the Master and began explaining what he knew and how he had learned it. Listening, the Zen master poured tea into his guest's cup until finally the cup filled to the brim and ran all over the table. When asked why he did that, the Zen Master explained that if a vessel is already full, it will not contain anything new. The professional's mind was like the full cup, so there was no point in telling him anything. It's tough to be a novice, especially after having attained a degree of mastery in a different technology. But in order to learn, you have to keep an open mind.

Corollary: Pick Your Gurus Carefully

Remember how big everything looked when you were a child? Your parents were nine feet tall, until one day you discovered they actually topped out at five foot six. (Usually this discovery occurs as a teenager.) It's very easy to overestimate how much expertise someone else has when the person knows more than you do. The best way to approach learning from others is to listen to what they have to say, and then weigh and measure how it applies to you. There are few true experts in any emerging technology, so it will pay off to watch closely to see where even someone with greater expertise may be off base. The last thing you want to do is take as gospel something that is patently wrong.

Learning Rule Number Five: Taking Things Apart Teaches How They Tick

Reverse engineering is easier than inventing it in the first place. When it comes to technology, get hold of a practical product that is built with the components and techniques with which you want to become more familiar. Learn it inside out and look for ways to apply those lessons to your situation.

Corollary: It's Harder to Get the Pieces Back Together

Other people's efforts can make something look easy. Remember to balance their resources with yours, including the amount of time and expertise available to make it work. Just because you can take a project or a product apart does not necessarily mean that you can duplicate the results.

These principles have helped guide me when approaching a new technology. I found they applied equally well to client/server, networking, UNIX, word processing, and even nonsystems activities such as martial arts and cooking. (Have you ever noticed how hard it is to reverse engineer a haircut?) I hope that this list is informative as well as being entertaining. I find it much easier to learn when things are not presented in a dry, fact-oriented fashion. The more fun, the easier it is to learn. Of course, any technology has more than its fair share of factual content. But if there is any way to make learning fun, use it!

Minimizing the Risk

First, it's important to understand that learning is an investment. When you spend money on training, you are in no way guaranteed to receive value for money. In many cases, I have seen employers use training as an inducement to get employees to join or remain with the firm, only to see them walk to a competitor for higher wages when the training was completed.

If you are a manager, architect, or designer, you will need to be aware of the expertise and deficiencies of the people on your project, and plan for those to be addressed. You may also have to be prepared to ensure that the people who are trained actually bring their new skills to bear on organizational problems. This is not to suggest for a second that your staff is actually out there looking to take advantage. Rather, you need to consciously manage the translation of learning into expertise and practical progress toward project goals. One of the most common failures to provide this management is when staff members are trained so far in advance of being able to work with a technology that their retention falls to almost nil. The investment is wasted at that point and certainly it is not the fault of the employees.

As a developer or project team member, you have a responsibility to review your role with the project and the organization, and then decide whether you actually should take any training offered. To knowingly take a course, intending to change companies immediately, is quite unfair, not just to your employer (whom you might despise), but also to the person who would have taken the course and done the job. Whether stated or not, you have a responsibility to look for ways to apply what you know or have learned to your employer's benefit.

Okay, now that I have had my rant that training is not a perk, I would like to describe some real-life examples of how companies and staff have tackled the Sybase learning curve creatively and effectively.

A New PowerBuilder Developer

An associate of mine got his start in PowerBuilder with a financial services client, designing and developing a life insurance telemarketing application. This was in early 1991 and PowerBuilder was not only a new product but also a new technology. Working with a SQL Server for OS/2, he read the documentation, reviewed the requirements with the users, and went on to code a prototype that, after review and refinement, the users accepted and moved into production.

The users themselves were new to Windows and unaccustomed to anyone being interested in their critique, let alone turn it around into new features and enhancements. They were very excited by the project and are still using the application today.

That's the official version of the story. One of the less talked-about aspects of the project was that the initial versions of the product did not use datawindows at all. Datawindows being the singularly distinctive feature of PowerBuilder, my associate elected to develop the entire application using embedded SQL instead.

Actually, that's unfair. My associate was familiar with embedded SQL development, so he stayed with what he knew and focused on developing an application that the users found acceptable. He became aware of the deficiency when he submitted his application to a code review by a couple of developers who were more familiar with PowerBuilder and its features. Of course, if he had built a technically elegant solution incorporating datawindows and none of the users' requirements, he would not have been around to finish the application.

The moral of the story? By focusing on the key deliverables, he was able to come back and address the deficiencies in his program, because it delivered a business solution.

Moving to SQL Server

On the database side, on my first SQL Server project, the developer given the responsibility for the database support had no relational experience at all. Instead, his background consisted almost entirely of dBASE and Clipper application development. After taking the Fast Track to Sybase course and a couple of one-day seminars on relational databases generally, the technology came in the door and we were under the gun to deliver a prototype system to the users.

At one point, the developer came to me with a problem. Given the need to port one existing C application to integrate with SQL Server, write another major module in PowerBuilder, and support the physical data model changes to support the rest of the team, he could not spare the time to learn and implement triggers and stored procedures.

The fact that one of the key architectural benefits of using SQL Server was the capability to incorporate business logic into the database directly through triggers went by the boards. So, too, did the performance benefits that were expected from stored procedures. There simply wasn't time to learn all of the aspects of the technology involved and get a fully functional prototype working.

Of course, trigger-based referential integrity along with stored procedures for common queries was implemented in version two. But by that time, the requirements were very well understood and, in any case, the application benefited from an extensive overall redesign.

Lessons Learned

The biggest temptation when dealing with an emerging technology is to focus too closely on its capabilities and features rather than on putting them to work. Ultimately, any tool is good only if it is used. That's what the whole concept of an *application* is about.

People who successfully move from one technological toolset to another typically follow a similar path. First, they get an overview of the features and capabilities of the tool in general. Then they identify the areas on which they themselves should focus at a more detailed level.

After gaining some understanding of those areas, they look for natural progressions. That is, they let what they learn lead them to the next set of features to work with. But most important, they measure the tool against an external objective and they meet that objective as effectively as they can with the resources available to them.

They do not, repeat do not, try to demonstrate any degree of sophistication, elegance, or efficiency their first time out with the technology. The motto "crude but effective" wins the day.

Summary

As with any subject as large as learning, it's difficult to be specific. I had thought that I might be able to identify the biggest obstacles with learning Sybase SQL Server and PowerBuilder in general, but in review with other people, it turns out that everyone's obstacles are different.

The hurdles that you encounter will depend on your background, the challenges that you face, and the support and resources available to you as much as the technology itself.

This chapter should have given you a better appreciation for some of the principles that affect people facing the very steep learning curve involved in client/server.

I hope this chapter has helped you identify the issues, if not tell you what to do. As we proceed with the development of the practical application, the pieces should fall into place.

If it's any consolation, keep in mind that engineers need to go back to school for complete retraining every eight years. In that short span of time, enough new knowledge, techniques, and information have been invented or made available to make their previous training obsolete. At least, all we're trying to do is build a Sybase application, not send someone to the moon.

2.5

Applying the C/S Development Model

Introduction

Throughout Section 2 you have been given a general treatment of how client/server projects can be described and broken into discrete sections. There are problems with moving from a more traditionally structured methodology with the waterfall approach to the iterative model. One of these problems is a tendency to gravitate back to the older model. You can find yourself thinking or saying things such as, "But we've already finished that stage." Of course, reiteration means just that—doing it over and over until you have a version of the product ready to ship. You must be constantly prepared to review and revisit any of the work done along the way.

In this chapter, I wanted to make the general description more concrete by applying the model to our particular development effort. As indicated earlier, we intended to go through the process of building a database and retrieval application for as many charitable organizations as we could get involved in this process.

Up to this point, I have described the application from a technical or tactical perspective.

Concept

Here I wanted to go into more detail on the conceptual aspect of the development lifecycle, because we are ready to deal with it not just in terms of where you the reader are, but also because of the stage in the process at which the development team was positioned.

After describing the concept in more detail, I will give you a broad-brush account of what specifically we took on in each of the other stages: design, implementation, support, and audit, specifically.

Management Mandate

In Chapter 1.5, I covered the background and strategy for the application. Obviously, the management mandate for the project came from Sams Publishing, in that if the editorial committee had not thought it a practical means of demonstrating the concepts, they would have insisted on another application. What is not so clear is that, as we progressed through the development effort and as you continue to read the book, the application must continue to provide this service.

Put another way, the editors of this book really did function in the same role as management, and their concerns were quite different from those involved in the development process or the users of the application once it's finished. From this you can see that we had to find a way to put the editors to work beyond making sure that the sentences made sense and the flow of the book was intelligible. In this case, the role of the editors was to make sure that the narration of the development effort actually did illuminate the development framework described in more general terms throughout the book.

Resources and Task Assignments

I would like to take this opportunity to introduce the people who have volunteered to help me in this development effort. As you can appreciate, developing any application, let alone one that accompanies a book written from scratch, is a large undertaking. Once I received confirmation that this project was a go, and had the concept written out, I approached a number of people who graciously agreed to lend me some of their time to get the job done.

The development team for CausesDB includes:

- Sue Carter
- Marie Worden
- John Daum
- Rick Wattling
- Dennis Kao
- Joe Unelli
- Jannette Anderson

At this time I would like to single these people out for recognition of their efforts, which was all done on a volunteer basis, in addition to holding down full-time jobs and lives of their own. Thanks!

Of course, I am the application designer and project manager. This whole thing grew out of my perception that we could actually build a useful application, for a good cause, while instructing people in the development process. Also, if any of you decide to actually use the application for research into the various causes, I take full responsibility for representing your requirements and for any errors or omissions that may have been made.

Sue Carter has taken up the role as project coordinator, ensuring that everyone is in the communications loop, and she has worked with the charitable organizations to sell them on the idea and get them equally involved in the process. Also, she has taken on responsibilities as a technical user or a user advocate. She's the person who would interpret the requirements of the users' organizations, based on her discussions with them and her understanding of their objectives.

Marie Worden is an experienced PowerBuilder development team leader and she has agreed to lend her considerable skills to ensuring that the various application components developed in various places by various people are not so variable that they won't work together. (Also, because she's my wife, I thought that getting her involved would gain me some points because I spend so much of my "free" time on this project! I'm in trouble now.)

John Daum has indicated his willingness to work on developing an application module, as have Rick Wattling and Dennis Kao. These are the guys who sat down and created the components that made up the CausesDB application described in depth throughout this book. They each developed an area of the application that stressed an aspect of either the tools side or the server side which should help you see the potential and the pitfalls inherent in the architecture.

Actually, Rick Wattling has been working as a Visual Basic developer, among other things, but more about that a little later in this chapter.

User Requirements

I have already established that there are three separate groups who must be satisfied with the CausesDB application: you the reader, you the application user and donor, and the charitable organizations themselves. At this point, we knew that without gaining the support and participation of the organizations themselves, we would not have much in the way of data to work with. So, for the first part of the application development process, we focused on the needs of the participating organizations.

The first step was to identify potential organizations and contacts within them. To this end, Sue drafted a letter describing what we wanted to accomplish and sent it out to 75 organizations. The letter follows.

Date

Contact
Charity Name
Address
City

Dear

We can help you raise awareness and funds for your cause. I am not trying to sell you anything and if you take the time to review this letter, you will find a tremendous opportuntity to help your organization.

First, allow me to introduce myself. My name is Sue Carter and I work for Word N Systems, Inc, a national systems consulting firm. Last April, the president of our company, Daniel Worden, wrote the best selling technical computer book, the *Sybase Developer's Guide.* This book has become very popular, with sales throughout North America and internationally. As a result, the book's publisher Prentice Hall, has asked Daniel to write another computer manual. This new book, *Developing Sybase Applications,* is due out in April 1995.

Mr. Worden is including a CD-ROM with *Developing Sybase Applications* that will demonstrate the techniques and methodologies used in the book. **The CD will contain detailed information of a wide variety of charitable organizations, hopefully including yours.** As well as learning about how this application was developed, readers are also able to look at data from a variety of different charities, and to identify which ones appeal to their particular preferences. This reference database allows them to research different organizations and make informed decisions on which ones to support. Another benefit is the ability for these potential supporters to contact the charities of their choice through on-line numbers and faxable donation forms.

Right now, we are identifying organizations that would be interested in participating as part of this charities database. The cost to you is minimal—a little time and some information about your charity. As thanks for your help on this project, we will include a free advertisement for your charity. Due to the capabilities of multimedia technology, we can incorporate any type of media: print, video, or audio, onto the CD. Any ad that you feel best represents your charity to our readers can be used.

If you agree to participate, we will need as much information on electronic format as possible. Our only requirement is that you have access to a PC, preferably a 386 with at least six megabytes of disk space and a VGA monitor. Any charity with a Macintosh is also more than welcome to take part.

If you would like to find out more, please contact me at (416) 597-9258 as soon as possible. We would like to send out an electronic survey to you by the middle of December.

As a part-time volunteer myself, I am excited about the potential of the project. I believe it will benefit everyone involved. It gives us a chance to demonstrate the technology and it gives your organization exposure to people who otherwise would not have the time to do this kind of research themselves.

I look forward to hearing from you and I thank you for your time,

Sue Carter

The letter was successful in generating contacts with whom the project objectives and potential benefits were discussed in greater detail. From these discussions, we identified "beta sites" who were really organizations interested in working with us in developing the application and providing us feedback on the app as it was developed.

The organizations who agreed to participate in the development process include:

United Way
World Wildlife Fund
Canadian Literacy Foundation
Foster Parents Plan
Canadian National Institute for the Blind
Ontario March of Dimes

At this point, we knew who the players were and who was going to do the work, but we weren't sure what they were going to do, or when. Because the development team had been asking me for a schedule, this point was really the best time to get down to it.

Development Timetable

As with many projects, we were working with two major dates, one flexible and one fixed. The flexible date was the start date, which was dependent on approval of the project and finalization of team assignments, identification of participants, and so forth. The fixed date was the delivery date for the application. As part of the contract with Sams for this book, I signed an agreement to provide them with particular portions of the book to be submitted at particular times. The final component includes the application software, which had to be submitted in time to go out for compact disk pressing. There was a specific due date for this, and given my experience with editors (sometimes known as Word Vampires), these dates were not up for negotiation to any significant degree. So, I basically took the deadline as a "ready or not, here it comes" milestone.

The major activities for this project were as follows:

- Develop book proposal (with case for CausesDB)
- Secure executive sponsorship
- Assemble project team
- Identify potential participants
- Secure participants
- Develop application design documentation
- Develop logical database design
- Develop physical database design
- Assign application modules for development
- Assemble modules
- Test
- Distribute to first-tier participants
- Refine application
- Distribute to general participants
- Receive returned data submissions
- Integrate data
- Develop reporting modules
- Test

■ Refine and revise

■ Test

■ Obtain user acceptance and signoff

■ Deliver to publisher

As I wrote this, it was close to Christmas. Because the delivery to the publisher had to occur on or about the end of February, CausesDB qualifies was a rapidly developed application.

The project plan for this application development effort is shown in Figure 2.5.1.

FIGURE 2.5.1.
The GANTT chart showing the project timetable for development of CausesDB.

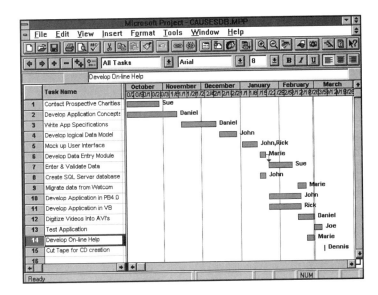

You can appreciate that everyone on the project team was concerned about our ability to get this application developed within the timetable allotted, especially with the software development being a volunteer effort. I believe this is a practical example of the kind of pressures that any of you can expect when you are facing client/server development in a RAD situation. Ultimately, we just had to get down to it and do it.

Toolsets

Earlier in the book, I discussed the rationale for developing the application with PowerBuilder and Build Momentum. However, a major development occurred in the client/server community that affected this book and our CausesDB application; Sybase announced the merger with Powersoft.

This little announcement caught everyone by surprise, but on reflection it makes a good deal of sense. I don't want to spend much time speculating on the implications of this merger to Sybase and PowerBuilder customers, but I think it's valuable to discuss how it affected this project.

First, PowerBuilder is now a Sybase tool. From the perspective of writing a book on developing Sybase applications, the decision to use PowerBuilder just became a good deal more relevant. However, the flip side of this is that Build Momentum has been moved into controlled release. Basically, this means that it has been shelved. Marie had been scheduled to take the Build training course just prior to the announcement, but the course was canceled, ostensibly for lack of registrants, but who knows? In any case, Build was no longer an option for developing our CausesDB application.

This is a perfect example of having to come back at any time and review the underlying assumption made during the conceptual phase of the development. The Build product itself had to be reviewed by Sybase in order to determine the viability of bringing it to market and competing with Sybase's newly acquired PowerBuilder tool. Naturally, the Build Momentum development team is disappointed that they worked so hard on a product that won't come to market. But the situation between Sybase and Powersoft changed to the point that it made more sense to can the product than release it. Your management will also make business decisions that affect your projects, and it can happen at any point in the process.

We were lucky. The timing was such that we had not invested anything in going the Build Momentum route. However, we were still faced with a decision: what other tool, if any, will we use to develop CausesDB?

The underpinning rationale still made sense. Demonstrate the openness of the SQL Server architecture by showing what you can do with a tool supplied by Sybase and one acquired from a competitor. It's just that, with the merger, the competitor actually became Sybase. Also, given that we already knew the PowerBuilder product, including its weaknesses, we wanted to demonstrate how the client/server architecture allows you to bring different tools to bear on the problem, each demonstrating their own strengths.

From that standpoint, then, we reviewed the various options; other power tools such as SQL Windows, down-and-in languages such as C/C++, and more popular approaches such as Visual Basic.

We decided that it made more sense to develop the application in Visual Basic. As Rick pointed out, there are a large (and increasing) number of object libraries and snap in controls available for Visual Basic. The number of developers is growing, and for RAD and prototyping, VB can actually be a useful tool. Because it's from Microsoft and enjoys a high profile, we thought, "Why not? Let's do CausesDB in both PowerBuilder and Visual Basic and see just how they play off against each other."

So, based on changing requirements and environments, we went back to our concept, reviewed our requirements, and selected a new toolset. What did not change was our deadline, though it would have been nice to take this development and use it to gain a little more time.

Design

I saved a detailed description of how we designed CausesDB to the end of the next section. At that point you will have been treated to the general description of various analysis and review techniques, and see how we applied those techniques to our development project.

It should be noted, however, that the design for CausesDB included a definition of all the data elements to be captured and manipulated, and a detailed description of how the application was to be structured, including menu hierarchies. Just as important, we identified the data dictionary and naming conventions necessary to have the application built by a number of developers working in geographically disparate places.

Our design process reflected not only the reality of rapid development, but also accommodated the principle that geography is irrelevant. That is, we designed the application to be built by a bunch of telecommuters. This added some interesting project management twists that reflected not only client/server but also some of the emerging work trends such as the virtual corporation.

Implementation

All the design and conceptualization in the world is practically useless unless something gets built. Even though the amount of time allocated to the actual implementation phase is quite constrained, there will be a number of hours and a larger number of challenges to be faced by the developers. As we work through implementation techniques in general, I will come back to the specifics experienced by the CausesDB development team and discuss what they were and how they were overcome. I hope this will provide you with some practical and applicable ideas for overcoming similar hurdles in your own environment.

Support

The development team recognized that we would have to provide support for the CausesDB product. Even though this is not a commercial product, we still had to address many of the same issues, such as user documentation and telephone support. Certainly, our early discussions with potential participants indicates that the level of computer literacy was low and that one of our support challenges would be to help the participants actually understand and work with the application. No doubt our experience will mirror those many of you have had.

Audit

Ultimately, you are the auditor. From feedback on my previous book, *Sybase Developer's Guide*, I know that any errors and weaknesses will be discovered and commented on. Because Sams provides a forum on CompuServe, there is an easy mechanism for us to get this feedback from you. As I mentioned earlier, an audit is really a project report card, and I look forward to seeing how you grade our efforts.

Summary

From this review of the CausesDB project, I hope my discussion of the five-stage client/server development cycle has been made more clear. I have worked with this model in many development projects and have found it to be simple without being simplistic and, most important, practical and applicable.

This chapter should have given you a better sense of just how much work goes into the concept and the degree of readiness you have reached at that point. I think the most important example of how the iterative model works is described in the implications of the Sybase/Powersoft merger. These things happen in the real world, and this example should show you how and why you have to be ready to come back and confront even the most basic assumptions.

The iterative model we are using here requires that you be prepared to relegate details to the appropriate level of abstraction. This somewhat turgid sentence simply means that you have to be ready to put things off to be dealt with at a later time. Sufficient unto the day are the details thereof. This model, if nothing else, will help you manage the anxiety of having to do a tremendous amount of work in a very short time.

3

Tools of Choice

Introduction to the Section

In this section you are introduced to the major client and server product offerings on the market as they relate to developing Sybase applications. The focus is on the tools offered by Sybase Inc.: the SQL Server product and Powersoft's PowerBuilder.

The Sybase product line has been built on the concept of openness, and the success enjoyed by the company in the marketplace reinforces that concept. Therefore, a good deal of attention in this section is placed on how Sybase products work on different platforms and the direction of these platforms in general.

The current state of the market for systems developers is a plethora of products that provides no real clear sense of which family will be the winner. Intense competition over brand recognition and alliances of products into compatible sets or families has dominated the systems trade magazines. This will likely continue into 1996 and 1997.

By addressing these issues in this section, I hope to demonstrate how Sybase applications can be positioned to take advantage of the technology on the market today. Also, I hope to show how any investment in this technology can be ported or migrated to another platform, if the need arises.

Last, I want to walk you through the process of selecting technology for CausesDB, our representative application. Often, it's one thing to talk about the technology selection process in general terms and quite another to get down to brass tacks and recommend a set of technologies for a given purpose. As you follow my reasoning and evaluation of the various offerings on the market, you should gain a better appreciation for technology issues from a buyer's perspective, and this will allow you to better assess the products on which you build your Sybase application.

3.1

SQL Server from Sybase

Introduction

In this chapter I cover the major architectural features and benefits of the Sybase SQL Server product line. In particular, you will be introduced to the System 10 SQL Server and you'll briefly tour the additional server products: Open Server, Omni Server, and Replication Server.

The purpose of this chapter is to focus on the unique features of SQL Server. Anyone in a position of designing and developing SQL Server applications should be fully aware of the product capabilities because a good designer takes full advantage of the products strengths. This chapter should provide you with a technical introduction to the product from the standpoint of application design; that is, what the product does and where you might use it.

I pay particular attention to the features that I have found to be most often used in real-world applications. You may have a requirement for one of the more esoteric features of the product, but because this chapter is an overview, it seems appropriate to address the mainstream requirements posed by most applications.

And in This Corner...

SQL Server System 10 is a multithreaded, programmable application that manages multiple users and resources as they access relational data stored in tables and rows.

The application is multithreaded in that it looks like one process to the server operating system on which it is installed, but inside that process, it is managing multiple processes itself. Without using SQL Server utilities and procedures, you have no way of knowing what is going on inside the database engine.

This means that on a UNIX box, when you perform a ps, you see a single process: dataserver. On a Novell box, you see the sqlsrvr.nlm or sqlsrvr.vlm, depending on which version of the platform you are using. Windows NT has sqlsrvr.exe, as does OS/2. Earlier I established that I was going to treat VMS as the mad cousin you keep in the basement, so I am not going to tell you what it looks like here.

From the outside looking in, SQL Server is not really that impressive. However, just because you can't see what is going on from the command line of the server platform, this doesn't mean that there is nothing happening. Far from it.

Every Sybase SQL Server engine ships with a basic utility for connecting to and looking inside the database engine. This utility is known as *isql,* for *interactive sql.* It's a brain-dead little utility, badly in need of some controls and enhancements, but as you work with SQL Server, you would not believe how frequently you use it. Nor would you believe how handy it can be. As with vi in UNIX or edit under DOS, having a common utility to allow access no matter what platform you are using provides benefits of its own. isql may not be elegant (okay, no maybe about it), but it works, and it works the same way under all platforms (well, not Windows NT, but there is the exception to prove the rule).

In any case, each SQL Server has a name, which consists of the identifier for the host platform and a particular number or query port for the database engine. The host is the address of the apartment block and the query port is the equivalent of the suite number, if you like. This approach to identifying SQL Servers is especially useful when you have more than one running on a single machine. In some cases, you may have development, testing, and training servers all running on the same box, but with different data and configurations. Each SQL Server is named in a look-up file that is kept in the SYBASE home directory. This file is called the interfaces file and it is an important key to connecting to your SQL Server. The name is really just an alias for the network number and query port combination to save you from having to type all those digits. For a TCP/IP network, the number might look like 190.149.232.21, and a query port is generally four digits, say 2025. For a server named SYBASE you would launch your isql session with the following syntax:

```
isql -Usa -SSYBASE
```

Of course, you could also launch the same session successfully with this syntax:

```
isql -Usa -S190.149.232.21,2025
```

Actually, that works only for isql sessions launched in DOS, but you can see why people prefer to use short, memorable names for their SQL Servers, because they end up typing the name a lot. For those of you still with the tour, -U stands for username, which in this case is sa, or systems administrator, the only user actually provided by Sybase upon installation of the SQL Server product. The -S is, of course, the server name or identifier. There are other options, but my intent at this point is to introduce you to SQL Server, not provide a tutorial in isql. The significance of the foregoing description is to give you some idea of how a client connects to SQL Server. isql is a completely separate application from SQL Server. It may be run on the host computer on which your SQL Server is running, or it can be run across the network, as most of your client applications will be. Even a straightforward isql session when you first install a Sybase SQL Server is a fully functional client/server application. Its just not a terrifically elegant example of the architecture at its finest.

All right, then, you are connected to your SQL Server. (To those of you who are well past this stage: thank you for bearing with me). If you want to see what processes are running on SQL Server, you can issue the following command:

```
1> select * from sysprocesses
2> go
```

You'll receive some gobbledygook (that's the technical term). The 1> and 2> are isql line numbers and are provided by the program; you don't have to type them.

Line one of the preceding command is a straightforward example of a SQL statement issued to the server through isql. This is probably the most primitive example of issuing SQL to a database engine; certainly, it is the most basic one I could think up. The reason for choosing this particular select statement is to demonstrate how SQL Server is programmable. For instance, if you really wanted to know what processes are running on the SQL Server, you would normally enter this command:

```
1> sp_who
2> go
```

You will receive some gobbledygook in a slightly more presentable form. `sp` stands for stored procedure. In the case of `sp_who`, it is essentially the `select * from sysprocesses` statement with some additional logic to translate the results returned into more meaningful information; specifically, who is doing what on the server.

Although this is a simplistic SQL statement, it does clearly demonstrate a few key characteristics of SQL Server. It is multithreaded. If you look at the operating system level, you will see only the one dataserver or sqlsrvr process. Yet when you look at the output from the `sp_who` or `select * from sysprocesses` statement, there are several processes running: checkpoint, mirror, network handler, and, naturally, your `select` itself.

SQL Server is programmable. In this very straightforward example, you see how a SQL statement can be turned into a stored routine that is run by name, in this case `sp_who`. In the same way that this procedure is supplied with the SQL Server, you can write your own routines of varying complexity and call them as you wish.

The other principle demonstrated here is that all data about the server is held in tables and can be accessed by regular SQL. It is not absolutely necessary to use these stored procedures to obtain information about the server; its just easier. In this particular example it is much easier to find out who is on the system by running `sp_who` than it is to remember not only your SQL syntax, but the system's tablesnames and contents.

The systems tables, like any other data tables, hold information in columns and rows. The sysprocesses table contains all information about status, i/o, cpu usage, sybase process number, and owner id, among other elements. `sp_who` gives you the actual name of the owner by performing a join of the sysprocesses table and the syslogins table to provide a human-readable translation of the process owner id.

From this example, then, you can see the basic end-to-end retrieval of information using Sybase in a client/server setting. It gets more complicated from here, but the underlying components remain the same.

System 10

The SQL Server System 10 database engine has a number of improvements over previous versions. At this time, Sybase has released System 10 for all of its major platforms, including Windows NT, Netware, and OS/2. My intent at this point is to give you a nodding acquaintance with the features and attributes of the SQL Server product. To gain a better appreciation of exactly what the product does and how you make it work, you should consult Sybase Developers Guide or review the SQL Server product documentation.

Without going into too much detail on the previous versions, the following sections describe the major database objects supported by System 10.

Tables

System 10 now supports the identity and decimal datatypes, while continuing its earlier support for character, float, money, datetime, binary, text, and image datatypes. By specifying tables to contain columns of these various attributes, built-in functions for manipulating and formatting the data according to its type are provided. Identity columns allow you to ensure a unique identifier value for each row in the table, whereas the decimal datatype allows you to determine the exact size of a number and to how many decimal places you wish it to be stored.

Clustered Indexes

Each table can have one clustered index, which consists of a physical sort of the data on disk according to the order of values found in the specified column or columns. Both clustered and nonclustered indexes can be made up of multiple columns to a maximum of 16, though normal usage tends to top out around 5 or 6. Indexes are the primary means of enforcing uniqueness for key values established for tables.

Nonclustered Indexes

Each table will support up to 249 nonclustered indexes, based on any given column or combination of columns (up to 16 columns). However, you can't index bit, text, or image columns. For larger tables, the use of indexes is the best way to speed query performance; however, indexes require a certain overhead when inserting or updating high volumes of data.

Defaults

Any given column can have a default value defined for it, which is entered into the row when a user or an application would write a null value. Because there is a great deal of argument in the relational theory and design community about the appropriateness of nulls, defaults allow you to enjoy the application freedom of not requiring explicit values entered into each column, while maintaining the performance benefits of requiring values for every field. A column may have a single defaults defined and applied to it.

Triggers

For any update, insert, or delete operation on a table, an action or set of actions can be automatically launched through a trigger. Triggers in SQL Server allow you to define logic or call stored procedures based on the modification of any or all columns defined in the table. Once a trigger is defined, there is no way to get around the trigger action for that particular operation without dropping the trigger. Typically, triggers are used as a means of enforcing business rules or database integrity.

Stored Procedures

These are precompiled programs that are held on the database and called by client applications. They can take parameters and may call other stored procedures. Because they are already compiled and called by name, they are faster than issuing the same SQL dynamically, and require less network traffic. Stored procedures are a highly effective means of ensuring that access to certain tables is handled in a uniform and approved manner. By making a stored procedure the only mechanism a user can have for accessing certain tables, you can completely control who and how that access is performed, including error handling and audit trails. Traditionally, SQL Servers provision of stored procedures has been one of its single most powerful features. System 10 offer extensive enhancements to the already powerful capabilities of stored procedures found in earlier versions of the product.

Other Features

Perhaps the most significant improvements have been made through the introduction of back-end cursors. Previous versions of the SQL Server product would support only row-by-row processing by declaring a cursor in the client application, such as PowerBuilder, or with a C program accessing SQL Server through Open Client DB-Library. It is now possible to do this with dynamic SQL or from within a stored procedure.

For those of you who are not programmers, the key point to take away from this discussion is that relational databases are set-oriented by nature. That is, you issue queries to the database and ask for a result set or group of rows that satisfy the condition. All processing is performed on those sets. For example, the condition might be to give all employees a raise who make less than minimum wage, or give the raises only to employees in GA (where the values stored for state are abbreviated). These criteria help filter out the rows until the set contains only the desired results.

Cursors reflect the more traditional approach to programming that consists of starting at the top of the pile, checking a few things, doing a few things, and then moving on to the next record. This more traditional means of processing information is still highly useful and familiar to most developers, and Sybase has included it to accommodate this type of processing.

Familiarity with the Product

My intention here is not to pretend that you can become familiar with a product as complex as SQL Server in a chapter. However, we are dealing with the process of development, so I thought it might be a useful exercise to at least make a note of the key elements or components of the products with which you will to build your application.

Actual implementation requires that you or your technical resources be very familiar with the technology and its capabilities and syntax. That is outside the scope of this particular book, but a little review of the highlights of the technology set is potentially valuable.

There are a number of solid technology books on the shelves which deal with the SQL Server database objects and syntax. The first technical book I wrote, *Sybase Developers Guide*, addresses many of these issues and an updated version of the book will be available soon.

Open Client (DB-Library and CT-Library)

One of the key differentiators between SQL Server and its competitors is the Open Client API (Application Programming Interface). The Open Client Library is available from Sybase for a nominal fee (approximately $150) and consists of a bunch of function calls that you can use to extend your programming language of choice to allow direct database access and data manipulation within your programs. You may make and distribute as many runtime versions of applications incorporating Open Client as you wish.

From the beginning, Sybase wanted its clients to be able to write their own application programs that made calls to the database and that could create a synergy between the client application and the database server. Open Client (also known as DB-Library and CT-Library, depending on what version of SQL Server is being discussed) has given rise to a great many third-party, shrink-wrapped applications that are delivered ready to connect to SQL Server and go to work. For those of you opting for a buy-not-build strategy, the inherent openness of the architecture, and the wide availability of this third-party software, means that you have a larger number of options when reviewing components with which to build you applications.

Open Client (Net-Libraries)

No overview of the SQL Server product would be complete without introducing some of the communications and connectivity features supported by Sybase. SQL Server was designed for networks and for access by heterogeneous clients. To support this, Sybase developed the net-libraries to provide access from client applications written with Open Client DB-LIB to the SQL Server, independent of which platform the server was running on.

This means there are net-libraries available for PCs, Windows, OS/2, Macs, UNIX, and other platforms. The role played by the net-library is to translate the SQL Server calls made by the DB-LIB-enabled application into something that can be understood by the networking and communications software loaded onto the client. For a PC, for instance, this means making Lan Work Place for DOS capable of understanding that the application wants to connect to a particular UNIX-based SQL Server, issue calls, and retrieve data. The communications or transport layer software must be capable of connecting to the host platform, of course, but Sybase requires an additional layer in order to connect to the SQL Server running on that platform, initiate a connection, and access the data contained within the server.

Open Server

Like Open Client, this product is really a set of extensions to a programming language, which allows you to make other systems look like they are SQL Servers. Open Servers have been written for a wide range of other database products such as IMS, DB/2, Oracle, VSAM, and many others. The key is that the Open Server products allow you to make every potential source of data look and act like a SQL Server from the perspective of the client applications, which need to access those data sources.

Naturally, this is a very technical product to implement. But from the point of view of those who must design and architect relational solutions, it is an important offering. The key advantage to this product is the facility to design applications that need to deal only with data from SQL Server, and then put the effort into making all of the back ends look like SQL Server using the Open Server software.

The alternative, of course, is to provide multiple connections for each client application and system that needs access to more than one server type. Those of you who are used to designing and deploying PC-based systems will immediately see the disadvantage of trying to manage several or many connections to servers from various vendors. The communications protocol alone will eat up most of the systems resources and leave you with very little left over with which to make the application itself work.

Other Sybase Products

There are a number of other products from Sybase that can be incorporated into an enterprise-wide client/server solution. These include the following:

> Replication Server: This product allows the propagation of copies of data across local and wide-area networks automatically. Essentially, Rep Server allows you to designate primary copies of the data and ensure a widespread distribution of that data automatically, but allows for problems in the communications linkages between servers. Rep Server also allows data to be moved from SQL Servers out to other vendors' products.

When combined with Open Server, it allows multiple SQL Servers to maintain copies of data that originate in other vendors' databases.

Omni SQL Gateway: This product is really a shrink-wrapped Open Server product for 17 different database backends including DB/2, IMS, Oracle, rdb, and others. All the services described as available with Open Server are also supported with Omni SQL Gateway, and this product may also be used in conjunction with Replication Server for distribution of data copies across many servers.

Navigation Server: This product is for the big guns requiring heavy-duty processing across an SMP (Symmetrical Multiprocessing) box. The Navigation Server is one of the first Sybase products to take full advantage of the SMP architecture and at this point works only with the AT&T GIS hardware.

Audit Server: This server product offers a means of providing full and complete audit trails and data security. Audit Server has been certified as being compliant with the ultra-secure lavender and orange books, which specify levels of security that must be contained in products to be sold into sensitive U.S. government applications.

SQL Monitor: A database administration tool for evaluating the performance of any given SQL Server and its resource usage, in terms of disk and CPU access.

Tools

There are also tools for building applications. At this point, however, I prefer to defer discussions on tools until you're actually ready to begin developing your application. It's appropriate, though, to at least note that you will see how Sybase-supplied tools can be used, as well as those provided by third parties.

Summary

This is the end of the nickel tour of the Sybase product suite. I hope that those of you who are already familiar with the product line have not been too bored, and that those of you who are unfamiliar with the suite are not too confused. The real reason for providing a chapter of this nature is to avoid the assumption that everybody already knows this stuff. The publisher tells me that this is neither a safe nor fair assumption.

I hope that, with this high-level fly-by of the product line and feature set provided by Sybase, you have a better feel for the technology. For those of you with more background in the technology and how it works, I suggest you consider this chapter a roster of the players with which you will work when it comes time to build the sample application.

To reiterate, the primary thrust and value of this entire book is from a methodological standpoint, as opposed to a technical reference. The main idea to be conveyed is how to work with the technology, not how the technology works.

If it seems like I am apologizing, I suppose it's true. I find it difficult to hit the highlights of a technology as rich in features (and exceptions) as SQL Server. I hope I have done justice to the basics, without boring those of you who already know this stuff.

For those of you approaching this from the architectural or application design level, you have now been introduced to all of the SQL Server features that this book will be dealing with in more depth. You may want to go to other sources and do some further research as the application demonstrated in this book progresses. In any case, I promise not to bring any ringers that weren't at least introduced in this chapter.

3.2

PowerBuilder 4.0

Introduction

As part of writing this book, I signed up for the Powersoft HeadStart program, which entitled me to a beta version of PowerBuilder, specifically version 4.0. In this chapter I will review the PB 4.0 product and describe not only the features of PowerBuilder, but focus specifically on PowerBuilder version 4.0.

Many of you may already be familiar with the features and functions of PowerBuilder, but because the common denominator for this book is Sybase, no doubt some of you are still wondering what the fuss is about.

I have been working with PowerBuilder as part of my client/server projects since version 1.0. This has given me the opportunity to get a good feel for the product's strengths and weaknesses in creating real-world applications.

In this chapter I will try to provide you with a "warts and all" assessment of the 4.0 offering. However, I think I should be clear about my pro-PowerBuilder bias, especially compared with other products such as SQL Windows or JAM. I think that Powersoft did a marvelous job positioning the product for the intermediate developers who needed to develop GUI-based applications without necessarily learning C/C++. I expect that some of my enthusiasm for the product will come across in this chapter.

For those of you who are skeptical about PowerBuilder, I will try to provide equal time on the things that it just doesn't do as well as other tools.

PowerBuilder is now a Sybase-owned, if independently managed, client/server development tool. After reading this chapter you should be familiar with the appropriate uses for the product and have a solid grasp of the features new to 4.0. As a result of the help of the real, live PowerBuilder developers who work with me, the treatment of the product will be based on how you can expect it to behave in reality, rather than an optimistic marketing review.

The PowerBuilder Product Suite

As of the first half of 1995, Powersoft offers a number of products which round out its development environment. This environment includes PowerBuilder, PowerViewer, PowerMaker, and the Watcom database engine.

Powersoft has expanded its product line to cover all the aspects of development—ad-hoc queries as well as the DOS/Windows back-end database to support the creation of all elements of a client/server application.

PowerBuilder

PowerBuilder, the flagship product, is offered in Enterprise and Desktop versions. PowerBuilder is a GUI/SQL application generator that theoretically allows a developer who does not know either the Windows Software Development Kit or SQL to create Windows client applications that integrate with SQL databases such as SQL Server, Oracle, and such.

The Enterprise version is required either for connecting the development environment to a database on the list, or distributing a compiled application with a deployment kit to allow native connection to the same database products.

The Desktop version of the product, on the other hand, supports integration and deployment of PowerBuilder applications with ODBC-compliant data sources. Of course, you may use ODBC to connect to a SQL Server or other major database back end; however, there is generally a performance penalty due to the extra connectivity layer that is part of ODBC support.

Between the Desktop and Enterprise version, there are no feature differences beyond the databases supported. The two products work identically and provide complete compatibility between the two environments. As a developer you can work at home on the Desktop version and expect your libraries to work identically when opened at the office using the Enterprise version. Of course, there may be a few differences between the database-specific syntax, which brings me to the next point.

Watcom

The original vision of the PowerBuilder product did not include a database with the development environment. After a number of marketing changes, which saw the extra charges dropped for runtimes and connection kits, Powersoft made a strategic decision and acquired Watcom, a Canadian company that developed and sold compilers and a powerful, PC-based relational database. This product is now bundled with both the Enterprise and Desktop versions.

Watcom is also available in multiuser configurations to run on Novell or other DOS-compatible LAN environments such as Windows for Workgroups, OS/2, and Windows NT. Watcom SQL 4.0 supports stored procedures, triggers, and cascading updates and deletes. It also sports a high-performance optimizer and clever self-tuning features. Perhaps the most attractive aspect of the Watcom product is its price. At this point, the way Watcom will fit into the Sybase workgroup products strategy is unclear, but the product is likely to be allowed to continue on its own, unmolested for the rest of 1995. A new feature in PowerBuilder 4.0, data pipeline, allows transparent migration of data between Watcom and Enterprise database sources. This will be covered in greater detail as you get into more of the PowerBuilder product features and functions.

PowerMaker

This product was introduced in late 1993 to be targeted at the technical end user who wanted to use a subset of PowerBuilder to access data but not necessarily build applications. The original concept was that PowerBuilder developers could create objects that were in turn used by the PowerMaker users.

PowerViewer

This ad-hoc query tool is positioned for the less sophisticated end user who wants to browse and retrieve data without having to understand the underlying data model or SQL syntax.

InfoMaker

InfoMaker is provided with the Enterprise version of PowerBuilder. It is described as a powerful, easy-to-use, object-oriented reporting tool that supports ad-hoc queries and custom reports. It also allows you to create forms to change data, pipe data from one source to another, and create applications that are distributed to other users.

The specific objects supported by InfoMaker include:

- **Query Painter:** Enables you to create queries that feed other objects such as forms or reports
- **Report Painter:** Enables you to create composite, crosstab, freeform, graph, grid, group, n-up and tabular reports
- **Forms Painter:** Supports the creation and use of interactive forms to view and change data
- **Data Pipeline Painter:** Creates and executes data pipeline definitions that move data between databases and/or servers
- **Database Painter:** Enables you to work with data in tables and views as well as define extended attributes including edit styles and validation rules

These products form the basis for the toolset offered by Powersoft. However, Powersoft has been committed to open systems from the first version of PowerBuilder, and there is no requirement to use all of the Powersoft tools. Powersoft does not use methods to lock you into its products.

Additionally, there are a number of other products, such as ER-Win and PVCS, which have been written to integrate closely with PowerBuilder.

Building Applications with PowerBuilder

The five-day introduction to PowerBuilder is a very full training session that introduces the student briefly to all the features and functions supported by the PB product. I will attempt to cover the basics of creating PowerBuilder applications in a few pages or less. Necessarily, this is a somewhat superficial treatment. Those of you already familiar with PowerBuilder might want to skip ahead to the "What's New in PowerBuilder 4.0" section. If you have never been exposed to developing GUI applications with PowerBuilder, this part of the chapter should help clarify how it all hangs together.

The Twenty-Five Cent Tour

After you install PowerBuilder and the requisite connectivity to a server, you must set up an applications library. The library contains all the objects that make up the application. This includes an application object that stores the name of the application, default fonts, the icon to be used, application open and closing scripts, and error handling and definitions for global variables.

Loosely speaking, the library contains the source code for the application. Actually, the library contains objects that have scripts to perform work given a specified event. Any analogy to mainframe or traditional coding or software development tends to break down quickly at this point. The script is the development language for the application. PowerBuilder objects use scripts written in the PowerScript language, which is proprietary to PowerSoft.

Figure 3.2.1 shows you a typical library and its contents.

FIGURE 3.2.1.
A PowerBuilder library showing contained objects.

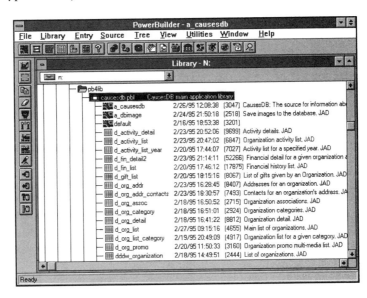

PowerBuilder supports a number of objects, most of which will be familiar to anyone who has ever used a Windows GUI application. Specifically, typical objects used in a PowerBuilder library include:

> Windows
> Menus
> Functions
> User objects
> Datawindows

From this list you might recognize only windows and menus, which are objects exactly like the windows and menus you see in any Windows application. PowerBuilder-specific objects such as datawindows are transparent to the user of the application but are of much value and concern to developers.

The datawindow is the single most important object supported by PowerBuilder. It is either a freeform screen or a tabular grid of data displayed on the screen and retrieved from the database. The data window is a live link between the Windows application and the data on the server. The datawindow allows you to define retrieval logic and actually makes a connection to the database and issues that SQL generated by the datawindow definition.

User objects are objects that you as a developer can construct to augment the PowerBuilder objects. Calls to external dynamic link libraries (DLLs) can be incorporated into a PowerBuilder application through user objects.

Functions are used to place processing code outside event scripts. You can call a function from an event script or from another function. Functions are used to move application logic into components held in a centralized location where it's easier to maintain and call from multiple applications. PowerBuilder provides a number of functions to perform particular tasks.

Controls

There are other objects that are not objects in the PowerBuilder vernacular, including such things as scroll bars, buttons, drop-down list boxes, radio buttons, check boxes, and all the other goodies with which real Windows applications are constructed. These are instead called controls, as they control what happens within the window.

Controls also have event scripts associated with them. The kinds of events that are incorporated into these controls include getfocus, which tells the control that the cursor has been moved onto it, or get clicked, which performs the scripts associated with the getclicked event when the application user clicks the mouse (or presses Enter) while the cursor is on the control.

How an Application Is Constructed

Programmers learning the C language for the first time typically start off by writing a program to print "hello world." Here you will see what it takes to construct a PowerBuilder application that prints "hello world" to the screen when a button is clicked.

First, you create an application library, in this case called "hello." Then you must establish the objects that will be used by the application. Because you won't be doing data retrieval or anything tricky with this PowerBuilder application, you need only to set up in the application a window and some controls. For even the simplest Windows application (for which distinction this probably qualifies), you must have a Close button to exit the application gracefully. This means you will need two controls on the window: one to print `Hello World` and one to close the application.

The application to reach out and welcome the whole planet looks like Figure 3.2.2.

FIGURE 3.2.2.

A simple PowerBuilder application to print `Hello World`*.*

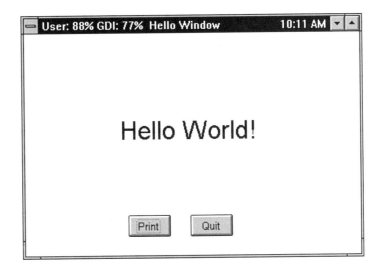

The way to get the application to do what you want is to turn the Hello World text to invisible and make it visible only when the Print button is clicked. The Quit button closes the parent window, which, because this is the only window, makes the application exit.

Using PowerBuilder, you can run the application without compiling it into an executable. If you wanted to distribute the application to users who didn't have PowerBuilder, you could create the executable as an activity within the application painter. The executable would then be distributed with the runtime .DLL files, and at that point the users would be able to run the application at their leisure.

Before creating the executable, though, one other thing that you might want to do is to associate an icon with the application. This is also done in the application painter by selecting an icon from a file. This could be any file with icons (*.ICO). PowerBuilder installs a bunch of icons in the PB4 directory as well as distributing them with its sample applications. Once the icon is associated, you may compile the application creating the .EXE for distribution.

From this relatively brain-dead application (after all, it doesn't do any work) you can see how event-driven programming in a GUI environment is handled by PowerBuilder. Obviously, there is much much more to the product, especially when you connect to databases and start to work with datawindows, but the intent here is to describe the whole process end to end, quickly and completely for a simple example.

From this example you can see how objects and controls are contained within an application, where PowerScript fits, and how an application associates resources such as icons. When taken with the capability to generate and run executables, that's everything needed to create Windows applications with PowerBuilder.

What's New in PowerBuilder 4.0

Many of you will already be highly familiar with the features of PowerBuilder through your work with PB 3.0. At this stage I would like to summarize a few of the key differences between PB 4.0 and earlier releases.

- **Greater support for Oracle stored procedures:** Given the title and audience of this book, the fact that PB 4.0 supports nonresult set stored procedures in Oracle makes me think, who cares? It's interesting to note, however, that up to this point it has been impossible to build datawindows populated with stored procedures under Oracle, whereas this has been possible with Sybase since PB was first released.

- **OLE 2.0 support:** You can now create OLE 2.0 Container Applications with version 4.0. PowerBuilder 4.0 also provides controls that allow you to place an OLE 2.0 object on any PowerBuilder window. Using new PowerScript functions, you can manipulate the control at runtime. Also, support for the automation of OLE 2.0 servers within PowerBuilder has been added. This allows you to access data from PB using the language of another OLE 2.0-compliant application.

- **Project Painter:** A new painter has been created for easier management of PB applications' resources and objects. Using the Project Painter, you specify the name of the project and resource file if desired. You can use the project painter to prompt you before overwriting .PBD and .EXE files as well as to regenerate the objects in the library before compiling the executables.

- **Nested reports:** You can now create reports that incorporate nested datawindows. This allows the more flexible creation of master/detail reports, each having their own database connection. This feature allows you to now print more than one datawindow on a single page. Reports may also be nested through the creation of a composite report that simply contains a number of other reports. Unlike nesting a report in a base report, the composite does not itself require a database connection.

- **Watcom 4.0 C/C++ object class generator:** The Watcom database engine is shipped with PB 4.0, allowing the creation of unlimited runtimes, but new with this release is the inclusion of the Watcom C/C++ compiler to support the creation of objects in that language.

- **Stored procedure data source:** It's no longer necessary to define the result set description before populating a datawindow from a stored procedure. The default is now for the description to be built automatically.

- **Remote stored procedure support:** You may now use object.function notation when calling nonresult, remote stored procedures.

- **CT-Lib Support:** PowerBuilder 4.0 now supports full access to Sybase System 10 through the CT-Lib application programming interface. It's not necessary to know CT-Lib calls to take advantage of access to such features as the Identity and Decimal datatypes and other specific enhancements of Sybase System 10.0.1 and higher.

- **Increased Performance:** Using bind variables and cached statements, you can improve the speed of your PB 4.0 applications by 100 percent over their 3.0a counterparts.

Rather than a comprehensive listing of the new features in 4.0, the preceding list reflects my assessment of the most interesting changes in the product. These features, taken together with the facilities for cross platform compilation of PowerBuilder Libraries, makes PowerBuilder version 4.0 an even more powerful offering for developing enterprise-wide client applications.

Summary

PowerBuilder continues to be positioned as a highly effective tool for generating GUI client/server applications. At this time, the elegance and robustness of the cross platform compilation remains to be seen, but there are still a great many enhancements with PB version 4.0.

The merger between Powersoft and Sybase will no doubt affect such services as training and support, though it is highly unlikely that Powersoft will move away from support for multiple databases. The underlying philosophy of the two companies remains consistently open and highly integrated with existing sources of data through direct and gateway connections.

The PowerBuilder product has found a solid niche in IS shops where a premium is placed on quickly coming up to speed with GUI client/server applications. With this new release there is no reason to believe that the momentum built up to now will be in any way lessened.

Although there are a number of features such as enhanced color support that would have been nice to get, focusing on performance and cross platform support makes strategic sense at this time. Look for a PowerBuilder 5.0 late in 1995 to further address performance and even tighter integration with SQL Server.

3.3

Visual Basic Product Description

Introduction

After the Powersoft/Sybase merger announcement, it no longer seemed appropriate to evaluate the Build Momentum product as part of the toolset for developing our sample application. The key attractions to the Build Momentum product were its highly object-oriented feature set and its ability to generate high-performance executables.

Having had to go back to the drawing board, I thought it might be wise to re-evaluate the requirements of our sample application and the nature of tools evaluation in a client/server environment. Put another way, it was an opportunity to review the kinds of things you folks are looking for when you look at the tools market.

In this chapter I will cover the general requirements of our development effort and how that relates to the typical requirements found out there in organizations such as yours. I will also go over the Visual Basic product and feature set, describing how it can be configured to connect to a SQL Server. Last, I will describe some of the strengths and weaknesses of a product such as Visual Basic, especially compared to a power tool such as PowerBuilder.

Introducing GUI Basic

The Visual Basic product was developed by Microsoft, which in itself makes it an attractive alternative for some people. Microsoft derived a great deal of its early revenues from GW Basic, so it's understandable that the company would go to some lengths to move the language from the character-based, line-oriented programming environment of the past. Today's Visual Basic bears little resemblance to the older Beginner's All-Purpose Symbolic Instruction Code, except in simplicity.

That is not to say that VB is a simplistic product; far from it. Rather, it's possible for individuals who are not familiar with various Windows controls and GUI objects to get up to speed with these development elements very quickly. The general feeling of the people I talked with about the product was that VB took half as long to become comfortable with as products such as PowerBuilder and SQL Windows. Of course, these products are also reasonably quick for initial efforts, especially when compared to, say, Visual C/C++.

Microsoft has leaked its intention to release a new version of Visual Basic later in 1995, which should provide an even more powerful development environment.

The choice to evaluate a platform-specific language such as Visual Basic is a reflection of the reality that Windows is the dominant environment in client/server systems today. Also, I am told that future Windows ports may provide the capability to migrate these applications from Windows to, say, the Dec Alpha platform, among others. Of course, the PowerPC means that Mac users can take advantage of the applications anyway, but for our purposes I will assume that most of you have at least a passing interest in developing client solutions within the Windows environment.

Visual Basic User Profile

Like many languages and development environments, Visual Basic has its share of vociferous fans. It's easy to use, it's open, it's powerful and feature rich, it does the job, and it's cheap. Come to think of it, that is an attractive list, which means that pretty much anyone could wind up being a Visual Basic developer. The key to understanding where Visual Basic fits on the food chain is the word *anyone*.

Visual Basic is often a choice of individuals rather than of organizations in general and Information Systems shops in particular. I have run into a great many people who develop their own single-user applications with the VB product, but comparatively few Systems Managers tell me that they have standardized on it as a development environment.

That being said, the same people who develop in VB at home also bring the product to work. By the very nature of being cheap and available, the product has found a high degree of acceptance on the bookshelves of corporate America. Power users gravitate to the product as well. This means that not only are third-party applications being downloaded, developed at home, or otherwise acquired, but also that end users are developing their own applications on the job.

If it's not the Windows development tool of choice for many IS shops, Visual Basic is the competition for the hearts, minds, and client/server applications that you want to develop and implement in your organization. As you review and work with the product, you will see that it is not a competitor to dismiss.

The Helicopter Tour

By now you should be familiar with my approach. I always like to get that high-level fly by of any new tool or technique to get an overview of its functions and features. Applying that approach to Visual Basic, you will see that there are a number of efficiencies that the product draws on, not the least of which is strength in numbers.

Visual Basic in itself consists of a number of screen painters, rudimentary database access through full ODBC, and the capability to put together Windows applications that can be compiled and freely distributed as runtime. Additional features of Visual basic include support for the MS Help compiler, Crystal report writer, full MS Access database engine integration, and the capability to write application wizards for distribution with applications. These features mean that anyone can create a professional looking application using Visual Basic.

But the real strength of the offering lies in its capability to easily incorporate third-party code as objects that are readily available to the VB developer. These third-party objects "snap-in" to the VB environment and behave as if they had been included with the release obtained from Microsoft.

Let me explain. The current (and previous) releases of Visual Basic allowed external functions not supported by VB to be written in C and made available to the VB environment in the form of a .VBX. These external visual basic commands could provide any service that a C programmer could contain in a dynamic link library (.DLL), which describes just about anything you might want to do in a Windows environment.

On installing the base version of Visual Basic, you have an environment that includes a dock, a blank screen, and a menu bar. The dock functions the same way as it does in most visually oriented development environments, containing most of the frequently used options for immediate access. In Figure 3.3.1 you can see how you can access the dock to allow you to build forms and applications in Visual Basic.

FIGURE 3.3.1.

The Visual Basic development environment.

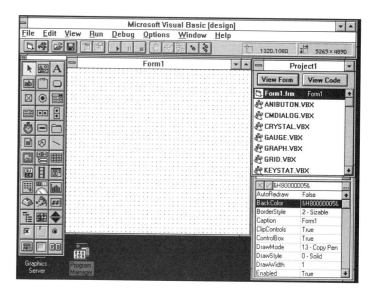

Any of the controls available within Windows can be painted on a screen, and these screens can be linked to create an application. Like PowerBuilder, these controls include scroll bars, drop-down list boxes, radio buttons, and so on.

When you add a third-party object to Visual Basic, you copy the .VBX into the VB directory and the object is shown on the dock.

To understand the significance of this capability, you need only to look at the third-party object catalog published by Microsoft. There is an industry of people who are writing VBXs and extensions to the Visual Basic product, and they focus on addressing weaknesses or omissions in everything from database access to multimedia support. This feature alone makes Visual Basic a force to be reckoned with in the client/server arena, and the reason is simple. In the same way that MS-DOS allowed people to take advantage of shrink-wrapped applications, Visual Basic allows developers to incorporate the most powerful developer aids.

With PowerBuilder or a more native development environment, you must wait for the vendor to add enhancements and come out with a new release. With Visual Basic, the market for third-party add-ins is a living, breathing entity of its own. If a need exists, it will be filled. If the third-party offering is weak, it will be replaced by a more powerful competitor. It's the intellectual equivalent of the law of the jungle. Whether this is good or bad is not the issue. The fact that you can acquire objects to do what you want is the significant point. And the really big news is the volume of options. There are literally thousands of third-party objects available for Visual Basic. Although PowerBuilder also sports some third-party object support, the difference is as great as between Windows and Warp, and you all know what that means. Developers flock to the greatest selection.

Comparing Visual Basic and PowerBuilder

I'll use the assessment of John Matthews, a senior corporate developer with in-depth experience with both products, who told me that he could list hundreds of differences between the two products, but the bottom line is that comparing Visual Basic Professional with PowerBuilder Desktop is like comparing a Ford Thunderbird with a Jaguar XJS. The options for the Thunderbird are cheap and plentiful but watch out in the curves. The options for the Jaguar are limited and expensive but provide a much nicer environment.

I recognize that PowerBuilder tends to attract its own kind of snobs, and certainly even I was leery of Visual Basic in the beginning (Basic? Basic! What kind of person develops in Basic?). But I had to include that assessment in spite of its seemingly elitist tone. The fact is that there are differences in the two environments and that PowerBuilder is the premium product. However, it needs to be noted that the T-Bird can still get you around, and depending on the model year, it can even do it in style.

Subjective assessments aside, the following are a few key differences in the features of the two products.

- ▪ PowerBuilder datawindows are the number one difference between the two products. Datawindows provide seamless access to databases, whereas Visual Basic needs third-party products to provide datawindow-like services.

- ▪ PowerBuilder provides check-in and check-out features to support multiple developers working on the same application. Again, Visual Basic requires third-party products to provide these services.

- ▪ PowerBuilder allows native access to Sybase and other databases. Visual Basic uses ODBC, which has a performance penalty associated with it.

- ▪ Some level of object orientation is supported in PowerBuilder with its Windows inheritance features. Visual Basic does not support inheritance.

- ▪ User objects are easily created in PowerBuilder, whereas Visual Basic requires C programming expertise to create VBXs.

To be fair to the Visual Basic product, some of these observations are nullified by third-party products. Version control with PVCS and Visual Basic is much stronger than with PowerBuilder, even when you integrate PB itself with PVCS.

Also, object orientation and PowerBuilder are two terms that have become less enthusiastically combined than they were at the beginning of the PB product lifecycle. Object orientation in PowerBuilder exists primarily as a marketing construct because you can't inherit datawindows. (There are ways around this, but we will have that discussion later.)

The performance advantages of native access to databases is a legitimate note, but you should keep in mind that this connectivity is not free. Far from it: street prices for PowerBuilder Enterprise connectivity kits range upwards of $1,000.

In both cases, the products will allow you to develop Windows front ends for client/server systems. The strengths of the Visual Basic product are price and available add-ins, whereas PowerBuilder has the higher end feature set for multiuser client/server applications developed for organizations.

From my point of view, they are both legitimate tools for developing an application such as CausesDB; therefore, as you will see, the two products allow different things to be accomplished, even while meeting identical requirements.

Connecting Visual Basic to SQL Server

I would like to take you through two methods of connecting Visual Basic to a SQL Server, first by using the features that come with the raw product, and second by using an add-in. In this case, the add-in is a tool called TrueGrid.

This connection assumes that you have a SQL Server on the network and that your PC is properly integrated with it. I was very surprised to discover that the largest number of people who called or contacted me about *Sybase Developer's Guide* were looking for free technical support on how to connect their PC to a SQL Server. That's what your system and/or network administrator gets paid to do. If your machine is not up and running on the network, call them in now.

Ready? Great. Because Visual Basic uses ODBC to connect to data sources, you must first configure your SQL Server to support ODBC. Typically, this means running the INSTCAT.SQL script and creating some stored procedures on the server.

ODBC Connectivity

Microsoft's ODBC, or Open Database Connectivity product has been touted by many, including Microsoft, to be the Swiss army knife of database tools. Guaranteed to fix everything. Like most tools, it has the potential to be misused. In some cases, however, you would be best to avoid using ODBC. The most important caveat has to do with performance. ODBC is slower than native database calls, so avoid using it in performance-sensitive situations. The same warning should accompany using ODBC with very large databases. You should certainly avoid it when a database volume reaches gigabyte sizes. I have heard some people advocating ODBC as a mechanism that is simpler for developers and end users alike to deal with databases.

In my experience, however, if you're bright enough to figure out ODBC, then you'll be fine with the native database configuration. If you're an application developer, you should be aware that it will be more awkward in most situations to make use of any back-end functions that a native database engine such as Sybase might provide. Database objects such as stored procedures can be difficult to use, depending on their function. This may end up making your client code fatter than it needs to be and also could lead to duplicating and maintaining multiple business rules within the client.

Configuring ODBC

ODBC allows a client application to insulate itself from the underlying database, which is ideal if your intent is to use the same client across multiple database platforms. Porting client applications from, say, Sybase to Oracle or verse visa can become much simpler. In any environment with any attachment to Microsoft, you can pretty much count on having ODBC available. The latest version of ODBC can be accessed as an icon within the control panel. This is a strong indication that Microsoft intends to make this an integral part of the operating system rather than an application add-on. Once started, you can choose between two sets of included drivers for Oracle or SQL server. Other database products could supply drivers that would appear on this selection list. Because we're mostly concerned with Sybase, you should select the SQL server option. You can configure ODBC at this stage for any of the various flavors of SQL server through this option. This includes the regular Sybase-supplied SQL server, certainly, and the Microsoft flavor as well. You also can configure ODBC to use the Watcom SQL engine from this selection. In fact, this is the primary configuration used to develop the CausesDB application.

You can choose to select an existing installed ODBC application at this point, or click the New button to prepare a selection that has not previously been set up. Depending on the type of configuration you're preparing, the detailed options will vary. All will require entering a name that will become the continuing tag associated with this configuration. You also can enter a longer, more verbose description at this point. I recommend entering one, but don't knock yourself out because it's not generally available outside of the setup screens. All the various flavors require establishing the various connection details.

For a regular SQL server connection, this becomes a similar connection string that you would use when setting up a direct Sybase Net-library connection, including the driver name, IP address, and connection port. In fact, ODBC provides the connection via the netlib interface.

Figure 3.3.2 demonstrates the complete dialog box that must be completed to set up an ODBC data source.

In our case, this looks like "WDBNOVTC, 129.9.32.108, 2200." This is replaced in the Watcom configuration with the path and filename of the Watcom database. You optionally can further supply the database to make a default connection to at this stage. If you choose this, you can expect a dialog window to appear prompting you for a user ID and password to connect with. Once that's completed, you'll be provided a list of the available databases to choose from.

FIGURE 3.3.2.
The ODBC data source setup screen.

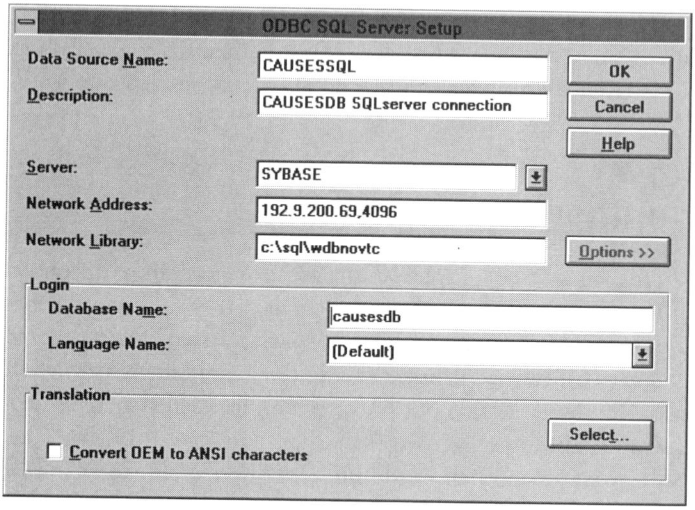

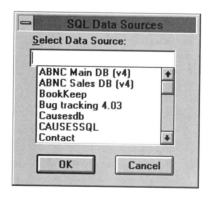

Figure 3.3.3 shows how the tag lines for data sources can be accessed.

FIGURE 3.3.3.
A list box of ODBC data sources including Watcom and SQL Server databases.

A word about these "magical" dialog windows that ODBC displays. When you initiate an ODBC connection from within an application and your connection string doesn't include all the required information, then the ODBC driver will display these dialogs automatically to collect what it's missing. This can be an added bonus or a pain, depending on your viewpoint. It can save you some coding in your application and allow your application to be more generic by allowing the ODBC dialog to solicit the required information. It's more transparent to unsophisticated users how to collect all the required information within the applications to build a complete ODBC connection string, rather than have these alien-looking windows pop up in your application.

The connection strings within an application are literally test strings that are passed directly to the driver by an application that supports ODBC. In Visual Basic, this can be either within the data control, or separate as part of an OpenDatabase call.

Other applications, such as Access, always allow the ODBC driver dialog to handle the connection.

Pulling Data into Visual Basic

Once the initial connection is established, data access is accomplished primarily using Recordsets. As the name implies, these are collections of records that are collected from the underlying database. Various properties and methods interact with the Recordsets. Properties such as the value of fields within a record and methods that allow you to move the current record pointer within a Recordset are quite useful.

There are several methods of creating Recordsets within an application. The most common is a Dynaset. A Dynaset allows changes that occur to the underlying data to be reflected within the Recordset. This also allows changes in the Recordset to be reflected within the data source. The second method is a Snapshot. As the name implies, it's a one-time copy of the data bundled into a Recordset.

The Visual Basic portion of the CausesDB application makes use of these techniques. Check out the source code for more details on the actual implementation of the concepts covered in this chapter.

ODBC offers tremendous potential for cross-database support for an application, although, typically, the conditions that ideally suit ODBC applications are more common in theory and you would be well served by learning the Net-library interface.

Summary

Visual Basic provides a very accessible and powerful tool for developing GUI applications. The capability to include a wide variety of third-party add-in controls makes the environment extensible and applicable to a great many diverse requirements.

The native ODBC method of connecting to SQL Server offers some convenience advantages that are offset by a performance hit. However, it's a highly useful means of developing an application that can be used across multiple databases, including Watcom and SQL Server, among others.

From this chapter you should have gained a sense of the strengths and weaknesses of the Visual Basic product and how it can be used to connect to SQL Server. For those of you interested in exactly what Visual Basic can do and how it accomplishes doing it, I recommend that you look on the CD enclosed with this book and check out the /VB subdirectory.

3.4

Client Environments

Introduction

In this chapter you will be taken on a tour of the major client software development environments as of the first half of 1995. The explosion of options for personal computers, workstations, and home computers, plus the inherent capability of Sybase to integrate these diverse environments, has led to considerable confusion in the client/server marketplace.

This chapter should give you a better appreciation for each of the major platforms, the characteristics that differentiate them from each other, and directions for the future. Given the scope of the chapter, this will be covered at a high level, rather than the down-and-in details about each product. However, by the end of the chapter you should be up to date with current trends and be able to identify each of the major players in the market.

For those of you who are reading this book long after it was written, I hope you will cut me a little slack on any of the predictions that turn out to be off the mark. Predicting technological trends is difficult at best, and my real objective here is to simply enumerate each of the major environments that you could encounter and incorporate as part of your client/server development effort.

State of the Art: Chaos

Unquestionably, the current state of the client environment market is quickly changing. Microsoft, always a dominant player in any client software market, has no fewer than five products for developers to work with. The introduction of IBMs OS/2 Warp did not catch fire right away, especially with the recall of the first few shipments due to bugs. At the same time, the product is highly capable and stable, which has a great deal of appeal for those who just cannot live with the General Protection Faults that plague the Windows environments.

The PowerPC was released to give Mac users access to DOS/Windows applications without having to run some lame emulator application. This platform has the endorsement of all my Mac-fiend friends.

UNIX continues to show up as a high-end client workstation choice for engineering, technical, and financial applications. In that area, Sun and HP continue to battle it out for servers and workstations, each backing their own flavor of UNIX, though HP supports X-Windows/ Motif, whereas Sun continues to push its own OpenLook environment. The OSF client software environment should be released imminently, and the DEC Alpha environment will be based on that operating system and windowing environment.

The end result is that people who are in a position of backing a particular standard for their applications have more choice, and correspondingly more complexity and risk, than ever before in the short history of information systems. As you proceed through this chapter, you will gain an appreciation for some of the advantages and implications of each of these major environments, which will either help you select one, or at least better understand where you might appropriately make an exception to any general standards set by your organization.

Microsoft: The Friendly Giant?

Many people have pointed out the similarity in positions between Microsoft's dominance of the PC software market and the traditional role enjoyed by IBM in the mainframe marketplace. The question becomes, will Microsoft make the same mistakes?

The claims that Microsoft stifles competition in the software industry by providing both applications and operating systems has been under investigation by the Justice Department. Because the wheels of justice grind so slowly, it's likely to be years before anyone reaches any formal conclusions. With the speed at which the software business evolves, the whole question could be moot by the time a conclusion is reached.

My more cynical industry watchers have observed that a conspiracy is unlikely simply because no company as large as Microsoft is managed well enough to support such coordination. "What conspiracy?" you may ask. Well, I've heard that Microsoft supplied the second gunman on the grassy...never mind.

By including undocumented features in the operating system and Windows environment, Microsoft has the ability to build in an advantage for its development teams that would not be available to third-party developers creating competitive products. Depending on the extent and capabilities of these undocumented features, Microsoft developers can save time, allowing them to bring their products to market.

Realistically, the published Microsoft Application Programming Interface must contain sufficient features to allow anyone to develop viable products, or people won't use it. Any undocumented features (and they definitely exist) must be considerably fewer in number than those contained in the published API. Sure, it would be advantageous to know *all* of the Windows calls, but I think we have to recognize that the user interface and feature set of software is what users buy, not the underlying programming language or structure. Look at Quicken, which Microsoft finally gave up trying to compete with in late 1994 and simply acquired the company, product, shares, and all. Knowing undocumented features didn't help Microsoft dominate the market for home finance applications.

Microsoft Market Share

Microsoft represented more than half of the entire software industry's revenues in the U.S. during 1994. This statistic alone brings home just how significant Microsoft products are when considering various client environments and options. In spite of how feeble the Windows 286 product was, Microsoft popularized graphical user interfaces on the PC, and there is no reason to believe that they will not have the same huge impact on PC-based operating systems and GUIs of the future. Microsoft may be the biggest player; however, it is by no means the only option.

Microsoft Products

When Windows 3.1 was the only readily available GUI for the PC, life was a lot simpler. You simply had to put up with all those GPFs or face a move to OS/2. Microsoft itself complicated the market by moving a number of products into the market, each with slightly different feature sets and, in some cases, very different operating characteristics, especially from an integration standpoint. This is especially important for those of us architecting and implementing client/server solutions.

As it stands now, the major Microsoft offerings consist of:

> Windows 3.1
> Windows for WorkGroups 3.11
> Windows NT
> Windows 95
> Windows NT/AS

The Windows 3.1 and WFW products are expected to be phased out in 1995 as customers move toward the Windows 95 environment. Windows NT clients are intended to operate as a discrete group. These two environments will provide the 32-bit operating system's offerings from Microsoft for the remainder of the decade.

After talking with several infrastructure people responsible for PC acquisition and standards in large companies, a number of concerns have emerged. At the moment, the key criteria in most minds is compatibility and stability, not enhanced performance or new applications.

New products that take advantage of the 32-bit capabilities of the operating system (extended memory addressing, true multitasking, support for multiprocessors, and so on) are just not on the market in early 1995, and the absolute key requirement is to keep life as smooth as possible for the vast army of existing PC users. If compatibility or stability are issues, most organizations will delay adopting this new technology on the desktop.

Of course, there are always the more adventurous, "gotta have the latest technology" people in any outfit. And this works to everyone's benefit as people adopt, experiment, and debug their new toys. A small group of such users can form the basis for the appraisal on which a more general rollout is based. Once the rollout of the new technology has begun, these people help promote and support the adoption of the new environments (if you pick the right people).

Most of the systems folks I talked with did not expect to see mass migrations to Windows 95 until 1996, and then only if the product works as advertised. They also did not see much of a role in their organizations for Windows NT on the desktop, as they much preferred to have a single desktop standard wherever possible.

As a server product, Windows NT has tremendous potential, but I will cover that later in this chapter.

Whatever the outcome of the various Microsoft environments, Microsoft has indicated that as long as you write to their API, your code will be portable across the numerous offerings.

In self defense, you should be evaluating the 32-bit Microsoft API, if only to familiarize yourself with the capabilities it provides. Although there may be undocumented features (grin), it will no doubt take some time to come up to speed with the features the API does contain.

OS/2 Warp

Any delays, problems, or confusion in Microsoft's product offerings work to IBM's advantage. Certainly, OS/2 does not expect to become the dominant operating system for the rest of the decade. At this point, everyone other than Microsoft is fighting over niches and market slices when it comes to client-side operating environments. However, that does not mean that these products are doomed to oblivion, or that there may be some applications that make more sense to develop under a more specialized environment. Competition in a market economy tends to keep companies honest and customers focused. Monopolies do not typically enjoy these attributes.

In any case, OS/2 has been reported to be solid since the introduction of version 2.1, and by all accounts, Warp builds on this base successfully. The most important attributes of this environment are its ability to run Windows applications and the stability of the environment. People have looked to OS/2 when their requirements simply would not support the frequent GPFs experienced under Windows 3.1.

Macintosh

The PowerPC provides an underlying hardware base to allow Mac users to continue to take advantage of their applications while becoming compatible with Intel-based applications (read Windows apps). Anyone who has had to work with extensive color requirements, image manipulation, or graphics design knows that the Mac has a powerful suite of third-party applications. Multimedia has typically found its high ground with Mac developers and hardware.

The Mac environment is sold as friendly, intuitive, and easy to use. Whether it is or not matters less than the degree of commitment the platform enjoys with its users. Mac users tend to feel quite passionate about their system, and this is unlikely to change over the next few years, regardless of new and improved services from other vendors.

If you have a stable of Mac users in your environment, chances are that you will have to integrate with them and develop some of your applications to run on this platform. However, the real potential benefit of the PowerPC is that these users can run non-Mac apps, while maintaining the advantages of the Macintosh environment and the software they have come to know and love.

Solaris for Intel

PC hardware has offered a great deal of promise and attraction over the past several years, especially when contrasted with RISC workstation pricing. Yes, workstation costs have come down considerably as well, but a cheap Intel clone still undercuts a RISC-based workstation by a considerable margin. There is a market for people who don't need the high-end hardware performance but still want UNIX on the desktop for compatibility with their user populations.

Enter Solaris for the PC. Sun committed to migrating its operating system from Berkeley 4.*x* bsd to AT&T System V release 4. Leaving aside a discussion of the differences between the two flavors of UNIX, the point here is that Sun committed to that migration and the Solaris offering (as of this data version 2.4) is the UNIX VR4 version.

The port to the PC hardware environment allows Sun software developers to run Solaris on their home systems. As mentioned earlier in this chapter, high-end applications that crunch lots of data, need to quickly display complex images, or are oriented to technical specialists are often very well suited to a UNIX workstation. By using Solaris for Intel, you can take advantage of a high-end client environment while still running on your inexpensive PC hardware. The other thing to keep in mind is that a number of leading software development tools and approaches are pioneered on these powerful workstations. In licensing the NextStep Interface Builder product, Sun has provided its customer base with the ability to work with a highly effective, object-oriented development tool. With the ability to run this on your PC hardware, it's now possible for software developers to take advantage of these tools for prototyping applications on their personal computers, instead of being chained to an expensive (however desirable) UNIX workstation.

Server Environments

On the server side, there are just as many options when looking to select a host platform for your Sybase application. One of the problems with the schizophrenic nature of some of the products on the market is that the same environment may be offered as either a client, a server, or both.

When evaluating potential products, it's always a good idea to know what criteria you need to meet for the selection to be a good one. Before addressing that, I want to take a look at some of the server-side trends that might affect your choice of a server environment.

Server Trends

There are a number of major factors to weigh when determining which server environment is most appropriate for any given purpose. Technical people always seem to have their personal favorites, based on criteria ranging from past experience with the vendor to elegance of the approach taken by the development team. To select a truly effective server environment, it pays to look beyond these personal preferences and pick a product that best fits your organization's requirements.

The major trends affecting server environments today include:

- Multiprocessing
- Communications protocol support
- Availability of networking and administrative tools
- Availabilty of expertise and support
- Scalability
- Interoperability
- Performance
- Stability

Some of you may feel that these criteria are common sense. The important thing is for you to fully appreciate which of these factors are most significant for your particular challenge. The best fit will be an environment that strongly delivers on your most important criteria and may or may not do well on the least significant areas.

To better understand how the various server environments measure up to these criteria, I would like to walk you through my appraisal of each environment relative to these factors. It's important to recognize that any evaluation could hardly be made in absolute terms, but rather in comparing one product to another. The availability of expertise, for example, is not something that can be measured in parts per million, but rather in terms of greater or lesser than another product.

Mulitprocessing refers to the capability of the product to take advantage of multiple CPU chips in the same box. OS/2 and Novell, for example, do not support multiprocessors. UNIX and Windows NT can be configured to benefit from the increased computational horsepower. Keep in mind that most Sybase applications are not CPU bound, so it's unlikely that this factor will be the most important one when determining which environment is right for your development effort.

Communications protocol support refers to the capability of the server to be configured to connect with clients over different transport mechanisms. The most popular communications protocols are TCP/IP, IPX, and named pipes. If your server will support only one or a limited set of protocols, then you must configure your clients to support mulitiple protocols. This places certain overhead requirements on the PC, often incurs increased cost, and, most important for a large implementation, can be a management and support headache. Some of the environments will allow connection of either TCP/IP or IPX clients without discriminating. Typically, this issue is more important to an organization with a large investment in UNIX and Novell servers. The idea of requiring your people to reconfigure their systems to also support, say, named pipes, does not hold a great deal of appeal and so mitigates against the attractiveness of platforms requiring this kind of rework.

The newer the environment, the less likely it is that there will be generally available tools to help you manage that environment. Performance monitoring tools, backup and restore products, and network management software are all vital components when it comes time to support the continuing operation of your client/server system. Of course, the vendors know this and frequently attempt to address at least the basic functions as part of their offering. The question becomes, what happens when that is not enough? The more mature environments have greater third-party product support, and that is especially important when it comes to add-in utilities and environment management facilities.

Expertise and support are typically available along with the third-party tools. The greater the mind and market share and the longer the environment has been on the market, the more likely you will be able to find people to help you solve your technical and educational problems. It's important to note that these factors really have nothing to do with the technology itself, but rather its position in the market. And it could quite easily turn out to be the most important criteria, depending on over how large an area you are expecting to deploy your system. Third-party support means that you can find ways for your remote sites to be supported, instead of having to implement some support mechanism yourself.

Scalability is the ability to grow your system. These days, almost all products support scalabilty to some extent. There are still a few hardware vendors who try to segment their product lines to protect higher-priced, higher-performance platforms by requiring you to change operating systems (the relationship between OS/2 and the AS/400 comes to mind). Generally, however, these environments have been designed to allow a highly flexible configuration ranging from a very small desktop environment to a large-scale implementation.

You should pay particular attention to how well the environment manages large amounts of resources. With the advent of client/server to replace mainframe applications, people are increasingly moving very large databases over to Sybase and client/server. Not all of these environments will function effectively with 1GB of RAM and 200GB of databases. On the other hand, some of the UNIX offerings handle the top end just fine, but are rather expensive for the smaller implementations, especially compared to the competition. You need to know what size your servers must be, and how many of each size you will be expected to implement. This will have an impact on the environment you choose.

Interoperability is a great term that refers to the elegant concept of being able to run a particular software service or integrate a hardware component with those from other vendors. Plug and play, as they say. While interoperability is still a practical problem, with long lists of bugs and incompatibilities, the industry continues to move in that direction. Sybase itself is interoperable, given its support for so many platforms. However, there are still restrictions on the capability to move databases from one environment to another. UNIX was always touted as the interoperable operating system and, compared to MVS, it is. The key point to watch here is whether you have a uniform hardware environment on which to run your servers. Sun Solaris may be interoperable to the extent that it will run on any machine that has a SPARC processor, but even though there are several vendors with this product on the market, the number is vastly smaller than the number of vendors offering Intel and competitive products. You will need to evaluate whether you should select a server environment that must run on a wide variety of hardware from many different vendors or else package the hardware and the operating system together for a combination that best meets your needs.

Performance is the watchword that gets the attention of most technical people. We like comparing statistics such as horsepower and RPMs—at least this is generally true of most technical people. We like the technology and we want the stuff that goes real fast.

Well, fair enough. But does the organization *need* that stuff? You can want anything (people in hell want ice water) but you should recommend the platform that best meets your company's overall requirements, which we've established may or may not have anything to do with technical merit.

At the same time, be advised that if you pick a technology for price or other considerations and it does not perform up to the requirements of the users, they will likely attempt to do you bodily harm. Performance is very important in any client/server environment, simply because the needs of the users (and developers) grow with their experience. What starts off as a perfectly reasonable configuration can turn into a very underpowered system as the requirements change.

Stability does not refer so much to the stability of the vendor as to the robustness of the product. Like exotic sports cars (I almost wrote Ferrari, but I wouldn't want to get sued!), high performance often has a cost in terms of reliability. At the very least, a high-performance system requires constant tweaking and attention. This translates into resources and operating costs. Before selecting any server environment, you should have a very clear idea of how much flakiness you are prepared to live with on your server. Because almost everyone in a client/server setting actually has to access the server at some point, an unstable server environment will bring you to general attention quite quickly. The facts of life today are that some of these products do offer great price/performance at the expense of reliability. It's up to you to determine which of the criteria is most important.

Each of these environments has its strengths and weaknesses that translate into an appropriate selection for any given set of processing requirements. The real key to successful application of technology to your business is to understand exactly what those requirements are, and then to position the technology that best supports them. You should contrast this approach to the more technical orientation of evaluating technology first and then looking for a place to put it.

Summary

This chapter has consisted primarily of name dropping, and I hope I have not left out any major player in the client/server marketplace. Certainly, from the perspective of organizational computing, you should have found all of the new products as of early 1995 with at least a brief treatment of their features and benefits.

One of the great challenges of designing and implementing client/server solutions that incorporate the SQL Server database engine is the capability to tie together a diverse range of clients with database servers. These databases can run on any number of server platforms, and from reading this chapter you should have a better sense of where each product is generally used.

On the client processing side, the issue of the day is multiplatform programming and support. For the past ten years, we have seen vendor products such as Excel, FrameMaker, and SQL Server provided for a number of target environments. With the introduction of cross-platform compilers, the expectation to support multiple environments is moving into end-user organizations.

All of this tends to push designers of Sybase applications into support for multiple server types and multiple client environments. This has its challenges, of course, but it is technically achievable and desired by our organizations.

To make it work, however, requires a methodology and management discipline. As you progress through the remainder of this book, these issues will be covered in more detail, allowing you to successfully address these issues within the context of your company's requirements.

3.5

Technological Environment for CausesDB

Introduction

So far in Section 3, you have been treated to a long, rambling review of a number of technologies with their features and potential benefits. In many cases, these technologies will be of only passing interest (OSF/1 running on a DEC Alpha, for example), especially if you are not responsible for recommending technology in your organization. For others, the discussion may help illuminate the underlying rationale for the tools in place at your shop. Wherever you fall in this spectrum, it has been my experience that technical people (if you don't consider yourself technical, how did you ever get this far into the book?) enjoy discussions about technology directions and trends.

On the more practical side, I had to work through a number of choices when deciding how best to represent a typical Sybase application. Even though it could hardly be considered a large-scale application, CausesDB will be reviewed by thousands of readers, and you all work with very different platforms, networks, and client environments. The pivotal point was to select technology that would be relevant to all of you to some degree.

In this chapter I will work through a description of the technology we chose for the development of the representative application, CausesDB. You will see not only why the choices made sense for this application, but also how we applied the various features of the offerings to the requirements identified to date as part of the objectives to be met by CausesDB.

You might want to keep in mind that, during the writing of this book, these chapters were distributed to the development team to help shape their understanding of the job to be done. At this point, not only do you not know what technology we decided to work with, but my development team did not know what technology we were going to use.

In many ways, this application exactly mirrors how client/server applications are built out there in the real world. One of those ways is that you usually do not know how the application will be built while you're deciding what to build.

As you read through this chapter you will gain a better sense of how technology can be applied to practical requirements, and become familiar with the techno-features of CausesDB on the supplied CD.

The Server

One of the most likely candidates for a database on which to run CausesDB was obviously Sybase SQL Server. In fact, if we did not choose SQL Server, you might very well ask, then what's the point of having a sample client/server application ship with this book? A fair question, but it does not address two distinct requirements that we identified already: first, some of you are reading this book to become familiar with Sybase development and do not actually have access to a SQL Server; and second, we need to be able to distribute the application to the charitable organizations who agreed to work with us in creating CausesDB. They do not necessarily have SQL Servers in their organizations.

So, you can take as a given that there is a Sybase SQL Server component to CausesDB. This takes the form of a script that installs the necessary stored procedures, tables, and data for the back end portion of the application.

The merger between Sybase and Powersoft provides another interesting option, however, when it comes to applying client/server technology: the Watcom database product.

Because this is now a Sybase product, it makes sense that you should be able to see how it can be used when developing Sybase applications. Additionally, the Watcom database addresses a previously unfilled niche in the Sybase product line, a Windows 3.x or DOS-compatible database engine.

No doubt, Sybase was not that interested in developing databases for the PC world for a number of reasons. But the reality of today's systems shops is that remote access to corporate resources is a little more restricted than what might be possible in an ideal world. This means that, in order to develop at home or to take applications on the road, some transfer of data is required between a SQL Server in the head office and a developer's PC.

By providing both a Watcom and SQL Server component to address the back end of our client/server application, we can accomplish several things:

1. You can run the application at home or on a stand-alone PC.
2. You can see the issues of transferring data between Watcom and SQL Server.
3. You are introduced to the database shipped with PowerBuilder.
4. I can distribute the application to the charities who worked with us.

Watcom, then, formed an important part of our database server strategy for meeting the requirements identified for the application.

On the SQL Server side, we had to look at an upgrade to our poor SQL Server 4.22 for Netware. Although most of the client work we do is with SQL Server for UNIX boxes, our in-house copy of the product was acquired during the developer's promotion several years ago, and like many arrogant small companies, we decided to save money on support and do it all ourselves. The upshot of that decision was that our SQL Server looked increasingly like the backward cousin, especially when compared to the new releases of SQL Server for various platforms.

Suffice it to say that, for this project, I recognized that it was time to move up to System 10. There is an important reason for this beyond just the new features in System 10. Since the split between Microsoft and Sybase, version 4.2 is more closely identified with MS-SQL Server, which does not have the System 10 enhancements. Because this is a book about developing Sybase applications, rather than generic SQL Server applications, I thought it more appropriate to go with the higher version.

Server Platform

Having made the decision to go with SQL Server System 10, that put me smack in the middle of the kind of issues that were described in Chapter 3.4, "Client Environments." Sybase had been offering its workgroup solutions for several months, which included System 10 for Novell, System 10, and OS/2.

The performance of SQL Server on the netware platform was always kind of problematic, and when the decision was being reached, people in my shop had been making noises about more disk space on the Netware server. I thought that by moving off the Novell server, I could wait a while before having to decide whether to migrate my file server to Netware 4.02 and avoid all the compatibility issues with NLMs and VLMs that might occur with SQL Server for Novell.

This left a choice between Windows NT, OS/2, and, of course, UNIX. We also looked at Sun and HP. But part of what we wanted to do with our investigation was look into alternatives to what our clients were using. Being very familiar with both Solaris 2.*x* and HP-UX, we wanted to have some fun with something new.

This took us over to the Silicon Graphics people to look at their offering. Very exciting stuff. Lots of cool graphics processing, and those folks own I/O processing when it comes to speed. The biggest problem was that SQL Server to Silicon Graphics is not a first-tier release. All new UNIX releases come out first for Sun, HP, and AIX. Sadly, we had to pass on the SGI machine, at least for this application.

At that point, I decided that it made more sense for an application of this size to look more at the SQL Server workgroup products. Some colleagues of mine took my temporary open-mindedness as an opportunity to bend my ear about Windows NT.

Frankly, I was skeptical about NT. I had only limited exposure to the product when it first came out and I admit to being reluctantly impressed with the stability of SQL Server, especially being a first release port to a brand-new operating system. At the same time, previous experience with LAN Manager and other attempts at multiuser products from Microsoft had left me cold. I was prepared to pass on Windows NT.

It was the support for multiple processors that finally got to me. The economics of putting Pentium chips and PC drives under a SQL Server where the platform actually took advantage of the processing power appealed tremendously. That combined with native support for both tcp/ip and ipx was just too attractive. I decided to go with SQL Server for Windows NT.

The Client Environment

In the first two chapters of this section, you were basically given all of the rationale for why CausesDB would be written in PowerBuilder 4.0 and Visual Basic. However, those chapters described the general features of the two products without focusing on the uses I thought we should put them to with our representative application.

PowerBuilder 4.0 allows the migration of applications from Windows to Windows NT, Macintosh, and Motif. Although I was not all that interested in NT as a client environment, the idea that CausesDB could be rolled out as a Macintosh application made a good deal of sense. In spite of the overwhelming presence of PCs in the institutional marketplace, Macintosh is still found in many shops, and I thought the ideal configuration for CausesDB would be one that supported both Mac and Windows. Of course, those Macs would have to be connected to a SQL Server because neither SQL Server nor Watcom runs on the Apple platform. In any case, PowerBuilder 4.0 boasts cross-platform capabilities, and I thought that many of you would like to see exactly what an application created in Windows might look and behave like when rolled out as a Mac or Motif application.

To support this plan, we had to register with Powersoft and get on their HeadStart program. As I wrote this, I had hoped to receive a version of PowerBuilder 4.0 that supports the cross-platform capability, but this did not turn out to be the case.

The other major area that the CausesDB client environment had to address was to show how BLOBs could be manipulated in a client/server application using Sybase. Specifically, we wanted to include some representative advertisements from the charities, which could be played back on any PC supporting sound and color graphics. To call it a multimedia application would probably be kind. Still, the idea was to provide an integrated application that would allow data search and retrieval, as well as displaying .TIFF images of print ads, playing .WAV files for sound, and even a couple of .AVIs to play back samples of commercials (subject to availability).

The key technical requirement was to be able to support retrieval of these various files and support playing back the stored files as part of the application. As you will see when we walk through the actual process of building the application, PowerBuilder and Visual Basic bring different strengths to bear on this requirement.

Network Access and Storage

It's difficult to think of designing a corporate client/server application without giving some consideration to the topology of the network linking client and server platforms. However, as indicated in the discussion about server platforms, I have no idea about your particular environment; the best position I can take is to minimize network traffic in case you're stuck with a slow communications link between the SQL Server and your client workstation. The way to accomplish this is through eliminating the requirement for a network altogether and allowing you to run the application from a stand-alone machine.

However, as you develop Sybase applications in the real world, this is not usually a suitable response, and the network implications must be addressed.

To accomplish this, the CausesDB application installs several large objects in the SQL Server tables, which are created and populated when you install the server component of the application. Most of the images are held on the CD itself, however, and the tables simply point back to storage locations on the CD. To give you an idea of how your network affects performance, there are several options within the application for viewing the same image. In one case, the image is timed as it is retrieved from the SQL Server. Another option shows the time to access the same image from the CD, and yet another from your hard disk. By running through this aspect of the application, you will get a quantifiable measure of how application performance is affected, depending on your network, workstation, and server processing capabilities.

Summary

You should now be able to follow my reasoning in selecting a set of tools with which we have built the CausesDB application. I hope that you also can start to see how your requirements will be addressed by this process, as well as those of the other interested parties.

One of the problems with developing Sybase applications is that so much depends on the specific requirements and environment in which the application is to operate. This problem is compounded when the group discussing developing approaches comes from as widely varying environments as those of you reading this book.

By walking through the rationale in picking PowerBuilder, Visual Basic, Windows NT, SQL Server Systems 10, and Watcom as the toolset, you should be able to see how the criteria were established and the features weighed. I don't expect that all of you will agree with my selections (beyond Sybase, of course); the point here is to show how the decision can be made, rather than to attempt to identify the right choice for everyone.

In fact, you should bear in mind that all of the opinions and technical prejudices expressed in this chapter are my own, and I am aware that there are always counter arguments that can be made. Ultimately, any organization or project must pick a set of tools and get to work or nothing useful will ever get developed. If I have made mistakes in selecting a toolset, I hope they will prove instructive to you as readers and will help you make better recommendations and decisions for your own environments.

On a more upbeat note, I obviously don't think that any of my technology picks are big mistakes. In fact, everyone on the development team for CausesDB was excited by the opportunity to create an application that stressed the technology and showed what it was capable of accomplishing.

As you work through the development issues faced and overcome by the team, you should get a sense that all technology has inherent problems and rarely works exactly as advertised. The bottom line is, select a toolset that has features relating to the job to be done.

You should now be in a better position to understand what we were trying to accomplish and the tools with which we intended to address these requirements.

At this point, how well we did remains to be seen.

4

Application Concepts

Introduction to the Section

In this section I cover all of the major steps and techniques that you can use to work from concept to detailed specification for the application to be constructed. This straddles the concept and design phases and, as you might expect from an iterative model, there is no real clear demarcation of where one stops and the other begins.

In fact, as you further define your requirements, you should allow for discoveries to be made that cause you to review your higher-level documentation. You might, for example, discover a use for data that makes you reevaluate the key benefits of the system. As you delve into the business practices to be reengineered, it's common to uncover both opportunities and obstacles that were not anticipated at the outset. The key to this approach is to not only tolerate this process of discovery, but anticipate and welcome it.

Most of these steps can be successfully performed without actually having taken delivery of any client/server hardware or software. The planning, modeling, and specification process typically involves such low-technology approaches as interviews and meetings. As indicated in Section 1, there are several real benefits to performing this work before getting sidetracked with training and practice with the new toys needed for implementation.

As you review the material in the following chapters, you should gain a greater insight into the specific documents and diagrams that you need to map out and plan your Sybase application before beginning development.

In keeping with our format, I first discuss the most general documentation, the feasibility study, and then assume that approval to proceed was received, at which point I move on to project planning, process modeling, data diagramming, and requirements specification activities. You will see how each of these steps should contribute to a greater understanding of what you need to build, and how each provides you with an opportunity to enhance and refine the earlier iterations of your model.

Although client/server allows you to develop applications rapidly, work side by side with your users, and create prototypes almost instantaneously, it does not eliminate the need for good old-fashioned analysis and design. The techniques recommended in this section have been adapted specifically to client/server practice, but they owe an intellectual debt to the decades of work performed by mainframe developers, who were also always looking for a better way to build software.

If you come from a structured background, you should feel as though you are on familiar ground. No matter what your previous experience is, though, remember that if you skip the analysis and design stages, your project is most likely doomed to failure.

On that happy note, let's get to it.

4.1

Establishing Project Feasibility

Another term for business case is a *feasibility study*. Whether you call your initial appraisal of the opportunities and cost inherent in any client/server project one or the other is up to you. The bottom line is that you must describe the business problem to be solved, recommend methods for solving that problem, and work out a cost-benefit analysis to support your recommendations.

Sounds simple, but in many organizations there is no real tie-in between the initial business justification for technology and the continuing analysis and design work for actually implementing the recommendations. The first step is to understand that the initial business case sets the parameters for all the following design and implementation efforts. As I pointed out in Chapter 2.1, after you have completed your implementation, you will be audited. Although the audit may raise questions about the process and efficiencies of your implementation, normally you are evaluated on how well you met the promises made in your business case for the technology.

The Importance of Managing the Process

Here is where the management process of your client/server application is most important. In many larger firms, analysis and business cases are performed either by business analysts or the units themselves. After management review, the new system becomes an initiative and is handed off to other people for detailed design and development. Those people frequently are more concerned with the technology than with understanding the business benefits to be gained by the new system. This is a mistake.

If you're responsible for developing the business case, look for ways to clearly express the business benefits of the technology and stay involved in the development process to ensure that the team is focused on applying the systems technology to meet the real requirements. Write the top ten benefits to be achieved on posters and plaster them down the hallways. Whatever it takes, make sure that the development team understands *why* the system was approved.

On the other hand, if you're a developer facing a client/server system, the onus is on you to research what your organization really needs to achieve with the system. More than any other factor (except user acceptance of your system), this should drive your focus as you build. Remember, you will be graded on how well the application provided the anticipated benefits, not on how clever you were in solving the myriad of technical problems that cropped up along the way.

Structuring a Business Case

Those of you who read *Sybase Developer's Guide* may remember a treatment I did on writing feasibility studies. Other people and myself have successfully used the following format to structure our business cases for client/server projects. Interestingly, this approach has a high comprehension factor with decision makers, and the approval ratio when using this approach is also high. You should keep in mind that the more clearly you focus the technology on the business problem and the more closely you align the solutions with management's priorities, the more likely your system is to be highly visible and supported. Succeeding with systems such as that is often a good career move.

The major areas to be addressed in a feasibility study or business case are as follows:

- Objective
- Terms of Reference
- Existing Situation
- Problem Statement
- Proposed Solutions
- Recommendation
- Gross Benefits
  (a) Quantifiable
  (b) Nonquantifiable
- Estimated Costs
- Net Benefits

By organizing your business case into these stages of analysis, you will find that you can create a document that logically flows and leads the reader to a natural conclusion. Naturally, the conclusion you want them to reach is to approve your recommendations.

The purpose of this document is to set the context for your new system. The document defines what you are trying to accomplish, delineates the must do's of any solution with the terms of reference, evaluates the existing situation, and summarizes that situation with a statement of the problems to be addressed.

Where the document begins to pivot away from simply being a business instrument or decision aid is in the proposed solutions section. This section describes a number of means by which the business problem could be solved. It is, in essence, a high-level description of the application before it exists. A gleam in someone's eye, you might say.

The recommendation is typically a single paragraph that indicates which of the proposed solutions seems to fit best and contains a firm statement asking for action. It is the benefits case that will interest management most, and the estimated costs that will intrigue the technical types. Well, at least the estimated costs will be of interest, because they refer to the gear and software to be acquired for the project.

You can assume that management is less interested in the gross benefits and more concerned with what's left over after the costs. In many cases, any amount of money to be spent can be approved, provided that the net benefits are sufficiently attractive. Systems people are accustomed to being cost centers and, as such, tend to try to minimize costs. This is especially dangerous with client/server because it can be very tempting to underestimate costs, and the last thing you want to do is go way over budget on a high-profile application.

Having discussed the business case overall, I would like to briefly describe each one of the feasibility study's components.

Objective

This should contain one or two sentences stating the objective of the study document itself. You don't have to describe the business problem to be handled by the system at this point, but rather introduce the reader to what you want to accomplish with the document. For example, *Objective: to evaluate the feasibility of integrating the operations of the company into a world-wide client/server architecture.* As you can see, even the most ambitious objectives can be stated succinctly.

Terms of Reference

These are the rules to be followed by any proposed solution. Terms of reference are very difficult to write for most systems people and require that you fully understand the business constraints under which any system must operate. In one organization for which I implemented a Sybase solution to replace their aging mainframe suite of applications, a term of reference was that any proposed solution must be financed with short-term operating leases. Capital leases required the approval of a bank committee to whom the management team had to report, as they were into the banks quite heavily for financing a leverage buy-out of the company. In any case, establishing a complete and accurate set of terms of reference ensures that you don't waste your time making recommendations that get rejected out of hand for business reasons. My advice is that you work closely with the Chief Financial Officer when working out your terms of reference for a big client/server project.

Existing Situation

This is a factual appraisal of the environment in which you expect to set the new system. Typically, you arrive at an assessment of the existing situation after spending some time with the users to review their operation and requirements. However, it's absolutely imperative to avoid the temptation to make judgments or imply that anything about the existing situation is good or bad. Express everything as a clear statement of fact—something that can be verified—and leave your opinions out of it. For instance, you would say, "The average order takes 14 days to be processed from initial customer contact to product shipment." You would not say, "There is a tremendous backlog of orders, which causes delay in getting the product out to the customer in a timely manner."

First, it's not up to you to establish in your feasibility study what constitutes timeliness. Let management review the document and arrive at the conclusion that 14 days is too damned slow. (Senior people hate it when you try to predigest their information for them.) Second, you are going to be recommending changes to the environment. It's not politically astute to point fingers or make implications that put your users on the defensive. By stating the facts, which the users likely supplied or assisted in gathering, you make it possible to be a little more objective, and you don't make work for yourself later by needing to overcome user resentment.

Problem Statement

Once you have set the context for the new system, having described the existing situation in a factual fashion, you are then in a position to clearly state the problems or inherent limitations. At this point you can use a few more adjectives to try to get your point across. *Customer satisfaction surveys indicate that the company is seen as being too slow to respond to complaints. The existing systems and communications processes simply do not support the volume or speed required to satisfy our customers.* That sort of thing.

Proposed Solutions

I have heard that doing nothing is also a decision. Personally, I have always tried to avoid describing nonaction as a proposed solution. However, it can be effective to describe the implications of each proposed solution, including doing nothing. In this way, you can address head on the implications of not taking action to meet the business requirement. Although systems people are typically there to support organizational initiatives, not make operational decisions, it's responsible to at least identify the costs of action or inaction, even if it is not politically wise to say I told you so later.

The proposed solutions should be complete descriptions of major methods of solving the problem. However, you typically do not work out either the benefits or costs of each proposed solution. That effort is made only for the recommendation. Of course, management may well come back and tell you to work out the cost/benefits for a proposed solution that you didn't recommend, buy why assume that they won't follow your recommendation to begin with?

Recommendation

This is where you put your career on the line. Don't waffle or equivocate, but make a firm statement and stand behind what you see as the best course of action. Remember that everyone has to sell his or her ideas in order to get the opportunity to put them into effect. Your recommendation is where you ask for the sale. My experience is that decision makers like to know that someone believes in a recommendation enough to be identified with it. If you make it too soft, they will frequently shelve the entire proposal in favor of some other course of action or opportunity for investment.

Gross Benefits

This is the big picture of everything the company stands to gain. Throw everything including the kitchen sink into this section. If it looks good, smells good, feels good, whatever, make sure that it gets into your benefits case. But remember to sort out the benefits into quantifiable and nonquantifiable. This is to say that you can actually put numbers to a quantifiable benefit. Real cash money, if you like. Nonquantifiable may still be tangible, such as the ability to recruit better systems people. Tangible, for those of you who don't have degrees in English, means perceptible but not necessarily measurable. This is why we refer to the benefits as quantifiable or nonquantifiable, because this is the word that refers to the ability to measure something.

Estimated Costs

Do yourself a favor. Identify everything you might possibly want to spend money on as part of the project and multiply it by one and a half. Some of my colleagues recommend doubling the initial estimate, but I think that is (1) extravagant, and (2) an indicator that your estimation skills are not so hot.

If your system can't justify the full amount that it costs, however, you should be asking yourself whether this is such a good place to apply technology. After all, opportunity costs money, and if you can write off only the time invested in coming up with the feasibility study, your organization will be ahead in the long run. Look for the high payback opportunities, leave yourself enough budget to experiment, and, in some cases, change direction. Flexibility and responsiveness to business change mean increased expense for which you should budget from the outset.

Net Benefits

This is sometimes known as the bottom line. This is where you clearly state what the organization will gain after all the costs and benefits net out. Keep in mind that this is where the audit will go first. The key questions asked by auditors are as follows: *What was the net result to be achieved by this investment in systems technology? Did the system actually provide them?*

Don't get all hung up with having to return a profit on the investment, however. There are many strategic benefits such as customer service, flexibility, or improved internal communications, for which you may not be able to quantify anything, but the costs and the system will be approved. The trick is to understand what it is that your management team *values,* and then structure your business case to deliver that. Of course, saving money is always appreciated; increasingly, though, people are recognizing that client/server doesn't actually save an organization any cash but does provide other very attractive returns.

Client/Server Cost Justification

If you're in a position in which you must do more with less, then obviously your feasibility study will have to show where you can save money over current expenditures. There are many places where an organization spends money that you may be able to save by migrating to a new system. These should fall out of your inventory of the existing situation and can include:

- Leases for obsolete equipment
- Maintenance and support agreements
- Supplies
- Communications links
- Reports (reproduction and distribution)
- Employee time

By distributing the processing power throughout your organization, you can often take advantage of the economies of small. That is, a large printer with an expensive support agreement might be replaced by a dozen distributed laser printers. This depends entirely on the nature of the work performed in your organization, of course, but opportunities for this kind of savings exist.

If you decide to justify client/server on the basis of freed-up employee time, you had best be aware that most management teams then want head count reduced. Cost avoidance is not a very palatable argument to a management group unless they have already agreed to hire more staff, or you are willing to reduce a budget for things such as overtime or temporary staff. However, in many situations this is exactly what can be achieved. A new system should smooth out backlogs and workload peaks, and this can translate to reduction in seasonal overtime or temp workers, which may be sold as a benefit to the user department.

This is exactly the kind of opportunity you should be looking to identify in your business case. If you're developing an application based on someone else's feasibility study, make sure that you have read it and that you look for ways to realize its objectives.

Summary

You have been taken on a tour of how I have successfully structured feasibility studies in the past. I have tried to not repeat the treatment of this topic covered in *Sybase Developer's Guide*, but instead to place more emphasis on the interpretation of how you might use this structure in your environment.

The feasibility structure recommended here has been used successfully for almost a decade. It can be applied to large or small systems, client/server or otherwise. The key to its success is in breaking down each major component of the analysis and leading the reviewer through the maze in a logical fashion. At the very least, you should find that it identifies the key areas to be addressed in any business case. No matter which format you decide will work best in your organization, these considerations will be vital to the success of your business case.

I hope that you find the template to be applicable to your requirements. Ultimately, you are the one who must identify the real costs and implications of any system for which you are given responsibility. I would like to point out that even if such a structured report is not necessary in your organization, you should go through this effort anyway. By applying yourself to a structured analysis of the business objectives, costs, and benefits of the system, you are in a much better position to align the technology with the business. And that, these days, is what good systems practice is about.

4.2

Modeling Techniques

Introduction

From the beginning of the commercial information systems industry, people have struggled with techniques to effectively depict and model systems elements. The move to client/server technology has increased the complexity of not only the technologies but of the methods we can use to deploy and integrate the systems tools with the business process. And we all know that senior management has been handing out failing grades to IS for responsiveness to real business requirements.

To address this problem, I have experimented with my own techniques and adaptations of established modeling techniques when developing client/server systems. My intent with this chapter is to share that thinking with you and to provide you with a basis for determining how they could be applied to your requirements.

I believe strongly that our industry has been in a state of transition, from the first explorations and efforts made by pioneers toward an established and respected profession. A necessary part of any establishment is codifying techniques and creating governing bodies to ensure consistent and proper practice. Whether client/server systems designers and developers should be certified, and how they could be if in fact they should, is beyond the scope of this chapter and the book in general. What does fall within the terms of reference for this book is a discussion of practical techniques.

By the end of this chapter you will have been introduced to several approaches to modeling the findings of your analysis into documents and diagrams, which will allow you to build the first iteration of your system—a blueprint for a prototype.

You will find a great deal of emphasis on abstraction, of delegating details to appropriate levels. The "not seeing the forest for the trees" syndrome is common when developing complex systems. Although there is no teacher like experience, with this chapter I hope that you will find a structure to allow you to approach your own complex requirements, as well as a logically consistent framework for developing a client/server application to meet them.

Setting the Context

In one of her essays, the novelist and philosopher Ayn Rand makes a remarkable observation. She refers to the process of "context dropping" as a flaw in the process of building a logical argument. Even the mention of Rand's name can generate heated debate, but I bring this up because it's a vital concept when laying the foundation for an information system. It does not matter how well you think through your analysis or specify your requirements from that analysis; if you have started from a faulty premise, it will fail.

"Context dropping" in this case refers to any attempt to begin your systems design without first understanding the base level at which it will operate. To properly understand the role and function of the system, you must first understand the environment in which it will operate and the underlying rationale for the system. This sets the context for the system as a whole and gives you a fallback position from which to rebuild in the event that some or all of the requirements change.

Tools of the Trade

Although we work with some of the most intricate and advanced technology ever devised, much of our work is still most effectively accomplished by manual means. As mentioned in Chapter 2.3, JAD sessions are most frequently based on a "chalk talk" setting, where ideas are thrown around and scrawled on a white board, erased, revised, and finally recorded by some scribe into a more permanent record.

There is still a temptation to consider all the case and modeling tools mandatory when developing client/server systems. I have found that a keen eye on the process and commitment to delivery during each stage of development is more likely to yield production systems than splurging on a vast array of systems modeling software.

This is not to say that a modeling tool in any way inhibits the development of good systems, but simply that, like any tool, how it is employed is what counts most, not the mere possession of it.

For these reasons I will emphasize a set of modeling techniques that are manual and can be automated but, most important, must be done, one way or the other. If you take nothing else from this book, take away a firm understanding and belief that you can build valuable systems by paying close attention to the fundamentals. Even the most complex system, built with the most leading-edge technology, needs to be based on a firm foundation to provide real and measurable benefits.

Developing an Integrated Systems Model

At various points in this book I have identified a number of different constituents, each with a role to play, something to gain, and a set of concerns. In many cases, the system must be described in terms that are meaningful to each constituency, in spite of the fact that those terms carry no meaning to another group. Systems engineers, for example, are unlikely to much care about the financing for the system.

What you need is a method of depicting the system in a way that these parties can review and take away the meaning important to them. Better still, if they can review the model and provide feedback allowing you to capture and revise assumptions and misconceptions, then you have a truly useful communications tool. Last, this tool or model must allow you to move forward and drive the development of an application that takes the form specified by the model.

The modeling technique that I use describes the system at three levels of abstraction, or planes. These are the following:

- Business Operations
- Application/Data Structure
- Systems Topology

The function of the three planes is first to provide an understanding of the business or operational context in which the application is to be employed. Second, the three planes identify a logical model for both the data and the programs that use it; and last, they provide a physical description of all resources incorporated into the system.

The methodology for arriving at these diagrams is based on a hybrid of JAD and RAD techniques. I assume that you have a commitment to the project by a small group of knowledgeable and committed user representatives, and I also assume that you are competent to lead a meeting of this group. To spell it out, I take as a given that you have effective listening skills, you have a grip on at least the basics of group facilitation, and you don't have a hidden agenda or an axe to grind. If this does not describe the qualifications of your team leader, please don't blame my methodology if your project fails.

Provisos, warranties, and qualifications aside, I think we can now get down to work.

Modeling Business Operations

There are three components to each element in the Business Operations model: Operational Task, Data View, and Application Module. The idea is that you must first identify discrete tasks, with each task representing a single function. Then you identify the data to be used by each function. However to keep the level of detail appropriate to this plane, consider the data to be views as opposed to specific tables. Last, identify the application module that will provide the services and data needed to complete the task.

The order in which you do this is also significant. The primary step is to list all of the business tasks that must be performed by the system overall. At the highest level, you could represent a typical order system with these components:

Order
Inventory
Supplier
Purchasing
Shipping
Customer

This could be represented by the diagram in Figure 4.2.1.

FIGURE 4.2.1.

Depicts the basic high-level work flow for a financial application.

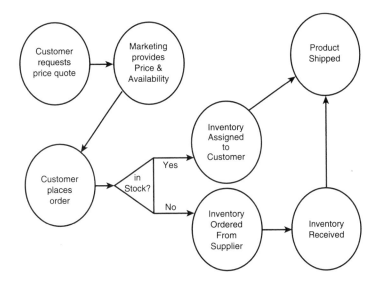

We have already dropped the context of our system, however. Where does this order system fit in? How do we know that all of the necessary entities have been included? Without the highest-level model, there is no way to ensure that we have actually identified all these players.

A sample context diagram in which the financial system could be contained is depicted in Figure 4.2.2.

FIGURE 4.2.2.

A simple context diagram.

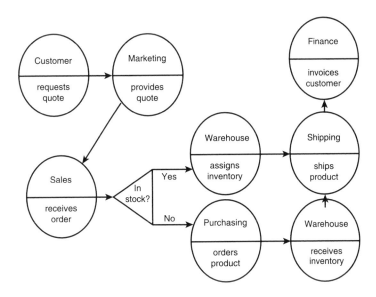

By creating this high-level context diagram, you ensure that you understand the basic building blocks of your organization's major activities.

This process of modeling tasks simply ensures that you have a work flow that can be structured around business units, departments, or individuals, depending on what level of detail you choose to reflect. This is very similar to more traditional diagramming techniques recommended by Yourdan, DeMarco, and others when modeling was in its infancy.

Once you understand the tasks, however, one of the biggest challenges ahead is integrating the tasks with the data required and the application to provide that data to individuals performing the tasks. At this point, the modeling process begins to get a bit more complicated.

The DataView Modeling Process

One of the key differences between my modeling approach and others is the emphasis on developing view definitions before modeling data. As you will see, standard entity relationship modeling and data flow diagrams have a role to play; however, they are not primary. As indicated previously, the very first step is to document the work flow and identify the operational tasks that the application will support. The next step is to identify the data needed by those tasks, without regard to data structures or ownership.

Users are always much more familiar with the actual data used in their business operation than any other group. Frequently, systems developers misunderstand a user's lack of comprehension about data storage and manipulation techniques, seeing this as a lack of knowledge about the data itself. When working with users in a client/server setting, it's vital to acknowledge their position as arbiters of their own procedures. You are there to provide them with computerized assistance, not drive down your definition of how they should work. Maybe this little diatribe does not apply to you, and if that is the case, then if you see someone else on your development team with that attitude, share it with that person. The users know what data they need to get the job done.

At this point, you should be able to see that the user view of the data is quite consistent with the level of understanding that a new or fresh development team would have. That is, users typically want to see data represented independently of any physical relational structure. They don't want to know about normalization, denormalization, redundancy, or replication. These things can be left to the second plane of abstraction: the logical model for both the database and the application modules.

What you need now is how to collect the raw data elements and relate those to the tasks. If you're working with a small group of user developers, you should be able to lock yourselves in a room and arrive at this. To accomplish it, use the technique displayed in Figure 4.2.3.

Each bubble contains a task and the name of a view for the data needed by that task.

FIGURE 4.2.3.

DataView title added to a task bubble.

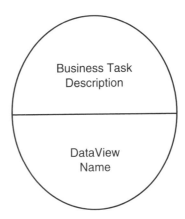

Of course, any relational database system strives to get away from the "one big table" concept. However, from a user's perspective, a spreadsheet is a familiar construct, and the challenge you present the user is to ensure that every cell needed is identified. The title of this spreadsheet is used as the name for the data required by the task. You should be able to see how the repeated columns across tasks will give you the basis for understanding how the data elements relate to each other. Again, you don't have to worry about modeling those relationships at this time. Here the key objective is to identify all of the data elements encompassed by the various operational tasks.

Figure 4.2.4 shows the DataView names and definitions that you might see for the mythical financial application for which we developed a task flow.

FIGURE 4.2.4.

The order systems tasks flow complete with DataView titles.

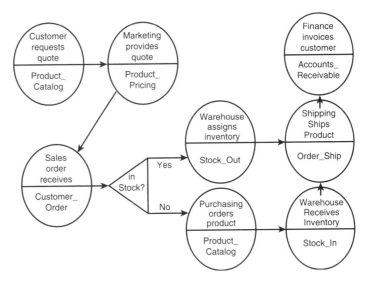

These titles describe specific data elements that will become the basis for column names in the next plane of the model. The DataView contents for this example might include that shown in Figure 4.2.5.

FIGURE 4.2.5.

DataView spreadsheet contents, including the names of each data element.

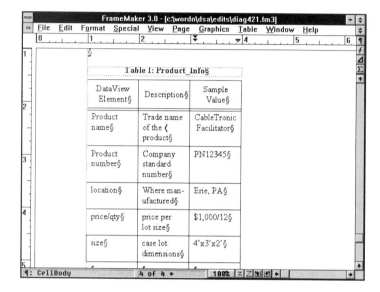

This is where the research that you have already done begins to take shape in the form of a model. You may remember the discussion in Chapter 1.4, "Taking Inventory," in which I referred to the importance of identifying all data used by the business unit or the application environment. When you performed your data inventory of all reports, forms, manuals, and such, you were preparing for this plane of the model. As the members of user group documents all of the data elements they can think of, you should be reviewing your findings from earlier research to ensure that the model does completely identify everything that is used. In keeping with the iterative technique and importance of user involvement, you would naturally also prepare a briefing for a wider audience, in which you walked them through the findings to date or circulated a report for their perusal. Remember that the key deliverable at this stage is completeness of the data sets to be handled by the system and their relationship to the task.

If someone identifies that data is needed to support a particular task, you may also find others prepared to argue that it is not required. This is your opportunity to allow the users to review their business process and challenge underlying assumptions. Certainly, you don't want to automate poor practices of the past. At the same time, you need to be sensitive to the idea that, for any significant change in practice to occur, it will have to be user driven. The whole point of modeling this plane in this fashion is to provide yourself with the assurance that you understand the complete set of tasks and data, but more important, that you arrive at an integrated business and data model that your users can understand and relate to.

The Importance of Nomenclature

In many cases, modeling at this level will cross organizational units and reporting structures. Another key deliverable at this plane of the model is to not only identify the complete data set to be used but to ensure that like data elements are given the same name across the application environment as a whole. This is not as straightforward as it might seem. Frequently, the users themselves may think there are subtle or even huge differences in "their" data versus that which comes from another department. In the next plane of the model, you'll see how to designate the primary source of data. When dealing with systems developed under earlier architectures, users sometimes invented their own names for data to avoid having to rely on coordinating with other business units.

The challenge in developing a Sybase application for your organization is to seek out and reconcile these artificial distinctions. The new client/server technology allows seams and relatively transparent access to data across the organization. But first you must understand the data. As you progress through the Integrated Task/Data Model, you'll see where the development of a data dictionary fits. From the outset, however, you should be concerned with ensuring that you are dealing with unique data definitions before you move to the next stage. Of course, you don't have to be 99.99996 percent correct. It's actually good enough to be aware of the requirement and remember to ask the question, "How is this data element different from this similar sounding one over here?" If they are in fact different, your users will let you know.

Grouping Application Functions

The next stage of defining the Business Operations plane of the Integrated Task/Data Model is to label the application module that will handle the data and systems functions necessary to support each separate task. At the highest level, you might assign labels such as Finance, Operations, Administration, or Sales. Because most of you won't be using this modeling technique to document enterprise systems (at least that's my expectation at this point), you will more likely label the tasks with module functions that break down the application into discrete components.

For the example I have been working with so far in this chapter, you might agree to break up the application to be built into components labeled as follows: Quotation, Order, Inventory, Purchasing, Shipping, A/P, A/R, and Shipping.

Naturally, with application modules of this scope, you can assume that the system to be built is reasonable large. We used a preliminary version of this model for a customer who replaced not only the organization's FIS but every operational system previously running on its mainframe system.

In some cases, the module label will help you determine which components you should focus on for timing reasons. Or you might use this model to help identify where tasks/data must be integrated with legacy systems. Anything that belongs to the accounts receivable or accounts payable subsystems might be remaining on a mainframe or other legacy system. By labeling the applications that support the business tasks and use data sets, you can use the model to review integration or data transfer requirements, which frequently form a part of the requirements for Sybase applications.

To document the application module labels, you can use the template format displayed in Figure 4.2.6.

FIGURE 4.2.6.
The model allows you to identify which application module supports tasks and uses data.

Integrated Task/Data Modelling Depiction Conventions

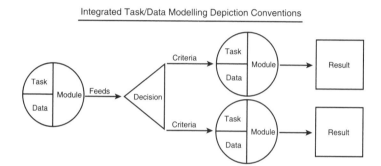

Putting the Model to Work

Once you have worked through your entire application area with this documentation technique, you actually have a good start on your system design, at least at a high level. Of course, it would be extremely dangerous to attempt to implement anything at this point. There is still a great deal of work to be done to logically lay out the data with which your application will work, and to identify application module functions and features as well as all the physical specifications that must be addressed in actual implementation.

You do, however, have a document that can be understood by management and by users. It defines the overall scope of the application to be built and provides a structure for the rest of your design.

At this level, the model is more of a process model, although using this particular technique allows you at least to identify what data you need and which subsystems must be built or integrated.

In terms of defining the overall modeling technique, I could now move directly into the Applications and Data Structures plane, defining entity relationship diagrams and menu hierarchies. In terms of the steps you would take to build a system, however, that part of the model is not what you would actually implement next. There are two other key elements to a systems design that have not yet been taken care of, yet must be to ensure a successful Sybase solution. These elements include developing a set of user requirements—specifically, systems specifications and a detailed project plan.

The work you do as part of modeling the Business Operations plane can be done without having installed any client/server technology. In fact, that is the best time to do an analysis at this level. You don't need to have people fully familiar and experienced with the relational model. They simply work through their understanding of the job to be done, the order in which it is done, the data required to get it done, and the name of the application module to do it.

From this documentation, you are ready to begin the more detailed processes required for a well-designed Sybase application.

Summary

In this chapter I have introduced the main elements of modeling a client/server system. The sheer number of variables to be balanced is always daunting. I have intended to provide a means of integrating the top to bottom elements of the plan.

Naturally, your client/server applications will require a great deal of time and effort to understand, model, and communicate. In this chapter I have shared with you the techniques that I have used successfully to build Sybase applications, and I hope they will work as well for you.

The key points to take away revolve around the means of tackling the problems inherent in building a new system and practical techniques to document them. Diagramming techniques have been around for years and, where possible, I have incorporated existing techniques, such as bubble diagrams. The real critical success factor is not to slavishly follow any one methodology, but to select from the alternatives available a method of explaining and documenting your system so that you understand it. Just as important, I hope that you have gained from this chapter a sense that these techniques aren't strictly for your own benefit, but also benefit the users and developers who will follow in your footsteps. These are the people who will make the most use of the models—the former group verifying your understanding, and the latter group building on it.

4.3

Project Planning and Resourcing

Introduction

Usually, you need at least some level of planning done before you ever ask management for money. That level typically reflects the true objective of the plan: to gain approval, not build a system. In my experience, the first thing a systems planner/architect does upon receiving approval to proceed is to review the promises made and work through a plan to make reality reflect the optimism on which those promises were made. (I will deal with the process of breaking bad news and renegotiating delivery dates in a later chapter.)

In the previous chapter, I addressed the process of modeling your business and application in such a way as to allow further development of your design documentation. In this chapter I will show you how you also can use that effort as input for your management documentation, specifically your project planning.

I would like to point out that this is also highly relevant for developers who have no management responsibility. Not only will you have higher "salability" if you present your timelines in a professional-looking chart, but more important, the technique of planning your tasks, allocating time, and determining dependencies at the detailed level will ensure that you stay on track within the development effort as a whole.

In any case, this chapter should help you become more familiar with the process of detailed project planning and task assignment. The emphasis will be on planning as part of the design and as a means of preparing for implementation, rather than as a project selling tool.

The Best Laid Plans...

The biggest problem with plans is that they change. These modifications occur frequently and to varying degrees. Usually, the process of updating the plan is considered too time consuming or unnecessary. As with all chores—filing, timesheets, what have you—it's easier for most people let them slide until it's either too late, the problem is too big, or it's an emergency. This approach to planning deprives you of the benefits that come from being organized.

I favor Microsoft Project, although there are any number of tools out there that can effectively help get the job done. One of the reasons I had for choosing Project was the facility to manage the same resources across multiple projects. The fact that I have never used the product to that level of sophistication does not detract from my perception that it is an excellent product. The important thing is that it has worked for us as a means of automating the project planning process.

But here's the rub: If you must scotch tape fifteen pieces of paper together to come up with a wall chart that everyone can see, it's no longer really an automated process. It seems that all systems are only as efficient as their least-automated link. If you're going to use a project planning program to help you with the planning process, try to ensure that you can fit some kind of regular reporting on a single sheet of paper. Usually, this means setting up the sheet to allow roll ups and printing detailed assignments only for the individuals involved. This might sound like an obvious or picky point, but I can assure you it will have an impact on whether or not you keep your plan up to date. But then, no doubt you already know this and I am preaching to the converted.

The Essentials

My father worked as a Systems Analyst and Project Leader when I first started in this business and he told me that there are really only five components to any successful project planning and status monitoring process. These are as follows:

- Identify single-step activities
- Assign one accountable person
- Estimate start and end dates
- Record actual start and end dates
- Reward performance accordingly

It doesn't matter whether you use a form or a slick project planning program to help you accomplish this. As long as you work through some semblance of this procedure, you have a fighting chance of actually implementing your design on some sort of schedule.

Let me explain exactly what he meant by these terms in a little more detail.

Identify Single-Step Activities

This has to be one of the trickiest processes to learn when working with information systems. Breaking tasks down into the discrete steps that must be taken to achieve a successful result comes from practice and experience. It's quite possible at the project planning stage to describe things quickly that take a great deal of time and effort to accomplish. For example:

Step One: Build the Great Wall of China

Any project plan that has a step of this magnitude is going to take a great deal of time and attention. For our purposes, it's not a practical method of working through a project plan. Ironically, it's exactly the kind of thing you want to do as part of your project plan for the feasibility study. At that level you are more interested in the overall costs and time and don't have a sufficient understanding of the details to break the project into single-step activities.

As a rule of thumb, a single-step activity should be no more than a day's work and no less than an hour. Otherwise, you will either become overwhelmed with details or you are back to the "Build a Pyramid" sized tasks.

Assign a Single Individual

In this era of teamwork and groupware, it's easy to forget that a camel is a horse designed by committee. All of the little sayings that indicate how important it is for individual accountability are absolutely true. Even for those tasks that require a team effort, you must know who is on the hook to deliver, or nobody is and that is almost always who ends up doing the job.

The other reason for assigning tasks to individuals is that it's a means of ensuring a fair and reasonable distribution of the workload. All too frequently, teams are made up of people with unequal skills, expertise, and competence. Usually, one person ends up carrying a greater portion of the load. One of the benefits of breaking things down to individual task assignments is that you can then minimize your risk that a person is overloaded (and as a result ends up not delivering), or that if they do take on the challenge and actually deliver, that you can fairly reward them for effort above and beyond the call of duty.

Beware of people who like to do their work as part of group. Give them an opportunity to stand out from the crowd and be recognized for their contribution.

Estimate Start and End Dates

This is the meat of project planning. How long is this particular task going to take? Of course, having reduced your tasks down to single steps means that you can more reasonably estimate how long each one will take. You can then add up the time required and discover that there is absolutely no way you can deliver what was promised in the time allocated with the resources as budgeted. But, hey, that's client/server.

Record Actual Start and End Dates

This is where the process typically breaks down. When a project slips off the rails, it's usually as a result of a missed step, an unforeseen technical problem, or a lack of delivery on the part of a particular individual or group. Who wants to have that as a matter of record? Unfortunately, the Hawthorne experiment proved that monitored behavior is changed behavior. The best way to minimize slippage is to record and report it. Also, if you want a reputation for on-time and on-budget delivery, you need to have monitoring tools in place to prove it. (Unless, of course, you want the credit without doing the work, in which case, forget I said anything).

Reward Performance Accordingly

When you actually demonstrate the discipline of proper planning and performance monitoring, your organization will typically reward you when you achieve results. This general observation may not apply to your particular employer's peccadilloes, but certainly you have a better chance of asking for a bonus if you can prove that you managed to stick to the plan. From the point of view of the people involved in meeting the plan, anytime someone delivers as agreed, it should be acknowledged. People who consistently don't pull their weight should also be recognized for what they are: a liability.

These are the essentials that make up any project plan. At this point, you should be ready to look at the process of breaking down client/server tasks into a representative project plan.

Translating the Feasibility Study into a Project Plan

Don't be confused by my overuse of the term *project plan*. This document is a key element of the design of your Sybase application. It serves as a map of the resources, activities, and timing that you must integrate to achieve the result identified as part of the systems concept.

It follows, then, that the project plan or design must be based on and built from the points identified in the feasibility study. However, if you could reasonably translate the study alone into a more detailed document, then you would likely be expected to generate that documentation as part of the business case prior to its approval. In fact, you need to marry the high level task/data modeling information into your project plan.

Look at the outputs from the IT/DM: you know what tasks must be performed, you know what data is needed, and you have descriptions of the modules to either be built or integrated. Most important, you should have some confidence that you have identified the complete set of elements, even if you do not understand them to any degree of detail.

The major areas to be addressed by a client/server project plan will normally include provision for the events described in the following sections.

Equipment Installation

One of the major causes of delay at the beginning of a project is inventory shortages and vendor delivery lag times for machines. Allow six to eight weeks for delivery and a couple of extra weeks for replacing parts that don't survive the initial burn in. Integration of new servers with existing networks and PCs can also eat up a considerable amount of time. Allow at least two weeks to accomplish this, unless you have access to people who are already familiar with all the issues involved.

Training

Training should be staged to allow your staff members to experiment and build on their new skills. One of the worst things to do is schedule all the training for one time. Allow enough time between courses for absorption. Also, you need to allow sufficient time for user training if you're implementing a set of new tools such as Windows or e-mail before releasing the new system.

Data Conversion

Trust me, unforeseen issues will arise once you actually start to move data from legacy and manual systems into your new database environment. Although even a large database can be populated over a weekend, the most frequent scenario is to have to take several kicks at the can, which means that something that takes a weekend on paper takes a month in reality.

Delivery Milestones

The people in my group specialize in commando-style, quick in-and-out client/server projects. Even with a focus on tight deadlines, it's possible (even likely) that some of your milestones will slip. Unnecessarily aggressive delivery commitments will be hard to meet and make you look bad if you need to reschedule. Whatever you do, try to schedule the major milestones so that they can slip a week or two without causing bedlam. I have seen Systems Directors schedule financial systems migrations for the weekend before a semi-annual report was due, or an annual inventory was scheduled. When the project needed to be pushed back (only by a week), the users couldn't deal with it and ended up rescheduling for the next quarter, a full three-month delay. Ensure that your milestones are coordinated with the activities in the business unit and other functional areas.

Access to Users

Also in keeping with the awareness of business unit schedules and commitments is the need to ensure that you will have access to users. All too frequently, business unit managers agree to participate during the concept phase and are reluctant to give up their resources when the design phase gears up. The last thing you want to have to do is fight for user time at this point because even if you win, you lose. If necessary, budget not only for user time, but for money to temporarily reassign staff to your project so that their involvement can be guaranteed.

Prototype Development

Even though the prototype is developed with the users as part of the detailed design process, you should plan for it separately because it's a high-visibility activity. The single biggest problem with prototypes is that they look too good, and management can become convinced that the system is virtually completed after a demonstration of the initial prototype. Make sure that you schedule lots of testing and debugging time after the prototype is reviewed the first few times, because this is where you get the most valuable feature and function design input. It's hard for people to imagine what a new system will look like and it takes a little while for them to process all of the implications, flaws, and weaknesses of a demonstrated prototype. Schedule lots of time for hands-on review of the prototype throughout the user group.

Application Design

Which came first, the application design or the prototype? The real work of putting validations, error and exception handling, and integration with other systems all falls out of the prototype review process. These requirements often don't even get identified in specific detail until after the users have an opportunity to ask questions about the new system based on their first few walkthroughs with the prototype. Make sure that you have these functions scheduled and assigned or you will end up looking to borrow time for them from other planned activities.

Data Modeling

For those of you moving from the relational databases on big iron systems (DB/2, anyone?), data modeling is not as big an issue as it is for those moving from hierarchical databases. You will find a great deal of time and resources consumed by the translation of the logical model to the physical, including tweaking (a nice word for redoing) indexes, views, and table structures. If you're dealing with data volumes in the gigabytes, this effort will be exponentially greater than if you are working with more modest table sizes. In very large database (VLDB) applications, the data model has a tremendous impact on performance that can't be solved by throwing hardware at it.

Testing

This is nice to have and it's not really a necessary activity (grin). As the guy on the TV commercial used to say, "Pay me now or pay me later." The amount of time you allocate to testing will probably be used to compensate for delays in development, but experience shows that the more testing you do, the less likely your application is to crash and burn. Even the most tolerant users have a low threshold for unreliable production systems. The sensible thing to do is to schedule a testing component after each stage of development, including the data modeling process.

Implementation Schedule

As the system is developed, you should be in a better position to assess the real impact of implementation. Part of your development plan should allow time to work through a detailed implementation plan, including user training in the new application, identification of additional (read temporary) support mechanisms and resources, as well as how any parallel operation of both the new and old system will be accomplished.

These major phases and their attendant details are most frequently represented in the form of a GANTT chart. A sample client/server GANTT chart is depicted in Figure 4.3.1.

FIGURE 4.3.1.

*A typical client/server
project GANTT chart.*

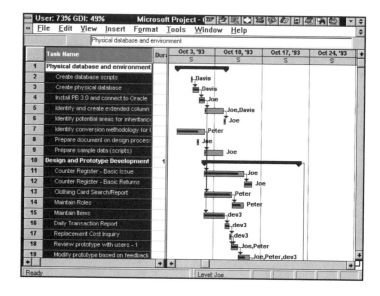

Tracking Progress

Earlier in the chapter I referred to the Hawthorne effect, an organizational behavior experiment conducted in the 1960s that is covered in first-year management classes. If you really want people to take project deliverables seriously, you must make it obvious what progress is being made and let them know that the progress is being watched by the "powers that be."

Most project planning programs have facilities to report progress in terms of percentage completed that you can express as a little line inside the task bar of a GANTT chart. The problem with this mechanism is twofold: the progress is task based, so it's difficult to see how the project as a whole is doing; and it's difficult to focus on upcoming tasks while abstracting the details of later phases.

Let's face it, most people never even bother to do more than glance at project plans and PERT and GANTT charts, and they most certainly don't let them affect them emotionally. Yet, if you want people to completely buy in to the project and its schedule, this is exactly what has to happen.

On one of my early client/server projects, I realized that the development staff and the users seemed to be working to their own schedule for delivery, which did not quite jive with the one I had received approval on from management. In spite of full-color GANTT project progress charts and weekly meetings, all I got were glassy stares when reviewing the plan and project status. I realized that I needed a new way of presenting the information to really get the team's attention.

It was about the time of the United Way fundraising drive, and my attention was caught by the donation thermometer. It was a quick reference method of explaining not only the target but the progress toward the target by particular dates. This is the kind of thing that you need to have to communicate the performance of your projects.

To accomplish this, I developed a progress charting method that I call a tunnel chart.

Tunnel Charts

The key metaphor underlying the tunnel chart is the light at the end of the tunnel; it could be daylight or it could be an oncoming train. The tunnel chart is designed to present progress in relation to the deadline date that has been set for the last major milestone typically considered to be the delivered project. During development, this is generally the target implementation date.

Encapsulating Details

Another aspect of the tunnel chart that works quite well is the encapsulation of details into simple headings. The biggest problem with traditional charting methods is that they treat all phases of the project equally. You can collapse activities into project headings, of course, but generally, people looking at a GANTT or PERT chart expect a consistent level of detail from the start of the project to its completion.

By now you should be able to see that client/server projects consist of a series of stages, some of which you will not understand to the detail level until it's actually time to work through that stage. The tunnel chart is designed to accommodate this feature of typical client/server development.

Tunnel Chart Structure

As you can see in the graphic, a tunnel chart consists of concentric rings with a date in the center. This date represents the key date on which you want the project team and management focused. You would normally update the chart at the completion of every major phase. I found that printing a large color poster version of the chart and hanging it on the wall of the common area worked to get people's attention. Remember that the key value is not that the details of the next assignment will be communicated to your project team (if they don't know what they should be working on you have a problem), but rather that everyone needs to know that the deadline is coming. By placing it front and center, you advertise it and increase the overall understanding that the deadline is real and not just an optimistic target.

The outer ring is the largest and contains the discrete deliverables on which everyone should be working. These would not be the single-step activities, but rather the combined result; for example, completion of the logical data model, prototype demonstration, and staff training.

The next ring contains major headings to indicate the upcoming major functions to be addressed. You want people to be thinking about what comes after the successful completion of their current assignments. However, the remaining rings typically are titled with a single term or phrase. During the analysis phase, you would detail all the review and documentation deliverables and refer to the key deliverables in the design phase, but the inner rings would simply indicate that development, testing, implementation, and support were activities to follow. The tunnel chart shown in Figure 4.3.2 represents this.

FIGURE 4.3.2.

A tunnel chart depicting the activities at the beginning of a Sybase project.

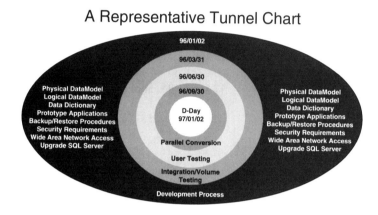

A Representative Tunnel Chart

Updating the Chart

As you progress through the project, the outer rings drop off the chart and the ring representing the deadline date gets bigger. Over time this has the effect of communicating that the delivery date is drawing closer. Toward the end of the development phase, where your deadline date represented rollout into production, your tunnel chart might look like the one in Figure 4.3.3.

FIGURE 4.3.3.

A tunnel chart depicting the activities to be performed just before deadline is reached.

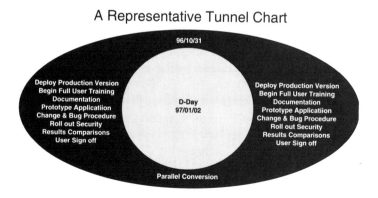

A Representative Tunnel Chart

Maximizing Impact

Depending on the resources available to you in your organization, you should consider having the chart printed in color because this allows you to convey a good deal more information viscerally. For example, when I used this chart the first time, I always had the center ring printed in yellow. Over time, the yellow dot grew until it was the largest feature of the wall on which the poster was placed. I noticed that developers and users did not pay much attention to the chart, but when we discussed the deadlines and what needed to be accomplished next, there was little confusion on the part of the people in the room.

When used in conjunction with a project planning tool such as MS Project, this makes a highly effective summary of what needs to be done and when it must be completed for the project to remain on schedule. Repetition works as a means of improving memory and it also works to reinforce commitment to a deadline, especially if that deadline is communicated well in advance and does not change. The tunnel chart is an excellent means of depicting what needs to be done next, and when, especially if your project has an externally driven target date that absolutely can't change. If you do a development project for the Olympic Games, for example, you aren't likely to get an extension if your systems are running behind schedule. For these kinds of projects, a tunnel chart gets the date fixed firmly in everybody's mind.

Summary

Developing successful Sybase applications is primarily a question of integration and balance. Not only must you balance processing requirements and workloads, but you must integrate business objectives, technical considerations, resource requirements and availability.

Project planning and monitoring is a necessary part of a complete methodology for developing client/server solutions. From reading this chapter, you should have a better appreciation for the elements that must be included in you plan and some of the options available to you for representing and communicating this information.

One of the critical success factors of working with as many variables as you must with a client/server project is the need to provide constant feedback to the various contributors. In this chapter I have tried to address all of the elements of successfully identifying, monitoring and reporting what needs to be done, when it needs to be done and who is going to do it.

If you operate in the role of project leader or systems architect, this responsibility will fall to you. As a developer you should seek out this kind of information and review it when it is made available to you. Understanding how the project as a whole will fit together is one of the more rewarding aspects of working with Sybase and client/server technology. You get to be a part of something larger than just your own efforts. However, unless you understand what your role is and how others are contributing, it can be difficult to be motivated by this involvement.

Client/server systems are a swarm of details. By reading this chapter, you should be in a better position to plan for these details and have a structure for relegating them to their proper time and scope.

4.4

Writing User Requirements

Introduction

By now you should be comfortable with the overview of the conceptual framework that I have defined for designing and developing client/server systems. The preliminary analyses that you perform as part of the inventory process, and then again to support your business case, will give you a good grasp on the overview of your own organization's requirements.

Beware of the temptation to become overconfident, and remember the old adage that a little knowledge is indeed a dangerous thing. Take advantage of the opportunities afforded by the development process to truly flesh out your understanding of the business.

In this chapter I will take some time to put forth my view of how and why to write a formal statement of users' requirements of the system. Also, you should see how this user requirements document fits into the overall methodology for developing Sybase applications. It provides a unique explanation of what the system must do to be a success and, as such, is not a trivial contribution to the development effort.

All too often, I see systems professionals placing too little or too much emphasis on written requirements. Wherever I recommend putting the effort into writing such documents, keep in mind that this applies only if your organization tends to minimize the creation of formal plans. If your organizational culture is one with high dependence on memos, plans, committees, and documentation, feel free to skip this requirements definition documentation process. Just don't skip the requirement's definition. Whether you write it into a formal document or not, all successful client/server systems meet clearly defined and well understood user requirements.

One last point: the users themselves will be the ones to tell you whether or not you have actually met their requirements. This document formally defines their expectations of the system, as opposed to management's objectives, or yours.

Why Bother Defining User Requirements

In many ways, the relationship between systems professionals and the users of their systems is like the stereotypical relationship between spouses. There is a familiarity (with or without the contempt it breeds) and, as in any relationship, this familiarity leads to assumptions. These assumptions can kill your project in the same way that they can lead a relationship onto the rocks.

The process of defining user requirements is one of clarifying what the users expect the system to do for them. This is different from modeling what their existing work flow does, and much different from the level of concerns addressed by a business case or feasibility study. A business case asks what benefits would result from the system being considered, whereas a feasibility study determines whether obtaining the desired result is viable from a cost, resource, and timing perspective. A requirements document, on the other hand, begins at the stage at which a decision to proceed has been made. The users will be getting a system that provides a result desired by the business. The question becomes, what do they want it to do in order to arrive at the desired benefits?

The user requirements definition process is an opportunity to start fresh and take a new look at the environment in which the system will operate. People and situations do in fact change. Or, more important from your perspective, maybe they would change if only someone had the ability to effect that change. In other words, changes are needed, but the capability has been lacking.

Our client/server technology is most definitely a force for change. It is in meeting the users' requirements that this force becomes an enabler and empowers the people who use it.

Empowerment: Beyond the Hype

There has been a tendency for some human resources types to misuse or overuse the word *empowerment*. It sounds good, of course. That is one of the reasons that it has become as notorious as the term *paradigm*. People frequently use it without a full understanding of what it means. It then becomes a hackneyed cliché that raises peoples hackles.

That being said, I will blithely carry on with my use of the word, because I happen to believe that it is a good jargon phrase that refers to something significant and of direct interest to anyone developing client/server applications.

At one point in my travels, I had some luggage containing a little more than 30 pounds of diskettes. For various reasons, I needed all of them in spite of their considerable nuisance value. While waiting for a delayed flight, it occurred to me that the contents of those diskettes represented an incredible volume of work in terms of hours, and even more if their contents were printed out on paper. The contents of my luggage were the combined efforts of hundreds of people and thousands of hours. I recognized that I could just tap into whatever relevant piece of work I needed at the moment and use it or refer to it to meet my own needs.

There is a direct corollary between this and how your users see the systems you build. All the time and attention of a development team is spent on creating capability. Like the diskettes in the sack, someone has to have a need for that capability and bring it to bear on a unique problem of his or her own. The purpose of the user requirements document is to determine from the outset what it is that someone might need done, and to provide an effective means of meeting that requirement.

Which is exactly what you do whenever you develop a system. The difference is whether or not you have identified what you think you would want done, or presumed that you already know what they will need done. At which point, off you go to develop a system. And this is where most client/server systems bog down to some extent.

To Thy User's, Not Thine Ownself, Be True

There was a commercial on television several years ago that quoted Ralph Waldo Emerson: "To know in your heart that what is true for you is true for all men, that is genius." Because most computer systems people are geniuses (just ask them, they'll tell you), it follows that what they come up with is necessarily inspired and superior.

Ironically, this is sometimes true. No new major development in applications software would have been possible without someone believing in an idea and pushing it out onto an unsuspecting world.

The world of developing client/server solutions does not so easily lend itself to this model. For one thing, when someone invents a new product, he or she offers it for sale and the market can choose to adopt or reject it. Your users are not in a similar position of strength. Even with the capability to snap on various client software, they are still pretty much at the mercy of systems providers to provide them with a system to do their jobs.

To give them power, or provide them with tools that allow them to be more effective (and thereby more powerful), you must understand what they need to accomplish. True, they need to understand how to operate the tools and some of the concepts necessary to make the tools work, but this happens after they identify what needs to be done.

The Importance of Individual Discretion

When I first got into the information systems business in the late 1970s, I was taught about the principle of soul-destroying work. This is the mindless repetition of tasks that is not suitable for humans to perform. Invariably, this work is of a step-and-repeat nature. In some ways this is worse when its mental drudgery as opposed to a physical fetching and lifting. At least physical exertion is exercise and contributes to a fit and healthy body. My trainers and mentors in the field said that repetitive clerical tasks were mind-numbing and should be automated as quickly as possible.

Over the years, many organizations have made great strides in eliminating and automating these repetitive tasks. With the advent of personal computers, many employees have been given opportunities to define their own methods of processing data. It should come as no surprise that if you try to integrate these people into a more corporate framework, they may resist.

One way to turn this potential resistance into collaboration is through the development of an in-depth user requirements document. By giving the users an opportunity to tell you what they need and want, you allow them to see you as a facilitator, as someone who can help them rather than as a restriction on their freedom.

The other value to working through a users requirements document is unabashedly political. Users are able to sign off only on business level descriptions of systems, not on the features and functions of the technology itself. Once you have developed a document on which they can sign-off, you then have a target for delivery. If you meet those targets, you have ensured that the users can't undermine the review of the success of the system. After all, it does what they indicated they wanted it to do, right?

Practical Considerations

There are reasons that go beyond political or psychological realms for creating user requirements. With the creation of your first plane of the IT/D model, you labeled the application module that would support a business task and provide the data belonging to the associated view. The user requirements document allows you to begin detailing the functionality and features belonging to each application module named in the model.

The user requirements are a statement of what the users require the system to do for them, therefore you can use this process to list the overall functions and features that the application must provide. Like the first plane of the IT/D model, it's still not necessary to have hands-on access to client/server technology. This portion of the documentation straddles and translates the systems concept into the beginning of the design process.

This pretty much sums up my reasons for bothering with user requirements. The next stage is to describe in some useful fashion exactly what these wee beasties look like.

User Requirements: A Template

First, you should be in agreement that user requirements must be in English. It's not my intention to recommend some esoteric or arcane diagramming techniques that only systems gurus would be able to decipher. Simply put, user requirements must be in the language of the users. As you have seen, one of the key objectives of performing this design task is to obtain user sign-off. How reasonable would it be to think that they could or would accept a document that they could not understand? Or worse, what happens if they are only pretending to understand the document? Now there's a scary thought.

Avoid the potential problem by ensuring that the requirements are clear and intelligible.

The following describes the key elements to be contained in any user requirements definition:

- ▪ Output and Queries

  The user requirements for data should be expressed in terms of the printed and screen reports that they must have to perform their operational tasks. Special requirements such as graphic output should be identified here.

- ▪ Data Manipulation and Calculation

  Most applications provide some of their value by calculating values for contrived columns or subtotals. Sales to Date calculations on a particular day is an example. A complete set of requirements will identify where data is required, based on calculation of data elements stored in the server.

■ Validations and Tests

If you accept that the users are the owners of their data, then it stands to reason that they should be able to tell you how they establish the validity of that data. These validations need to be incorporated into the requirements and subsequently bound into the application at the client workstation, the database, or both. Tests refer to conditions against which input is reviewed to determine whether or not it falls within the ranges of stated business rules.

■ Format and Presentation

The business unit for which the requirements are being developed may have unique needs for data presentation. These formatting requirements would be identified as part of the user requirements document. This consists of a note about the required formats, not an attempt to diagram, model, or otherwise graphically depict the format. That step occurs as part of the actual systems design plane.

■ Replication and Ownership

The scope of the data handled by a particular operational unit must include a designation of which data is to be generated and owned by that unit and which data is to be replicated from another source. Typically, it's more straightforward to identify which data will be published for consumption by other systems or departments and to which existing data the application should subscribe, instead of trying to define all of the places that will use data published by this application.

Once again I want to stress that the trick is to deal with these elements at an appropriate level of detail. The user requirements stage allows you to explicitly note any exceptions or requirements specific to the applications being developed for a particular operational group. Let the group members tell you what they want and worry about how to provide it later in the development process.

Using the Format and Presentation section as an example, you should be able to see how you could get bogged down trying to do screen design before you actually have enough information to successfully complete the process. In fact, there may not be any requirements relative to any of the sections identified in the preceding paragraphs. When you discuss the users' formatting and presentation requirements, they may simply shrug the whole issue off. It's perfectly permissible for the users to have no unique requirements, without this meaning that they don't need the data or the systems functionality. They just may not particularly care how you present it, for example. However, by reviewing your IT/D model with your users while developing requirements, you give them the opportunity to identify such things as data that must be presented together, or must be validated by a calculation, or is derived from data obtained from a different department or subsystem.

Remember, the user requirements consist of a list of needs from an operational point of view. Ultimately, it's just a statement of what the system must do in order to be useful from a nontechnical standpoint. One of the challenges of putting user requirements together is keeping them from telling you how the job is to be done. Frequently, you will run into reasonably technical end users who are not as focused on what the system is to accomplish as they are on how it should be done. By structuring your user requirements process according to this format, you should be able to defer any detailed technical discussions, while still getting the insights you need to round out the user requirements and set the stage for the more detailed design activities.

The Requirements Definition Process

Now that you know what needs to be contained in a user requirements document, I would like to spend a little time on the order of the activities. Typically, systems people are highly linear and these things are approached often on an A to B to C basis. With the user requirements documentation process, it's often best to begin with the final outputs required from the system and work backwards.

At this point in the life of organizational computing, most of you will not be in the process of automating manual systems so much as migrating existing mainframe and PC applications to a Sybase environment. This means that there are already output reports provided by the existing applications.

This may come as a shock, but some of the reports that the users currently get may meet their requirements just fine. It's an important critical success factor that you not only give them the new things they want and need, but that you also do not take away anything they already have and use.

This is a more subtle issue than it first appears. The process of migrating to a new environment carries with it a momentum that can easily sweep people up into a widespread belief that everything must be changed. Of course, this may be true, but it's more likely that continuing some things in the same way will provide more benefit and allow for time to be spent reworking those activities that can actually benefit from reengineering.

Once you pose the question, Which reports can't you do without?, you give the users an opportunity to tell you what data they use and value. And you provide your project with a target list of reports that must be duplicated in the new environment to provide the same (and, with luck, more) value than the application being replaced.

Defining Processing Requirements

The calculation and manipulation of data by applications is the kind of thing that should interest users. In fact, this is one of the areas in which you can co-opt the users and put them to work with their own subcommittees and work groups. You can then ensure that they have worked through all their business logic and have spotted all the opportunities to take advantage of the new system.

Business rules don't actually change all that much (depending on the nature of your business), but what does change dramatically is the capability of systems to enforce or incorporate those rules. Your users may actually have procedures that are essentially manual verification of data that is fed into or held by the system. By working through the user requirements to explicitly identify these rules, you may uncover the need for the users themselves to work on a more detailed definition of what they want, simply because they could never get it before. Put another way, the capabilities of your Sybase application could drive opportunities for refinement in the way they do business. This is not your job, although ensuring that the users are fully aware of what you can do for them most certainly should be in your job description.

At this stage of the user requirements, you're simply informing the users as to what is possible and allowing them to define how they can best take advantage of the capability. This covers both the validation and test requirements, as well as the calculation and manipulation capabilities that the system must provide.

Data Replication Definition

This is way too early in the process to get into methods of modeling replicated or distributed data. However, it's not too early to identify sources of data within an application area. If your users know that what they really want is timely data generated by another business unit, this is definitely the place to make that note. The system must provide timely data from sources x, y, and z for further processing.

Just as important, the unique data generated by the application that may be of interest to other groups also must be explicitly noted at this point. When other users outside the application area review the requirements definitions, you may be surprised to learn that there are two places that primary data is generated, and which location is truly primary must be established. Again, I want to note that these are business issues that revolve around systems, and resolving these issues is not typically the responsibility of systems people (unless no one else is willing to take responsibility for it).

Summary

I hope that this chapter showed you the utility of having a written document that defines the users requirements of the system. Certainly, you should see that this level of analysis is not actually addressed by any other aspect of my methodology. The process of defining user requirements, in the language of the business, is a vital component when it comes to developing successful Sybase solutions.

The key is to work with the users to ensure that they have every opportunity to tell you what a successful system will look like and what it will do for them, before you begin building it.

Like many of the approaches to building systems, client/server or otherwise, success is in the practice of these recommendations, rather than simply going through the motions. If you are not actually interested in finding out your users' requirements, it won't matter whether you have a document that contains all of the relevant sections.

Much of the value of this process is that it provides a structured forum to get the users involved, and forms the foundation of trusting that you intend to give them something of value that they can use to make themselves more effective. This is really what people mean when they talk about user buy-in. The requirements definition process is a real opportunity for you to obtain that buy-in, even before the technology arrives on your doorstep.

Remember that there is a practical value to be derived from this process as well. By defining the five components of user requirements, you give yourself the basis for developing validation formulae and edit masks at the column level, and for defining output reports and calculations to be performed on the data. In short, you get a quick look at exactly how much work is involved to meet the objectives of the application.

In my book, this is of considerable practical value.

4.5

Modeling the Sample Application

Introduction

By now, you should be aware of the approach I've taken to reinforce the material discussed in more general terms throughout the book so far. I have mentioned in a number of places that the sample application was being developed by a team who used these chapters as the basis for their development efforts.

Actually, I would like to be able to tell you that I did all of this stuff myself, but because we've been through so much together, I have to be completely candid. Even the smallest Sybase solutions require the combined efforts of a team and this application is no exception.

I'm the one who designed the application and managed the development team, however, so I guess I should get down to the business of not only applying what we've covered so far, but lay out for you the requirements and project plan with which the developers themselves had to work.

In this chapter I will detail the users' requirements and identify the specific steps taken as part of the project plan for the development of CausesDB.

These requirements were handed off to the developers I mentioned in Chapter 3.5, "Technological Environment for CausesDB," who turned these documents and diagrams into a prototype by following the development methodology I have sketched out to date. As I evaluate the results of these efforts, you'll be able to see just how the methodology works and what level of delivery and detail is appropriate to the design phase.

User Requirements

As you should remember, there are several groups of users for the application I am developing here. However, at some point there will be a hands-on operator of the application, which is different from the organization that benefits from the application; this operator is our end user. Namely, you. For the remainder of this chapter, I will deal with defining the requirements, data, and task modeling strictly from the point of view of the end user. I do this on the assumption that if you're happy, everybody else involved in the process will be happy, too.

You should be aware that whenever anyone makes assumptions prior to the design, they had best be prepared to revise their position when those assumptions are tested. I am just as interested as anyone whether the application developed here will actually provide hands-on features leading to the benefits identified as part of the initial concept for CausesDB.

In any case, you the reader will also get to see how this process unfolds, as it mirrors real-life development projects.

User Requirements for CausesDB

Unlike most real development projects, CausesDB has no real client. Other than the promise to deliver a representative application to the publisher, there are no users anxiously awaiting the delivery of the system.

At the same time, I firmly believe that anyone who has ever considered donating money or volunteering time to help a worthy cause has wondered about the alternatives. To assist in this investigation, we wanted to provide a database application that would not only show how decision support systems could be built, but would be practically useful as well.

Output and Queries

The following reports and forms will be available from CausesDB:

- **Donation Form:** This form is to be completed on screen with user contact data, which automatically populates fields with charitable organization data and prints to paper or fax/modem. This form must also support targeting any aspect of the charity to which the funds should be put, such as an unfunded or underfunded initiative.

- **Organization Search:** This screen form allows users to view the details provided for each charitable organization contained within the CausesDB database.

- **Advertisement Browse:** This screen form retrieves available radio, print, or video ads for selected charities and allows the user to review the associated advertisement.

- **Mission and Purpose Review:** This screen form allows users to select target groups assisted by various charities to short-list organizations for a more detailed review.

- **Financial Report:** This screen form displays the financial profile of selected charities, including their overall budget, costs, and shortfalls. This report should graphically depict total revenue history for the past five years (growth or decline) as well as percentage of operations funded by government.

- **Unfunded Program Report:** This screen form displays details on initiatives that the charitable institutions would like to launch but for which they have insufficient funding.

These queries should be available from a menu or allow a drill-down approach as the user focuses more clearly on an area. The data is related on the basis of assisted groups and then primarily it is organization specific. All the screen forms should be available for printing data, and numeric data should be exportable to a spreadsheet for further manipulation.

Data Manipulation and Calculation

The CausesDB application is primarily a decision support application and, as such, is not computation intensive. However, one of the key objectives of the application is to generate donations for charities, so the Donation Form will require some data manipulation.

Additionally, a report of growth and decline in donations, plus the impact of government funding, should be derived from hard dollar values rather than from the percentage values submitted by the charitable organizations.

The following calculations will need to be performed:

■ Financial Report

   (a) Year-Over-Year Performance - Report percentage growth/decline for each of the past five years

   (b) Cost Allocation - Calculate the percentage distribution of proceeds according to administration, advertising, and operations

   (c) Government Funding Impact - Report percentage growth/decline for each year of government funding as a portion of the overall revenue base for each charity

■ Donation Form

   (a) Calculate tax credit or deduction for donor based on estimated taxable income and total estimated charitable donations. Express percentage of the donation as tax relief to the donor

These calculations and data manipulation activities supported by the application will directly affect the usability of the application and its effectiveness in meeting one of the key deliverables— to generate funds for participating charities.

Validations and Tests

CausesDB is not numbers intensive, so there are relatively few data validations that must be performed. However, the following validations must be established on the database and validation processes incorporated into the data entry process. Additionally, care must be taken to ensure that information pertaining to the solicitations of donations is absolutely correct and verified to eliminate the possibility of funds being misappropriated by people outside the participating charities.

■ **Charitable Organization Tax Number:** Must be provided and verified accurate before donations can be requested.

■ **Charitable Organization Contact Name:** Providers of data must be identified and verified.

- **Charitable Organization Contact information:** Must be verified to ensure correct address, telephone, and fax numbers. This includes validating zip codes and postal codes, and checking validity of area codes.

- **Financial Totals:** Must total 100 percent and relate to other subtotals provided as part of the data collection process, such as government funding and cost allocation.

- **Donor Taxation Information:** Must provide literal quotes of relevant tax information for Canada and the U.S. (reprinted from the Tax Act). The application can't provide validated tax implications reports or advice; this must be clearly stated and responsibility legally waived.

The validations will primarily be implemented through the use of look up and validation tables on the database. Additionally, validation tests will have to be run on submitted data prior to its acceptance into the CausesDB database.

Format and Presentation

To ensure that collected data is entered as quickly as possible, the data entry process must be based on an automated process. This will eliminate the need to process paper forms at both the charities and by the development team, who would prefer not to have a data-keying component to the application.

The format of the data entry module will be a form-based application, where data is stored in a stand-alone database. The data collection application must run off a diskette that can then be returned for data extraction and validation before loading the data into the CausesDB database. We don't anticipate that any of the charities will have users sophisticated enough to support Internet access or other online data transfer.

The data collection executable must run with satisfactory performance on a 386/33MHz personal computer with 4MB of RAM, because many charitable institutions don't have the latest technology. However, the CausesDB application itself can expect to run on a multimedia-capable PC, configured as a 486/33 SX with 8MB of RAM.

The format of the CausesDB application must conform to Windows 3.*x* standards for applications. Keyboard shortcuts, though desirable, won't be necessary for this application.

In general, the application should take full advantage of color, while conforming to the rules of good user interface design and graphics presentation.

CausesDB will be distributed on a CD-ROM and will contain installation scripts for the creation of SQL Server database objects such as tables and indexes. Due to the storage intensive nature of BLOBs (such as those used to store .TIF, .AVI, and .WAV files), inclusion of these objects on the database will be minimized. Instead, users will access the database to determine which object to browse, and the application will load the selection from the CD-ROM directly.

Reviewing the User Requirements

From the preceding breakdown, you should have a much clearer picture of exactly what the CausesDB application must do to be successful. Virtually all of the preceding definition is not oriented to the technology but relates directly to how the user will see and interact with the application. Some discussion of disk format is necessary because it directly affects how the users will address the application and what they will need to make it work.

The key consideration is that the application is to be broken into two discrete parts: the data collection process, which involves the charitable institutions themselves; and the data review process by the end users of CausesDB, which includes, I hope, you.

The development of user requirements, like most aspects of a Sybase application, is an iterative process. While writing the requirements, you will frequently think of an additional point and include it in the material already created. Also, as part of the development of our representative application, I circulated these requirements to the development team to solicit input and feedback. With their questions in mind, I enhanced and expanded the requirements to make them as clear and complete as possible before moving into the design phase of the development.

From this you should be able to see that you as a developer are a key user of the user requirements document. To understand why you are building the application, you need to look at the business case, but to understand the basic shape and structure of the application, you turn to the user requirements document.

Modeling the Tasks and Data

Using the IT/DM approach, you can see exactly how the application fits into an overall workflow and what data is required to make it all work. The highest plane of the IT/DM appears as shown in Figure 4.5.1.

FIGURE 4.5.1.
The CausesDB Context Model expressed in Integrated Task/Data Model format.

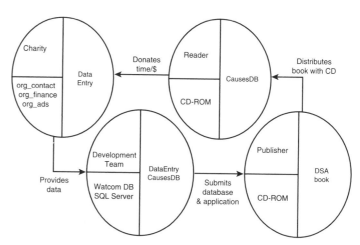

From this you can see how the overall application functions, from the identification of participating charities to the preparation of the data collection modules and collection of data, integration of the data into a database, and distribution of the application where it can then be used.

The most important aspect of this model is the manner in which it breaks down the work to be done and identifies the people who are assigned to performing those tasks. In this sense I mean the systems development tasks necessary to create and support a module, or to collect and massage data, rather than the operational task itself.

From our development of the IT/DM model for CausesDB, I have identified the following modules:

- Collection
- Extraction
- Validation
- Distribution
- Browse
- Donation

The resulting output of the application is a donation. From the model, you can see that all of the processes are linked together and ultimately end up at the point of donation. Of course, every user must make an active decision to donate time or money to any charity; however, the application itself supports that process.

As well as having identified the modules that must be created to make the application work, I have also identified the data needed to support the process. The DataViews refereed to in the IT/DM consist of those shown in Figure 4.5.2.

FIGURE 4.5.2.

A collection of DataViews necessary to support CausesDB.

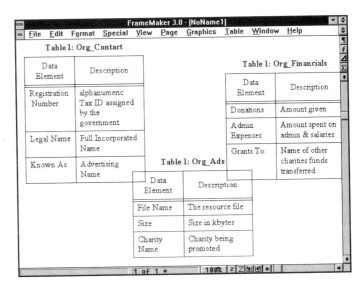

Between the overall model depicted in the diagram and the user requirements, you should now have a fully defined concept of the functions that the application will perform, and the data resources necessary to provide that functionality.

Understanding the Data

The point behind modeling the DataViews is to understand the overall collection of data elements that need to be incorporated into the application. In the case of CausesDB, at this point we can see that the data we need consists of the following major groups:

> Organization "tombstone" data
> Contact Information
> Program Data
> Financial Data
> Advertising Data

Within each of these major areas there is a number of specific data items that will need to be collected and massaged as part of the application. At this point we do not have to know what tables and columns will be created on the back end; however, to move into the design phase, we will need to know what specific data will be available. The purpose of the DataViews is to provide an overview of that data.

Summary

In this chapter you have seen how the modeling techniques discussed in the section apply to a specific project. Possibly the most difficult part of learning any new technology and/or set of professional practices is applying the concepts to any specific situation. By working through the ideas covered in this book and through the sample application, you should get a better idea of how these ideas can work in reality.

I don't expect that the methodology recommended here will be the last word in client/server development techniques. At the same time, I have found that working through this process with my employers and clients has actually led to the development of workable and effective client/server systems. By checking your own development techniques against the format and approach suggested here, you may be able to identify a few holes or areas that could use further development.

In terms of the CausesDB application, we tried to accomplish a number of objectives simultaneously. Of primary importance was proving the validity of the techniques recommended in this book. The last thing I want to do is suggest some kind of academic, ivory-tower approach to building systems that does not stand up in the real world.

A number of other important objectives also may be achieved by this application. From the requirements, you should be able to see how the funding needs of worthy causes can be researched and ultimately supported by people who use the application. If this does in fact turn out to be the case, it will mean that the CausesDB application is representative of your Sybase application on a higher level. That is, the application built as part of this book is important in some way and of practical benefit. This is the opposite of using technology for technology's sake.

The requirements for this application have been created for an imaginary user: someone who has access to powerful PC technology and has an interest in how he or she can provide resources or work with an organization to accomplish something particularly meaningful.

As a reader of *Developing Sybase Applications*, your use for this book as a means of instruction has been of utmost importance to me. On the other hand, if you know someone who might be interested in actually using the CausesDB application to research potential support of a worthy cause, please pass it on to them. Ultimately, these people are the end users of the CausesDB application.

5

Design

Introduction

In this section I will take on the unique challenges posed by integrating GUI-based PCs with relational database servers over sophisticated communications networks by detailing new techniques for designing client/server systems.

There are many expressions and sayings that deal with the phenomenon of underdelivering on one's promises. Some of them are even polite, but they all come down to one essential truism: anyone can talk about it. Client/server systems are inherently difficult and the only way to maximize your chances of making your Sybase application a success is to properly design it prior to implementation.

I would like to point out that I fully realize the importance of design; many of my client/server projects are really implementations of the concept, turning prototypes into production systems. Although these have succeeded, I have become convinced that there is a better, safer way to accomplish the same result, and that is what this section will cover.

The role of the mock-up and prototypes as a method of establishing detailed design documentation is addressed at this point in the book. The process of using the prototype to focus the development team on standardized techniques for combining efforts and ensuring that the system's modules will work together is also covered in this section.

Defining essential elements such as naming conventions, base objects for inheritance, error handling procedures, and coding standards will be detailed for those of you expected to write code.

For those of you with network design or administration responsibilities, your role and methods of anticipating network traffic and growth, as well as capacity planning and load balancing techniques, will be discussed. Continuing operations activities such as backups and recovery strategies will also be addressed as part of the design phase.

My intent is to provide you with a comprehensive view of all the issues that must be covered before you can consider your system designed and ready to begin implementation. As promised, it will reflect the iterative model of development, and will provide ample opportunity to reflect and enhance your understanding of your application requirements as it grows. (Your understanding, that is, not your requirements.)

This is an ambitious undertaking. You will be taken through the end-to-end process of developing a Sybase application at a detailed design level as opposed to a general and conceptual overview. Over the course of this section, I will make specific recommendations on how to take advantage of the Sybase architecture and how to deal with PowerBuilder and Visual Basic capabilities at a detailed level.

I hope it proves useful to you as well as interesting.

5.1

Virtual Design

Introduction

I have pointed out on many occasions that there are a great many things we can learn from the experience found in the mainframe world. One of these is the importance of prototyping. On the other hand, there are just as many things that you can turf out without feeling too great of a sense of loss. An example of this would be the voluminous written specifications that passed as design documentation under structured development methodologies.

Of course, I can't argue that a complex, large-scale development effort with hundreds of programmers won't result in binders and binders of design documents. What I want to challenge here is the assumption that any of that approach results in useful guidelines for building Sybase applications.

In fact, as I mentioned in the introduction to the section, it's possible to develop software that will survive and adapt through the implementation process with no structured design documentation. The trick is to focus on the features and services provided by the application that are actually useful to the business, and to provide a working application in sufficient time to address requirements before they become obsolete or redundant.

In this chapter you have the opportunity to look at the role of the prototype and relate it to your experience. One of the problems of any methodology is to be adaptable to a wide range of situations without being so general as to be of no practical value.

I also describe the mock-up and prototyping of a Sybase application in relation to the level of skills and experience you have, which can dramatically affect what deliverables you expect to gain from the prototyping process.

By the end of the chapter you should be comfortable with the definition of a prototype and understand its role in translating the systems requirements defined in the concept phase into the beginnings of an application design.

Mock-Up versus Prototype

I believe that it was the software engineering people who first proposed the development of a prototype before developing production systems. At least it makes sense to me that this group of people would be behind such an initiative, as it mirrors the tried-and-true practice of manufacturers who have a great deal of experience in turning ideas into production units.

If that process is indeed the inspiration for all these systems prototypes that I hear about people working on, perhaps you might benefit from a closer look at that process.

Like the software business, the manufacturing industries have wide-ranging business practices and approaches to turning out products. However, also like developing software, there is a fundamental transformation of a concept into a tangible product.

Mock-Up What?

Successful product development teams start with the people in the marketing department, whose byword is, "If we build it, they will buy it." The parallels with developing successful Sybase applications should come as no surprise to you, because you have already gone over this as a systems input during the last section on development concepts.

Wait a second, before you dismiss this with a "Yeah, yeah, I know," there is an important but subtle implication in allowing the marketing department to define the product to be manufactured. How often have you seen truly stupid products manufactured and offered for sale, only to be marked down and finally yanked off the shelves altogether? Who out there is really enthusiastic about investing the time and energy necessary to build an application with all the functionality of a pet rock? Just because somebody says that people will buy it does not necessarily mean they are right. And that's why you go through the process of building mock-ups and doing market research.

Market Research at Home

Within your own organization you have both an advantage and disadvantage when it comes to doing this sort of research. First, someone in your IS organization has to take on the role of marketing and come up with the initial idea. Second, your user population is more contained than that of the general buying public, so it's a little easier to reach the users, but they may have more entrenched (and less flattering) ideas about what you're capable of doing.

Creating a prototype without having first mocked up your application and touring it around Userville is as potentially fatal of a mistake as implementing your concept without first undergoing a design phase. Sure, it can be done, and people have survived going over Niagara Falls in a barrel, too.

Defining the Mock-Up

The mock-up has a role to play in giving a tangible shape to the application to be; however, it's usually characterized as having no real functionality. Like the architect's initial three-dimensional rendering of a retirement village, there should be some similarity with what finally gets built, and also like the model, you will not find people trying to live there.

Typically, a mock-up is the first go-round at defining a user interface with menus, screens, dialogue boxes, and radio buttons. It's oriented toward the GUI application side of the client/ server equation and can be developed with no database component at all. It presents to the users an approximation of the application, something to assist them in visualizing the final product.

Do me a favor and refrain from referring to a collection of screens without functionality as a prototype. A prototype is different from a mock-up, as the prototype has functionality. Typically, what a prototype lacks is scale and robustness, where a mock-up of the application just provides a starting point for the users to provide critical feedback as they rip your entire concept to shreds.

Redefining the Mock-Up

As hard as it is to believe, this is a good thing. You actually want them to tear it apart. After all, it should not take that much effort to knock a mock-up together, and it follows that you should be able to change it pretty quickly as well. As I have pointed out already, the real key to success is getting your users to believe that you will change the system to meet their demands, and fast. The mock-up is the place to start that process.

The Mock-Up as a Design Aid

At this point you are actually using, hands-on, some of the client/server technology with which you expect to build your Sybase application. Until this point, everything I have described can be handled with a white board and a word processor. And it probably should be, even if you have shelves full of shrink-wrapped technology crying out to be played with. Do your homework first, then play. It worked when you were a kid and it still applies to developing successful Sybase applications today.

Just because you have finally been able to get to a point in the process where you can use some of this stuff, however, does not mean that you're done with the word processor. The feedback you get from the users must be documented. Screen captures should be made of every screen, menu, and dialogue box and the components listed and explained. This will become vital when the people responsible for the database design have to figure out how to provide your application with the data it's expected to retrieve, manipulate, and save.

More important, it will give you as an application designer the basis for reviewing how you arrived at a particular screen, and why it contains the elements that it does. Equally as important, it captures what you know while it's still fresh in your mind. Remember that one of the key aspects of a client/server system is that the applications can be duplicated in many environments. By creating a mock-up, obtaining user feedback on it, and rapidly changing screens, you can design the application on the fly. With appropriate documentation of this process, you can ensure that the design documentation explains what the users wanted as they provided that feedback. This may then be used by a different group responsible for creating an identical application with a different application development tool.

The Mock-Up as a Developer's Aid

The mock-up has another important contribution to make for you as a developer. By allowing yourself time to become familiar with the way the application looks, you give yourself an opportunity to learn more about the way GUI-based applications operate.

I have noticed that the complexity of mock-ups and prototypes changes with the level of experience of the design team. If you're an experienced GUI designer and developer, what you do as part of the initial development process will be significantly more detailed than someone who is new to the technology. The challenge for me is to define the steps that must be taken in an order appropriate to both groups.

As you become familiar with tools such as PowerBuilder or Visual Basic, it takes much less time to knock together a mock-up or prototype. At that point, you can take the time that is usually consumed more by user review and discussion to modify the approach with which you build these initial descriptions of your application.

Contain the Scope

The first few times that you create a mock-up, you should limit your scope to simply painting screens that contain appropriate list boxes, radio buttons, scrolling windows, bitmaps, and so on. However, as you gain familiarity with these controls, you should take advantage of the early stages of a project to define your ancestor objects and to build discrete functions that can be snapped in place later.

There is an important decision point here, which you as a developer have to face. It's human nature to say to yourself that you should do all the same steps that the most experienced professional would take, but when developing GUI-based Sybase applications, that is a very risky proposition.

If you take on the challenge of designing windows for the first time, and trying to define an object inheritance strategy at the same time, you will end up being less responsive to your users' demands for change. As the old saying goes, you eat the elephant one bite at a time.

Based on the level of experience available to your team, you may focus more at this point on the value of a mock-up and prototype as a design aid, rather than as the first steps toward the creation of a usable application. This means that you absolutely cannot be shy about throwing out the work done to date and starting from scratch, while incorporating what you have learned.

I just can't stress this point enough, because I constantly see projects during which people have nodded sagely, fully believing that they understand, and then off they go, trying to incorporate their first cuts at the technology because they can't bring themselves to start from scratch.

> **TIP**
>
> Throw the first version out!

The Benefit of Using Mock-Ups

The value of the mock-up is as a user research vehicle and initial design documentation. When you look through the design docs for a successful client/server project, you very often see a large number of annotated screen captures that exactly reflect the screens of the production application. This makes sense if you consider that the purpose of the design documentation is to define exactly what the application is supposed to look like and what it's supposed to do before it's built.

Most people don't stop to consider that this documentation is not hauled together as part of some catch-up documentation exercise when the production systems is in testing or ready for production. The screens contained in the documentation have only to look like they work; they don't have to actually perform any functions themselves. Therefore, you can design your initial version of the application using PB or VB for the mock-up and the production system itself might be written in a lower-level language such as C.

Translating the Mock-Up into a Prototype

As you have already read in this chapter, the key distinction between the mock-up and the prototype is the level of functionality. A prototype must do some useful work and is what the users will expect to see after they have signed off on screen layout and design. From the mock-up you should know what options need to be presented as part of the application. However, you won't have defined what goes on behind the buttons, and you most certainly won't have a firm grip on what is to happen on the back end.

All of these things must be designed and, depending on your level of experience with the technology, you can choose to address it as part of the prototype or later in the design process.

Regardless of when you decide to address the details, it must be done prior to implementation. In general, the flow of development from concept to design at the detailed level includes the steps shown in Figure 5.1.1.

The steps progress logically from the initial requirements definition and form the basis for a detailed systems design that can be reviewed by users and technical people alike.

FIGURE 5.1.1.

The detailed design process for GUI-based client/server applications.

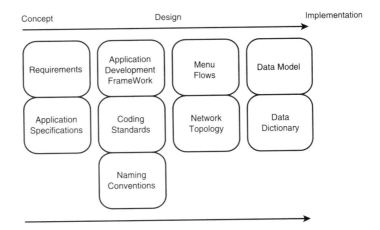

Translating Specifications into a Prototype

If you choose to create paper-based applications specifications, you can do this by using your mock-up as a template for the applications processing and data manipulation facilities. For example, during the course of building your mock-up, you may decide that the screens and menu structures as developed will actually work for the production application. Of course, at this point, all the buttons do is bring up a dialog box to indicate what they *will* do once they are programmed with some functionality. As part of the documentation, you can capture the screens and associate approximate logic with each button. This takes the place of writing structured English or pseudo code under more traditional structured development methodologies. The resulting output will allow you to see at a glance, not just how the user will perceive the screen, but what steps must be taken when any given object is selected or activated.

The example in Figure 5.1.2 demonstrates how this process could look.

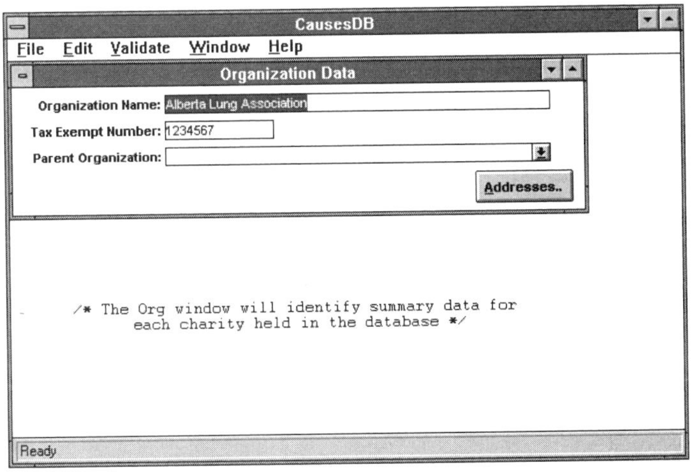

FIGURE 5.1.2.

Attaching commented application specifications to mock-up options.

Of course, you could always choose to simply write the scripts associated with the window objects and controls, and then print them all out to create your documentation. The problem with the direct approach is that you immediately become enmeshed in the lowest level of detail. By sketching out the processing steps associated with each window option, you create the equivalent of an outline, which you can use later to ensure that you have allowed for all of the features that the application has to provide in order to meet its requirements. Consider this step an intermediate step between defining what your application will do and spending the time necessary to actually get it to perform those functions.

Perhaps the easiest way to get started on this process is to create comments that describe your understanding of what the widget or control is supposed to do. By writing these comments in English, you enable your users to review and approve them while they gain a better feel for what the system will look like once it's actually completed.

Building a Prototype

By now you should be more than clear on the difference between a mock-up and a prototype. But what about the differences between a prototype and a production system? As I have indicated already, it's possible to implement your prototype (and live to collect unemployment insurance), but you should still be making a conscious decision to take this rather risky step and fully understand what your system will be doing without.

The key difference between a prototype and a production system is not in what they do; a prototype will frequently handle 80 percent or more of the features that will ultimately be put into production. The real distinction is in the exceptions and error handling. Prototypes typically handle only the most common errors and a few exceptions.

This makes perfect sense if you consider the role of the prototype to be primarily a proof-of-concept, on-the-job training tool for users and developers. After all, if you can work out how to trap and mask one error message from your SQL Server, it stands to reason that you can do the same thing for the other 25,000 potential errors. The same holds true for exception handling in the application. Your users may have (read should have) defined a very long list of exceptions to the rules they established for their business processes as part of the integrated task/data modeling exercise. Once you demonstrate that you can handle a few of them, it follows that, with time and effort, the system can be expanded to include the remaining ones as well as any new ones they may determine necessary.

You can see how dangerous it is to implement a prototype. Sure, it may accommodate 80 percent of the processing that falls neatly into predetermined procedures, but the other 20 percent represents 80 percent of the time spent by the people in the business unit. This means that your application addresses the wrong part of the 80/20 rule.

From a developer's point of view, the prototype is probably the first time the development effort gets interesting. This is where you can actually write code (usually scripts, but I will cover that in more depth later), issue queries, retrieve results, and juggle variables, just like real application development.

This is also where you will want to get your technical users more heavily involved.

At some point you will be making decisions and trade-offs based on your perception of what the users want the application to do and the restrictions under which you are developing. If you can work through your application logic with your technical users, they will be the best ones to tell you where you can compromise or take a different route.

During the development of the prototype is the most appropriate time to do this. As a general rule of thumb, a prototype will take between 6 and 12 weeks to develop. If you are already quite familiar with the technology, you might be able to knock one together in a shorter time, but I recommend instead that you take the full amount of time available and use it to define what needs to be done later in the design phase.

Prototyping the Back End

I just love working with people who specialize in data models (wink, wink). Perhaps I've been unlucky, but I generally find that they hate making changes to the model unless there is some abstruse or arcane normalization rule to justify the change. They can be as challenging to work with as the users.

Seriously, though, you should be prepared to prototype the database design as well as the application itself. If you reflect on it for a second, it makes sense. Client/server applications have both front- and back-end components. You must address both ends during the prototyping process.

One of the advantages of working with the Integrated Task/Data Modeling methodology is that you identify the data you will need at the same time as specifying applications functions. This in turn forms the basis for a coarse data dictionary that you can hand off to your favorite data modeler/administrator for translation into tables and views.

Avoid a Database Focus Too Soon

I want to make one point very strongly, however: do not use stored procedures during the prototyping process. I bring this up for several reasons. First and foremost, stored procedures should be created by a central entity, usually the database administrator. This is absolutely not the person to get involved in your prototyping effort, except in a peripheral way. Later in this section you will see how the lower plane of the IT/DM involves a great deal of effort and implication for a DBA, but the top plane does not require any involvement from database specialists. The reason that stored procedures should not be used is simply because developers will (should) want to change them continually during the prototyping process. Funneling these changes through a central point is not such a good idea.

The other way to handle this is to allow each developer to have rights for creating stored procedures. Depending on the nature of your organization and the way your security policies work, this may or may not be an idea you can entertain. Even if you could implement this concept, take time to consider whether it would be such a good thing to do. Personally, I think developers should focus on the things that provide the greatest yield, such as good interface design and application functionality. Database features can be dealt with later, when the actual SQL has a chance to stabilize.

The real contribution to be made by the DBA is to optimize and tune the performance of your databases when you move into production. Typically, the last thing any DBA wants to do is have to spend a lot of time working through an application to figure out what part of it is hitting the database hardest. If you can provide a test SQL to run against a relatively stable data model, you will probably get the greatest degree of cooperation from your DBA. In the meantime, treat everything as if it could change tomorrow, and keep it within your scope of operation.

Preparing for Production

You don't end up with a fully functional production application by accident. The mock-up and prototype are concrete deliverables that reflect your understanding of both the requirements and solution, as well as your mastery of the technology.

At this point you should clearly see how the iterative approach works. Every step you take brings you closer to your ultimate goal and at no point are you ever actually finished with anything. Even with a production system, you must be able to differentiate features that must be included in fixes and those that can wait for a new version.

Defer What You Can

The phased approach to software development is far from new. However, it's useful to think of versions as "job jars" for future features. During the course of the development effort, you will frequently run into suggestions that are good ideas, but there is no one in a position to implement them, for any number of reasons. However, if you decide to toss these ideas off, you do so at your peril. People will offer suggestions only if they feel they are being taken seriously. To this end you should identify a set of features to be included in "version two" of your production system.

This is a bit more significant than it might seem at first glance. The real point is that you must be careful to ensure that you have identified an achievable set of features for your production system or you will be seen to have underdelivered on your promises.

There is a very real and seductive temptation to imagine that you will be able to finish everything toward the end of the design and beginning of the implementation phases. The development of mock-ups and prototypes are usually gratifying experiences during which users and management provide a great deal of positive feedback on the look and feel of the application. As you have seen, the real work is under the covers and, as such, is not appreciated by these people.

This means that you have to walk a bit of a tightrope, balancing between what the users would like on the one hand and what you can practically get done given the available time and resource constraints. To assist in this, you should make a point to have a clear vision of what your second cut at the production application is going to look like, and clearly communicate that at each stage of the project.

Summary

In this chapter you have been introduced to my definition of mock-ups and prototypes and where they fit in the development cycle. Certainly, there is no substitute for detailed design and application specifications. With emerging client/server systems, the question becomes how to successfully incorporate that discipline into the new technologies.

This chapter should have given you a solid understanding of how the prototyping process is conducted and its role concerning application design and specifications. If you take anything away from this chapter, I hope it's a clear differentiation between a mock-up and prototype. For that matter, I hope you're now in a better position to see how the prototype is really an embryonic production system. It may have an uncanny resemblance to its ultimate configuration, but it's not a sustainable system on its own.

The true benefit to be derived from this approach is the ability to build on work that has already been done. If you mock up good screens, you can keep them in the prototype. If the application logic works well in the prototype, chances are that it will migrate unchanged to the production system. The idea is not to redo things so much as to appropriately layer features and functions on top of each other. Of course, the facility to catch and correct misconceptions and errors in design always pays if done early in the development process. I hope this chapter has given you a solid approach to doing just that.

5.2

Application Specifications

Introduction

In the previous chapter I recommended an approach to design that included building mock-ups and prototypes, and fleshing out your application specifications documentation as you went through the development cycle. This chapter covers exactly how to define specifications when developing Sybase applications, including specific recommendations for naming conventions, coding standards, and how to define an applications development framework.

You may choose to either use your own standards or adopt wholesale the recommendations made here. In either case, the benefit to your project will be in defining the standards and creating development specifications from the beginning, instead of allowing the key development practices to emerge along with the application itself.

After reading this chapter you should gain a solid insight into all of the elements that must be defined, detailed, and documented before you can consider your application designed.

For the purposes of ensuring specific and valid details, I focus on defining standards for developing with PowerBuilder and Sybase SQL Server. The conventions and techniques are in keeping with that focus. For other products, you'll need to take the time to identify the specifics that relate best to the tools with which you will build your client/server application.

This chapter is critical in that it shows you one method of breaking down the application into the objectives to be accomplished and structuring the methods by which the application will be built. All too often, systems people spend a great deal of time understanding the business without ensuring the proper degree of preparation and coordination among the development team.

I have written this chapter on the assumption that all client/server development projects involve the efforts of at least a small team and, in some cases, large groups of people. The need for structured design documentation and application development specifications is exponentially compounded by the number of people involved.

Project leaders, managers, and systems architects will gain a great deal from reviewing this chapter, but it will be the most valuable for Sybase/PowerBuilder developers. If this is your role, you should spend extra time on it to ensure that you can create similar documentation for your own projects.

On that note, you are probably ready to get down to it.

Setting the Appspec Context

There are two perspectives that must be addressed by your application specifications: what to do and how to do it. These two outlooks correspond neatly to an external and internal view of the application. The users are most concerned with what needs to be done, because the application is a tool for their use; whereas the development team is most caught up in how it is to be accomplished. This makes sense when you consider that, as systems professionals, the development team has the objective of tying the technology to an organizational purpose.

Consider, then, that application specifications consist of two layers. The outer layer is comprised of business requirements and functional definitions, the inner layer of technical models and standards.

As a developer you must understand the outer layer well enough to build a systems product that is useful to the business, but you must completely understand the inner layer if you are to successfully take advantage of Sybase and other client/server tools.

Conversely, it's unlikely that any but your most technical end users will even see your internal documentation. The inner layer of specifications allows you to set the development standards and practices to be followed by the technical people involved in your project. It should be at a level of detail that makes it impossible for anyone not familiar with the technology to understand it. This is important simply because it forms the basis for a technical practices review by independent software development specialists, and the most frequent use is to bring new staff up to speed with the development approach in use by a particular project.

Your documentation needs to be complete and comprehensible by any contractors or consultants you bring on in a last-ditch effort to meet the big deadline. In fact, you might want to keep that scenario in mind as you evaluate whether your level of documentation is sufficient. If you had to bring on three top-notch freelance developers for two weeks just before the due date, would your internal documentation provide enough of a starting point to allow them to go to work? The last thing you want to do is take time out explaining your development standards *et al* from scratch. Just as important, you don't want to have developers out there doing their own thing; this results in highly unmaintainable code that even they might not be able to figure out again in three months. Even if the resulting output is exemplary, chances are high that it will be quite different from that of the developer in the next cubicle.

The point, then, is to have detailed development specifications that can give your project a uniform set of standards used by all involved to build their part of the application.

The Outer Layer

If you have done the recommended modeling, analysis, and reporting recommended to this point in the book, I would say that you already have a reasonable set of outer specifications. You should have a pretty clear idea of the application, who will use it, what data is needed to feed it, and how it fits into the business. What is needed at this point is a way to bring that description down to actual functionality within the application.

This can effectively be accomplished by commenting the functional requirements into the scripts associated with the window objects defined as part of your mock-up. This step is the intermediate one between defining menus and window layouts, gaining user approval on the look of the application, and setting out to build the prototype.

In many cases, however, you will have mocked up your application without having spent the time to define the internal technical standards to which the application will conform. Like most of the client/server development techniques covered in this book, this is not a linear "Do Until" approach. You should be looking at internal specifications at the same time that you are working on the mock-up. You should also find that, at various points in the project, you go back and add things into the internal standards as they come up. Both sets of documentation should reflect your understanding to date, rather than the view at a particular time.

I would like to reiterate a point made in the preceding chapter. If you're already familiar with the toolset, you could choose to define the internal project documentation prior to the development of the mock-up to reduce the amount of disposable work. However, here I am operating from the assumption that you have not yet defined the internal documentation and work on the mock-up has already begun.

In any case, the most appropriate time to begin work on the internal standards is before developing the prototype, after signing off the mocked-up application.

The Inner Layer

The kinds of standards, conventions, and frameworks you will need to define as part of your Sybase development effort include:

- Naming conventions
- Coding standards
- Inheritance definitions
- Error-handling standards
- Layout guidelines

Any developer should be able to refer to his or her internal application specifications to determine how to handle development of any given module or feature of the system. The key to success for this kind of documentation is not correctness in any absolute way, but consistency. It's important that everyone follow the guidelines, not that they are the latest and greatest sorts of notation and that recommended by XYZ vendor or some consultant.

To give you a practical idea of what this kind of documentation looks like, I have included samples of each for PowerBuilder and Sybase. I have attempted to make the examples as complete and relevant for these two products as I can, but you may find it helpful to extend the list to be more consistent with your toolset or your organization's practice.

Naming Conventions

The following are representative naming conventions to be followed for all PowerBuilder and Sybase objects in use for Project X. (More detailed examples of naming conventions follow later in the chapter.)

Standard Prefix	Object Type
d_	datawindow
sp_	systems procedure
u_	user object
psp_xyz_	project specific stored procedure
m_	menu
tablename_idx	index
v_	view

As you can see, the naming conventions recommended here closely follow the standard practice for both Sybase and PowerBuilder. There is really no good reason to use obscure naming conventions, as the more common sense or intuitive they are, the easier it will be when reviewing database or library contents. The idea is to be more effective than clever, and you won't go wrong staying with a naming convention based on common sense.

Coding Standards

The coding standards section of your application specifications or development principles document is the place that you will define the programming practices that you expect to see uniformly followed in your development efforts. For example, you might consider adopting the following coding standards, among others:

■ Avoid using RetrieveRow event in a datawindow control unless absolutely necessary. This event fires for each row retrieved into the datawindow and can seriously slow down performance. A common use of this is to count the rows being returned. This can be done after the retrieve by performing a datawindow.RowCount( ) function. If you need to know how many rows will be returned before doing the query (say, to limit the number of rows returned from the database), consider trapping the outgoing SQL in the SqlPreview event and replacing the selection criteria with the SQL Count. This will tell you how many rows match the selection criteria, and, if acceptable, you can then issue the original select.

■ Never use the Other event unless absolutely necessary. This event fires for any event that does not fit within one of the predefined events. Use custom or user events instead.

■ Datawindows aren't just for database activity. You can use a Script, or External, datawindow for nondatabase-related functions. It will perform better: 20 controls on a window use a lot of resources, but 20 objects in a datawindow appear as a single control to Windows. You also can take advantage of all the events and features of datawindows (validation, itemerror, and so on).

■ You don't have to set up a transaction object (`dw.SetTransObject( )`) for External datawindows. If it never accesses a database, why bother?

Always check return codes from functions for the possibility of errors. Even the simplest of function calls (for example, `dw.SetItem( row, column)`) should be checked. You never know when a function will fail, especially in the MS-Windows environment.

■ Don't use function calls that return the same value in a loop. For example:

```
For CurrRow = 1 to dw.RowCount( )
   .
   .
Next
```

instead, use:

```
Count = dw.RowCount( )
For CurrRow = 1 to Count
   .
   .
Next
```

■ Use shared datawindow buffers for fairly static tables used on many windows in an application (for example, Provinces, States). Consider retrieving the information at application startup time into a hidden datawindow, and then sharing that datawindow buffer each time you open a window that uses the information.

This gives you a pretty good idea of what your coding standards document should contain.

Along with coding standards and naming conventions, you will want to incorporate all other elements of good Sybase applications design that you expect your application development team to follow. I'll give you an example of what kind of detail you'll need. In order to make this chapter more meaningful, I have referred specifically to what we will use for the guidelines in developing CausesDB. This means that our primary development environment will be PowerBuilder.

Graphic User Interface Standards

Because CausesDB is developed in and for a Windows environment, it uses Windows standards where possible. The purpose of this document is to identify the standards to ensure that the interface has a consistent look and feel.

General Interface Description

CausesDB uses a multiple document interface (MDI) with an associated pull-down menu. This is a Windows standard interface style and is used by Windows products such as Microsoft Word and Microsoft Excel. This interface provides an application desktop, or *frame*, and allows for several windows, or *sheets*, to be open at one time within that desktop. In PowerBuilder, the frame is actually a window of *MDI Frame* type. For the remainder of this document, the terms *sheet* and *window* are synonymous. Any one of the open sheets may be the *active* sheet at any point in time.

To give you an idea of what an MDI frame looks like (as if you didn't already know), take a look at Figure 5.2.1.

FIGURE 5.2.1.

A representative MDI frame.

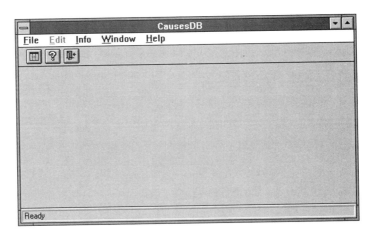

The title bar of the application uses the current Windows setting for active and inactive colors. At the bottom of the MDI frame there is a space provided for *microhelp*. This will provide the user with hints and information. If the user wishes to switch to another Windows application, the Desktop application can be minimized or moved behind Windows applications. The menu bar may be augmented by an associated *toolbar*. The toolbar is useful for mouse navigation and can be made hidden or shown, depending on user preference.

Each pull-down menu discussed here has several items, including the following:

- ■ File - Save, Save As, Print, Print Setup, Close, Exit
- ■ Edit - Undo, Cut, Copy, Paste, Clear, Select All
- ■ Causes - Access to query and data entry windows
- ■ Actions - Retrieve, Add, Delete, Add Detail, Delete Detail
- ■ Maintain - Code maintenance and user preferences system defaults maintenance
- ■ Reports - All available reports by category, Export

- Window - Cascade, Tile, Layer, list of currently open sheets, Toolbar control
- Help - Index, Search, System Resources, About

Existing Windows applications such as Microsoft Word have been used to set precedents for menu item accelerator keys (underlined character) and short-cut keys (control or function keys).

General Window Features

One of the key values in providing a consistent user interface is that people familiar with the environment but new to the application will be able to learn how to operate the application much more quickly. Naturally, we want CausesDB to take advantage of this principle, so, as much as possible, we designed it to contain all the familiar Windows features. Generally, all Windows applications include the following features:

- **Printing:** If data is displayed in the window, that data may be printed to the user's default printer. The File menu includes Print and Print Setup options.

- **Window management:** The control menu allows the user to minimize, maximize, move, restore, resize, and close each window. If a window is minimized, it will show as an icon within the Causes Desktop. Additionally, the File menu includes a Close option with an associated toolbar item.

- **Text editing:** Any user-enterable field in a window may be addressable by the features on the Edit menu. These features include Undo, Cut, Copy, Paste, Clear, and Select All. Undo reverses the last typing operation, if possible. Cut, Copy, and Paste work with the Windows Clipboard. Clear deletes any selected text. Select All selects all the text in the current field.

- **Navigation:** When the user is working in a window, any other window may be opened from the menu. This allows the user to work on several things in parallel, or research data in other windows while entering data during a data entry session.

All data entry and maintenance windows include the following features:

- A series of fields to allow the user to specify or change the data. This area is known as the datawindow. Some windows may have two or more datawindows if they are master-detail in nature.

- **Database save:** Any changes made (data edited, new rows added, or rows deleted) are saved to the database. The Save option on the File menu implements this feature. The Save option may be disabled for some users.

- **Local data save:** The data currently displayed on the window may be saved to the user's local disk drive in the user's default directory (as specified in user preferences). This Save As option on the File menu implements this feature.

- **Database query:** The appropriate select window for the data being entered can be invoked at any time to allow the user to query new data to work on. The Retrieve option on the Actions menu implements this feature.

■ **Add new data:** This sets up a new row for the user to type new data. The Add... option on the Actions menu implements this feature. For master-detail windows, an additional Add Detail option is available from the menu. This feature does not automatically update the database or hold locks on the tables.

■ **Delete data:** This deletes the row currently displayed to the user. If several rows are displayed, the selected row (or the row with the cursor, if no rows are selected) will be deleted. The Delete... option on the Actions menu implements this feature. The Delete option may often be disabled for most users. For master-detail windows, an additional Delete Detail option is available from the menu. This feature does not automatically update the database or hold locks on the tables.

All select (query) windows include the following features:

■ A datawindow to allow the user to specify selection criteria and show the list of entries resulting from the query.

■ A Search button to allow the user to query the database based on criteria entered. This button changes to Query after rows have been retrieved from the database. The Query button returns the datawindow to the selection criteria specification mode.

■ A Cancel button to close the window. This can also be done using the control menu or the Close option on the File menu.

■ An OK button to open the main information or detail window for the selected item. The opened window will automatically show the item.

■ A Sort button to resort the retrieved rows.

■ A New button to open the main information or detail window with a new row set up for entry. This button may be disabled for some users.

■ **Navigation:** A list of possible windows to open for the selected data.

Keyboard Input

Because the data entry function is keyboard intensive, the interface is designed to accommodate keyboard control. Although complete mouse support is provided, each menu option has a standard shortcut key to accelerate keyboard operation. For example, the function of adding a new row is supported by the Ctrl-N keystroke.

In message boxes, dialog boxes, and response windows, one button will be designated as the *default* button, which maps to the Enter key on the keyboard. The default button in a window is designated by the bold border around the button. In all dialog boxes and response windows, one of the Close, Cancel, or OK buttons will have the *cancel* attribute, which maps to the Escape key. This means that, by pressing the Esc key, a user may close the window.

Error Handling

Three levels of error handling are defined: system errors, database errors, and internal logic errors. All errors may be printed to provide easier troubleshooting when required.

System errors are trapped at the application level and presented to the user in a consistent message box on the screen. This kind of error will be triggered when an event occurs that Windows can't resolve. An example of the system error window is shown in Figure 5.2.2.

FIGURE 5.2.2.

A representative systems error handled in a Windows application.

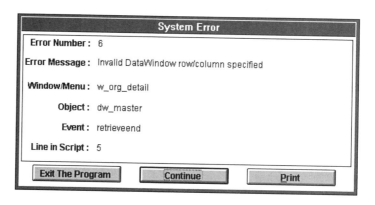

As a matter of course, all SQL Server errors will be trapped by the application and interpreted for the user, complete with recommended courses of action. For any errors that aren't mapped, the message `Please Print this screen and call your Systems Administrator` should be displayed along with the error text from the server.

Database errors are trapped at the datawindow level (and whenever a SQL statement is executed) and presented to the user in a consistent message box on the screen. This window automatically appears when a database error occurs. The database error may not be presented directly to the user, but can be displayed for technical analysis. An example of the database error window is shown in Figure 5.2.3.

Internal logic errors are trapped after each function is executed and presented to the user in a consistent message box on the screen. This type of message indicates an unanticipated event that can't be handled by the program logic. A prefix of `Logic error:` in the text indicates to the user that a bug may be present and should be reported. An example of the logic error window is shown in Figure 5.2.3.

In addition to error handling, data validation errors are also presented in a message box on the screen. If data in a field causes an error, after the message has been shown and the user has responded, the cursor is moved to the field in error. If a message is shown that requires a decision from the user, a direct and clear question is presented. Wherever possible, the user is given the option to cancel the operation in progress upon error. Most validation message windows use the title from the sheet to which it applies. This ensures that the context of the message is clear if many sheets are open.

FIGURE 5.2.3.
A window displaying a returned database error.

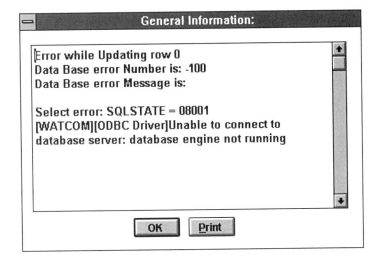

FIGURE 5.2.4.
A logic error displayed in an application window.

Colors

Any definition of the user interface standards should recommend how colors will be defined, even if that is simply to acknowledge that user defaults will be picked up.

- ■ MDI background - application workspace (a)
- ■ Window, enterable datawindow background - light gray
- ■ Select list datawindow background color - window background (w)
- ■ Enterable fields and select datawindow background - window background (w)
- ■ Nonenterable fields background - light gray (transparent in datawindow) (t)
- ■ Text (field headers and user-entered data) - window text (wt)
- ■ Colored text or background and icons are used to draw attention where necessary

Fonts

Except for buttons, all text in the application appears in Arial, 8 point. Bold is used for headers. Italic is used to draw attention to items where necessary.

Borders

All buttons appear in 3D raised by default. Generally, datawindow controls use no borders unless there are other controls on the window (select windows, for example). Windows that have no controls other than datawindows should take advantage of the inherited "resize" feature of the ancestors. This resize feature automatically sizes datawindows to take up the entire window surface at runtime. In the case of the master-detail ancestor, the master datawindow sizes itself down to the top of the detail datawindow. All datawindows that can hold more than one row at a time have a vertical scroll bar. Datawindows that are too wide for the window have a horizontal scroll bar.

The user-enterable portion of CheckBoxes, RadioButtons, input fields in datawindows, and ListBoxes appear 3D lowered.

For input fields in tabular datawindows, the 3D lowered border is expensive in terms of space, so the field borders are underlined and the fields are placed as close together as possible. In these datawindows, the background is the window background color (w).

Buttons

In general, buttons appear only on dialog boxes, response windows, and message boxes. MDI sheets use the menu to implement standard functions such as Retrieve, Save, Close, and navigation to other windows.

All buttons are a standard height and font. A user object is inherited to ensure consistency. In some cases, the width of a button is overridden when the required text does not fit.

Response windows, message boxes, and dialog boxes may have the following buttons:

- ■ {OK, Cancel, Close} - Any combination to acknowledge and/or close the window
- ■ Additional buttons required for window navigation or to perform specific processing

Contextual Information

The organization or charity name and other contextual information is shown in the title bar of each window. This allows the context to show up when a window is minimized on the application desktop. Other contextual information and configuration controls are positioned at the top left of the window.

Capitalization

All user-entered data is automatically converted to uppercase to facilitate queries. On each window, the first letter is capitalized for all control text, field headers, and static text. Acronyms are presented in uppercase.

Justification, Edit Masks, and Formats

On freeform datawindows, header text is right justified with the corresponding input fields. In the input fields themselves, numeric data is right justified whereas character data and dates are left justified. CheckBoxes and RadioButtons are justified as appropriate for the window design.

On tabular display datawindows, numeric fields and headers are right justified. Character and date fields are left justified. Character and date headers are left justified or centered as appropriate for the window design.

Date fields use the YYYY/MM/DD edit mask with no spin control. Numeric field formats are determined by the database definition of the underlying column. Monetary amounts are always presented with the appropriate currency symbol.

Query Processing

Information windows are accessed from a select window. Query windows allow the user to narrow the list of items of interest, and then the information windows can be opened to review the details. Figure 5.2.5 shows how a query window looks to the application user.

FIGURE 5.2.5.
An example of a recommended query window.

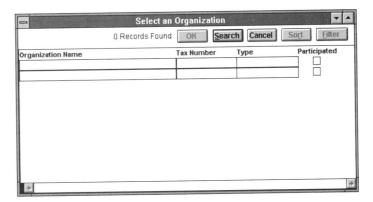

Window Linkages

All windows are managed separately by the user. This means that there is no linkage between windows at close time. If the user opens a window, the user also must close that window explicitly.

Commit Processing

The database is updated only by explicit command from the user. In every window, if any changes have not been applied to the database before the window is closed, the user is asked about updating the database.

Control-Specific Attributes

Each application object and control has an intuitive internal name. Application objects also have an associated comment indicating use or special features. The following naming conventions are applied to internal names of PowerBuilder controls and objects in the application:

Prefix	*Objects*
w_	Windows
m_	Menus
d_	datawindows
u_	UserObjects
f_	Functions

Prefix	*Controls*
dw_	Datawindow Controls - default number; names may be used in some cases
cb_	CommandButtons
pb_	PictureButtons
p_	Pictures - default number; names may be used in most cases
em_	EditMasks
gr_	Graphs
rb_	RadioButtons
gb_	GroupBoxes - default number; names may be used
cbx_	CheckBoxes
sle_	SingleLineEdits
mle_	MultiLineEdits
lb_	ListBoxes
ddlb_	DropDownListBoxes
st_	StaticText - default number; names may be used
uo_	UserObjects (custom user objects only)

All controls use the default PowerBuilder attributes with the following exceptions:

- ■ **DropDownListBoxes:** Always show arrow, V scroll bar, Auto H scroll (if required)
- ■ **DropDownDataWindows:** Always show arrow, V scroll bar, H scroll bar (if required); may increase width beyond 100 percent
- ■ **MultiLineEdits:** Auto V scroll, V scroll bar
- ■ All fields allowing character data editing enforce the limit according to the database column specification and allow Auto H scroll if the width of the field cannot accommodate all the characters

■ The Required Field attribute is not used in any circumstance; instead, mandatory fields are checked manually before Save

Datawindow Style

Tabular-style datawindows are used wherever possible to allow the user to see as much data at one time and make better decisions. In some cases, a tabular-style datawindow with horizontal scroll bar (defined on the datawindow control on the host window if the columns are wider than the host window allows) is a better choice than a freeform-style datawindow because of the nature of the application.

Application Defaults and User Preferences

After the user has connected to the database, some application defaults are retrieved from the database. These application defaults act as operating parameters for the application. Storing the values in the database eliminates the need to hard code these parameters into the application. Maintenance of the system defaults is a secured function.

Similarly, there are some parameters that may be configured differently for each user. These parameters are automatically retrieved after the user connects to the database. A window is provided for the user to maintain his or her preference.

Validation Rules

Validations, such as range checks, are implemented in the PowerBuilder application to provide instant feedback to the user. Where appropriate, these other validations are also implemented at the database level using rules, defaults, and referential integrity triggers. PowerBuilder allows validation rules to be defined as extended attributes to the existing database columns. Where possible, this technique is used to allow datawindows to automatically inherit these validations.

Help

The application provides online access to help information using the Windows standard help documentation access facility. The contents of the help are created in Microsoft Word and then converted to a Windows help document. In the process of help conversion, words that are used for searches and topic headers are tagged for the help hypertext search facility.

The Libraries

PowerBuilder library files contain the application source code. PowerBuilder's inheritance capabilities are employed to reuse application logic. The following library files contain entries developed and gathered from a number of sources.

■ GRANDPA.PBL - Includes the oldest ancestor objects. These objects have been custom designed by the CausesDB team to include all the basic logic required in most windows. The use of ancestors not only reduces redundant code but also helps maintain a standard look and feel. None of these objects is actually presented directly to the user when the application executes. Instead, other objects are inherited from these and customized for a particular purpose.

You can see from Figure 5.2.6 how an ancestor library contains base objects.

FIGURE 5.2.6.

A PowerBuilder listing of ancestor library contents.

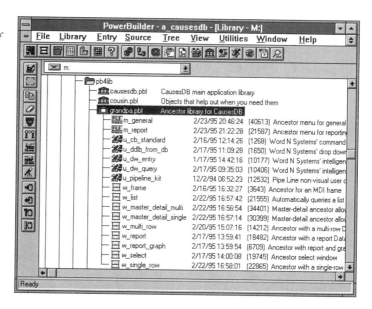

■ COUSIN.PBL - Includes objects that support any application. These objects are referenced at various times during application execution to perform error handling and general processing. Many of these objects are provided with PowerBuilder's application library.

■ Powerbuilder displays information about objects contained within an application when you access the library option, as depicted in Figure 5.2.7.

■ CAUSESDB.PBL - Includes the application object, windows, menus, datawindows, and other objects that are actually presented to the user when the application is executed.

FIGURE 5.2.7.

A PowerBuilder listing of application library contents.

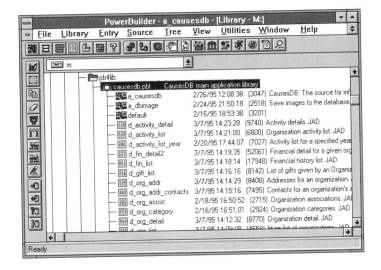

Summary

From this chapter you should be able to see what kind of detailed effort is involved when creating a proper set of GUI application specifications. Developing Sybase applications may provide you with much greater flexibility and power when it comes to the toolset, but to build truly effective applications, you must have coordination with every member of the team.

You should also be able to see how this methodology allows you to take advantage of the expertise gained by the more experienced members of your development team. Through the creation of detailed specifications and published expectations, you save all the other developers from having to reinvent the wheel.

This is also a key deliverable to be exacted from consultants and contractors. You can exploit their experience and expertise by having them recommend detailed development guidelines, which then form the development bible for your shop.

As you work through the CausesDB application, you should be able to see how successful we have been in the incorporation of these principles in our own application.

5.3

User Interface Design

Introduction

Merging several previous, disparate disciplines into the client/server systems architecture requires that developers be more well rounded than ever before. It's no longer enough to have a good grasp of a development language, or to be a specialist in particular hardware. Today's systems need people who can appreciate a wide range of skills and expertise. Appreciation is probably the best word to use, because even if we as individuals don't possess a particular skill, we can learn to appreciate something that is well done.

In this chapter I want to discuss the various skills and techniques that make for excellence in user interface design. Much has been made of the move to graphical user interfaces, and equally as much press has been given to emerging technologies, as if these new tools have no parallels or historical background from which to draw.

In terms of graphics, there is a tremendous body of work that has already been done, and there is no question in my mind that the move to GUIs will only enhance the role of graphic artists, as opposed to automate them out of existence. Interestingly, Apple is reputed to hire strictly artists (not tech types) to develop their bitmaps and icons. Remember that, even if you feel that you have a talent for design, we all think we have a sense of humor, we all think we have good taste, and we all think we're good kissers. (Somebody has to be wrong.) All of these things may be true for you, but even if they are, you can only benefit from paying attention to the rules of thumb developed by professionals and craftsmen over the years.

Beyond the layout and design considerations, developing effective GUI applications involves an appreciation (there's that word again) for ergonomics. The art and science of making users more productive through technology is the pinnacle of a client/server developer's trade, and this chapter will address the issues that you'll face when taking on this challenge.

Look and Feel

A long time ago (about seven or eight years, which is a long time in our business), Lotus sued Borland over the interface used in Quattro Pro. Apparently, the Lotus people felt that the /FR (slash file, retrieve) interface was proprietary and belonged to them, the copyright holder of 1-2-3, where the interface originated. I don't recall how the lawsuit ended, but the point to take away from this little diatribe is that your interface is something with which people can identify.

Microsoft, on the other hand, has no illusions about the role of its interface. It may not be the best (okay, it is definitely subject to criticism on a number of counts), but it *is* consistent across all of the Microsoft applications. And this consistency does in fact pay big dividends for users who must move from one application to another with a short learning curve.

This will no doubt apply to the applications you develop as well. If you want your users to come up to speed with your application as quickly as possible, stick with what they know: the Microsoft standard interface.

This doesn't mean that you won't have the ability to show your particular talents and design flair. I just want to reinforce the point that you don't need to invent new scrollbars, minimize and maximize buttons, and other objects. Reordering the menus to your own taste is also not advised. The maxim here is keep it consistent, which has its own simplicity.

Designing Your Windows

If you work with data retrieved from a database, you are already familiar with the two main methods of representing data: tabular and free form. Tabular data is the most straightforward, as it contains simply the retrieved columns and rows consistent with tables in the relational database. Forms, on the other hand, are a different story.

The use of forms goes back hundreds of years and their primary purpose has been to identify and organize data to be recorded and reported. Does this sound at all like the uses we put it to on screens? Forms design is a graphics arts specialty in its own right, and although it may sound tedious, hey, those artists probably don't want to be programmers, either.

The point is that there are a number of rules that apply to good forms design, and this also applies to screen forms.

These rules are subordinate to general forms design, so I will cover them later in this chapter, after I've had a chance to review what makes for good graphics interface design versus simply *awful* windows. I have even seen examples of someone placing a giant Close button in the middle of a final screen and pointing to it like a proud parent.

Graphics Design Rules of Thumb

Perhaps it would be useful to make some concrete suggestions that you can incorporate into your GUI development efforts. To arrive at some useful guidelines, I talked with some of my graphic artist friends who provided the following insights.

Provide a Focal Point

Choose where on the screen you want the user's attention to be focused first. There should be only one focal point per screen, because too many important things to look at makes the screen appear busy and cluttered. This in turn leads to eyestrain, headaches, and ultimately tumors and death. Okay, that last part is ridiculous, but your users will complain if they have to work with busy screens.

Allow Lots of Whitespace

This leads to the corollary that the best screens are clean and simple. On a more practical level, this means that there is sufficient space surrounding any of the words or icons on the screen. Look at the format of reports and screens that you find particularly inviting. Chances are that they have a tidy font with large margins and lots of space between lines and paragraphs. You are developing screens, not documents, but the same rules apply to screen form development. The key criteria is that the text must seem easy to read, not cramped. Most people hate to read anyway (how many developers ever read their manuals?).

Lead the Viewer

If you want to create effective screen forms, you need to lay out the screen in a fashion that allows most people to process the information in a logically consistent format. For instance, the tab order on columns should match the order in which they are presented. But what about left to right versus down one column and up the next? In most cases, it will depend on the nature of the information with which you're working. In any case, group related pieces of information together so that people can take the group in at one pass.

Use Color Properly

In the PowerBuilder documentation there is the suggestion that you use color judiciously. I love that...what does it mean? Of course, most developers leave the application users to set their desktop color and pick those up as defaults in any application they build. This makes sense because, even if you have better taste than your users, you will just annoy them if you force a change of colors on them. Other considerations include using Windows standards such as grey for disabled options and black for text. A friend of mine is a Color Applications Specialist for Xerox and he has shared a couple of interesting points when it comes to incorporating color into your applications.

- Red is the most aggressive color in the spectrum. People always look at it first, and you must use it sparingly to avoid saturation.

- People are generally more receptive to certain color combinations. Blue and white or blue and yellow are at the top of the list.

- Limit the number of colors used in any given screen to five or fewer. (Less is more in fashion and GUI design.)

- Remember to check how your color combinations display on a monochrome monitor. Although color subnotebooks are coming, there is still the chance that some executive will try using your application in black and white.

- Pastels or somewhat muted colors are generally more attractive than primary colors such as white, black, red, or yellow.

■ Sixteen-color screens are still the norm for many PCs. Don't spend too much time working out color combinations on a 32K color system without checking how they map on the lower common denominators.

■ Senior managers do like vibrant colors. Relate your application's colors to the level of the user you expect to encounter it. An Executive Information System should use a lot of navy blue as a base color (I know that sounds stereotypical, but apparently it holds up statistically). Lower-level employees frequently enjoy something a little more lively.

■ If you plan on printing color from your application, remember that the paper output never matches the screen colors unless you have an elaborate pantone-matched color system (which you probably don't have and can't afford anyway). Just don't be surprised if the pretty screen colors look dreadful in print.

I think this is what Powersoft people mean when they refer to the judicious use of color.

Fonts

If you ever have trouble getting to sleep, try reading some detailed design specifications for designing fonts. Maybe it's just me, but talk about detail! However, even a cursory understanding of fonts can help you avoid creating an application that just looks silly, while at the same time giving you an opportunity to show some of that personal flair.

For short lists such as menus, a san serif font such as Helvetica (Arial in TrueType) is frequently used. However, if you have more than a paragraph of text and it is of a reasonably small size (like the font used in this book), you should consider using a serif font such as Times Roman. The reason that so many books are published in this or New Century Schoolbook font is that, for voluminous text, it's easier on the eye.

Don't use more than three fonts...*ever*! If you must, try changing the emphasis to bold or italics. In any case, be consistent and do not change fonts in buttons or other objects from one screen to another.

Window Size

You should develop your GUI applications with window and object sizes that work on the coarsest resolution likely to be found in the deployment area. If you develop a compact and tightly organized set of screens on a 1024×768 system, you'll find that some of the windows are not viewable under a 640×480 monitor. Keep in mind that most laptops and notebooks still use the lower resolution.

An application designed for a lower resolution screen will look fine on a higher-resolution system. People who work with very high resolution screens get used to having tiny fonts and objects. The trick is to design for the largest number of users, not just the high-end systems.

Summary

Good graphic design makes for attractive advertisements, product labels, and GUI applications. If Apple hires graphic designers rather than systems people to develop icons, you might want to take a leaf from their notebook. By focusing on the art and science of appealing images, you can ensure that your Windows applications never make the 10 worst-dressed list.

Like wearing dark suits and white shirts, it's hard to make a design or image mistake by playing it conservative. For the more adventurous of you (who like maroon suits and black shirts) remember that there are rules to be followed, or you may not like the reactions your applications get.

If you intend to become a serious GUI developer, I suggest that you invest in some layout and design training. It can't hurt to know the basics, and if you don't know, it will show.

5.4

Testing Your Application

Introduction

I have worked on several projects in which the operating philosophy was that testing is for wimps. I think you can file this one under the category of Don't Try This at Home, Kids. The people implementing their systems without testing are trained unprofessionals who rely more on good luck than good management.

This may sound a little harsh, but it's certainly harsher for the users when they end up with a production system so unstable that it can't withstand a stiff breeze without falling down.

In this chapter I will cover the testing practices that I have observed in the most successful Sybase development efforts. Those of you coming from a mainframe background will recognize many of the techniques as being consistent with the development disciplines of traditional large systems. However, there are a few wrinkles created by the client/server technology, so I hope the chapter will be relevant even to those of you who subject your applications to rigorous testing regimens.

In any case, no book on systems development of any sort would be complete without due respect paid to the testing process, and this is what I will be addressing here.

The Testing Process

In MacDonalds restaurants, you can often see a sign posted in the kitchen area that reads, "Clean As You Go." The theory underlying this is simply that it's easier clean to up a bunch of little messes than it is to put everything off until the end. This is true for documentation and testing as well.

Certainly, no one wants to have to revisit two million lines of code to determine the cause of the half million bugs identified 24 hours before going live with an application. The feeling is very similar to that of a teenager who wants to get out of work as quickly as possible in order to get to a hot date. Let's face it: human nature being what it is, no one is going to work that hard to get everything operating at the highest level of quality. Instead, people often do the minimum they can get away with.

For this reason, client/server systems don't have a separate testing phase, as such. You have to test iteratively in the same way that you develop. In essence, you test as you go.

There are a number of project management benefits to this as well. Not only do your testers become more familiar with your application while there is still time to change it—testing can identify design flaws—but developers can address the little defects as they go without compiling a huge list of fixes to be made.

This, too, contributes to the perception that as developers your team is committed to incorporating suggestions and observations from the users into the application quickly.

As a separate component of the systems development process, there are several aspects to testing:

- **Function Testing:** Determines whether the application actually does what it is designed to do
- **Integration Testing:** Determines whether the application modules fit together without causing other systems elements to fail
- **Volume Testing:** Determines whether the application handles anticipated data volumes within acceptable time limits
- **Load Testing:** Determines whether the application handles the number of users required
- **Failure Testing:** Determines the outcome of failures of various aspects of the system, such as network outages, hardware failures, or user error

Each of these aspects of the testing process must be thoroughly reviewed before releasing a system into production. The outcomes of each of these tests will be highly valuable to developers to ensure that the application will meet the business requirements once it's rolled out into production, and in the project audit to determine how well potential problems were identified in advance and fixed prior to initial release of the application into the business unit.

Function Testing

You also can consider this as basic feature testing, in which the objective of the endeavor is to determine whether the application provides the right answer, consistently and in the format required by the user. This also can tell you which scripts need work, or which calculations are not completely understood. Additionally, by testing the application functions one by one, you should be able to determine whether the error handling is effective.

Typically, function testing is performed first by the developer and then by a selected small group of people who will be users or have the same background as the users. In some cases, it's not possible to assign actual members of the business unit to the testing team, due to business processing cycles and resource constraints. In cases such as these, it's important to go out and find people to do testing who will approach the application from the same background or perspective as your application users.

If you're planning to release the application to a bunch of financial analysts, for example, recruit summer students from a Commerce program or accountants preparing for their article phase (whatever it's called), as opposed to hiring temps.

Remember that, as a developer, when you try to test the application yourself, you'll fall into the trap of trying the same approach every time. Users always find ways to break applications because they try to do things you never dreamed they would be stupid enough to try, and sometimes it works and sometimes it breaks.

If you have to do this kind of testing yourself, make the objective to successfully kill your application. Do things for no particular reason, approach the application in strange ways, randomly click a bunch of buttons, and see what happens.

Also, compare the output of various reports and calculations against known answers. Bugs will always work their way into programs, and the more complex the program, the greater the number of bugs.

Look at the kuffuffle over the MS-Windows Calculator program. If you subtracted .000 something from 17 you got the wrong answer. I saw someone demonstrate the bug a week ago, and I have been trying to duplicate it while I write this, but I can't quite remember the number. This is a perfect example of testing. I know there's a problem with Calculator, but I can't duplicate it. Anyway, it's been fixed.

Integration Testing

Not only do the application modules written by the various members of your development team have to work together, but the application, database, network, and platforms have to work together as well.

In my last book, *Sybase Developer's Guide*, I included a PowerBuilder-based shareware utility for managing SQL Server. I also distributed it on the various courses I taught throughout 1994. Interestingly, some PCs would have a great deal of difficulty running the application successfully without getting GPFs. Other systems never had a problem at all. What was different about this from any normal application I had worked on was the sheer number of users and systems on which the application was run. We had not tested the application on any more than a handful of different machines and different configurations, but when released to the great wide world, we found a number of conflicts with certain hardware and software combinations (these have subsequently been fixed!).

The main point here is that integration includes your application with the client workstation on which it will run. If at all possible, you should try to make your client workstations as similar in configuration as possible. However, like the situation with DBA@Win, there are times when the configuration of the client is completely outside your sphere of influence. In those cases, you should make a point of testing the application with as many machines as possible to identify potential conflicts.

Integration testing also involves ensuring that the application will integrate with legacy systems and business practices.

In many situations, I have seen integration testing scheduled well after the prototype has been approved and the production version is in development. Integration testing typically involves determining whether the application has been made suitably robust to handle the often unexpected behavior of the rest of the systems with which it interacts.

The kinds of issues identified during integration testing include:

- **Connection Time-Out Issues:** In some cases, the length of time required to retrieve a result set may have the application drop the connection to the SQL Server. I have seen this especially with ODBC connections to Sybase.

- **Datatype Incompatibilities:** You may need to code explicit convert statements to handle formatting of certain datatypes, or to deal with datetime values to accommodate the behavior of other tools, such as Access.

- **Processing Window Implications:** Batch processes such as BCP or nightly backups can affect whether or not your application has enough time to process data without interfering with or being interfered with by some other regular process.

- **Network Delays:** For developers who access their back end on a high-speed LAN, performance issues experienced by WAN users may not be caught until the integration test.

These are the sorts of issues and problems that you can expect to identify during the integration testing phase.

Of course, there is also the more traditional issue of how well the various modules work together. One of the major nuisances of client/server projects is discovering that new release X.1 is incompatible with old release Y.9 of some other module. One of the features you'll be looking for when managing development across multiple developers is the facility to manage the release of versions that include various versions of subcomponents.

Although there are software tools that will manage this process for you automatically, you should, at the very least, have a spreadsheet to indicate which module versions were included in the various releases of your application. Not only does this greatly assist in the support process, but it's vital from an integration testing standpoint as well.

Your application version 1.5 may work great against SQL Server 10.0.1, but what about System 10.0.2? This is not so hard to manage for a small number of applications with a few components, but the larger the project, the quicklier (no, that's not a real word) you will lose track.

Volume Testing

Frequently, developers work on databases that are smaller than the ones that their applications will be expected to handle in production. Of course, working with the pubs database can be a quick and easy way to determine whether the logic or syntax in an application is valid. What it won't tell you is whether that same logic or syntax will work when you go up against a table with five million rows.

If you're working on a relatively small application, say with a database of five hundred megabytes or less, take heart. You will probably still want to do some testing with production-sized volumes, but things should work pretty much the same as they do in development.

If you're planning, however, to roll out your applications to work against databases of tens of gigabytes and work with tables with millions of rows, well, I hope you're sitting down, because volume testing is very, very important to you.

In discussions with various Sybase clients who have developed VLDB (very large database) applications, the word is that SQL Server can get a little flaky when pushed to DB/2-sized databases. I have personally observed some such strangeness and I am here to tell you that it isn't pretty.

Back end cursors, for example, may not behave the way you think they should when they have to operate on millions of rows at a time. Forget just erratic performance—hey, you can get used to that. It's when the results that come back are different from when they are run against smaller volumes that the whole thing takes on a twilight-zone air.

In talking with the Sybase tech support folk, I'm told that the customer *must* have done something different (this is me shrugging). VLDB applications can occasionally pose very Bermuda Triangle-like symptoms, and I am sure you will agree with me that it doesn't matter whose fault it is, it just has to get fixed.

My point? You absolutely must have the facility to duplicate your environment database for database, table for table, especially if you're working with large volumes. This will have some implication for resourcing, as disk may be cheaper than it was, but if you buy it in the dozens of gigabytes at a time, it still requires some budget. This is the second major point to make about volume testing: make sure not only that you have time for it (and sufficient time to process the results), but that you have the finances to allocate for the gear to support it as well.

Load Testing

The number of users pounding against your Sybase environment is a completely different kettle of fish than the volume of the data to be handled by your application. At some point prior to production, you really should have both the anticipated number of users and the anticipated volume of data loaded on a server and processed by your application. Wouldn't it be nice to know whether your application just won't work with production demands on it?

Perhaps the most important element of load testing is correctly mimicking the mix of transactions. Obviously, these transactions don't have to be real. You can test whether the data model will support the application by inserting or updating fake data. The important part is to determine whether the locks conflict.

When you have a number of users updating databases as part of the transactions to be handled by their business unit, and when that data is of interest for decision support or reporting purposes, you can create a real bottleneck in performance.

The scary part is that, functionally, the applications may work fine. The performance may be quite acceptable against a large database. The various client workstations, networks, and server platforms may pose no problem at all, yet the whole thing can melt down when a dozen users try to run the application.

The kinds of solutions to problems identified by load revolve around upgrading resources, replicating or distributing data, and denormalizing the data model. You will definitely want to know whether any of these are necessary before you roll out your application into production.

Failure Testing

All mechanical things fail; this is a sad fact of life. And Murphy's Law says that it will happen at the worst possible time. The question is: how is your application protected against catastrophic failure? Using hardware devices such as RAID (redundant array of inexpensive <ha!> disks) to provide automatic mirrors of the disks, or using software facilities within Sybase such as mirroring logical devices, are some solutions. These should also be tested in a safe environment to ensure that they actually provide the protection you think you have.

Network bypass procedures and loading databases from backups should also be drilled at least once to ensure that the practical considerations are all met. For example, if you do backups without performing DBCC operations on the databases, you may end up with a backup that cannot be reloaded. The only way that some people find out about this is by trying to restore databases after they've lost one. Not a pleasant learning experience at all.

You should ensure that, before signing off your development as completed, your application has undergone some rough stuff to see just how Tonka Tuff it really is.

GUI Testing Tools and Utilities

Most testing is still done manually and is generally a highly labor-intensive process with a great deal of potential for duplication and waste of effort. As the popularity of Sybase and other client/server solutions grows, more shops are looking to automate their testing process. The pressure to do this increases as client/server moves towards providing solutions for the enterprise as a whole. To meet this need, a third-party marketplace is burgeoning that provides testing tools and assistance. To date, the principal user group of such products is independent software vendors (ISVs), but more organizations are looking at the benefits case for testing tools as they move more heavily into client/server development as their norm.

The most widely known GUI testing tools include:

- Enterprise Quality Architecture from Mercury Interactive Corporation supports both GUI and stress testing of the application environment.
- SQA TeamTest from Software Quality Automation is focused on testing PC applications, and incorporates an object-oriented approach to developing tests.

- Microsoft offers Microsoft Test, which was originated as an internal tool to help Microsoft test its own GUI applications.
- Segue Software offers QA partner, which supports testing of applications under multiple operating systems, including Macintosh, OS/2, Motif, and Windows NT, among others.

Additionally, Sybase provides a RUNGEN utility to test the physical data model on the back end, simulate workloads, and provide server side statistics.

Many of these products integrate to various degrees with development products such as PowerBuilder and Visual Basic, and CASE tools such as LBMS and ProTeam Case.

Although these products are still new and the market for automated testing facilities is growing, the general consensus is that manual testing will still be required. Like the other aspects of client/server development, these tools represent an opportunity to increase development team efficiency. More important, they allow companies to keep expertise and lessons of experience in a formalized format and not just in people's heads.

Last, one of the primary benefits of automated testing tools is the capability to run regression testing. When you have set your tests up with the tool, and a user identifies a bug to be fixed or a change to be made, with regression testing you run the test suite to ensure that what used to work still works. This is very difficult to do in a manual testing environment because of the amount of work and discipline required to run the complete test suite again.

SQA TeamTest

In the PowerBuilder/Sybase development arena, one product has gained considerably more momentum and recognition than its competitors—SQA TeamTest. One of the key reasons for this acceptance is the focus provided on PowerBuilder objects and the range of tests supported. Specifically, SQA TeamTest supports six main areas: test planning, test development, execution, results analysis, defect tracking, and reporting.

The product allows you to configure the PowerBuilder Object Recognition Model, customize reports, and develop rules to manage workflow. SQA TeamTest incorporates a 3-D graphics engine and supports object state test cases and any other basis for comparison.

This focus on the GUI object allows the tester to work with what the object does, rather than how it looks. A dialog box, for example, is affected by the system font, default colors, and screen resolution of the system on which it is running. In testing with the object model versus record/playback technique, the internal logic associated with the dialog box is tested without displaying irrelevant and distracting information such as how it looks on any given workstation.

Let's look at how SQA TeamTest handles this specifically.

The description in this chapter of SQA TeamTest is not intended to be an endorsement, simply a treatment of a representative tool of this type.

In any case, you can build your own customized utilities for testing the elements of the application that you anticipate will be most applicable for your particular site.

For some of our clients, my company has written PowerBuilder applications that simulate data retrieval, calculation, and updates to the database to test the data model. The key element to making this approach work is to clearly understand exactly what kind and how many operations will be performed by the users in order to correctly simulate the selects and updates across the appropriate number of application client connections.

If, for whatever reason, you're not interested in a structured testing environment, you may find that documenting the trials and tribulations of the users is made somewhat easier with utilities such as ScreenCam from Lotus. This utility allows a user to record exactly what is on their Windows desktop, including all of the steps taken and messages displayed. It's very handy for people who cannot articulate their problems exactly, or who get confused by the terminology that is necessary to describe the problem symptoms to a developer.

Another approach for remote testing is to provide dial-in or remote access that allows you to view what is being done on a remote screen. Most of the popular communications products such as Carbon Copy and AW Remote will support this feature, allowing you to observe the remote tester's approach to using the application, as well as whatever happens when something goes wrong.

Summary

For really small departmental applications, testing need not be a tremendously time-consuming task. You may be able to handle most of it during the iterative development process with your user partners, and handle the integration during implementation support.

For enterprise-wide client/server systems, however, or for any project affecting more than a handful of people, testing will be the assurance that you are not committing corporate suicide by releasing a half-baked application.

The last thing you want is to have to perform a recall on your application. It implies shoddy workmanship and demonstrates a couldn't-care-less attitude to your internal customers. A rigorous testing plan will ensure that you have built the quality into the application, or at least that, if you didn't build it in, you caught the problems before releasing them to the world at large.

Testing is more than just making sure that you handle error conditions and process the data correctly. Testing is about the overall quality of your application as a product and its fit against your organization's requirements.

By budgeting sufficient time and resources to the testing phase, you will show that you are committed to quality work, and this can hardly be criticized by your management and users. In spite of the pressures of deadlines, you should be sure to perform adequate testing, and if that is not possible, at least go on record that specific kinds of tests should be performed.

Even if you're overruled in the interests of business expediency, you will at least have your testing plan to fall back on in the event that fingers get pointed and voices get raised.

Some organizations are more interested in quality that takes time than mediocrity that allows speed (but not all, I know). By addressing the testing issues covered in this chapter, you should have a higher level of comfort that your application will not only do the job, but it can be relied on to perform well as the demands increase.

From this chapter you should have gained a few practical tips for testing your applications. I have pulled out what I feel are the most important aspects of application development and ways in which you can evaluate them before putting the application in production.

As I stated in the introduction, I expect that a good many of you will see this sort of testing process as being *de rigeur* and will wonder whether client/server developers really need to be told such things.

There are many ways in which the novelty of the client/server architecture and tools makes itself felt, and the lack of rigorous testing methodologies is one of the most obvious. This is perhaps the single most important contribution that experienced mainframe developers can make when they are in the process of migrating to client/server.

The software development efforts in the client/server arena need to be subject to many of the disciplines developed the hard way over years of experience in big iron shops. If you're developing a Sybase application that doesn't have a testing process planned and documented, I hope this chapter helps you stand up and be counted.

5.5

Capacity Planning

Introduction

Most of the discussion of planning done so far has been at the architecture, or design, level. In moving towards the implementation of Sybase applications, however, you must at some point address the need to allocate physical resources. Of course, it's helpful if you have had some prior idea of how much in the way of resources you're actually going to need.

In this chapter I discuss the issues of estimating resources for your system. Arguably, some of this capacity planning or estimation must be done as part of the business case process; after all, how else would you identify how big of a server to buy? Even with a solid basis, however, for choosing a server configuration (like take your best guess and double it), at this stage you should begin preparing for the allocation within the server. This is probably the best time to find out that you have underconfigured the server, as it gives you time to sell the idea to management, order, and install the upgrade.

In this chapter I review all of the elements that need to be accounted for as part of a capacity planning exercise for a Sybase application. The focus will be on the server, as opposed to the client or the network, because this is typically where constrained resources are felt by all, and PC upgrades are a little easier to come by than a new server.

Resources to be Managed

In a typical Sybase installation, there are a number of resource issues to be managed, specifically:

- Disk
- Memory
- CPU
- Network connections

The easiest one to deal with is CPU, as you have a choice between opting for a single- or multiple-processor configuration, depending on the server platform on which you are implementing your application. In a large environment, for example, you might decide to opt for a half-dozen 60MHz processors and allocate two to the OS and four to the SQL Server to handle a large number of user connections. Any real change to the CPU configuration should come about as a result of performance monitoring, when you discover that a particular server is CPU bound. This is not usually the biggest single contributor to performance bottlenecks, but, hey, it could happen.

Memory is a more significant contributor to the performance of your SQL Server. You will need to allocate enough memory to the Operating System, and then give the rest to SQL Server, assuming that you're not running any other applications on the server. Keep in mind that the RAM allocated to SQL Server is consumed as you add users and logical disk devices. Only after the RAM required for the dataserver and for managing user connections and disk devices is allocated is there memory for data and procedure cache.

Network connections require your server to handle a number of client connections and manage the throughput to those workstations. If you have remote users, these connections may involve routers and other communication servers that will all contribute to potential bottlenecks. Once you decide how fast your network needs to be to support your application and install it, there is really little you can do to increase network speed and capacity without hardware changes.

Disk, on the other hand, is the real resource that requires continuing management. From an estimation perspective you will want to be sure you have enough disk for the various tasks to be handled by your Sybase server.

Disk Resource Allocation

To ensure that you have ordered and installed enough disk to run your application, you need to check the estimates of disk space for the following purposes:

- **The Operating System:** A UNIX operating system installed with all the options can take 500MB of disk space. Swap space will be more, depending on the size of your server.

- **Sybase SQL Server:** To install Sybase and its attendant languages, help docs, utilities, and so on requires approximately 50MB of disk. If you're running multiple languages or installing Sybase tools as well, you will require more.

- **SQL Server Database Devices:** As explained in Chapter 6.5, "Physical Database Implementation," the logical database device sizes get allocated first, not the databases. These devices need to be at least as big as the databases and are frequently bigger to allow easy expansion.

- **SQL Server Dump Devices:** For speed of backups and restores, most sites dump databases first to disk and then to tape. The dump files are compressed but still contain the entire database and all its objects. You must allow space for all of the dump files for each of the databases if you wish to be able to restore from disk.

- **Work Space:** When loading or unloading data from a table using bcp, you must have space to contain a text image of all of the tables that you wish to manipulate. This could be mounted across a network, though performance will necessarily be slower than if the disk was local.

- **Tools and Utilities:** If you're planning to work with companion products such as SQL Monitor or datatools for Sybase backups, you will have to allocate space for these files and their resulting output.

If you're in the process of trying to determine how much disk to install on your Sybase server, you must account for disk consumption by all of these elements.

Database Size Estimation

There are a number of rules of thumb that you can apply when determining how much disk space a database will require. As you have already read, you will gang this number up into the size of the logical database devices overall.

These rules of thumb are as follows:

- Allow 20 percent of your database size for the log
- Allow for the creation of clustered indexes, which require an additional 150 percent of the table size to be free for working space in the database
- Allow five percent of the table and index size for overhead from systems-required internal pointers and so on
- Allow for the fact that text and image columns automatically allocate one 2K page per row even when empty

Other than using these rules, you need to sit down with a spreadsheet and work out the size of the row and estimate the number of rows you will have at any given time.

Transaction Modeling

To arrive at capacity estimates with any kind of relevance, you must have a good grasp of the kind of transactions your users will be running against the system. This means that, for most client/server applications with a Decision Support requirement, you are in for a rough time. Ad hoc queries are difficult to predict in terms of resource consumption, because generally you have no idea what the users are going to attempt to do once they get their hands on the system. However, there should be at least some representative queries defined as part of the user requirements, and you should use these as a baseline for determining whether your server configuration is up to the task.

To determine the resources consumed by any given application, you must allow for the following:

- CPU resources consumed by each transaction
- Disk resources consumed by each transaction
- Number of transactions per user per unit of time
- Number of users on the system
- Overhead resource consumption required by the system

As you can imagine, the likelihood of arriving at exact numbers when modeling a system not already in production is not good.

As you can see, the development of a capacity planning model for Sybase applications could be as time consuming as it is valuable. This approach is most likely to appeal to people who already have an application running in their shop; they can do a forensic analysis to determine the real values.

For those of you who are moving to Sybase for the first time, you will no doubt have some parallel experience with those who have gone into the jungle before you. We all recommend that you get the biggest configuration you can afford and cross your fingers.

Doing the Math

At some point, you will no doubt be unwilling to trust to luck your estimation that you have sufficient resources for your SQL Server databases and attendant objects. To assist you in dealing with this anxiety, I have talked with a number of data modelers responsible for just this function in their projects, and compared notes. Here I would like to share that common view of what practical capacity planning means in a Sybase environment.

First, everyone agrees that you can't have enough disk. Put another way, databases expand to fill the disk available. However, you must still have some reasonable idea of how much constitutes the minimum amount of disk space that you can get away with.

To arrive at this, you must first review your data model to determine exactly what datatype and size each column in the database will be. If you have not developed your logical model sufficiently to determine this, than you really will have to trust to luck, or opt for some kind of contingency—such as, buy more disk.

Anyway, you can see from the rules of thumb covered earlier in this chapter that percentages can be allocated to account for indexing, working space, and overhead. However, all of these projections are based on the estimates of table space, and ultimately that is a function of column width and row count.

By way of example, take a table with eight columns, `fname char(18)`, `initial char(4)`, `lname char(30)`, `phone char(12)`, `fax char(12)`, `addr1(40)`, `addr2(40)`, and `favorite color char(12)`.

The length of any given row in this table would be at most 168 bytes. A varchar datatype will conserve space, but for purposes of estimating disk requirements, you are best advised to err on the side of pessimism. Allowing the average 5 percent for pointers and other overhead, the row moves to a size of 172 bytes. For a table with a million rows, the table would consume 168,945K or 168MB. (I know that you know already, but divide 172 million by 1024 to get the kilobyte count, or 1,024,000 to get the megabyte count).

The point is that even a tiny table starts to consume serious disk resources when you start getting row count. A seven-figure customer list may be highly unlikely for your organization, but a million transactions may not be and you must be very careful when you start talking about storing historical data, even if you keep it in summarized form.

Good Fences Make Good Neighbors

There is an expression in the West that "good fences make good neighbors." This most likely stems from the somewhat territorial attitude of cattle barons in the last century, but who knows for sure? I like it because it fits the theme of this particular discourse.

What you want to guard against in your capacity planning is having your databases blow up under daily use. Now, I hope that the expression "blows up" conveys the sense of urgency that I feel this phenomenon deserves. It most definitely can feel that way when your job does not complete and the errorlog fills up with messages such as `Cannot allocate sufficient space in syslogs`.

More than any other single event, filling the database log can cause a developer or user headaches difficult to explain, let alone assuage.

The key to success in this arena is to work with some of the SQL Server settings to help you jealously guard the space that you do have, when transactions threaten to overrun the boundaries.

In older versions of SQL Server, the default activity when a transaction filled the log was for the transaction to fail. With the introduction of System 10, a new feature was introduced, namely the last-chance threshold and associated `sp_threshold` action for each database.

Server and Database Options

Under System 10, the default is now to place any transaction that fills the database log into "log suspend," giving you the opportunity to alter the database and increase the log, or to drop the transaction log with `truncate_only`, which clears the transaction log, possibly allowing the offending transaction sufficient room to complete. After doing either of these operations, you select the `lct_admin` option desired (in this case "unsuspend"), and the transaction carries on as if nothing happened. Remember, the default in non-System 10 or later SQL Servers is for the transaction to be aborted, forcing you to start from scratch.

This is important because one of the areas of disk for which you will have to manage capacity is the transaction log. It's much easier to allocate database space in smaller chunks than to accurately guess from the outset.

Another database feature that you'll want to manage is the `truncate log on checkpoint` option. This works with the recovery interval option set in `sp_configure` to determine how long your SQL Server will wait before automatically checkpointing each database. A typical option sets the recovery interval to 5 minutes, meaning that the SQL Server will checkpoint each database every five minutes, writing dirty pages to disk and thereby ensuring that all committed transactions are in fact reflected on the data pages rather than buffered in memory.

Don't Be Afraid to Commit

The really interesting point here is that after this occurs, a database whose truncate log on checkpoint option is set to true will then flush committed transactions out of the log and thereby maximize the log space available for transactions to follow. However, to take advantage of this, you must ensure that you write frequent commit transaction statements into your client applications. If you're a PowerBuilder developer, pay particular attention to the autocommit option in your PowerBuilder applications. (An option of true does not issue a commit until the end of the session, sometimes creating very long running transactions.)

Another way of managing this is through the `sp_threshold` action, which might dump the transaction log to a file. Because it's not necessary to dump devices any longer with System 10, you can use a naming convention such as `dump transaction dbname to trandump+(select getdate())`, allowing you to keep incremental logs without overwriting older transaction log dumps. Take note that `sp_threshold` action does not work when certain database options are set (such as `trunc. log on chkpt.`), so some planning will be required.

The Use of Segments

One of the main thrusts of this chapter is to give you ways to protect your project against unexpected increases in the size of database objects that can cause difficulty in development or worse, in day-to-day operations. There are some other database options which you can use that will contain, if not control, runaway tables and indexes of other database objects. Here I am thinking specifically about the use of segments.

In many IS shops, you'll have a very clear idea about how much data you need to store. The variations will be in the amount of additional tables created by technical users, user/developers, or other people on your team with more of a cowboy mentality when it comes to consuming disk space.

Where this most frequently becomes a problem is where regular uploads, updates, or bulkcopy operations are planned as part of the application. You may have estimated perfectly well how much space you required, but come in one morning to find that your bcp failed due to insufficient room, the root cause being that someone created a bunch of user tables using select into, thereby duplicating data for his or her convenience but causing you headaches due to lack of room. This also can occur with indexes.

You can get around this risk by creating user and index segments within the database. By using `sp_addsegment`, `sp_extendsegment`, and `sp_dropsegment`, you can allocate certain disk slices to particular tasks. For example, if you drop the default segment from all but one of the disk slices, you ensure that no one can create a table larger than that segment unless the table is created explicitly on a different segment name. If you code your create table scripts with the ON SEGMENTNAME extension, you can ensure that your disk space is available and can be poached only by someone with as much Sybase savvy as you. This should at least narrow down the culprits when it comes time to uncover the individual responsible for taking away your room.

Summary

From this chapter you should have gained an appreciation for an approach to estimating the size and configuration of your server in advance of ordering it. This discipline is usually carried out in a more formalized process by larger shops looking to move VLDB applications off their mainframe and down to client/server.

Unfortunately, the tools for estimating transaction rate and database sizes are not as mature on the client/server side. This is one more area in which our systems must become more mature.

Realistically, most of you will simply want to ensure that you have enough disk and that your server is upgradable to meet the demands that will be placed on it.

One of the key elements of capacity planning is to have a contained, not widely variable or growing workload. When it comes to client/server systems, however, you must keep in mind that you are enabling your users with technology to allow them to do things that were previously impossible. For this reason, you aren't likely to have a firm grip on usage until it actually occurs, and even then it will change as the users become more familiar with the technology.

This is one area in which increasing the freedom of data access to the users has created a much more difficult job for systems professionals trying to keep on top of the technology.

5.6

Balancing the Workload

Introduction

Perhaps the single most arcane subject in the black art of client/server systems is the process of determining how much work should be done on the server and how much should be performed by the client. The optimum balance is a blend of performance, security, maintainability, reusability, and flexibility. In short, a whole series of trade-offs.

In this chapter I discuss the various techniques that I have seen used in load balancing for Sybase applications. I also cover the trade-offs and implications inherent in the features in Sybase and PowerBuilder specifically, such as stored procedures and cursors.

Last, you will have the opportunity to review my rules of thumb for architecting client/server systems with a processing balance appropriate for the application.

Actually, I think this topic should be the subject of an entire book, rather than a mere chapter. Obtaining the right balance during the application's architecture phase is critical to the sustainability of any Sybase application. However, given the amount of ground I have covered in this book, a chapter will have to do.

From this you should be able to take away an appreciation for the issues involved in program architecture and the implications for performance and future development.

Prerequisites

To cover this topic, I need to make a number of assumptions. First, that you are already familiar with the hardware and software environment in which you expect to deploy your client/server application. Second, that you have some idea of the priority of the technical options open to you. This includes understanding the relative importance of security versus open access, for example. You need to be aware of the kind of importance your organization puts on the following:

- ■ **Application performance:** The performance of a particular or set of applications. You need to know whether the architecture is to be generic or specific to an organizational function.

- ■ **Data security from unauthorized access:** Establish the philosophy underlying the particular application regarding access permissions and protection.

- ■ **Data integrity:** Define how important is it to ensure that the data is 99.99999 percent pure.

- ■ **Flexibility in manipulating data:** Identify the requirements to slice, dice, and distill the data in different or unpredictable ways.

- ■ **Investment in hardware resources:** Look at the organization's commitment to expenditure. Maximum performance and flexibility can be had for a high price; all else is a trade-off.

- **Geographic distribution of data:** Identify the potential user population of the application and their locations.

- **Communications costs:** Evaluate the sophistication of the organization's communications infrastructure.

- **Centralized vs. decentralized control:** Review your company's commitment to keeping control in the hands of a few or providing data as tools throughout the organization.

- **Accountability:** Based on the centralization required for the application, look at who will be accountable for the management of the application. Will it be the users or a centralized IS group? This can make a big difference to the architecture of the application.

Each of these parameters has a different implication for the way you design your application in terms of the emphasis on the client or the server. That is the heart of finding the appropriate balance in the workload between the two.

The Feature Set

Familiarity with the technology is an important aspect of balancing the workload. This is true, first, because individual designers tend to emphasize the features with which they are most familiar, and second, because without knowing how a particular processing option works, it's impossible to take advantage of it.

Here I will identify the factors that I have seen most frequently used to perform the processing work to achieve the objectives of the user requirements within a framework that balances the organization's infrastructure priorities. The feature set consists of the options or tools available to us as application designers to perform the work. The work of the application is, of course, to meet the users' requirements (which you really better have a grip on by now). However, the other set of priorities to be satisfied is the organization's requirement for security and maintainability. These, among others, make up the considerations that are part of the computing infrastructure of your organization and are not, strictly speaking, part of the application requirements. However, to properly balance the workload, you must be fully familiar with both sets of concerns, because much of the balance is due to competing pressures between these two areas.

The typical list of features, techniques, or systems elements to be addressed when constructing Sybase applications includes:

- **Stored procedures:** Precompiled database programs that are invoked by name and that return results

- **Triggers:** SQL or stored procedures that are automatically fired when update, delete, or insert operations are performed on tables for which the trigger was defined

- **Back-end cursors:** A method of processing row by row through a table or result set on the database
- **Indexes:** Pointers to rows based on values in an indexed column or columns
- **Locks:** The automatic database permissions that are assigned to data based on read or write operations
- **Cache:** The RAM allocated to data and procedures to allow SQL Server to manipulate results in memory without having to retrieve from slower hard disks
- **Denormalization:** A process by which redundant rows are stored for increased performance
- **Replication:** The process of managing guaranteed data synchronization across multiple servers
- **Network bandwidth:** The speed and capacity of the link between client and server or multiple servers
- **Application generators:** Products used to create applications quickly without having to deal with lower-level coding issues, such as optimum performance
- **Structures:** In PowerBuilder, a method of temporarily storing data for further manipulation
- **Disconnectibility:** A facility that allows data to be retrieved by a workstation, disconnected from the server, manipulated, and later restored to the server
- **PC configuration:** This covers the hardware/software resources available to the workstation

From this list you should be able to see that there are a number of potential contributors or inhibitors to any given requirement. The reason for listing these is to ensure that you're familiar with all of the things one could suggest when attempting to address a particular issue. For example, if you indicate that data integrity is mandatory in your application, a systems architect might ask whether you have implemented triggers. Each of these elements has both a contribution to make to the equation and a penalty to apply.

The list that follows represents the typical advantages/disadvantages of each of the preceding elements.

Feature	Benefit	Cost
Stored Procedures	Speed, Accessibility	Server Resources
Triggers	Data Integrity	Performance
Cursors	Processing	Accessibilty
Indexes	Performance	Maintainability
Cache	Performance	Server Resources
Denormalization	Performance	Server Resources
Replication	Accessibility, Performance	Money, Maintainability
Bandwidth	Performance	Money, Stability

App Generation	Development speed	Performance
Structures	Accessibility	Client Resources
Disconnectibility	Accessibility	Maintainability
PC Config	Performance	Money

For every advantage, there is an opposite disadvantage. Whether they are equal depends entirely on the priorities set out for your application environment. If you have distributed low-end personal computers for clients and a really tricked-out server, the server resources consumed by stored procedures is not really that unattractive and certainly isn't equal in cost to, say, implementing holding data in local structures.

I left locks out of the equation because they are automatically applied against data, depending on the operation you're performing. They are mentioned simply because they have a tremendous impact on accessibility and performance when you implement other features such as triggers and cursors.

Balancing the Box

The competing concerns can be expressed as a box (an octagon, not a rectangle). You need to determine how much pressure is exerted on your application from each point. The workload balance box is depicted in Figure 5.6.1.

FIGURE 5.6.1.
The application's attributes to be balanced.

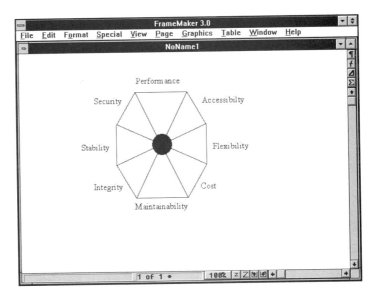

If you go to your management people and ask them which of the above is most important, they will probably tell you they are all equally important, but, of course, they are not. However, most users and executives are not particularly thrilled at the prospect of discovering that, although they saved money (for example), they have no performance. Or perhaps they decided to provide access to as many people as possible, and then discovered that the system had been tampered with due to less emphasis on security.

These things are trade-offs and there is no way you can have it all, though it is possible to end up with none of it (you'll probably have to change jobs if your application turns out that way).

If you look at the octagon carefully, you'll notice that some of the points are diametrically opposed. That is, if you move toward one, you must move away from the other—integrity and accessibility, or security and cost, for example. If you want to have a system that anyone can access, it will necessarily be less secure. If you care most for your data integrity, then you'll have to make update procedures, among other things, more restrictive. This is simply the way things are. Every feature has a trade-off, and the trick is to determine what is most important to your organization, in advance of putting the effort into developing the application.

Rules of Thumb

I have given a great deal of thought to the best way to represent the various trade-offs and implications of each Sybase client/server feature. Application architecture is hardly an exact science, so much of what gets recommended is a result of research and investigation into site specific elements.

In any case, to simply leave it at that won't be of much help to you, so I thought that the best way to encapsulate my opinions on workload balancing would be to create a series of If...then rules.

In discussions with other client/server developers, I have discovered that it's quite easy to argue for or against any of these positions, and that it's possible to describe hypothetical scenarios in which they are either valid or invalid.

At the very least, these rules should give you a basis for reviewing the features and determining what to look for when trying to apply them to your own application architecture.

- If your server environment is resource rich *and* your client environment is resource poor, then do all of your processing on the server.
- If your client environment is resource rich *and* your server environment is resource poor, then do all of your processing on the client.
- If your client environment is resource poor *and* your server environment is heavily used, then do most of your processing on the client.
- If your application requires a high degree of flexibility in connecting multiple client platforms, then use stored procedures extensively on the server.
- If your application requires a higher degree of data integrity than performance, then use triggers extensively to ensure that the transaction completes all updates, inserts, or deletes on all tables.

■ If you use triggers extensively, then incorporate extensive process status and error-handling messaging to keep your client informed of progress.

■ If your server is heavily used by a large number of users, then keep your transactions short to avoid locking conflicts.

■ If your server is heavily used by a large number of users *and* data integrity is critical, then use stored procedures rather than triggers to enforce integrity and business rules.

■ If your users are high-level knowledge workers, then provide them with maximum flexibility on the client with access to data.

■ If your users are low-level systems operators, then provide them with maximum stability with defined procedures and messages.

■ If cost is the primary driver, then do most of your processing on the client.

■ If access to data for decision support is required to an OLTP database, then look at data replication to offload the data to another server.

■ If large result sets or complex images need to be manipulated by an application, then invest heavily in the client configuration.

■ If your users require disconnectibility from the server, then use triggers to enforce data integrity on synchronization.

■ If you have a read-intensive application, then put clustered indexes on the database tables.

■ If you have large databases, then avoid incorporating `having` or `group by` in select statements within the server logic. Do this on the client instead.

■ If maintainability is a key driver, then do most of the processing on the server through stored procedures.

There are situations in which these rules of thumb will not apply. You may have a large number of users for a database that is highly normalized and data integrity is vital, forcing you to use triggers and/or having long-running transactions. The expected result of a situation such as this is that you will have transactions blocking each other, and performance will be an issue.

Whether this works for the application is a trade-off between performance and integrity. This is naturally something that you must know in order to determine how best to implement the client/server features and options available to you.

No doubt there are many more appropriate guidelines or rules of thumb that could be discussed here. I hope to start a collection and add to them over time. However, the main point for you to take away from this discussion is simply that you can't just use stored procedures extensively in all cases. You must first determine what the application must provide to be deemed a success, and then incorporate the features that most support that.

For example, when client/server is a new technology and management wants to contain costs, it's easier to justify powerful personal computers than it is to get a powerful server, because the

PCs are considered reusable whereas a Sybase-specific megaserver might be authorized only after the value of the technology has been proven.

In such a case, it makes more sense to do much of the work on the client, rather than on the server, even if the application will have to be rearchitected after a megaserver is approved. The reason for this is that if you take advantage of stored procedures, say, and load the work up on the server, performance on a workgroup server will suffer and the technology will look ineffectual. The natural result is that even if the application has been well architected in a theoretical sense, the requirements of the application were not met (as in response time) and the system is deemed a failure.

From this discussion I hope you can see that it's always possible to provide sufficient details and twists about a specific application to require a unique combination of server-side and client-side processing.

Summary

In this chapter you should have gained a sense of exactly what the issues are underlying any workload balancing act you might have to do with your Sybase application. In many of these situations, people look for hard-and-fast rules that always apply, but with the technology as it stands, this just isn't practical.

The one thing I have seen consistently in successful Sybase applications is a healthy respect for the uses and benefits of stored procedures. Triggers frequently prove problematic when nested, but I have never met a Sybase applications designer who regretted using stored procedures. On the other hand, I have met people who lost their project (if not their jobs) for having promised the capability to connect multiple platforms and then invested all their time and effort in developing for one client platform. This approach naturally requires performing the same effort for each platform, which puts the organization no further ahead in terms of developer budgets or application maintainability.

The key to any successful Sybase application is to understand what the system must provide to the business, and then to support that. Workload balancing is no different. Relate the features of the technology back to the benefits derived and the application requirements.

From this chapter you should have good grasp of the high-level costs and benefits of the main architectural features inherent in any Sybase application.

Perhaps the last point to keep in mind is that if your application meets its business requirements, is stable, and provides data integrity, you can always throw hardware at the application to gain improvements in performance. If it is fast but without integrity or stability, chances are that you focused on the wrong area and the organization will be reluctant to embrace your Sybase application.

5.7

Designing the Sample Application

Introduction

The purpose of this chapter is twofold. First, you will be able to see how each of the steps identified in the design section applies in a practical sense to our representative application. Second, the development team will have used this chapter to begin the process of mocking up, prototyping, and documenting the application itself.

This chapter shows you exactly how the external design documentation (including the requirements laid out in Chapter 4.5, "Modeling the Sample Application") gets translated into screens, functions, and features. Perhaps more interesting, you will also see how we set up our own development environment for the CausesDB project.

The Outer Layer

From the requirements set out in Chapter 4.5, you already know that the application must support the following features:

- **Donations:** Support on-screen completion of a form allowing users to designate charities to which they would like to donate funds
- **Organization Review:** Allow users to view the details provided on each charitable organization contained within the CausesDB database
- **Advertisement Browse:** Retrieve available radio, print, or video ads for selected charities and allow the user to review the associated advertisement
- **Mission and Purpose Review:** Allow users to select target groups assisted by various charities to short-list organizations for more detailed review
- **Financial Report:** Display the financial profile of selected charities including their overall budget, costs, and shortfalls
- **Unfunded Program Report:** Display details on initiatives which the charitable institutions would like to launch but for which they have insufficient funding
- **Data Entry:** Capture data on-line which can be transferred to the database and accessed by modules which address the above requirements

At this point in the process, the development team had a clear idea of the purpose and nature of the application while not having a clue as to what the systems itself was going to look like, or how it would work.

In reviewing the requirements, however, it became clear that the data entry module was separate and distinct from the other parts of the application.

When looking at our project plan, it also became obvious that data entry was the first component that had to be completed to get the data ready for uploading to the database.

The contingency plan was to fax the questionnaires and have the organizations complete them and fax them back, at which point they were to be entered manually into the database. If the press for time became really tight, we recognized that this could possibly be done by temporary data entry staff. However, were that necessary, our development team would have to provide access and support for the data entry module. In any case, the data entry component had to be developed first.

Now I'll work through that component and then come back to the rest of the application.

The Inner Layer

I thought that it made the most sense to use the standard development practices guidelines laid out in Chapter 5.2, "Application Specifications." In short, the development team focused on using the naming conventions that are commonly used for PowerBuilder and Sybase applications. The coding standards used were also those identified in that chapter.

The first step in actually doing the work was to define the application development framework. I will cover this as soon as we have reviewed the mock-up, which will show you how the application functions were to be organized. This also shows how we expected the users to get around within the application.

Data Entry

The intent for the data entry component of the application was to create a stand-alone or disconnectible application capable of running off of a 3.5 inch diskette and containing information entered directly by the charitable organizations. Actually, the need for the application to run off a single diskette was questioned in our design meetings and we thought it would provide the highest degree of ease of use. We decided that if performance became an issue, or if size wouldn't permit running off diskette (and with the size of the runtime .DLLs needed for PowerBuilder, how could it?), the application could be installed to the users' local hard disk and a facility would be required for copying to diskette the data saved to the Watcom database. The users were then to ship the diskette back to the development team, who intended to migrate the data from Watcom to SQL Server.

I'll look at a first draft of the menu for the data entry module. Obviously, this isn't a complex application. However, you can see from the master menu that a number of basic functions must be provided—specifically, Validate and Help. It's not unreasonable that we would include online instructions for the users who must complete this online questionnaire; after all, it's a new application and I couldn't be sure that they were all that familiar with Windows. At the very least, the online help had to include a discussion of what the questionnaire was for and what had to be entered for it to be considered completed.

Speaking of which, the Validate option may also be new. However, as you may remember from our user requirements, there are a number of data elements that are mandatory before the questionnaire can be considered complete. Although there is a number of ways to address this, I prefer to give the users every opportunity to complete the form in their own way. For this reason, I would rather avoid forcing them to enter fields such as charitable organization number before moving onto the next component. In other words, I think it makes more sense for the users to be able to validate their responses to the questionnaire in one pass. This could be tied into the save feature, so the application could be up, allowing them to enter whatever data they have available, but not allowing them to save the data until it has been validated. At that point, the validation process would print a message informing them of which data elements were still needed and asking them if they wanted to save anyway. The validation report could then be stored in a database column and its status could be checked by the development team when the diskette is returned. Where a user forced a save without completing all of the mandatory fields, we could then actively follow up with the users before processing their returned data.

To support these requirements, the options contained below the File option on the master menu include the following:

> New
> Open
> Close
> Validate & Save
> Print
> Exit

By the time we had reviewed the requirements to this point, the development team had an idea of how the menus should be laid out. The next step in designing the mock-up was to provide some direction on how the body of the questionnaire should be represented within the application.

The questions to be represented in the questionnaire itself were detailed in Chapter 4.5. Each of the sections to be completed represents the source for the data that will be viewed and reported as part of the main CausesDB application itself.

Creating the Mock-Up

Remember, the whole point behind preparing the kind of documentation we have done so far is simply to provide some direction to the developer who is responsible for creating the mock-up screens. Because I have some idea of how I want the data to be represented, in this case in accordance with a form, it's appropriate to at least sketch what the screen should look like.

In some cases, you'll be better off to simply have your user interface specialist meet with the users, gain a sense of what they want to do first, and then logically organize the work into screen forms. There will be no easier time to change the overall look and feel of the application, so this is when you should schedule frequent reviews, and feel free to toss the whole thing out and start over if your users don't like it.

For our situation, we were not working in proximity to the users, so we selected a small group of them to review things such as the mock-up and give us feedback. This process is described in greater detail in Chapter 6.6, "Implementing CausesDB," in which I discuss the implementation of the CausesDB application.

In any case, how the development team translated the screen layouts and menu options into PowerBuilder screens is shown in Figure 5.7.1.

FIGURE 5.7.1.
A mock-up of the main menu and first screen of the data entry module.

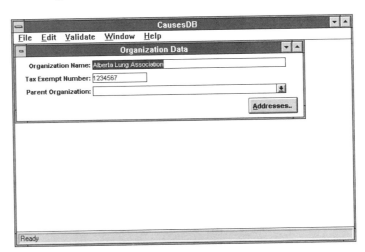

Now that we have a mock-up, we can begin the process of commenting the functionality to be associated with each screen. The key point here is that the comments are derived from the users' understanding of what the screens will do, and they are described in common English. Later, these comments will be handed off to a developer who may or may not be the same person who worked out the function descriptions with the users. Certainly, anyone who must maintain the application will want to know what the functions were intended to be without necessitating a laborious review of the application specifications with the users.

You can see one method of documenting specifications with mock-ups in Figure 5.7.2.

At this point, the mock-up for the data entry component could be prototyped. Actually, that is almost true. In other chapters in this section, I pointed out that, during the prototyping phase, you have an opportunity to define all of the inheritance and base objects with which you will develop your application. The development team was now ready to do that for the data entry module. However, even in the context of our rather small and contained application, there was more work to be done before we could move to the next stage of design for data entry.

FIGURE 5.7.2.

An annotated version of the main menu and first screen showing desired features.

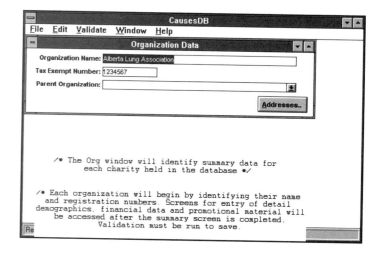

Specifically, we still had to mock up the CausesDB application itself. Like most application designers (and all technical writers), at this point I would like to dismiss the need to do this with a casual comment such as "you get the idea." My Sun workstation has a fortune cookie program that runs whenever I log in, and it recently asked me this riddle:

Q. How many hardware engineers does it take to change a light bulb?

A. None, they'll fix it in software.

Q. How many software developers does it take to change a light bulb?

A. None, they'll document it in the manuals.

Q. How many technical writers does it take to change a light bulb?

A. None, let the users figure it out.

After seeing this, I decided that I could not just let you figure it out, and besides, at this point, my development team for CausesDB was getting a little antsy (ANSI?) about the specifications to which they were supposed to develop this application in record time.

So Here Goes...

At this point, the book you are reading is obviously finished, as is the CausesDB application, at least in its first version. However, you should keep in mind that since it really was to be a representative application, the development team reviewed this material as it was written, and then got to work on making the application real. It was at this point that the team actually got down and started to work on creating the application, a few short weeks before the delivery deadline.

Preparing for the CausesDB Mock-Up

Because GUIs are one of the driving forces behind the move to client/server systems generally and PowerBuilder specifically, I was convinced that CausesDB had to demonstrate some of the real power of GUI applications. Additionally, I intended to show how you can work with BLOBs (or at least some of the multimedia objects) within a Sybase application. For this reason, the layout of the screen was a critical element of the success of the application.

As discussed in Chapter 5.3, "User Interface Design," one of the key characteristics of good user interface design is adherence to the rules of graphics design as worked out by graphic artists over the past hundred years. The traditional graphic artists did not have the facility to simply click or double-click a picture in order to navigate a document or obtain more information.

Because this was a cornerstone of the user requirements for CausesDB, this had to drive the layout of the screen.

Please appreciate that, as I wrote this, there was no screen layout or other guide for the CausesDB application. This was the point at which all of the research, analysis, report writing, and other narrative needed to take on a visual representation. Of course, once the development team took a look at the layout I sketched, no doubt it changed. But past experience tells me that developers will typically work within the application in at least the rough form passed to them by the designer.

Naturally, I wanted the design to be a good one. In reviewing many professional multimedia applications that incorporate graphic image displays and data retrieval, I have seen many different approaches to screen design that I feel would greatly assist the users of CausesDB. I mention the other products because I think it's important for you to realize that you don't have to be a genius to recognize something that can work. Speaking pragmatically, it's often effective to survey the market, see what works, and then adapt it.

Because we typically develop PowerBuilder applications with Multiple Document Interfaces and toolbars, these Windows design features will drive the way CausesDB that will be constructed. Working with this in mind, the main screen layout for the application will be based on the following specification.

From the rough sketch of the main CausesDB layout, you can see how we have allowed for the integration of the text and various graphic images that need to be displayed at the same time, Also, each region has its own controls, though logic will have to be implemented to keep the two coordinated. For instance, if a new organization is selected through the database results area, the logo of that organization should be displayed in the graphics region, if available.

During the mock-up phase of the CausesDB development, the application team came up with this screen shown in Figure 5.7.3 based on the rough sketch.

FIGURE 5.7.3.

The mocked-up main screen for the CausesDB application.

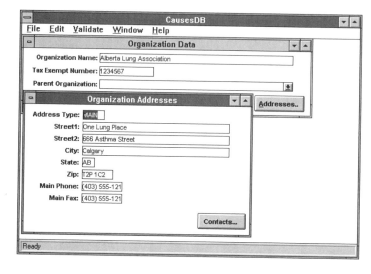

The main purpose of the window at this point was to ensure that we allowed for displaying all of the attributes to be managed as part of the application. For our sample application, we knew that we had database forms, graphics, and sound, and that we had to provide a facility for querying and browsing the data. In reviewing the mocked-up window, it appeared that all of these requirements at least had an area or a button to provide a home for the necessary logic.

The Application Development Framework

CausesDB is made somewhat more complex by the fact that it was developed by people working on sites from Denver to Toronto to Calgary. This means that the definition of an effective application development framework was of even greater importance than it would be for your project, presuming that most everyone on the team works in the same office.

In this era of distributed computing and mobile offices, however, that is not always the case and that certainly applies to this application.

As a rule of thumb, we knew that we wanted to take advantage of inheritance, not so much for improved maintainability (will we have to maintain this application?) but to minimize the development time and effort.

During the move from mock-up to prototype, we could work out the specific attributes, events, and functions to be contained within the objects that made up our base classes or ancestor objects. However, as part of the instructions to the design team, we designated one individual, John, as the keeper of the application framework and gave him the responsibility for defining what the base classes should be.

Because he worked from this chapter to begin that process, I define here at least a high-level overview of what needed to be contained in the framework. John, of course, reserved the right to change the actual base classes as we got closer to developing the application, but this served as a starting point.

Library Name:	CAUSESDB.PBL	
Ancestor Object:	d_stateddw	Provides state list for drop-down datawindows
	f_checkcomplete	Reviews all required columns in dw for completion
	m_menumain	SDI ancestor menu object
	m_menumdi	MDI ancestor menu object
	u_cbclose	Modifiable close command button
	u_toolbar	Modifiable toolbar with picture buttons
	u_dwbase	Base datawindow with error handling & messages
	w_baseresponse	Base response window
	w_basesdi	Base SDI window
	w_basemdiframe	Base frame for MDI applicatoins
	w_basemdisheet	Base sheet for MDI applications
	w_baselaunch	Base windows for CausesDB application launch
	w_basegraphics	Base window for displaying graphics
	d_baseform	Base form for displaying CausesDB data results

From this description of objects required for our applications development framework, we were able to come up with approved objects that formed the base on which the CausesDB application was built.

Preparing for the Prototype

Once we had reviewed the application development framework, menus, toolbar, and display layout in mock-up format, we were ready to begin developing the prototype. At this point, we began working in PowerBuilder to create our application object and preliminary screens, which we then walked through to comment into the scripts the functionality required.

After completing this process for all of the windows and controls developed as part of the mock-up, the work was farmed out to various developers to put the functionality into the prototype. Once completed, the various objects were e-mailed back to John, who put them all together into an integrated prototype. This was reviewed and tested by several members of the team before shipping it out to the beta sites for further appraisal.

Summary

In this chapter you have been shown how each of the application development steps applies practically to the development of an application. During the course of developing the CausesDB application, we uncovered a number of steps that had been previously glossed over or omitted altogether. This should tell you that it's not absolutely mandatory to follow this (or any other) methodology slavishly. Like cookbooks, they are merely a guide to help you in creating your own application.

PowerBuilder provides its own application development framework, and the fact that we developed our own for CausesDB is more of an indication of how small our project was. As part of an enterprise-wide development standard, you should adopt or develop your own framework. Equally important is creating and building on the coding standards and naming conventions.

As you can see demonstrated in this application, due to the geographic distribution of the developers and the somewhat piecemeal approach to development, definition of the framework, as well as establishment of conventions and standards, was vital to eliminating wasted effort.

You should also be able to see how the development of the prototype is truly a reflection of your understanding of the application requirements and a method of conveying specifications to developers as well as functionality to users. It's a mirror of your application, and it changes from one stage of development to the next. I hope this is one of the clearest examples of how iterative development works in a practical sense.

5.8

Logical Data Modeling

Introduction

To create a complete set of documentation that will allow you to build your Sybase application, you will at some point need to create a logical data model. In this chapter I cover established techniques for modeling data prior to physical implementation.

You will see how ERwin, a data modeling product frequently used in Sybase shops, approaches the data modeling process. Also, I demonstrate how the logical data model pulls information from the highest plane of the Integrate Task/Data Model methodology and prepares the path for the lowest plane, the physical data and application model.

As you go through this chapter, you will see methods for preparing entity relationship diagrams that depict the data to be held in your database and used by your application. You also will see the benefits of using a CASE tool such as ERwin (and there are many others) to help document and manage your project.

Data modeling is an integral part of any relational database application, and my intent is to introduce you to not only the value of this function, but some practical tips for how you can go about it in your environment.

A Data-Driven Approach

One of the key benefits of any relational database management system is the facility to pull data out of the database that was not anticipated when the database was first created. Obviously, it's necessary for the data to actually be held in the database, (with the exception of data derived from calculations performed on existing columns), but it's not necessary to know what queries will be required before establishing the database.

This is quite a bit different from the more traditional approaches using hierarchical and network databases. In those environments, information systems were typically application driven. A business requirement was identified, an application proposed, data sets required to feed that application were also identified, and the entire thing was implemented as a block. As you have probably seen, this led to tremendous duplication of data in various applications, as well as a great deal of difficulty in getting access to data from an application for other purposes.

With the introduction of relational systems, a new approach to implementing systems emerged alongside the database technology: data-driven systems design.

IDEF Modeling Techniques

The ERwin logical data modeling tool is based on the IDEF modeling techniques. These techniques themselves are based on the Integrated Computer Aided Manufacturing project initiated by the U.S. Air Force. IDEF itself stands for *I-CAM Definition* methods. The original intent of these definitions was to develop a method for capturing and depicting graphically all of the processes and data requirements for manufacturing systems.

The methods and techniques that have emerged from this project have a much greater applicability than simply manufacturing, or, for that matter, developing, systems. However, you will see that they are quite well suited to modeling relational data to be used in Sybase applications.

Benefits of Logical Data Modeling

Whichever modeling tool or approach you choose to use, the major benefits of logical data modeling remain the same. Specifically, they include:

- Reducing data redundancy
- Simplifying changes to data structures
- Isolating changes to systems applications
- Providing a data model for use by multiple applications
- Identifying improvements prior to implementation

The data modeling process is essentially a design process. It's appropriate for this effort to take place well into the development process, when your concept for the application is more defined. To derive the benefits of a logical data model, you would complete these activities before you tried to actually build your system.

By creating a model of your data, you increase the likelihood of data reuse, which correspondingly decreases the occurrence of data redundancy. Like the potential of object orientation, the key to reusability is in knowing about the existence of the desired data before developing an application to acquire or create it.

The model allows you to simplify changes to data by identifying any of the places that data is held. I suppose that this is only common sense, as the data model becomes a clear method of documenting the contents of your databases. In the event that you need to change a data element name (or whatever), the best way to simplify this process would be to know all of the occurrences of that data in your various databases. Without a logical data model, this is quite difficult to accomplish quickly in an environment of even moderate complexity.

Changes in systems applications are data independent once the data has been moved out of the application and into the database. Looking at this from the logical modeling perspective, you can take advantage of the client/server architecture by focusing strictly on application logic or functionality changes without being concerned with impacting the data. This is really a function of the client/server architecture, but the logical model allows you to quickly see the impact of any changes to the application on the data.

As an extension of this, the logical data model can be used by many applications. In fact, the key benefit of a logical data model is that it can conceivably cover the entire enterprise so that *all* applications use the same model.

Last, by working through the logical data modeling process, you will be able to identify any missing data elements or attributes that are required by your application. In some cases, the application requirements indicate that data is required where that data is not readily available—reference data, for example. The modeling process itself ensures that you have created a model of everything you'll need before you try to build it.

Scope of the Data Model

At the highest level of the Integrated Task/Data Model, you have identified the business requirements and provided a brief description of the data sets to be used and the systems application that will use that data to meet the requirement. At the next level, you want to define the data in much more detail, and to place restrictions on or definitions of how that data can or should be used and validated.

The data model contains not only detailed descriptions of the data, but identifies how the data is related and defines the business rules that govern that data.

As part of the logical data model, you will define the following:

■ Data Dictionary - A list of all data elements and their associated attributes, such as underlying data type and size

■ Entity Relationship Diagram - A graphic depiction of entities described by data and what data elements they have in common as well as the cardinality of the relationship

■ Validation Rules - Any methods of determining good or valid data

■ Business Rules - Any guidelines or policies for how data must be handled to be relevant to the business

Taken together, the definition of these things makes up your logical data model.

Definition of Terms

To understand the data modeling process, it will likely be helpful to define the terms used. These are covered in the glossary at the end of the book, but even for those of you familiar with the data modeling process, it can't hurt to review what I mean when I use these terms.

Entity - A thing, tangible or abstract. Represented as a noun (that is, person, place, or thing).

Attribute - A characteristic or descriptive element (an attribute of a person might be hair color, whereas the value None is for bald people).

Data - Raw facts that have no context (data in the context of a question becomes information).

Key - An attribute that identifies an entity uniquely.

Cardinality - The number of occurrences (none, one, or many) that an entity may have in relationship to another.

Rule - A procedure that must be invariably followed or adhered to (for example, zip codes must have five or nine digits).

With these definitions in mind, it should be easier to understand the logical data modeling process that I describe in greater detail.

Data Modeling Tools

It's quite possible to develop a data model on a white board, graphically depict it using a drawing package (or, heaven forfend, with pen and paper) and create a data dictionary as a text document. In fact, some of the most heavily used data dictionaries were actually just documents rather than data held in some automated tool.

By and large, however, when people approach data modeling, they look for assistance from a CASE tool.

It's not my intent to get embroiled in the debate about the validity of CASE tools and whether they have a future, provide value, have lived up to their promises, blah, blah, blah. (I like this expression better than *etc.*)

For practical purposes, I have seen CASE products used most successfully for documenting the data model, creating entity relationship diagrams, and generating data definition language scripts for the creation of databases and database objects.

Products such as Silverrun, Systems Architect, Excellerator, and IEF provide a great deal of value if you know how to use them. I have gravitated more towards ERwin simply because the product does a good job, but more important, it's integrated with PowerBuilder to a higher degree than the other products. For this reason I cover the actual description of how to use ERwin to automate the logical modeling task. When combined with other packages for developing data dictionaries, ERwin becomes in essence a CASE tool. For those of you who have more stringent definitions of the term CASE than I, please excuse me. (Wait until you get to the object-oriented chapter; that should really give you something to chew on!)

Defining Entities

Having defined entities as basically nouns, you can identify the basic entities that would be used by any business. For example:

- Customer
- Product
- Supplier

- Order
- Shipment
- Invoice

These entities conform to the nomenclature that is typically used when defining ER diagrams. The entities are easily identifiable, unique, and expressed in singular form. The relationship is used to described or link two entities.

- The Customer Places an Order
- The Supplier Ships a Product
- The Customer Pays an Invoice

You get the idea.

At this level, you can probably take much of the definition from the higher-level modeling you did as part of the business analysis. The logical data model begins to get a little more complex when you define attributes. For example, the entire customer entity might include attributes such as the following:

- Company Name
- Head Office Address
- Contact Name
- Contact Address
- Ship to Address

And the list goes on. Actually, even from this short list, you can start to see one of the core problems that is addressed in the logical data modeling process. It's quite possible that there will be multiple contacts within one company. If you were to store the name and demographics of each contact for each company, the physical table in the database that stored the customer information would soon get very messy. Customer name would no longer be unique, for example. (This is what I mean by messy.)

To avoid this, you create a new entity called Contact and you relate it to Customer.

Each Customer may have zero, one, or many contacts. However, a contact must have one company to be valid. From this example, you can see the role played by cardinality in depicting the entities and relationships for the data to be held.

Using ERwin, this relationship would be depicted as follows in Figure 5.8.1.

At this point you can see how the attributes are much more cleanly represented. For instance, Customer might contain the head office address, telephone, and fax number, along with the company's legal name. However, the contact entity would be fully attributed with the names and contact information required for each member of the customer entity with whom you have contact. This is shown in Figure 5.8.2.

FIGURE 5.8.1.

A one-to-many customer-contact entity relationship diagram.

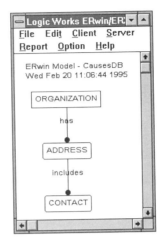

FIGURE 5.8.2.

A fully attributed customer-contact ER diagram.

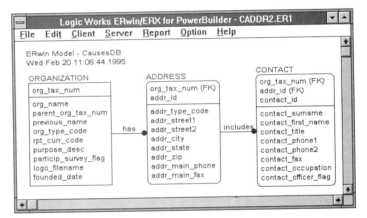

The process of eliminating duplicate entries by moving data into its own entity is called *normalization.*

Keys

Now might be the best time to introduce the concept of keys.

Primary Keys

If you were the tax department with a table consisting of every individual in the country, you would definitely not want to have to scan through every single record to find a particular person. To uniquely identify every given person in the nation, our governments have thoughtfully provided a unique number. Your social security number (social insurance number in Canada) is yours and yours alone. In a data model for citizens, the key would be this number.

By indexing this key and searching on it, speedy retrieval of a particular person's data is vastly improved. If you place a unique index on the key, you ensure that there can be only one such value in the table.

Composite Keys

Sometimes, of course, there isn't a thoughtfully provided unique identifier. In databases of the population outside the government, you can't insist on people providing their SSN, so you must come up with another method of uniquely identifying rows. One such method is to create a composite key consisting of a group of columns. Any given value in a column may be the same as another row. However, the collection of columns identified as part of a unique composite key must be, well, unique. For example, although a company might have a unique primary key that consists of an internal, company-assigned number, this may not be enough. Another approach would be to create a composite key consisting of last name, first name, and zip code. That might be enough to uniquely identify most of the people, but what about a father and son, Sr. and Jr., when Jr. still lives at home. No good. So, add birthdate to the composite key and, presto, everyone is uniquely identified.

Foreign Keys

Once a particular table has been identified with a primary key (which may or may not be composite), other entities could also use this key, especially dependent entities. Previously, I stated that a customer might not have a contact but all contacts had to have a company. The primary key for a customer would likely be `customer_id`. `customer_id` is also an important attribute of contact. However, if the customer id is changed for any given customer, the dependent contacts would also have to change. They are foreign to that entity, as they depend on another entity for valid values.

Parents, Children, and Orphans

Another way to describe this is that the entity with a primary key that relates to another entity with that key as a foreign key is a parent. The entity with the foreign key is a child entity of the parent. If the parent row is deleted while values exist in the child tables, those values would be orphaned.

When you set up mechanisms such as triggers in Sybase to ensure that this cannot happen, you are enforcing referential integrity. All of these issues are handled under the process of logical data modeling.

A demonstration of how this relationship would be depicted for the customer-contact example is provided in Figure 5.8.3.

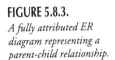

FIGURE 5.8.3.
A fully attributed ER diagram representing a parent-child relationship.

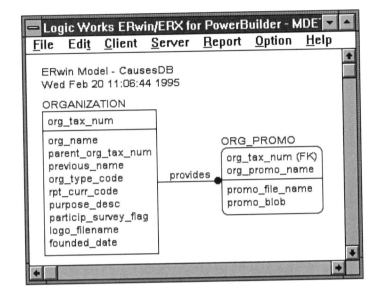

Tying It All Together

For systems people, none of these concepts is all that complex. Of course, when the number of entities grows to the hundreds or even dozens, it can become very complicated to keep it all straight. Therein lies the value of having documentation and appointing someone to develop a high level of expertise in the application-, departmental-, or enterprise-level data model.

Although the description of data modeling may seem somewhat simplistic, it may be helpful to keep in mind that some of these techniques will be highly technical and a great mystery to end users. These are the very people who will expect to be able to create ad hoc queries that run against the database and answer any question they might choose to pose.

Your challenge becomes to clearly define and communicate the data model to anyone who might be tempted to write these kinds of queries. This might be handled by creating practical examples of common queries and breaking down each system component. Once users see how all of the logical data model basics work in a real-world setting, it will be that much easier for them to understand the more intricate data relationships that they will no doubt want to address as time goes by.

Summary

I hope that those of you who are already familiar with the principles of data modeling don't mind the somewhat superficial treatment of the topic. Obviously, preparing a logical model is an important and intricate part of developing Sybase applications. It's also the subject of many in-depth books and courses and can take many years to become really proficient.

My intent in this chapter is to simply introduce the main concepts of logical data modeling and to define terms for those of you who don't have to perform this function as part of your contribution to the Sybase application development process.

We use ERwin because it also allows us to define the extended PowerBuilder attributes that a particular data element is supposed to have when used in PB applications. This is another way that modeling helps demonstrate the data before effort is expended in its physical implementation, and makes sharing data between modelers, administrators, and developers more efficient.

And the last note. Typically, end users are not either prepared or qualified to interpret a logical data model when they create their ad hoc queries. Of course, a lack of understanding of the underlying data model will make it very easy to create the query from Hell. Being able to quickly and easily communicate logical data model basics will make end user access of data through *ad hoc* queries much more achievable than just turning them loose with a query tool.

6

Implementation of the Design

Introduction to the Section

Implementation is my favorite phase of any project. This is the point at which you find out whether the whole thing is going to fly. In a nutshell, this is the point at which you make it real. I operate a consulting firm that specializes in what we call implementation consulting, so I have a number of observations and stories. I hope you find these directly applicable to your own situation and therefore of some value to you.

In any case, implementation of client/server systems is directly analogous to battle in a war. The generals make the plans, the officers make arrangements, resources are acquired, objectives are assigned, and ultimately, somebody goes forth to make it happen. On the *Great Commanders* series shown on the A&E network, I have seen that all generals feel dread when an army goes into battle, because at that point there is nothing more they can do. Winning or losing all comes down to the individuals involved.

This Is How I Think of Implementation

The unforeseen and unexpected are daily events. The unbreakable breaks, and Murphy's Law is shown once again for the truism that it is: anything that can go wrong, will.

By and Large, It's a Lot of Fun

The key to understanding a successful Sybase implementation is to view each of the stages as necessary contributors to each other, with one being the single most important: implementation. Without actually putting the system in place, there can be no users to support nor any outcomes to audit. All the concepts in the world become so much talk, and design efforts are wasted when the blueprints are shelved.

Implementation Is What It's All About

In this section, I share with you some of the practical tips and the sense of enthusiasm with which I have always greeted this particular activity. I hope it's contagious.

6.1

Managing the Implementation Process

Introduction

When developing systems, there are few things that have the pressure and excitement of the implementation process. Analogous to an organ transplant, implementation is the surgery itself, where the old system is removed or bypassed and the new application is grafted into place.

In this chapter I discuss methods of managing the risk inherent in the implementation process. If you have already gone through one or more client/server implementations, you know what to expect. Implementation is a combat zone, where you are constantly under fire from problems, glitches, defects, and flaws presented by the technology and the people involved.

From reading this chapter you should take away a complete agenda for change, which is the pivotal point of any systems implementation. Having conceived and designed a new and better way to do things, during implementation you actually make it so.

There are a number of potential pitfalls, which I will address in this chapter, as well as ways to spot and avoid them. One of the key points you should take away from this discussion is how to use the implementation process to compensate for any unforeseen deficiencies in your design. And you can be sure there will be at least a few.

As I have mentioned elsewhere in this book, implementation has always held the most interest for me as a systems designer and developer. In the past, I have used the implementation period to complete unfinished design specifications, a sort of build-as-you-go process.

I'm not actually advocating that you do that yourselves, but what you can expect from this chapter is a highly practical, proven-in-the-field treatment of techniques that you can use to ensure that the implementation of your Sybase application is a success.

The Importance of Morale

At various times in this book (and everywhere else in the systems world), you have been told that it's important to get the users on your side, that everyone has to buy into the process; in other words, everyone has to believe that the project can be done.

If you, or other members of the development team, or, worse yet, the users, feel that the implementation of the new system is doomed to failure, the chances of success are next to nil.

As you prepare for the implementation phase, you must check the spirits of the parties involved. Establish how many people in the business unit are sick or exhausted. Make sure that your key players have an opportunity to rest during the runup to implementation. This may take the form of a day off to make a long weekend, or a week's vacation prior to the big push. I have even gone so far as to nag people to take their vitamins.

The point here is that implementation is more draining and demanding than any other single period in the systems development lifecycle. To maximize your chances of success, you must be sure that you are building with people who have the internal resources to give to the project. First and foremost, they must have the right attitude, which you should have been cultivating every step along the way. Second, be sure that they are not already completely used up from the analysis and design efforts. Even when you have pushed hard for completion of deadlines prior to implementation, as long as your people have an opportunity to rest a little before getting down to the real work, they should be fine.

If you're not in a position to look after the interests of the team as a whole, check your own internal resources. And if you see any morale or attitude problems in your team, at least make the effort to make your project leader or manager aware of them. Management may not be able to do anything about it, but at least these people will have been given the opportunity to take care of the problem in time.

The bottom line is that a committed team made up of systems people and users can compensate for any design deficiencies or technical problems that arise. An uncommitted group of individuals will not.

Identify the Targets

One of the key values of using a tunnel chart is that the date representing the light at the end of the tunnel is usually the planned implementation date, and this date becomes fixed over time in everyone's mind. As the date draws near, people may be apprehensive or nervous or pressured, but the point is that the date cannot sneak up on them. They are psychologically prepared.

As well as the timing of the project, you must ensure that everyone has the objectives of implementation firmly in mind. This means that everyone must know what the checkpoints are, and how they will be measured for success.

In a financial system, for example, one of the key indicators might be the capability to balance various accounts at month's end. If this is the case, then the people on the project should be aware of that as the litmus test, even if they are not directly responsible for performing that work. The systems administration and networking people frequently are not made aware of what the developers and users will be focused on, for example. Therefore, they won't be in a position to ensure that data is properly backed up for those critical databases, or that sufficient disk space has been allocated. This also applies to your software and hardware vendors, and integration partners. Make sure that they are aware that you have a big deadline coming so that they actually have the resources around in case you need them. Depending on the size of your project, Sybase is probably not going to staff its technical support group around your implementation schedule. However, if your account rep knows about the big day, the rep can take steps to ensure that some additional technical resources are available in the event of a problem. This also applies to Systems Integrators or Value Added Resellers with whom you might be working. Giving them a heads-up before demanding support can pay great dividends.

The point here is that not all data or applications components are created equal, and it's critical that everyone involved in implementation be focused on the elements that are most significant. This, of course, implies that you have already identified what these are.

Communicate the Measures

It's vital for people to know how well they are doing. If at all possible, your implementation plan should include measures for success or failure. If an application GPFs once, does that mean that the whole project should be scrubbed? What about once a day? Client/server systems are frequently unstable, and this means that you need to set some expectations, and monitor performance against those.

During the course of your testing, you should have done some performance benchmarking to ensure that your data model and network was up to the anticipated levels of traffic. This would have allowed you to coarse tune the system against any obvious areas of contention. However, there is no substitute for real experience. Implementation may well turn up weaknesses in your platform, model, or network that would have gone unnoticed under less strenuous conditions.

To support this process, you should have published performance guidelines to your users. The last thing you want is for them to report that the system is slow, relying only on their perceptions that it is slower today than it was yesterday. To get around this, you should establish response-time targets for queries and put them in the position of timing them. By having the users identify how things are working, and providing quantified statistics for application components, you can isolate which areas need improvement rather than respond to whimsical or unfounded perceptions.

More important, by establishing performance measures, you put the onus of proof on the users. This may not sound as though it's in the spirit of total user support that I have talked about previously, but, believe me, during implementation you want as many ways as possible to winnow down the complaints to a manageable number. If there is a real problem, and you have provided methods for clearly demonstrating that problem, any user who goes to the bother of documenting the case probably has a point. This gets around people pointing to features of client/server computing and calling them problems—things such as spontaneous reboots and widely varying systems performance, depending on the phase of the moon.

Develop Contingency Plans

For every endeavor as critical as the implementation of a new Sybase application, you should have fallback positions and contingency plans in case things go awry. You can't predict everything that might go wrong, but you should at least have some idea of what you can do if critical deadlines are not met, if data gets out of synch, or if show-stopping bugs emerge at the last minute.

In some cases, this will simply be a new date to begin implementation. In the event of a show stopper, roll back procedural changes made to support the implementation of the new system and reschedule implementation for the new date. Frequently, I have seen project managers reluctant to discuss renegotiated deadlines because they were afraid that the later dates would become self-fulfilling prophesies. That is, if they admitted that the project might be able to go into implementation at a later date, that date would become the new target and the project wouldn't get out of the starting gate before then. However, even if these fallback positions are not broadcast to the project team at large, they should at least be developed. The last thing anyone wants to do when an implementation is in flames is to try to dynamically determine when the whole thing could be done again.

Iterative Implementation

Everywhere these days it seems that people are talking about iterative development versus the waterfall approach. Nowhere is the power of iterative development demonstrated more clearly than in implementation. The biggest reason for this is that implementation is the proving ground for design. All of those "good ideas" and improvements get the opportunity to show their practical value during the implementation phase, and, guess what, not all of them survive.

This means that, during the course of the implementation, it's possible for the feature set of the application to shift dramatically—usually in the direction of what is workable and valuable to the business on a practical level. The single biggest critical success factor to your implementation is to identify changes from your users and incorporate those immediately into the application.

This is not that different from the process I recommended for the iterative prototyping. The difference is that implementation involves a much larger group of people than the contained group you worked with to create the prototype. Not only that, but the implementation group will also consist of the people who, deep down, really don't want to change. These are people who will delight in showing your application's defects and presenting all of the nasty implications of not being able to handle things the old way.

I'm making the assumption that, because you're reading this book, you couldn't possibly be one of those people. But I have seen developers, typically ex-mainframe people, who have resented the migration to client/server so much that, although they are not vocal during any other period in the development, they jump all over the problems in implementation.

Regardless of who identifies a real problem or what their motivations are for bringing it to your attention, the critical element is how quickly you can respond to it. Even high-quality vendors such as PowerSoft and Sybase (whoops, that's one company now) end up releasing version X.0a or X.0.1 within a few months of general release. I make this observation to underscore the point that the initial implementation phase is really the proving ground for the design and an opportunity to identify the biggest bugs in the application.

Implementation is never a smooth process. You should count on having to identify problems and develop patches and solutions to them, especially in the first few weeks of initial implementation. This is one of the reasons that preparation and team morale are so important. The constant barrage of criticism and problems will drain even a well-equipped and rested team.

It's a grind and you should be prepared for it.

The Implementation SWAT team

The term *SWAT* stands for Special Weapons and Tactics, and you should have identified a group to take on this role. Personally, I think the term applies especially well for a small group dedicated to eradicating bugs, but then I'm rather fond of puns.

In any case, one of the reasons for having a special group to fulfill this function is the relief they provide to the rest of the team. In the event of a major problem, you have trained and qualified resources to bring to bear on the problem, and everyone else has the feeling that there are reinforcements for them to fall back on.

Most implementation problems fall into the following categories:

- **Holes in the application design:** The biggest problem by far is that implementation will show you where you neglected to cover a particular set of real requirements. To deal with this, you must conceive, design, and implement an add-on to the application that can quickly turn your system into a kludge. Better to get the complete design down up front.

- **Inadequate platform resources:** This only costs money to fix, but it can make your life a living hell. If the server or workstation products that you have used for your application are not up to the task, you must either replace/upgrade the equipment, or scale down your application.

- **Unstable products:** Many client/server products don't work as advertised. This is an annoying fact of life. Much of this should have been worked out in the prototyping/ testing phases of the development, but real-world workloads will sometimes point out previously unnoticed product flaws.

- **Insufficient user training:** Ad hoc queries can become major resource hogs, and if users are not sufficiently familiar with any of the technology with which they are expected to work—uh oh. During implementation, you also identify staff who took training but just didn't "get it." These people need remedial training and clinics as well as continuing support.

- **Inappropriate coding technique:** Related to inadequate resources, because there are so many ways to approach development, there are also many ways to write programs that just won't work well under pressure. First, you should have addressed this with your coding standards, and second, you should find any of these cases when you do volume testing. Ultimately, though, there will be cases when it just doesn't show up until implementation.

When you assign staff to the SWAT team, you should consider how well rounded the team is and how well the team can address problems that fall into any of these categories.

Summary

Implementation is the proving ground for any system and with it come all of the headaches and rewards of creating something new. In this chapter, I discussed the need to prepare the ground for your application, to ensure that the users are ready to receive it.

Like an organ transplant, the real risk is that the host will reject the new component. You may well have created a superior product to the old system, but if the users are unwilling to embrace it, you will really find out in the implementation phase.

One of the key points that I want to make in this section is that many of the objections to be raised by users will be brought up only during implementation. When they see what you mean by the system, then they will understand the significance to them, and there is always the potential that they will not like what they see.

The techniques described in this chapter should prove useful to preparing the ground for implementing your Sybase application. One of the real keys is to have identified in advance the satisfactory performance and quantitative measures for what the system will provide. During the design phase there is a tendency for people to gloss over difficulties, and in implementation there is an equal but opposite tendency to want to drop features and functions that pose difficulties.

By identifying what your application must do to be ready for implementation, you avoid a disappointing reconciliation of the reality with the expectations generated during the conceptual and design phase.

6.2

Conversions

Introduction

Whenever you migrate to a client/server environment, there is some element of converting from one system to another. Occasionally, it's not necessary to incorporate legacy systems or traditional technology into a new system. I encountered a project such as this once when a company launched an entirely new subsidiary with a charter to develop new applications to support it.

That, however, is the exception rather than the rule. Most of us must replace either mainframe or PC systems that already provide some level of service or disservice to the users. This provides a set of unique challenges to be addressed.

In this chapter I cover the process of migration, with special emphasis on the transplantation of the old systems with Sybase and related technology. There are a number of considerations to be addressed; specifically, how to determine that the new system is ready to be moved into production, how to prepare for the work of managing both the old and new systems in parallel, and when to simply throw the switch and cut over to the new system.

By reading this chapter you should become more familiar with the issues that surround replacing one system for another. You may already be familiar with this process from having replaced manual systems with PC or mainframe applications. Client/server, however, with its characteristically complex and interrelated components, provides a number of unique challenges.

In this chapter I try to address those in a way that you will find thought provoking and applicable to you particular situation.

Setting the Stage

Typically, the first stage in a conversion of an existing system to a client/server system is to migrate a preliminary copy of the legacy data from the old to the new platforms. You may want to do this by mapping the old data formats directly into the new relational tables. It's more likely that you will have to take a couple of preliminary steps to accomplish the migration to your satisfaction.

The first step is to catalog all of your existing data, including the format in which it's currently stored. You may have done this as part of the development of your data dictionary. In any case, you'll want to perform this step before moving the data over to your Sybase database.

Frequently, naming conventions and column lengths will change with the move. If your older system required all uppercase-character data, you may decide to convert this to take advantage of case insensitivity in your SQL Server environment.

The best way to document the data map is with a simple spreadsheet layout, as shown in Figure 6.2.1.

FIGURE 6.2.1.
A format for your data migration map.

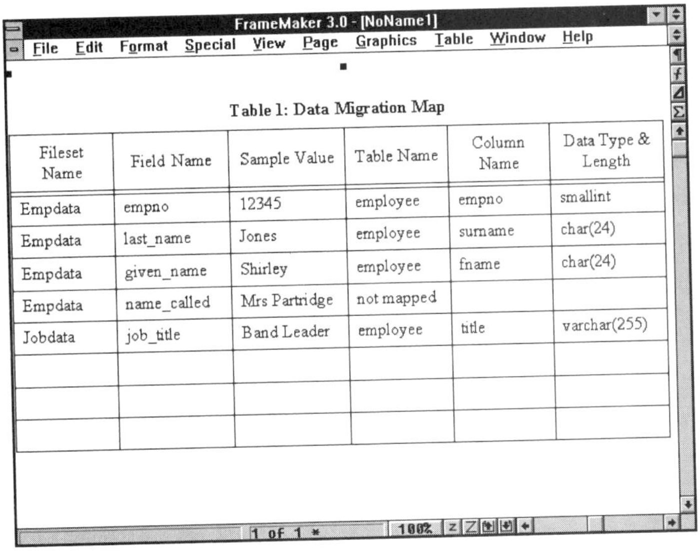

FrameMaker 3.0 - [NoName1]

File   Edit   Format   Special   View   Page   Graphics   Table   Window   Help

Table 1: Data Migration Map

Fileset Name	Field Name	Sample Value	Table Name	Column Name	Data Type & Length
Empdata	empno	12345	employee	empno	smallint
Empdata	last_name	Jones	employee	surname	char(24)
Empdata	given_name	Shirley	employee	fname	char(24)
Empdata	name_called	Mrs Partridge	not mapped		
Jobdata	job_title	Band Leader	employee	title	varchar(255)

1 of 1 *   100%

From the figure, you can see the old fileset or table name, the field names, the data type, and a sample value as well as the corresponding table name, column name, datatype, and sample value in the new format. This flags any changes that may need to be made.

Migrating the Data

The biggest problem with moving data of this nature revolves around size. For smaller volumes, it can be relatively straightforward to use whatever tool is available on your legacy box to create a text file, use a communications utility such as `ftp` (file transfer protocol) to move it to the new box, and then use bulkcopy to add the data into the new tables.

For large volumes of data with questionable integrity, however, this may not be the fastest method overall. In some cases, you'll want to opt for reporting the data out, transferring it over, and bulkcopying it into straight character columns with no indexes, rules, or triggers. As you may already know, slow bulkcopy is a great deal slower than fast bulkcopy. To activate fast bulkcopy, you have to make sure that you have no indexes, triggers, or rules on the target table. Because this means that there will basically be no integrity checks on the data, you may not want to take this route.

Instead, it might be easiest to bulkcopy the data into temporary tables and then use an insert with a subselect to pull the data out of the temporary tables and populate the tables with indexes, triggers, and rules to enforce data integrity.

Another advantage to this approach is that you can create the holding tables in the exact format of the original fileset and then apply SQL logic to break the records up into a more normalized data structure.

You also can take advantage of this technique if you're running low on disk space. To create a clustered index, for example, requires an additional 150 percent space above and beyond the table to be indexed. If you have pulled the data across into an operating system text file, you then must allow space for essentially three copies of the data. This is not typically a problem for small files, but for databases with detailed transaction tables with millions of rows, it can easily become an issue.

If the clustered index already exists on the unpopulated target table, the additional space is not required to build the index, though the insert is necessarily a real pig for performance.

The main point here is that you need to check on the space you have available before performing your migration. Many Sybase sites don't necessarily have triple the disk space of the estimated databases available for working overhead.

Legacy Data Integrity

In many projects there is an implicit assumption that the data on the mainframe (or other legacy system) is correct, which is kind of funny when you think about it. Isn't the legacy system being replaced? And isn't that at least partially because the application code can't be trusted to post reliable results?

Even if the rationale for migrating is entirely economic, not architectural, what many projects discover is that when they compare data that has been processed through the new application with results of the legacy system, the results differ. You may not find that surprising. After all, software under development is not always reliable at first. What is surprising are the reasons frequently uncovered after a detailed investigation into the results from both systems: the legacy system is often in error.

This is not only a time-consuming process but also throws doubt on the validity of the new application, something that can be disastrous depending on the levels of user commitment to the project.

One of the ways to avoid this is to triangulate all results used to validate the new application with results from a manual process as well as those from the legacy system. This may sound like a lot of work, but you end up doing it anyway if the results from the two applications disagree, and it's safer to do it in advance so that you can be sure that you actually know the correct answer.

Another way to do this is to determine what the tests will be in advance and restrict your comparators to those things that you have an extremely high level of confidence in as correct from the old system. Many legacy applications work just fine but need to be replaced because of a lack of flexibility rather than errors or instability. You could opt for validating the results of new applications manually and skip the mainframe comparison process as unreliable anyway.

In any case, I think it's worthwhile to make the point that you can't always rely on the results from the old system. I have seen cases when this has come as a radical shock to user management, who had previously taken all answers from the system on faith. If you have a requirement to operate both systems in parallel, this can change management's commitment to running both systems concurrently. Usually, management increases the pressure to bring the new application online as quickly as possible.

Parallel Conversion

Perhaps from the foregoing you get the impression that I'm not fond of parallel conversions. Not so. I just think that people often overlook that running two major systems in parallel is at least twice the amount of work, and more if you consider the learning curve involved in moving users to a whole new computing environment.

Frequently, the extra financial resources required have not been budgeted or available, and there is an expectation that the existing resources will be able to keep things afloat while users make the move to the new system. Taking this approach can very seriously jeopardize the success of the new system.

On the other hand, it often isn't about money. If you look around your application environment, sometimes there just aren't people trained and ready to take on the role of operating either the old or the new systems other than the people in the area already.

This means that you have to very carefully plan the period of time you expect both systems to be operated. And the people expected to do this work must be more than just accepting of the amount of effort involved; they have to be inspired to carry the workload.

This applies to developers as well. Expecting people to develop new applications while supporting old ones about to be replaced is a very big requirement indeed.

To make this work, there are a number of things that need to be put in place.

Freeze Changes to the Legacy System

It never ceases to amaze me that projects can be planned and funded without any kind of review for common sense. Implementation is difficult enough without having to deal with two moving targets. Systems scope and design will change as implementation reveals the omissions and flaws in your understanding of the job to be done.

It's not necessary, however, to compound the problem by continuing to make changes to your legacy system and data at the same time.

It can be very seductive to the users to insist that you "just make this little immediate change" to the legacy system. After all, they are still dealing with it while you plan, design, and develop its replacement. But it's vital that you focus your efforts on the new system, and this will mean drawing a line in the sand and telling users and management, "That's it. No more changes to the new system."

Consider What It Means if You Don't Get This Commitment

First, it means that you will likely have to divert attention and resources away from development, documentation, and implementation in order to support something that is supposed to be discontinued. Second, it means that any changes to functionality or processing logic in the old system has to be synchronized with the matching module in the new system. Third, it indicates that your users are not entirely certain that the new system will actually be ready to replace the older system.

Implementing client/server systems can be like juggling while standing on one foot. If you don't make the rest of your environment as stable as possible, it's like adding a requirement to jump at the same time.

Freeze the Specifications

The biggest problem with the iterative development process is knowing when to stop. And, in truth, you never do actually stop, because you must capture deficiencies, bugs, and flaws and convert those into new requirements. But what you must do at the time of conversion is pause in the development process and put what you have to work.

In Chapter 6.3, "Release Management," I covered the need to identify enhancements as a future release. The time to insist on this is during the actual conversion from the old system to the new. For a period of weeks for small departmental systems to several months for large-scale systems, the applications must be implemented as specified.

One of the reasons for this is to provide a reasonably stable definition of what needs to be done. The main focus of implementation must be getting the new system to take hold in the environment, not continuing to discuss what the new system should do. One of the ways to support this focus is by freezing the specifications for the implementation period.

This is especially useful during a parallel conversion, where you must synchronize the functions provided by the old and new applications, validate the results, and make a decision to turn off the old system.

Cut-Over Conversions

In many cases, it won't make sense to attempt to run two applications in parallel. These conversions require a leap of faith at some point, when the users must review the new applications in development, test their results, and give the go-ahead for implementation.

At that point, you throw the virtual switch and all eyes are focused on how well the new system holds up to the demands of production. If you have done all of your volume, load, integration, and function testing, there should only be a moderate number of meltdowns. If you're using implementation as your testing ground, you should be prepared for all sorts of bad news and short weekends with long nights.

From the requirement to cut over, you should see exactly why the partnership with your users is vital. They are not going to the store to buy an application in the box. Instead, their role is really in codevelopment and certainly in support during implementation. If they are not confident that the system is robust enough to use, or don't believe that you are committed to doing what it takes to change it, they absolutely will avoid making that leap of faith.

The Pivotal Point

At some moment in time during every conversion there emerges a requirement for a system-supported function or data that cannot be met by the new system, and the users discover that they can no longer obtain the desired result from the old system. Usually, somebody freaks.

When considering implementation, you should have this moment, the pivotal point, uppermost in your mind. It's the challenge that must be met if you want your new system to actually take hold and become the new production system.

All the iterative development and new technology in the world won't help you if you can't get your users to say goodbye to the old ways, take up the new system, and walk. To help survive this baptism by fire, you need to develop a change process.

The Change Process

I have identified several major stages that must be addressed in order to successfully introduce radical change into an organization.

- **Notification:** The process by which people become aware that a change is intended
- **Internalization:** Occurs when people realize that the change will affect them
- **Valuation:** People's attitude toward the change, whether good, bad, or indifferent
- **Reaction:** Ranges from acceptance to rejection based on the valuation

These stages are all quite distinct, though they may happen over a long or short period of time. You can frequently predict the reaction you users will have to the implications of a new system based on the way the other stages have been handled.

When you're in the position of managing the introduction of a new system, and you must deal with the conversion issue, you should be very aware of your responsibilities as an agent of change.

I Use the Term *Radical Change* Advisedly

Client/server technology offers a great deal of flexibility and potential for individual empowerment. By themselves, these represent radical changes from the older ways of doing things.

As such, it's important to manage the change process in order to maximize the chances for success. After all, who wants to bust their chops working on a project that never gets implemented?

One of the ways to accomplish this is to develop a written (though frequently private) document that walks you through the change process and deals with each of the stages in terms of the practical steps you will take during each.

It's often best to do this prior to implementation when you're not in a position of being overwhelmed by details and can see the forest in its entirety.

To give you a better idea of what this change process document should encompass, I take you through the definition and implication of each of the change stages.

Notification

How people find out about change is as important as *when* they find out. Communiques from senior management indicating that there is a very serious commitment to moving to client/server is one technique frequently used. Another is to hold launch or kick-off meetings with the business unit members most likely to be affected by the change.

If you hold these meetings or send out such documents very early in the process, most people will shrug and wonder what it has to do with them. Frequently, people don't see the implications of change until the change is right in front of them. However, you need to be aware that they will try to understand how they will be affected as soon as they hear a change is in the works.

Issues such as reduced workforce need to be addressed. Is the intent to lay off half the workers in a department as a result of the move to client/server? Even if it's not, people will wonder about the hidden agendas unless such issues are specifically dealt with during the notification process.

The most effective tool to use with notification is repetition. Not only is it a great aid to memory, but people become more comfortable with the familiar. Change is necessarily unsettling, but if the fact that it's coming is reinforced over a long enough period, people tend to see it as inevitable. Surprise is generally a very bad way of notifying people of change if you expect them to accept it.

Internalization

Even if you try to spell out the implications of a change during the notification process, there will be some users (and management) who just don't take it to heart until later. Then, at some moment, they realize that this change is going to affect their daily lives.

It's not wise to expect people to focus on the good things that they will gain from the new system. You have to sell the benefits, as most people tend to discount good news and exaggerate the effects of bad news. This is how the notification process contributes. When someone actually internalizes a major change such as a move to client/server, some will ask others or review material to determine how well they understand the implications of the change. Concerns about staff reductions are common and some people will consider such upheaval an opportunity for advancement.

You need to ensure that everyone involved in making the change occur—all the developers, designers, managers, and user partners—have answers for concerns that emerge during the internalization process.

For most of the actual business unit staff who will ultimately accept or fight the new system, this internalization process only occurs during the conversion or migration to the new applications. In spite of all the notification, they just won't get it until it's right on top of them. Your change process document must give you concrete steps to take at this point to address the process of internalization. For example, you should:

- Ensure that all development team members understand the implications to the business unit
- Communicate criteria for changes in staffing or reassignment
- Prepare a short list of the main benefits to each individual involved in implementation
- Provide hands-on access to demo software
- Focus on techniques to support the implementation process—lunch-and-learn briefings, and so on

The main point to take away here is that it's not sufficient to communicate that changes will occur and then leave people to deal with how it will affect them. You want to be reinforcing the new system's benefits while the target group is grappling with the implications of the change. In this way, you bring your strongest case to bear at the most critical time in the conversion process.

Valuation

This is a separate and distinct process from internalization. First, people discover that a change will occur and then they work through how it will affect them. Once they have identified that, they will decide whether this is a good or a bad thing.

People can be quite funny. Sometimes, a change that should be unsettling is welcomed (usually by someone who is bored), or a change that should be seen only as beneficial is seen as a problem (usually be someone who prefers the status quo). Perhaps the most difficult part of this process is that it occurs hot on the heels of internalization and most people are not aware of it because it happens subconsciously.

As an agent of change, you're in a position to affect the valuation that the user group puts on changes represented by conversion to the new system. To do this, however, you must understand the nature, character, and background of the people who will be affected. It's often a mistake to assume that they will see things the same way you do. In fact, perhaps the best thing to do is to build on the understanding of the new system by your user champions. Because you are an agent of change, your opinion will be discounted and your motives suspect. People from the same line of work and background typically have more credibility. Let them help your users reach a positive valuation.

Reaction

This is, of course, the part of the change process that most directly affects the success of the new system. No one can really know the private motives of an individual—how a person sees something, or why—but you can definitely see the effects of their reactions.

What you want is for people to be comfortable with a coming change, to know that it's supported and that the organization has planned it carefully. You want the users to realize the potential in the new situation for them, to understand that there are rewards and opportunities. And you want them to desire these rewards more than they fear the loss of the status quo, because then they will have a positive reaction.

You should realize that, when implementing a new system, there is no benefit to be gained from a neutral user. Like blackjack, when the house wins on a draw, a neutral user will favor the old way of doing things. You need people who are positive, if not downright enthusiastic, about the benefits of moving to the new system.

Only then will the reaction contribute to the long hours and long-suffering patience that is usually associated with a migration to client/server technology.

Unique Challenges of Client/Server

Most people have experienced changes in systems at some point in their lives. Whether their organization migrated from manual to automated systems, or some employees changed organizations that had very different systems, most people have encountered this process in the past. They bring their memory of that situation to your particular project and that is part of their individual valuation process.

The unique thing about the move to Sybase and its related technologies is the openness of the architecture. The combination of front-end products, which is what most end users see as the system, with the power of the server and pervasiveness of communications networks, means that things are now possible that were never possible before.

That means that people must learn to work with the technology. Older systems froze during implementation and for the most part stayed frozen. With client/server tools, people can jump on the next bandwagon that comes along, complete with its object-oriented, user-friendly, seamless, transparent (fill in your adjectives of choice) features that never existed before. The implication of this architecture is that things never really stabilize, and that, my friends, is a very different situation from the one with which most people are familiar.

In his groundbreaking book *Future Shock*, Alvin Toffler describes the difference between static decisions and dynamic ones. When you move to a new neighborhood, you must decide the best route to get to work. This requires a higher level of attention and effort than choosing from the various options that you're used to from the old neighborhood. That requirement for attention translates into a kind of stress.

With client/server technology, people are constantly having to reevaluate the best way to approach a problem. They must learn how to view each problem that comes up as a new entity and bring a constantly shifting range of solutions to bear on it. This is inherently more stressful than surviving a change from one static set of procedures to another. Yet to fully gain the benefits of implementing a Sybase solution, you must change the way your business users see their supporting technology and what they can make it do. This may be empowering, but it's also stressful, and you will need to manage their internalization of this stress if you want them to see the change as valuable and react accordingly.

Summary

From this chapter you should have a clear definition of the cut over from the old systems to the new applications as the defining moment of the implementation process. Whether you are the systems architect or a developer working in the trenches, you must pay close attention to the way the process is managed at all levels.

Change is resisted by people generally, and no less so when moving users to client/server applications. I hope this chapter helped illuminate the issues that must be dealt with to ensure that your systems implementation goes as smoothly as possible.

In this chapter I have chosen to focus on the issues that I feel are most frequently overlooked and yet offer the greatest potential payback: data conversion, freezing systems changes, and the change process.

The most significant aspects of implementation are not actually technical. Most of those issues will have been addressed in the design of the application architecture. The human factors are the ones that cause most implementation efforts to fail.

I have read that most strategies fail in implementation. That is to say, you can have a great idea, timing can be on your side, you can have all the resources you need, and still somehow the benefits of the strategy fail to materialize. Moving to Sybase and related technologies is almost always part of a business strategy and always has tremendous implications at the Information Systems strategy level.

By paying close attention to the change process and managing the user perceptions during the critical period when the technology is handed off to the users, you can minimize the chances that they will ultimately reject your system.

This is what a successful implementation is all about.

6.3

Release Management

Introduction

The iterative model for software development provides you with an opportunity to incorporate a very short time frame between releases of new software. In this chapter you will see two basic approaches to managing releases. First, there are the techniques that you can use to release bug fixes or functional enhancements to your application users quickly. Second, there are the issues surrounding planning and managing major version releases.

To ensure that this discussion is relevant to working at your site, I also cover the features and functions of some related version management software that integrates with PowerBuilder, specifically PVCS. This will provide you with an idea of how such software might be incorporated into your development effort.

Also, I quickly cover some of the version management issues within Sybase. Database objects such as stored procedures and triggers must be managed like any other type of code, yet the automated check-in and compare features available in other programming languages are not provided with the product.

Release Management in a Side-by-Side Development

When you work very closely with your users in a small group setting, it's not all that difficult to manage the promotion of a new .EXE into production. Part of managing the release process is related to testing, of course. You wouldn't want to simply throw a new executable into the production environment without having some confidence that it will actually work without major bugs. At the same time, one of the advantages of developing departmental or workgroup applications in a small team setting is that the same degree of rigorous discipline on releases is not mandatory. You can walk around and tell everyone to log off the application for ten minutes while you copy over a new version of the application.

As you move toward more complex projects, however, the advantages of this technique vanish and the problems become more apparent. With larger teams of developers comes the requirement to avoid duplication of effort as well as a greater requirement to integrate software modules written by different people. This usually leads to some degree of incompatibility that must be resolved.

Before I move on to the techniques that you can use to manage releases of applications or development of multiple versions of modules, I would like to emphasize the importance of speed in deployment.

When you work side by side with your users, it means that they have a better understanding of some of the technical difficulties you face. It also gives you an opportunity to gain valuable insights into how the application can be made more useful. Many of the changes desired by users are not complex and don't require major rewrites. Instead of waiting to roll all these changes up into the mother of all releases, I recommend that you take every opportunity to make changes to your applications and roll them out.

This is especially important when you're at the beginning of your working relationship with the users. It's absolutely vital that they see you as being committed to timely delivery of an application that meets their requirements. The best way to do this is to constantly make improvements to the application based on user input, and reflect those changes immediately.

Don't put release management policies into effect that in any way impinge on this, or you may easily find yourself fighting a losing battle for the confidence of your users, all the while instituting professional and effective release management practices. You can be too right when it comes to controlling changes and versions. On the other hand, without some kind of version control, you can quickly find yourself in a swampy morass of bugs and incompatibilities.

Version Control and Release Mangement

Although PowerBuilder and Visual Basic may make creating GUI applications faster and easier, one of their limitations is in managing successive versions and various modules to make up a release. This area has been addressed, however, by several vendors who sell third-party products to make up for these deficiencies.

This kind of tool is vital when you are releasing your in-house application to a large number of users, or if the application must be constantly running.

In addition, a high degree of professional discipline is required to take full advantage of any object-oriented approach to software development. Without librarians and object custodians, its very difficult to stay on top of which objects are already created to perform services X, Y, or Z. To move your shop closer to being one that can move into the object-oriented development model, you should first get control over your existing software development efforts.

Although there are a number of products on the market that can help you achieve this, PowerBuilder 4.0 has integrated support for three such products: PVCS, LBMS, and ENDEVOR.

ENDEVOR

This product is offered by Legent Corp and was first developed to support automated control and administration of software assets for the HP 9000 in the 1980s. The company's focus has been on providing enterprise-wide systems management solutions.

The product offers automatic inventory, change, and configuration management as well as release management features for development and maintenance environments. The current or previous version of software can be retrieved from a compressed format, which minimizes storage requirements.

Who has made changes, when, and why they were made are captured automatically by ENDEVOR. The product provides merging and notification of any conflicts in source code.

The reporting capabilties allow you to monitor your inventory of software and work-in-progress. You also can allocate your developers into security classes to help manage access to source code and the capabilty to make changes.

LBMS

LBMS (Learmonth and Burchette Management Systems), based in Houston, TX, offers a number of CASE and version control applications that work in conjunction with PowerBuilder and Visual Basic. The SE/Open product for Visual Basic integrates VB 3.0 with the LBMS Systems Engineer 5.1 application development tool. This combination allows users to create, analyze, and design for either the client or server side of an application developed with VB.

In essence, the product turns Visual Basic into an development tool that can support multiple developers working on the same project.

As well as version control, the LBMS product provides database generation facilities and configuration management services by integrating the front-end development tool with its back-end object repository and CASE functions.

For example, the PowerBuilder link to LBMS is bidirectional between the System Engineers repository and PowerBuilder's extended attributes. The PB Library painter is linked to the LBMS Library Services Application, allowing you to maintain objects automatically within the repository and see them within PB. Also supported by the link is a reuse management feature, allowing developers to model and control their objects for reuse within other applications.

PVCS

Another major contender for the hearts and minds of PowerBuilder and Visual Basic developers (I am, of course, assuming that you would choose Sybase as the back end for these tools), is PVCS from Ingtersolv. The most recent release of PVCS for Visual Basic supports an interface for teams of up to 20 programmers.

The version of PVCS for PowerBuilder provides greatly extended check-in and check-out facilties for multiple developers.

What You Can Do

Obviously, my intent in this chapter is not to provide a complete review of these three products.

Each of the three (and their competitors) have powerful offerings with features sets that may be more or less desirable to you. Part of what I want to achieve here is give a quick introduction to how Sybase applications can be more oriented to enterprise development through the addition of third-party products. It's not my intent to recommend one product over another.

Because we have been using PVCS for version control on some projects, however, I thought it might be useful to walk you through some of the features to see in more detail the use that you can put version control products to.

The Procedure

The following paragraphs give you a high-level overview of what a version control process will let you do.

In PowerBuilder the version control process is managed through the library painter, which, as noted in the section on LBMS, allows you to transparently access the source through either PowerBuilder or the version control program. However, you choose which objects you wish to integrate by registering the objects after installing your version control software. Once the object has been registered, it must be checked out before it can be modified. This ensures that no one will attempt to modify the registered object at the same time. It's possible, though, to open an object that someone else has checked out, and you will be warned and will be unable to save any changes made over the top of the checked-out version.

The registration directory will give you a list of all objects that have been registered (as if you wouldn't have been able to figure that out from the name). By clicking one of the objects registered, you can see its modification history.

The version control software actually saves successive versions in case you need to view or rework something from a previously saved version. As you can imagine, the manual equivalent of this process involves a great degree of discipline and adherence to a naming convention. (What am I saying? Practically speaking, there is no manual equivalent to this service.)

You can review the registration directory to determine whether there is a new version of an object that you use in your library. To update your library to use the latest revision, you select the object from the list in the Library painter and issue the synchronize command from the source menu. PowerBuilder recompiles the objects in your library from the definitions in the repository of the version control system. In this way, you can include objects that are being continually worked on by other developers or other teams.

It's also possible to deregister objects from the version control system, but I think you can see that the idea is to be rather more than less inclusive in placing objects under version control.

What to Include

Up to this point, I have discussed integration of tools to allow developers to control the objects that make up the application modules on which they are working. I have not yet addressed the methods by which you determine what should be included in a particular version.

When you look at professional software development houses responsible for the development and sale of third-party, shrink-wrapped software, you can see a group of developers who are (or should be) driven by their market. They will have competitors who release products with new features, or their own development schedule will call for the inclusion of new features by certain dates. PowerSoft, for example, takes great pride in shipping a major release every year.

When you develop internal applications, the same pressure is not usually brought to bear. Although I have harped on the need for user involvement (as does everybody) and being responsive to user needs, at the same time I would like to take a moment out and deal with how you find out what needs to be included in your software product.

In Chapter 5.4, "Testing Your Application," I discussed testing, and you may remember that I stressed the importance of reacting to bugs and enhancement requests when and as the users find them. Of course, a certain amount of discretion must be used by the project management. A complete redesign of the product is unlikely to occur unless the business has changed enough to make your original design obsolete.

Realistically, though, implementation always uncovers areas for improvement. It's wise to incorporate these fixes and enhancements into versions that are tested for new bugs before releasing the revision to the users. The key is to encourage your users to provide this feedback.

One way to do this is to incorporate a change request form right into your application, and then integrate that with your electronic mail or fax procedures. By automating the process of identifying desired changes and funneling those through a prioritization process, such as the project leader, you can arrive at a list of changes to be made, some immediately and some to be included in a future release.

Application changes, combined with the new functionality that your users and management tell you that the business needs, should provide more than enough material for a major release.

Summary

The version control and release management facilities provided by third-party software are a mark of the maturation of the client/server tools market. As you develop your Sybase applications, you'll see practical problems that can be resolved by acquiring and implementing solutions based on these technologies and incorporating the associated discipline.

Ultimately, your testing procedures and user walk-throughs will identify features and functions that must be either fixed or incorporated into your application. As the size and scope of your development effort increases, it's difficult to succeed without the use of such tools.

From this chapter you should have a clear idea of where CASE tools, release management, and version control software fit into an overall toolset for your Sybase application development team. Of course, such tools are often expensive, at least when considered a nice-to-have as opposed to a must-have set of utilities. However, you should be careful to appraise the value of eliminated duplication of effort and the creation of higher-quality code, all of which comes from using these software development tools in conjunction with SQL Server and GUI development tools such as PowerBuilder and Visual Basic.

6.4

Troubleshooting Methodology

Introduction

The more experience you gain with client/server systems, the more problems you see with the technology. Or perhaps it's just that to gain experience you have to encounter technical difficulties. After all, if every installation went smoothly, client/server systems expertise would not be so valuable.

In this chapter I would like to share with you some of the worst-case scenarios I have experienced or seen personally. You could see this as an "all the better to prepare you" kind of chapter.

The value you should be able to take away from reading this will be found in the systematic approach to dealing with these problems.

Specifically, you'll see how to diagnose symptoms, isolate problems, determine what sources of assistance are available, and take advantage of outside expertise to solve the problems. Frequently, it's the old "Doctor, it hurts when I do this....So, don't do that" approach to alleviating trouble with the technology. Wherever possible, I have focused on providing a means of helping yourself.

You have already read that client/server is an immature toolset. Nowhere is this lack of standardization or breadth of experience felt more than in the technical support arena. After you read this chapter you should be able to apply specific recommendations for preparing for technical difficulties and troubleshooting them in as quick and painless a method as possible.

If You've Got Trouble...

There was a television commercial for a board game in the sixties that said, "If you've got trouble, wait, don't run. This kind of trouble is lots of fun." Well, when it comes to troubleshooting client/server systems, nothing could be further from the truth.

Let me be perfectly clear. Most strategies fail in implementation, and when you're working with client/server technology (this includes Sybase and PowerBuilder), you'll encounter situations when things just don't work as advertised. At the worst, this can threaten your entire applications migration strategy. At best, it's a frustrating learning experience.

It's all too easy to take this frustration out on the technical support people, or to have unrealistic expectations of outside consultants who parachute in to identify and fix your problem. In this chapter, I want to show you how to prepare for trouble and the preliminary steps that you can take to address it.

When it comes to technical support, you're always in the best position if you can solve the problem yourself.

Just the Facts

One of the first things that any technical support call will require from you is a clear, concise, and accurate review of your situation and environment. This is generally at odds with the cranky and frustrated feeling you'll experience when facing a problem that threatens you with a bad day at best and a new job opportunity at worst. Yet, without documentation of the problem, no one can help you.

I mention this first because this is where you usually end up breathing a sigh of relief that you took the time out to assemble your documentation before trouble occurred.

That's right, this is where putting together all user accounts, passwords, directory structures, file listings, customer contact numbers, site IDs, support agreements, configuration values, server maps, and backup histories into some sort of humanly readable format is absolutely vital. If your system is down, the last thing you want to have to do is hunt around for the Ghostbusters' number.

I hope that you get the catch-22 here. Virtually no one wants to invest the time and effort into documenting the system. Yet, without documentation, you're flying blind when the server is crashed and you're trying to get things back online. So, usually what happens is that you don't have it the first few times and after a while, you internalize that it really is self-defense, so you assemble the materials you're going to need. Later in this chapter, I give you a checklist of the most important things to have documented for dealing with Sybase and other technical support groups.

What's It Like?

Just to be sure that we're talking the same language, I'll share an example of a typical Sybase trouble call with you. In fact, I had this situation occur yesterday (as of this writing, my yesterday, not yours) and I feel that it's a tremendously representative experience. It will no doubt irritate my buddies at Sybase, but in this case I'm on your side, not theirs.

On Friday afternoon I was at a client site working with their Infrastructure and Database Administration group setting up a new server. We had just completed the process of installing SQL Server 10.01 and creating 30 gigabytes worth of databases. One of the analysts needed to run a script from a third-party vendor that installed another set of databases. He came to us to get a list of valid logical devices, and off he went. Within an hour he was back, complaining of an error message.

Apparently, he had restarted the job a couple of times and was getting a `no space left on log segment` message for the master database. No problem, thought I, and issued a dump trans master with `no_log` to clear some space. At that point, the system blew up.

Consulting the *Troubleshooting Guide*, I looked up the 605 error message, which basically said, "This could be serious, call tech support."

After restarting the SQL Server and duplicating the experience, I did just that.

Because I had a down server situation, I was called back within two hours. At that time, I was asked to fax through the error log indicating exactly what the server had been experiencing. By then, it was five o'clock Pacific Time and my tech support contact went home. My server was still down.

To be fair, I did get a call back to say that the problem had been handed off to the Background Group for a review of previous cases and that I would have to restore master from backup in order to clear the problem.

Because this server was a few days old, I didn't have many backups and the one that had successfully completed the night before turned out to be corrupted. No particular reason; just one of those things. Bad luck and worse timing.

After spending several hours with the server on the weekend, I ran buildmaster to recreate the master database, and loaded an earlier backup. At that point I had to run disk refit and reinit to capture the hours of work that it had taken to create the big databases, but by Monday morning, the server was back up and the client reran his scripts. At this point, the log full condition occurred again. This time, however, I had a good backup of master, so I managed to restore the database, and then altered it to provide more log space to allow the guy to get on with his job.

Monday afternoon I got a call from tech support in Emeryville. It turns out that on Sun and IBM, there is a known bug for System 10.01, which can cause databases with the log on the data device to get an unclearable log full condition. Syslogs loses its end of log marker and can't get it back. Because both master and sybsystemsprocs are databases with logs on the data device, when the situation occurs to these databases, you must reload from backups or rebuild the databases.

Rebuilding the master database is not a trivial undertaking. At the time of this writing, there was no fix available because Sybase had not been able to recreate the problem, although there had been other customer reports of the situation.

The Moral of the Story

So there you have it, the typical tech support nightmare. I don't think it's fair to blame Sybase in any way; my customer's tech support agreement was for Monday to Friday, and Sybase people did get back to me within the performance guidelines as well as confirming a course of action for me to take. They just didn't solve my problem for me. You'll find that this is frequently the case with any client/server technology. You're the one with the problem, and it's up to you to identify the cause and fix it.

You should also be able to see how vital the documentation becomes in a situation such as this. When the server is down, you don't have time to investigate such basics as the name of the device where the master database is located, or the exact allocations of every database on the system.

When it comes to getting a server back online, every minute you spend pulling together documentation is a minute longer that the server is unavailable. This might not be a problem for your users, but chances are, you'll feel some kind of pressure.

What You Need

There are several things that you should have as an absolute minimum for any Sybase application. These include:

- A printed listing of sysuages, sysdatabases, sysdevices, syslogins, sysservers, and sysconfigures. (The easiest way to do this is capture the output from `sp_configure`, `sp_helpdevice`, `sp_helpserver`, `sp_displaylogin`, and so on.)
- A recent disk dump of the master database. Any changes to the SQL Server that would involve a write to a systems table in master should result in a dump of the master database.
- Recent dumps of all user databases. There are always unrecoverable situations that require you to go back to the dump. It pays to have the dumps.
- A case book with all customer ID and tech support numbers, outstanding and closed problem cases, and descriptions of problems, plus a history of contact. Who called back and what did they say?

There are varying degrees of elegance to which these items can be implemented, but the key to success is just having and using them. The case book, for example, allows you to flip through and identify where a similar problem had occurred and review the steps that had been recommended then, without having to wait for a return call from tech support.

A lot of this is common sense, but it's the translation of the idea into a procedure that allows you to gain the benefit of it. These practices are usually found only in shops where lots of problems have occurred and they finally got organized concerning the tech support process.

Especially where your environment has been reliable, stable, and robust, you need to have recent backups. There is a tendency to put this kind of work off, but when you need them, wow, do you ever need them and you need them now. Don't wait until it's too late.

Complex Problems

With a down SQL Server, you pretty much know who to call first; technical support at Sybase. But, frequently, it turns out that the cause of the problem is not so easily identified. There can be any number of contributors to serious technical difficulty. The server hardware is a frequent culprit, as are OS bugs requiring patches. Or the network can lead to outages in the application, and even unreliable power in the computer room can be the cause of down time. These things obviously fall outside the purview of Sybase technical support to identify and fix.

This is where things get complicated. The whole point behind moving to an open architecture is to integrate third-party offerings into a cohesive system. But there's the rub. The only one motivated to have the expertise in all of your products is you. Complex systems lead to complicated problems, and there is no single 1-800 number to call for support unless you acquired a turn-key application from a Systems Integrator and you pay for that support. Most of you, though, are probably on your own.

Symptoms versus Causes

One of the trickiest aspects of client/server computing is determining the exact source of a problem. Hardware problems such as flaky power supplies or backplanes frequently manifest themselves as software glitches. Generally unrepeatable ones. This makes diagnosing the problem accurately one of the big challenges of troubleshooting a Sybase application.

A certain amount of voodoo is involved in understanding your application as a whole. You have to listen to the technology and let it lead you to the root cause of the problem. The most effective approach that you can take is to break the problem into constituent parts and use the process of elimination.

An Approach to Troubleshooting

One of the worst temptations when faced with a systems problem is to change a few things and see whether that helps. The usual outcome of this is to introduce even more problems into the situation, or worse, to break things that were working fine. Then you have to work backwards to determine what you did that caused the new problem.

The key to success is to follow a few basic rules:

■ **Review all recent changes.** When you're faced with new problems or undesired behavior in a client/server application, first establish what changed. Server upgrades, O/S patches, network loads, client card swaps, changes to system.inis, and DOS upgrades all can have unexpected effects. Don't assume that something is broken; instead, determine whether something incompatible was introduced with a recent change.

■ **Start at one end.** If someone complains about performance or the system is down, start there and work along the system to the other end. Can the workstation ping? Can it connect to other servers? Can neighboring workstations connect? Do they have the same problems? Is the server up? What is the load? By reviewing the components from the client back to server, you can usually pick up the information you need to zero in on the problem.

■ **Isolate the problem.** Once you track from one end of the client/server system chain to the other, focus on the area that seems likeliest. If all other workstations on the network can connect to your server without complaint, and Windows was upgraded on a workstation that is dropping connections, that's the place on which to focus your efforts.

- ■ **Repeat the problem.** If at all possible, get your users (and yourself) trained to shake off one-time behavior oddities. General Protection Faults in Windows, panics or time bombs in other environments are facts of life. Complicated systems are less than totally bulletproof. If a problem is repeatable, though, you have the basis for working out a solution.

- ■ **Use benchmarks.** Not all problems are as cut and dried as an inability to connect to the server. If someone complains about server performance or is waiting forever for result sets, it's very helpful to have a few tried-and-true statements to run for purposes of comparison. This also helps you isolate the problem.

- ■ **Take a different tack**. If you can't find the source of a problem, try using a different tool, workstation, database, or server. Swapping components in and out of the equation can help you isolate the problem and, by revising your approach, you can sometimes find that something you took as a given doesn't work quite right under all circumstances. There is more than one way to skin a cat.

A Case in Point

Let me give you a real-life example taken from the trenches of support in a client/server environment.

A developer came into the office where I was working and ask whether the server was up. Because I had been doing a number of administrative tasks such as dbcc operations on the databases all morning, I knew it was and told him so. The developer maintained that his workstation was taking upwards of 45 minutes to retrieve a result set that normally took a couple of minutes.

To prove that the server was working normally, I issued this set of statements:

```
select getdate(*)
go
select count(*) from big table
go
select getdate(*)
go
```

This counted the rows in a large unindexed table, which usually took around five to seven minutes to complete (as I said, it's a large table). In this particular case, it took eight minutes. The server seemed to be operating fine, if not like greased lightning.

At that point, the developer asked whether I could take a look at the behavior on his workstation. He sat down and issued a command and we chatted about the colors he had selected for his desktop. After fifteen minutes of hourglass, this process got kind of boring, so I conceded that there really was a problem. After going back to the system console and looking at the load,

I noticed that one of my colleagues was performing a dump of some of the big databases. It turned out that the nightly backups had not worked the night before.

At this point, you have to imagine three people standing around trying to figure out where the problem lies. A quick sample of the other developers indicated that yes, most people were noticing performance problems and the ones who didn't were using X Windows to get sessions right off the server. This led us to think that the server was all right, but something was choking the network and causing retries and time-outs. Again, after kicking around the potential culprits, we realized that the dump database command was writing across the network.

Our network guy was adamant that there was nothing wrong with the fiber ring and that 100MB was fast enough to handle the load, but we decided to experiment, because we didn't want to reboot the server (which is the commonly the first step whenever there's a problem <g>). We waited until the backup finished, then checked with the developer to try his query once more. This time it came back within five minutes. Not fast, but then again, not the better part of an hour.

Our network guy shrugged and ordered a sniffer to be put on the fiber ring so that we could take a look at just how much stuff was being moved around.

The interesting thing happened later that day when the server crashed and an error writing device message was found in the error log. Tempdb had filled up and the server had not taken it well. After rebooting the server, everyone we checked with indicated that performance was much better. Our developer with the query from Hades was reporting results in a minute or two. The combination of a full or close-to-full tempdb and the network utilization had driven performance to its knees. Of course a count(*) in isql operates directly on the server and is unaffected by network performance, and because it wasn't using tempdb, it returned values consistent with expectations. So, you can see a practical example of how problems in one area can point misleadingly to another aspect of the technology.

Successful troubleshooting is very much a case of sleuthing through the clues until you find the real culprit.

Just recently I had the opportunity to sit through a conference call with one of the Performance and Troubleshooting gurus at Sybase in Emeryville. I thought it was interesting to hear his questions as he tried to diagnose the problems we were experiencing at my client's site. Part of what was interesting about this is that we were convinced that we had uncovered a Sybase bug, whereas his first assumption to be eliminated was that we had made a configuration or process error.

Naturally, it was perfectly fair for him to eliminate the possibility that we had done something erroneous before admitting that there could be a problem in the SQL Server code itself. To accomplish this, he asked the following questions:

Q: What is the procedure or process that is bringing the system down?

A: A suite of queries run concurrently to arrive at some performance benchmarks before going live.

Q: Is the problem repeatable?

A: Absolutely. It happens every time we run the query suite.

Q: Have the queries been tuned?

A: Each query has been run successfully on its own and checked to ensure that the query uses an index and does not perform a table scan.

Q: Are the queries blocking each other?

A: The output of `sp_who` and `sp_lock` is showing that the queries are not waiting for another to complete (status is running or runnable, I/O and CPU is growing, and the BLK column in `sp_who` output shows which processes are blocking completion for any given SPID).

Q: What EBF (Emergency Bug Fix) are you at?

A: The most recent release of Sybase (at this time version 10.0.2) and EBF number 666. (You can find this info with select @@version.)

Q: Are there any error messages on the box itself?

A: We checked both the server console and in /VAR/ADM/MESSAGES for complaints. There were none.

Q: What OS patch levels do you have?

A: We checked with Sybase tech support and got the list of all OS patches required to run our SQL Server version. They are up to date.

Q: What has changed recently in your server environment?

A: We added some disk arrays in the past week, but everything worked fine up until yesterday when we ran the benchmark suite of queries.

Q: I wonder what could be causing the problem?

A: We were hoping you could tell us!

I included this transcript because it shows a pretty reasonable set of questions to expect to answer when you actually get on the phone with Sybase technical support. You also should use these questions as an internal guideline to satisfy yourself that you actually have a problem before registering a frustrated or angry support call. The more that you can help eliminate potential causes of problems, the more likely tech support is to take you seriously and help you solve the problem. (This is not to say that they don't take every single problem seriously, just that it helps if you can keep from phoning in basic problems. Chronic complainers get a bad reputation everywhere!)

Accessing Outside Resources

Beyond the help desks and support services provided by Sybase and other vendors, there are a few key methods of obtaining assistance when it comes to troubleshooting. First and foremost, you should focus on anything that you yourself can find that is relevant to your situation. Don't invest a lot of time waiting for a call back from tech support, for example, when there are things that you can do to identify solutions for yourself.

- ■ **CD-Based Databases**. Sybase and PowerBuilder now both provide not only documentation, but a tech support database published in CD-ROM format. If you have never worked with this kind of technology, give it a try. Sometimes the problem you have is known but buried in an avalanche of detail. CDs are great for sorting through the volume and looking for something that matches your situation.

- ■ **Search the Net.** Other users find applications-related problems and work out solutions more frequently than vendors. I use CompuServe navigator to follow threads on the technologies that I'm responsible for hands-on. Other colleagues use Archie or Gopher and access the Internet to search out information on particularly irksome problems.

- ■ **Hit the books.** As amazing as it sounds, sometimes the answer to your problem actually can be found in the documentation or is referred to in a third-party book (such as, say, this one!) or in a developer's journal. If you organize your library into more than a stack of things to read, it can come in handy when you've got to get to the bottom of something sticky.

- ■ **Call your friends.** Professional courtesy being what it is in our business, we sometimes just end up flailing on problems. The most effective troubleshooters I know have a little black book of numbers of people with similar backgrounds and they are not afraid to call up and compare notes.

These are just a few ideas for ways to bring outside expertise to bear on a particularly pesky problem.

Summary

Necessarily, any discussion about troubleshooting will be general. Without referring to specific symptoms and situations, it's impossible to get down to any level of detail and still be relevant. In this chapter I have tried to show the practical application of the approach with examples from real life. From these I hope you take away a sense of how problems are handled by others.

One of the most frustrating things about working with client/server technology is how problems creep in and out of the system, often without apparent rhyme or reason. It's important to recognize from the outset that this stuff isn't nailed down, and you can't expect it to behave with the maturity of a 20-year-old environment such as MVS. Perhaps in 15 years, but as of today, no.

I hope that you have acquired a sense that the best approach to troubleshooting is to keep an open mind and take an organized approach. Keep notes, do your homework, and above all, evaluate the effects of one change at a time. It's just too easy to fall into the habit of throwing a few software switches to see whether one of them takes, and then spending a whole lot of time trying to back out of the changes.

Good luck with your own troubleshooting challenges, and I hope this chapter helps you in your approach.

6.5

Physical Database Implementation

Introduction

At some point, you actually must create databases and objects to reside within them. This is as physical as data ever gets, and it's the lowest plane of the Integrated Task/Data Modeling methodology. In this chapter you get the grand tour of the plumbing when implementing a client/server application with Sybase.

I cover the strategies that you can use to identify the most appropriate allocation of data to resources, as well as recommend a method for documenting your physical model.

Typically, the database implementation is the province of a database or systems administrator. As a developer, you may be completely insulated from these activities; however, this chapter should help round out your understanding of the back end. This can come in handy when you're looking for ways to optimize application performance.

Bear in mind that, without an adequately configured and properly balanced server and database configuration, your client/server application is likely doomed. For those of you addressing the overall needs of a Sybase application, don't underestimate the impact of the physical database implementation. This chapter gives you a complete treatment of the issues and some practical tips for addressing them at your site.

Welcome to the Machine

The server is the machine to be reckoned with when it comes time to implement your data model. From your logical model developed as part of the middle plane of the the IT/DM process, you know what data you want to store, and the datatypes and length, as well as having identified the various keys and redundant data desired. In other words, you know what you want to store in the database. What you need to establish at this plane is where you're going to store it.

The configuration of a new server is infrequently a trivial task. If you are highly familiar with the hardware, operating system, networking, and user account services, as well as the various peripherals such as tape backups and printers, then you still have to take on the unique approach that Sybase takes to managing server resources.

On the other hand, if you're already experienced with the technology, in order to properly configure a Sybase server, you will need to learn something about the way the applications will access the databases. And this is where it gets interesting.

Competition for Resources

The key element to keep in mind when approaching the physical implementation of a SQL Server is that there are finite limits to the resources available. You may have a Goliath of servers, complete with mulitiple processors, vast RAID disk storage, reams of RAM, and a fiber-optic network with tremendous throughput. But chances are that the application architects have also determined that you will support a horde of users and serve multiple applications.

For any size of application, you must be aware of what processes share the resources of the server. This includes the operating system and any non-Sybase applications that might be hosted by the server. Most often, systems designers opt for a dedicated database server, though occasionally people decide to "maximize" their investment in the server by loading it up with applications. This only makes the physical implementation of the database more difficult, and application performance usually suffers.

The main point to bear in mind is that whoever is responsible for the physical implementation must be in a position to understand all of the elements of that server from the ground up. Otherwise, it's unlikely that your physical implementation will be stable, and reinstalling your server is a high-risk, low-payback proposition. Anything that can go wrong will twice, and when you finish the ardous process of reinstallation, people will ask why you just didn't do it that way to begin with.

The trick is to balance the competing applications to spread the utilization of resources across the server as a whole.

The Ground Up

Part of the physical database implementation is understanding how much RAM and disk resources are to be allocated to the database. As part of your logical model, you will have derived estimates of the column sizes and row counts. These are ganged up into broad guesstimates of the database sizes. Of course, you can grow databases by altering them at any time, but as I proceed through the implications of disk usage, you'll see why this should definitely be a planned process and not occur on the fly.

Before you can even begin to create the databases, you should have installed and configured your SQL Server. As you will no doubt know from your training and experience in the Sybase product, the SQL Server architecture is multithreaded and highly insulated from the rest of the operating system. Although this is less true of platforms such as Novell, it is most assuredly the case with UNIX servers, which still form the vast majority of Sybase server platforms. Because the UNIX environment is also the most difficult, I'll use it as the example for purposes of discussion of the physical database implementation.

In any case, SQL Server is allocated RAM resources, which it uses for its own kernel process and for data and procedure cache as well. The sizes of these cache are based on percentage values and are configurable. If your application will use a large number of stored procedures, you might change the size of the procedure cache. These values can be made effective quickly after monitoring actual performance, so I don't mean to imply that they are a big deal at this stage. I'm just saying that this is one set of resources of which to be aware.

For example, if your server is hosting X-Windows sessions, you should keep in mind that this requires memory on the server side as well as on the client, so allowing X-Windows clients to run off of the same server as the Sybase databases can create a real resource crunch.

The real competition for resources occurs at the disk and controller level. The nature of database servers is to be I/O constrained. That is, the slowest link in the chain is the physical reading and writing of data to and from the hard disks. As a result, this is the key area to be managed as part of the physical database implementation.

As part of the server implementation, there usually is a number of discrete hard disks that are operated by a few controllers. Depending on the number of requests to access files and the amount of data to be retrieved, some disks will be working and others idling. When a great deal of data is pulled from or written to drives managed by the same controller, the controller's buffers may get full, and the system has to wait until the changes are caught up before proceeding. Like a bucket brigade, the trick is to keep the flow smooth and the amounts manageable.

Allocating Disk Resources

I mentioned previously that you needed to know how big the databases would be in order to proceed with physical implementation. This is really true for raw partitions in the UNIX environment.

A raw disk partition is actually a formatted slice of a disk that the operating system does not have the right to access. Sybase prefers to manage the reading and writing of data directly rather than broker these changes through the operating system. The reason for this is that the operating system might hold the data in a buffer and, although the Sybase transaction has been completed, the dirty data pages have not been physically written to disk. In the unlikely event of a crash landing at that point, the data is gone and the database is out of sync. Not good.

To get around this, and because Sybase has done a good job of getting UNIX servers to write its data, SQL Server works best on raw partitions.

The operating system does not know about the existence of the Sybase partition except through the ownership, which must be changed to "sybase" from "root." In some operating systems (such as Solaris), the ownership still shows as root, even though it has been changed to the Sybase user. It's quite possible for someone to unwittingly allocate that slice to an operating system filesystem or to another application, thereby writing over the Sybase data held on it.

The key point here is that there are few tools to easily report on the coexistence of Sybase-owned raw partitons and UNIX filesystems. Typically, this is managed by a single person who makes changes very, very carefully, because no one wants to have to restore an entire server from backups just because they clobbered a disk partition.

Sybase and Disks

SQL Server can operate with either operating systems files or with raw partitions. In the workgroup server environments (OS/2, Windows NT, Novell) only the operating system's files are used, so these discussions are not germane. In the workgroup environments, however, it's quite possible for someone with supervisor authority to simply delete the database device and blow away the data contained within.

As I mentioned earlier, I want to focus on the raw partition approach, as this is where the physical implementation is the most difficult.

SQL Server performs a number of activities when it handles requests to read or write data. First there is the data itself, which must get written to the data pages. Then there is the log of changes that must be maintained for any updates, inserts, or deletes, in order to roll back the transaction if for some reason it cannot be completed intact. Last, there are indexes that are searched to speed the identification of matching data for selects.

If you put the log, indexes, and data all on the same disk, that means that for changed data the hard disk must do a pass first for the log (Sybase uses a write-ahead log technique), and then write the changes to the appropriate data pages. For selects where an index is used, the same applies: first, the disk heads must move all over the disk searching the index, and then they begin the process of seeking the data that satisfies the query.

Keep in mind that this physical process of moving disk heads from track to track is the slowest component in the entire transaction chain. Instead, you want to move the logs onto one disk, the non-clustered indexes off to another, and the data to be kept to its own disk slice.

What is true for a single database is compounded when you must allocate multiple databases across a set of disks. To balance the load and ensure that optimum performance is achieved, you must allocate the slices to noncompeting uses. This implies that you have some idea how the data will be used. For example, you might put a busy database on the same disk as another database's log segment, if that database is updated only at night or infrequently. Or, you might determine which will be the busiest tables and move them to their own dedicated disks. I cover such situations later in this chapter.

Sybase Disk Components

As mentioned previously, Sybase manages disk devices in its own way and with its own set of utilities and commands. This is great if you happen to work with Sybase across multiple servers (which I do), because you can apply the same commands and labels wherever you go. On the other hand, if you're already an expert on a particular environment, it can be a bit of a nuisance because the commands are completely different from UNIX, Novell, or any other operating systems environment.

First and foremost, you must declare logical disk devices to your SQL Server. The primary disk device is the master device and it holds the master database. Many first-time installations put a bunch of user databases on the master device, which is not the best thing to do in case you have to recover the device, among other reasons.

In any case, a disk partition (which I have been also calling a slice) can have one logical Sybase disk, in the same way that it can have one OS filesystem. You use the format utility to set the sizes of the partitions.

> **TIP**
>
> You must be careful to start raw partitons for Sybase on track one, not zero, because that is where the disk label is kept and Sybase would overwrite it, causing the disk to fail on the next hard boot.

When you create a database, you do so on the logical disk device. A Sybase logical disk device can be used to hold any number of databases until it is full.

Once you allocate a disk partition to Sybase as a disk device, however, it can't be used for anything else. For this reason, you need to work out the physical data model in advance because you must define the partitions and logical disk devices appropriately before creating any databases, let alone tables, indexes, and views.

Another key ingredient in the Sybase disk management process is the creation of segments. These segments are defined in addition to the disk devices and the databases, and they are used to move particular indexes or tables onto specified disk slices.

I said earlier that you could move your busiest tables off to their own designated disk, one that you knew was used only for, say, archival copies of operating system data and files. In other words, a little-used disk. In that case, you would first need to ensure that there was a raw disk partition available, create a logical disk device identifying it, create or (more likely) alter your database to include it, and then define a segment for that database pointing to that particular logical device (in reality, that particular hard disk).

When you create your table (or index), you would create the table on that segment. All the data for that database object would then be written to that particular disk.

If you don't use segments, SQL Server decides to allocate the database objects to the various devices any which way it wants. This usually means that it fills one device first and then allocates pages on the next device. You use segments to ensure the spread of database objects across all of the devices declared for a particular database.

Considerations

Before I get into the how to of the physical model's implementation, there are a few considerations to bear in mind. First, there is the issue of size. When you're working with very large databases, you find that it takes time to even create a database, let alone restore a database into it or load tables through bcp. When a database is created, the entire size of the database is taken over by SQL Server through an allocation process. Sybase initializes the entire database with extents consisting of eight 2K pages. If you like, it checks out all of the disk from top to bottom. This makes sense if you consider that a raw partition is just that, raw. This process is essentially formatting the disk to Sybase specifications.

It takes time, however. On the order of 500MB an hour. When you're dealing with databases of 10 or 20GB, this means a wait of 20 to 40 hours, and that's on a powerful multiprocessor machine with fast disks. (Actual performance may vary.)

The main point here is that you should create the databases at the size you really need and alter them to larger sizes as the need for space grows. You start to believe this when you invest your weekends in babysitting the creation of a bunch of large databases so that people can work with the data on Monday.

(Yes, there is an option in the create database statement <for load>, but then the database goes through the same process when it loads the database from the dump, so it's pay now or pay later.)

Another consideration is whether you'll want to mirror your disks with the Sybase mirror facility. This requires that you have double the space, obviously, but you'll also want to ensure that you move the mirrored disks off to a different disk and controller to isolate yourself from hardware failures.

For large tables that will be hit by many queries, the primary tool for speeding performance is to stripe the tables across multiple devices. For this reason, you might prefer to have six databases, each taking a sixth of six devices, rather than allocate one database per disk.

Last, you need to be aware of the location of multiple SQL Servers on the same server, even if you're not the administrator for that server. It's possible to select a disk partition in use by another SQL Server and accidentally appropriate it, causing a disaster for the other server. SQL Server will warn you that the disk slice is in use by another SQL Server if that database server is running, but if it happens to be down, you won't be warned. Sybase shows its UNIX background here and assumes that you know what you're doing, so off it goes without complaint, writing on top of the other server's database device.

Modeling the Physical Database Environment

At this point, you should have enough background to see why the various database and disk components must be mapped out. For smaller implementations, you could conceivably hold this information in your head. However, for a VLDB environment with 40 or more 2GB disks, each with 6 partitions, trust me, you need to have some pretty effective documentation or you'll waste a lot of time.

In fact, this modeling technique was developed while working in just such an environment. I found it useful then, and I hope it works for you as well.

The first step is to develop a worksheet that identifies all of the databases that will be required, their anticipated sizes, a map of the disks on the server, and the allocation of the OS filesystems. As the physical database modeler, you can then work through your assumptions about usage and access with someone more knowledgeable about the application. That person can help you understand which databases will be subject to nightly or periodic updates, which will be query only, and so on. If no one knows this kind of information because it's a new application, make sure that some performance review and tuning time is allocated as part of the project plan. You will definitely want to tweak (if not completely overhaul) the layout of the disks based on real experience, so you might as well plan for it.

The data to be captured should be represented as shown in Figure 6.5.1.

FIGURE 6.5.1.

Spreadsheet with partiton information partially completed.

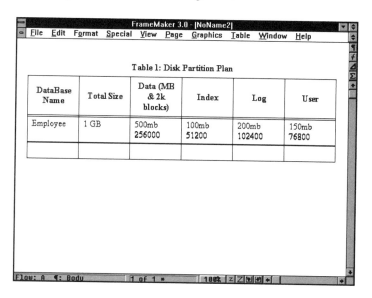

This tells you what you'll need to incorporate into the server's hard disks to accommodate the SQL Server.

You can see that all of the information you could possibly get about the database environment can be displayed here, though you won't know some of it until later. You have the physical device name, the database logical device name, and the databases that are to be created/altered onto that device with their allocated sizes. From your work with the logical data model, you'll have some idea about the approximate size of the tables that you would have worked up into disk space requirements during the capacity planning section of the middle plane of the IT/ DM methodology. If you are using some other methodology, I can't be sure when you would do this step, but obviously you have to at some point. So, I'll take it as a given that you know the sizes of the databases to be created.

To complete the worksheet, however, you'll need to know what disk resources you already have. To do this, you must take advantage of the techniques supported by your particular vendor's implementation of the operating system. Most recently, I have been working with SunOS5.x, so I will refer to the conventions used for Solaris.

Figure 6.5.2 demonstrates the partition information held by a Solaris server for a given disk.

FIGURE 6.5.2.

A printed partition map from a Solaris server.

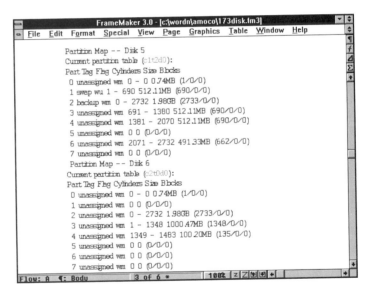

From this diagram you can see how the first track has been removed from the equation. In this case the disk has four usable partitions, three with 512MB and one with 492. The smaller partition may be used for OS file systems, for dumps or text files that will be loaded with bcp into a database.

In order for SQL Server to be able to use the disk partitions, a command that looks like [chown sybase /dev/rdsk/c1t1d0s1] will have to be issued by root, otherwise an error will come up when you try to create the logical disk.

From here, I will try to limit my remarks to what you do, and why, rather than the syntax for executing it, because I have no idea what server environment you'll be running, and you probably have access to the manuals if you don't already know.

At this point, you're ready to begin creating a model of your server before writing the scripts to implement it.

A graphic depiction of a large server environment might look something like that shown in Figure 6.5.3.

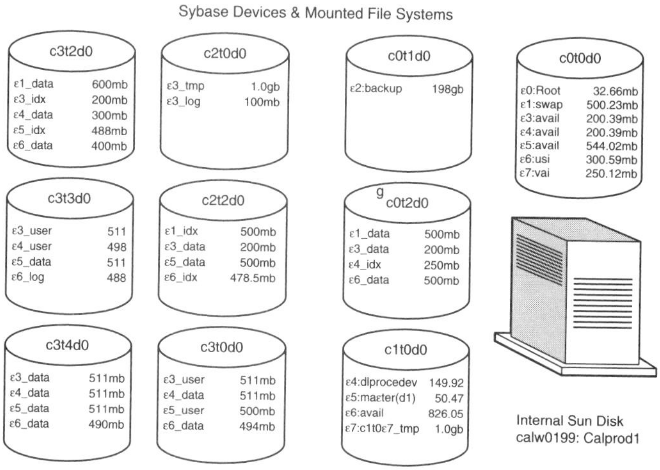

FIGURE 6.5.3.

An integrated model of UNIX and SQL Server database devices.

Sybase Devices & Mounted File Systems

c3t2d0	
ε1_data	600mb
ε3_idx	200mb
ε4_data	300mb
ε5_idx	488mb
ε6_data	400mb

c2t0d0	
ε3_tmp	1.0gb
ε3_log	100mb

c0t1d0	
ε2:backup	198gb

c0t0d0	
ε0:Root	32.66mb
ε1:swap	500.23mb
ε3:avail	200.39mb
ε4:avail	200.39mb
ε5:avail	544.02mb
ε6:usi	300.59mb
ε7:vai	250.12mb

c3t3d0	
ε3_user	511
ε4_user	498
ε5_data	511
ε6_log	488

c2t2d0	
ε1_idx	500mb
ε3_data	200mb
ε5_data	500mb
ε6_idx	478.5mb

g c0t2d0	
ε1_data	500mb
ε3_data	200mb
ε4_idx	250mb
ε6_data	500mb

c3t4d0	
ε3_data	511mb
ε4_data	511mb
ε5_data	511mb
ε6_data	490mb

c3t0d0	
ε3_user	511mb
ε4_data	511mb
ε5_user	500mb
ε6_data	494mb

c1t0d0	
ε4:dlprocedev	149.92
ε5:macter(d1)	50.47
ε6:avail	826.05
ε7:c1t0ε7_tmp	1.0gb

Internal Sun Disk
calw0199: Calprod1

You can see at a glance all of the disks and their allocations to both SQL Server and the operating system. You can see what is available and what it will compete with. If you have more than one SQL Server on the box, you easily can add a column to identify which SQL Server owns which logical database devices.

From the initial diagram, you can then pencil in the various allocations to specific databases as you determine the optimum balance across the entire server based on the way the applications access the resources.

Documenting the Model

One of the biggest problems with documenting systems is keeping the stuff up to date. Most of us hate to write (though some of us get paid to hate it) and put off doing it if at all possible. Yet there is a penalty to not having your design documentation current. When it comes to the physical data model, the penalty takes the form of wasted time and effort. Usually said effort is required when people are furious because the system is down and they want it back up immediately if not sooner. This is not the time to be researching the configuration of your box.

The key to keeping documentation current is to ensure that it's used on a daily basis. The best way to do that is to put it online and distribute it to a number of people. They will either nag you into it, or you can guilt yourself into keeping it up to date. Most people will not, however, do it just because it's a good idea and will save them time in the long run. Maybe you're different.

Anyway, the how to is what I want to address at this point. By taking your documented model after you have determined that you want to implement it, and running a help compiler against it, you can put your physical model online.

This is especially useful if you take the time to set up the hypertext links between pages. In this way you can navigate much more easily from a view of the server as a whole to a particular drive if you want to see the partition map or the details of a particular database. In most cases, it's difficult to predict exactly what you will want to know next when evaluating performance or resource allocation issues, and using this method really helps cut down the amount of time it takes to look things up.

Typically, you'll want to have reports that define the following:

- All databases with size and allocation
- All logical devices, sizes, vdevnos (Sybase virtual device number), and corresponding physical names
- All logical devices with space used and space free
- All segments and locations within each database
- All disks, partitions, sizes, and addresses
- All disks complete with allocations to OS and SQL Server logical devices

By allowing yourself to move among these reports quickly and easily, you are more likely to (a) create the documentation, (b) use the documentation that you have created, and (c) keep the documentation up to date. The larger the server environment and the number of servers in play, the more you need this kind of documentation to protect yourself, let alone make your operation more productive.

Naming Conventions

Like your application objects and the data itself, you should employ naming conventions and standards wherever possible. At one client site, I encountered a particularly effective naming convention for SQL Server logical disk devices that I would like to pass on to you here. The logical devices should point to the physical devices but have the intended database use appended to it. For example, a logical device on c1t1d0s1 to be used for logs would be named c1t1d0s1_log. If you expect to have multiple SQL Servers on the same physical server, you could incorporate a short form of the server in which which the logical device belongs directly into the name, for example FIN_c1t1d0s1_log, for the finance server.

Creators of databases who are not administrators will grumble at an apparently arcane method of naming disk devices; however, they must deal with the name only if they are allowed to create databases, which should be infrequently. The advantage of this convention is the ability to immediately know exactly where on the hardware the database has been located. This can be quite a benefit when you're looking at output from sp_helpdb!

Segments are specific to the database and are mapped to logical devices when they are created. Therefore, it's not as necessary to incorporate the hardware location into the name. Instead, try naming them according to their intended use; for example, index_segment, data_segment, image_segment, or big_bad_table_segment. This way, you insulate developers who have permission to create tables from the need to understand the underlying physical implementation while still providing the advantages of a properly laid out environment.

The Importance of Scripts

Some people use graphic tools to replace isql as a method of interacting with their SQL Server. And why not, considering that isql is generally ugly and there are more effective ways of viewing SQL Server database contents. You should avoid creating databases, segments, and logical disk devices interactively, however; first, because you lack a documented history of *exactly* what you entered, and second, because (and this will happen to you) you want to be able to quickly recreate the environment when you lose a disk and have to drop the database and reload from backups.

Scripts can be run directly against the server on the same machine; when a SQL Server is damaged or a network goes down along with the server, it can be awkward to connect PC clients for administration and recovery procedures. With isql scripts you are assured of being able to get the server resources recreated. Additionally, by putting `select getdate()` commands into your script and redirecting the output to a file, you can review exactly how long the creation (or re-creation) process took. This will help you estimate recovery times and work out appropriate backup and restore procedures.

Monitoring Tools

You'll want to schedule a time to review how well your estimates of performance and application usage actually panned out in reality, and make appropriate adjustments. Because SQL Server is essentially an environment unto itself, it can be difficult to get an accurate and complete assessment of how much work the server resources are doing and why.

The basic UNIX utilities, iostat, mpstat, and other facilities for monitoring disk performance (see administration manuals for your specific environment) will tell you at the highest level what the cpu and disk utilization is across your server. It will not, however, tell you which database objects are the most popular or which server is generating the work if you have more than one sharing the same physical devices.

There are tools that provide information for you to use. SQL Monitor is a utility sold by Sybase that provides detailed information about SQL Server's utilization of disk, memory, and CPU resources. SQL Spy, sold by Platinum Technology, which provides related feedback.

In any case, based on real experience, you'll want to make the determination in order to tune the performance of your application back on the server, where the greatest impact is usually felt.

Summary

In this chapter I covered the basic elements of a Sybase database environment at the physical level. You have been shown a method of depicting the physical environment at the planning, implementation, and support stages of the development effort. Also, I covered some of the considerations that you'll want to take into account if the responsibility for physical implementation falls to you.

Developers are not typically given root, supervisor, or systems administrator level of access. This is partially because of the interaction with the hardware. Most developers don't have a good grasp of hardware issues, in the same way that the typical administrator is not really comfortable with application design or writing GUI applications. I hope this chapter has given you at least an appreciation for the back-room portion of developing Sybase applications.

Some of the ideas recommended here are nice to haves, not must haves. That is, I recommend that everyone spend the time documenting his or her application's environment. And I must say that the people who do that are often the most organized and the fastest to respond. At the same time, I have to acknowledge that it's difficult to keep on top of such things in the fast-paced world of client/server.

At the very least, the concepts laid out here and the recommendations I have made should give you some ideas for the kinds of things you can do to document the infrastructure of your SQL Server project. Like most structural things, it's not the most glamorous work, but without it, everything falls apart.

By addressing the issues raised here, you should be able to avoid falling down, or if you do fall down, you should be able to get back on your feet quickly.

6.6

Implementing CausesDB

Introduction

Throughout Section 6, I've covered at length the kinds of flexibility required when actually implementing client/server systems. In this chapter I go into what kinds of compromises and changes in direction we took while implementing CausesDB.

Ultimately, when you're evaluating a systems project, even one as small as this, the question comes down to whether or not a workable product was created. When you fire up CausesDB, you can see the answer for yourself.

The approach I have taken in describing this application has been to comment on the actual experience of the team as we developed CausesDB. As I wrote this, the deadline for submitting the last part of the first draft of the book has passed. The application, on the other hand, is still in the final design stages. The deadline is looming closer. Talk about a representative systems application!

At the same time, it's not that we have not been doing any work on the project. In this chapter I cover the actual unfolding of the development effort and relate that to the points made earlier in this section.

CausesDB — The Users

Please don't get the idea that we just pushed back the development of this application to the last possible minute. In fact, during each phase of the development of the book, corresponding work was performed on preparing CausesDB. The only thing that got left to the last minute was the actual coding itself (which is not supposed to be a bad thing, as long as the additional time is spent on design, right?!).

One of the more interesting elements of this project was the reaction of the users we talked to about participation in the process.

First, we had a little difficulty identifying organizations that would actually qualify as charitable institutions. One of the initial reasons for picking the CausesDB application was to prove that information has its own momentum. As it turns out, there is no easy reference guide to worthy causes, and even creating a list of organizations to approach had to be done manually. One of the members of the development team went through the reference material that we could find, selected organizations that seemed to fit the bill, and mailed them an invitation to participate.

For those of you who are on the less idealistic side, you may be interested to know that a listing of tax-exempt associations (a category within which a "cause" is classified), includes a couple of associations for Ethnic Seeing Eye Dogs (who knew?), the OverAchievers Association, and (get this) the Anarchy Association.

By and large, most of the organizations that we approached were friendly, helpful, and interested in seeing what this new application could do for them. But not all of them.

Implementation Shock

There are two elements to the shock of implementation, especially as we experienced with CausesDB. For us, there was the shock of actually having to get this application built and shipped on time (publishers are less accepting of missed deadlines than any management committee I've ever seen <G>). But for the potential participants the shock revolved more around having to fit within a tight deadline for participation. Most charities are run, to a large extent, by volunteers. As you might expect, volunteers have other priorities and frequently this means that things get done when they get done and not when some arbitrary deadline has been imposed by an external agency (except the government).

Add to this the fact that we didn't receive our copy of PowerBuilder 4.0 until the general release of the product. The first thing we did was evaluate the product for Chapter 3.2, "PowerBuilder 4.0," and determine whether the product would stand up. Being a first release of a dramatically new version, this was hardly an automatic decision. But as you no doubt remember, the verdict was favorable.

The bottom line, however, was that with only four weeks to evaluate PowerBuilder 4.0 and organize our participants, there was not enough time to take the approach originally intended. If you remember from the concept and design of the application, we expected to be able to generate an online questionnaire for the participants and have them complete it.

Well, we worked with the "Betas," the group of people enthusiastic enough to want to work through each phase with us, and they had some good feedback about the questionnaire. A couple of organizations, however, took one look at the kind of information we wanted to report and indicated that they were no longer willing to participate.

More Than One Way to Skin a Cat

The withdrawal of any organization from this "experiment" really made me curious. The whole point of the project in the larger scheme was to create an application that can be distributed to multimedia PCs so that people with higher disposable incomes and systems talents could determine whether they wanted to support any given cause with time or money. How could any organization decide that they didn't want to get involved?

As it turns out, there were two reasons given. Some organizations simply didn't have time to fill out such a comprehensive questionnaire in the amount of time available. Others didn't want to report the detailed financial data that we had thought to request as part of the questionnaire. In not so many words, they really didn't want to go public with their finances.

That got us thinking. Maybe there was a better way to get the financial information without having the participants dredge up financial statements and spend hours completing a questionnaire.

I should point out that by the time we were considering this alternative we were also reaching the conclusion that we would have to develop the online questionnaire for data entry from faxed or mailed hard copy questionnaires. We just didn't have time to create an application in InfoMaker to ship to the participants. However, we knew that a data entry module was needed; we just developed it later and kept it in our offices. That still left us with the requirement to find another way to get detailed information more easily from the participants. So we called the Internal Revenue Service and Revenue Canada for help.

I'm from the IRS and I'm Here to Help You...

No doubt you have all heard jokes and horror stories about dealing with the tax people. Well, our experience with CausesDB was vastly different.

As it turns out, charitable organizations are tax-exempt associations (such as the Anarchy Association). Being tax exempt does not exempt them from a requirement to complete a tax return at the end of the year. In fact, there is a special tax return that must be completed for organizations of this nature. And this information is available to the public under the freedom of information legislation in both Canada and the U.S.

Although the information may be accessible, the tax people in both countries did not have to be as helpful as they were, and helpful they were indeed. Sue, our project coordinator, contacted representatives of both organizations in January to see whether they could be of assistance. Within days the answer came back that they most definitely could participate. All they needed was a listing of the tax-exempt organizations for whom we wanted last year's tax returns and they started sending batches of the returns right away.

We did notice that the IRS was a formidable organization to deal with. Certainly, the people were very helpful, but whereas the Canadian tax authorities were interested in the project itself and enthusiastic about participating, the IRS took a very structured position. First, they established that any private citizen (or organization such as ours) had the right to request and take copies of this data. Second, they reviewed our requirement with their public relations people to determine whether there would be potential problems with the use to which we intended to put the data. After this review, which was quite speedily performed, the IRS indicated that we could have the data within six weeks. This put us at the very end of the period that our publisher indicated that we could have the application and database finalized and ready to press onto CD for incorporation into this book. The timing was tight, but then, when is any Sybase application completed with time to spare?

Modeling the Data

Both organizations immediately provided us with blank copies of their questionnaires so that we could begin the process of modeling the data. John, our data modeling wizard, spent some of his free time while working on a project in Denver to break the form down into constituent data elements and model those with ERwin. The data model for CausesDB is shown in Figure 6.6.1.

FIGURE 6.6.1.
A high-level view of the CausesDB logical data model.

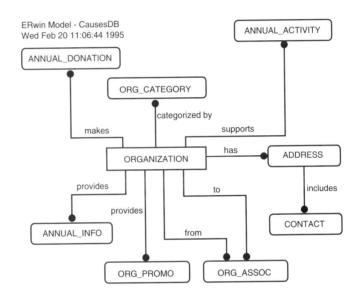

As you can see, the questions that are posed by the taxation people in both countries map quite easily to the data model. Apparently, both organizations are interested in the same sort of information that we defined as desirable at the conceptual stage of this project.

Revising the Questionnaire

Although the tax people could provide us with a great deal of financial data, there were still some major areas that we were interested in establishing that could only be provided by the charitable organizations themselves. Specifically, this was information relating the volunteers, contact data, advertisements, or promotional material, and last but certainly not least, what the organizations would do with increased funding. Remember, one of the key objectives of this project was to make it easier for these volunteer organizations to move their funding from public-provided donations to time and money contributed from private individuals supportive of the organizations' objectives. Even our team, with lots of experience in developing Sybase applications, had to stop from time to time and remind ourselves of exactly what we wanted to achieve here.

To accomplish this side of it, we revised the questionnaire to focus participating organizations on the data elements we still needed. Naturally, we took out a lot of the financial reporting and description of the target audience, because both of these were completely covered in the tax forms. We did emphasize the volunteer requirements and contact information along with the descriptions of unfunded programs. At the time of this writing, I still had no responses, so the completion rate will have to be determined from querying the database itself.

What's In It for Me?

A good question that you may very well be asking at this point. Of course, an equally important objective of the application was to provide an illustration of exactly how a Sybase application can be built. Also, it was always my intent to provide a variety of options for handling larger image files, such as .TIFFs, .BMPs, and MS video clips. This was the whole reason for the advertisement component of the application.

During implementation, however, we found that there was some confusion on the part of the participants as to how this would work.

One organization, the Canadian National Institute for the Blind, indicated that they wanted to develop a multimedia promotion component for their entry. Other organizations didn't indicate they had any appropriate materials at all. This left me wondering how we would meet our commitment to you as a reader. To address this requirement, we took a trip to the zoo.

Image Capture and Digitization

One of the more interesting aspects of the CausesDB application is the integration of image data. Because the local zoo in Calgary, where we have an office, is considered one of the best in the world, and because it's a charitable institution, I thought it might be of interest to show you some of the attractions.

To capture the images, our cameraman, Marsh Duncanson, used a Hi-8mm camcorder. (The company that makes these also makes our color photocopier, and because we're mad at those people at the moment, I am not going to mention their company's name.) In any case, the camera works fine.

To digitize the video into Microsoft Windows .AVI format, I used a VideoBlaster card from Creative Labs, the makers of SoundBlaster cards. This card provides the necessary hardware interface to hook up a VCR with RCA jacks to the computer.

The software I used to capture the video clips contained in CausesDB was Microsoft Video for Windows. This provides some basic capture and editing features that really provides all of the functionality I needed for the CausesDB application. You could consider this configuration the most basic multimedia production kit you can get. Certainly, I knew I wasn't going to knock you out with my videomaking talent with this application! In any event, the real objective was to show how the clips worked within a Sybase app, right?

Figure 6.6.2 shows one of the subjects captured within an .AVI file as part of CausesDB.

FIGURE 6.6.2.
A snapshot of the Video for Windows application.

By playing the tape through the camcorder directly connected to the VideoBlaster board, I was able to capture the segments that I wanted to include for your perusal as part of CausesDB. Perhaps you haven't looked through the application yet, but I have to say that my two favorites are the Siberian tigers and the baby gorilla. Check them out. I have to apologize for the torpid polar bear. As it turns out, he was on Prozac when we did the filming.

Data Entry

As it turned out, we didn't have enough hands to deal with the amount of data the tax people provided. So, we had to go outside and recruit a temporary data entry person. This was an excellent test of just how robust the data entry application actually was. After a reasonable amount of tweaking and coaching between the application and the data entry person, everything settled in nicely.

To make the best possible use of resources, and partially to provide a bit of rest from the drudgery of data entry, we convinced Stephanie (our data entry assistant) to act as the application tester for the CausesDB application.

Testing

The biggest thing we were looking for during the testing process was whether the modules actually worked together. To get the project finished in time to make the publisher's deadlines, we had to job out various modules to different people working all over North America.

Assembling and testing took place in Toronto under the watchful eye of Joe Unelli, one of our PowerBuilder project leaders.

Once we had what we thought was close to the final product, we sent copies to our Beta Test sites to let them have a go at the runtime version. Their review was rather more rushed than I would have liked, but at least we got a chance to incorporate their more modest changes before cutting the final executable and sending it off to Sams.

Migrating the Application

Just to make things interesting, we wanted to have a port of the PowerBuilder application to the Windows NT client platform. As covered in Chapter 3.2, one of the major features of this release of PowerBuilder is the capability to create executables for a number of different platforms. As soon as the Mac and Motif versions of PB4 executables are supported, I'll post the cross-compiled .EXEs to the PHCP forum on CompuServe. Check the databases topic for any relevant threads.

The other major challenge was translating the design specifications and the working prototype into a working application under Visual Basic. Rick Wattling worked some long hours under the gun to create the VB version of the CausesDB application.

The Contents

As part of the CD, we wanted not only to provide you with a working application and data to populate the necessary tables, but also to let you have a look at the actual code used to create the application. To that end, you will find the GRANDPA.PBL and CAUSES.PBL on the disk. Also, you'll find a Visual Basic executable that demonstrates how the design documentation could be translated into an identical application using a completely different front-end tool.

Summary

The CausesDB application was built using the design and development techniques described in this book. If you like the application, this in some small measure proves that the methodology works. By reading this chapter, you should have a solid sense of exactly how we built the CausesDB application.

Like most Sybase development projects, things did not go according to plan and we definitely had to keep to the schedule. The participation of the tax authorities was an unexpected but very welcome opportunity of which we took grateful advantage. You should think of this as a reasonable example of just how quickly the situation can change in your own organization. Sometimes you just have to take a different path.

7

Client/Server Applications Development Support

Introduction to the Section

When it comes to client/server, support comes in two flavors. First, there is support for the applications development process; second, there is support for the application. In the chapters in the implementation section, I briefly referred to a number of technical support techniques and issues that revolved around the applications development process.

In this section you will be taken through the start up and continuing support requirements to ensure that not only can you successfully develop and implement a Sybase application, but that it continues to provide value to your organization.

From the discussion about online help, as well as the ways to approach user training, you'll get an overview of the kinds of issues that must be explicitly handled during the application support phase. On the other side, I also cover systems administration issues to ensure that you have sufficient and appropriate backups to restore applications that get blown away in development. Other items covered in this section include how to organize your application development effort into one capable of taking advantage of object-oriented development techniques, and practical tips for supporting applications across multiple platforms.

You should find that this entire section was written with a view to getting a leg up on the support process. Maintenance and enhancements ate more than 80 percent of the lifecycle resources during traditional mainframe development efforts. By incorporating object-oriented techniques, focusing on polymorphism and reusability, you will realize significantly greater flexibility in your systems and cut down on the costs of supporting applications.

7.1

Help!

Introduction

It seems that application users fall into two main categories: people who use online help and people who read manuals. Of course, whenever a problem is sticky enough and the push to solve the problem sufficiently hard, most people will use whatever methods are available to them to get an answer to a technical question.

At the same time, look around your shop. When a quick reference point comes up—say, the exact syntax for a little-used command—does your group reach for the manual or browse the help? Teaching people to use online help effectively should be one of the specific deliverables of your change process. Give them the tools to resolve difficulties on their own, without having to involve another person, and you will make them much more productive.

In this chapter you are taken through the role of online context-sensitive help screens and techniques for developing these subsystems, as well as getting your users to take advantage of them effectively.

Also, I address the issues that surround the creation and operation of a telephone support desk, which may involve the part-time efforts of a single resource, or a team of people logging and tracking myriad problems. Anyone who has called a vendor for technical support knows that there are good help lines and there are bad ones.

If your application development plan has not identified exactly how you propose to help your users, then this chapter should give you a few ideas. On the other hand, if you're in the implementation process, you should be able to take away from this chapter a few tips and techniques for rolling assistance out along with the requirement to change.

RTFM...

At one point in Section 6, I referred to the need to create and maintain documentation. And I hope that my impassioned plea was not treated with the typically curt dismissal that stating the obvious usually receives. Look, I know that everybody acknowledges that you have to have documentation—that's not what I'm talking about. What I am trying to get across here is that it's not enough to plan it, it's not enough to talk about it; you actually have to apply the same discipline to doing it that you would to fixing bugs. No, it's not fun, but it's got to be done. And no one should have to nag you to document your code, or your application, or whatever your particular deliverable happens to be; you should do it as a matter of professional discipline.

The other reason for doing it is more practical and a great deal more self serving. By creating documentation, you give away responsibility for coming up with an answer, thereby reducing the support you must provide for your work.

I was once in a meeting with a hard-boiled veteran of the information systems wars when we were interrupted by a developer who had a question about one of the old programs. The old timer snapped at the developer to "RTFM" and shooed her out of the office. When I asked what RTFM stood for, I was told, "Read the Freakin' Manual." Apparently, this expression has been around for years. He went on to explain that the reason he had written the manual was so that he wouldn't have to remember some obscure application years after he developed it.

So, there you have it. The reasons for creating detailed and appropriate documentation range from the somewhat idealistic position of professionalism and pride in your work to a more cynical and jaded method of ensuring that you can continue to work for a company without your old applications coming back to haunt you.

Automatic Documentation

The reasons for bringing up the documentation process is that this usually serves as the basis for invoking a help engine to create online help. You can generate hypertext links and provide online access to your help document, but that presupposes that some kind of document actually exists. You have to write the thing first.

So, let's assume that you've been well behaved and written all your documentation as you go. As I mentioned in the implementation section, I believe that the best place to start with online help is during the development process itself, when you collect the design and development docs and turn those into online applications that developers can browse.

As a quick aside, if you're interested in how practical this approach can be, you should research what the people at the large aircraft manufacturing facilities are doing. Engineers who work on developing commercial aircraft must refer to literally hundreds of thousands of documents as part of their continuing work. To expect this to be done manually is just not practical, so some of these firms have implemented highly organized technical writing and specification publishing applications that coordinate the creation of engineering drawings and technical specifications, and provide online access to them.

Because this has been proven to work for very large projects for which the costs of mistakes are high, doesn't it make sense to do it for a smaller project for which the costs of failure are particularly high for you?

Okay, so you're convinced. And you have written your documentation. The next step is to create an online document out of it. To do this, you can use several products, as described in the following paragraphs.

Windows Third-Party Help Generators

Virtually all of the Sybase applications I've seen with any kind of application-specific online help have created the help file with a third-party generator.

Although there may be other ways to do this, such as crafting the document in hypertext yourself, I'm not convinced that this is the best investment of your time.

To identify some of the options and features available in the third-party help world, I've put together a review of the most commonly used third-party products.

WinHelp Toolset

Produced by BlueSky Software, the WinHelp Toolset is designed to allow you to create Windows-based multimedia documents including animation, video, and sound. The toolset works with a help generator such as Robohelp (a product produced by BlueSky) or any of its competitors.

The product allows inclusion of .AVIs, .BMPs, and .WAV sounds directly inside a .HLP document. Animation is achieved by playing a sequence of BMPs.

Distribution of the multimedia documents is achieved by including two .DLLs if required. A Video for Windows runtime is also provided, along with utilities such as WinHelp Hi-Rez, WinHelp Finder, and WinHelp Suitcase. The Hi-Rez utility allows the display of 256-color bitmaps, which allows much better help screens than the maximum 16-color bitmaps supported by WinHelp. Finder shows an outline view of the help document allowing speedy navigation, and the suitcase utility eases distribution of sample files as part of the .HLP document.

RoboHelp

Also from BlueSky, this help generator takes .RTF files or Word documents and creates .HLP files that can be handled by the Windows help generator. Version 2.6 of RoboHelp can automatically convert files bidirectionally, creating an editable document from existing help files. The features of the product include quick creation of standard help features such as pop-up windows, topics, and hypertext jumps from one subject to another.

Doc-to-Help

WexTech Systems provides another well-known Windows Help generator, Doc-to-Help. Like RoboHelp, the main function of Doc-to-Help is to generate .HLP files from word processing documents, complete with readily identifiable section headings and subheadings, keywords, and hypertext links between related topics.

HyperPerformance Tools, a .DLL that ships with Doc-to-Help, works with macros to support the seamless inclusion of 256-color bitmaps, background graphics, support for .WAV files, and playback of .AVI videos from within help.

Help in Real Life

I wanted to give you the benefit of one of my team's recent experience with help compilers—including the dark side. As part of the *Sybase Developer's Guide* book, I included an administration utility called DBA@Win. In response to reader feedback,we recently upgraded the package and put it up on the Sybase forum under SA/SQL Server tools. One of the enhancements included a much more comprehensive help facility, including detailed syntax and examples for stored procedures. In all, the help document comprises some 130 pages.

To truly support navigation through a document of that size, it was imperative that we work through an extensive heading, subheading, and referencing strategy. Once completed, we compiled the help, which was a bit problematic because the help would not compile until we tried it on a machine with more than 16MB of RAM.

On review of the successfully compiled document, we noticed that a necessary editorial change had not been made. After updating the reference, we compiled the help again, which completed without errors or complaints.

It would have been nice if it had complained, however. As it turns out, it's very difficult to directly edit a compiled help document without ensuring that you also update all of the subheadings that reference that change. Even though the help package digested our document (we were using Doc-to-Help), when we tried to actually use the help we started seeing messages such as See: Reference not found. After a while, the help document completely melted down, causing GPFs and ultimately making the document incomprehensible.

We had to go back to our backup document, make the reference change there, and recompile the document. The moral of this particular story is that like any compiled application, help must be tested as well. And you may have to go back to your original Word or .RTF document, so be sure to make backups!

Summary

From this chapter you should begin to see the very real payback from including multimedia as part of your online help. As I mentioned, help should be encouraged as a point of first reference, to reduce support requirements, downtime, and the costs of misused applications.

By taking the concept of online help one step further, you can easily distribute the application specifications, data dictionaries, and development standards for your shop.

Let's face it, most of us got into the systems business because we got to play with neat toys. Instead of being drudgery, the move to multimedia provides the potential for jazzing up your documentation and support reference material in a way that makes it much more likely to be maintained and used.

The real benefit is to the business because support and maintenance costs drop, whereas coordination between developers and users improves.

I hope that from this chapter you can begin to see that sometimes the biggest benefit of these new technologies is the elimination of some of the traditionally boring aspects of working with data, such as writing extensive online help.

7.2

Systems Administration

Introduction

In any project, whether a startup or one in progress, there is a requirement for infrastructure and systems administration support. Developers don't like to have to spend time fiddling with printers, network connections, and modems. Even if you do enjoy this activity, you have to ask whether it's a good use of time.

To assure yourself of a successful Sybase application, you need to establish a comprehensive set of guidelines and procedures for the administration of your system. This chapter will provide you with a review of exactly what this consists of, as well as making recommendations that you may find suitable for your site.

In this chapter you will be exposed to backup and restoration issues, security and database access considerations, the implications of multiserver sites, and requirements for server redundancy. Also, I address disk space and log full procedures along with the never ending problem of coordinating upgrades. All of these issues typically fall outside the developer's bailiwick while causing all sorts of difficulties if things aren't quite right.

After reading this chapter you should be in a much better position to set specific accountabilities if you are responsible for project leadership, and to identify what you require if your job is straightforward application development.

The DBA

I usually think of the DBA as the person who has the keys to the car. This is the individual who has the root or supervisor authority on the server, is the sa when he or she logs in to SQL Server, and most important, cares about how the applications are interacting with the hardware and the network. Most frequently, this is the capacity in which I work when developing Sybase applications for our company or clients.

You can expect, then, that I have a certain sympathy for administrators who typically have a definite antipathy towards developers. At the same time, like any customer, developers who rely on administrators to provide service have rights (though the developers I've worked with were definitely not always right!).

In any case, these administrative tasks and responsibilities fall to someone who has to do more than just build an application. This person is accountable for up time, performance monitoring and tuning, backup and restoration of files, and databases and objects, as well as creating and managing user accounts and countless peripheral devices and interconnections. The administrator is the keeper of the machine.

Because you as a developer rely on the machine to do your work, you need to be able to express your requirements clearly and ensure that your application is getting the resources and support that it (no doubt you would say richly) deserves.

This chapter is going to help you get just that.

The Top Ten Services

At the client sites where I have worked, the following are the most frequently requested and valued services provided by the infrastructure or administration groups.

1. Sybase Tech Support - Most support programs funnel all calls for tech support through one or two names. Although you can all call 1-800-8SYBASE and pretend to be the same guy, typically it works better if there is someone who tracks all calls and knows what already has been fixed or resolved.

2. Allocating Disk Space - As you should know, because SQL Server most frequently uses raw partitions, it's possible to get thoroughly confused about what goes where and accidentally add a logical device that clobbers a file system (or vice versa). Whether people need increased work space for tempdb or bigger databases, usually this is a job for...Super DBA.

3. Restoring Databases - Especially in development, being able to restore database objects is a critical administration support facility. Everyone on the team should know who is familiar with these procedures.

4. Backing Up Databases - If you want to be able to restore the stuff, you better have made a recent backup.

5. Killing SPIDs - Sometimes your own processes need killin', and sometimes just for the fun of it you request that someone else's Sybase process be killed. To avoid anarchy, this should be handled by one person (or a very small group).

6. Performance Diagnosis - On occasion, your query will go away and stay away. Your administrator might have some opinions about server load, or how it uses indexes. This kind of analysis and feedback is a critical component of an administrator's duties.

7. Performance Tuning - Where a particular database is heavily hit or transactions are blocked, the dba may opt to create a redundant database, or, more frequently, the busiest tables are striped across disks through segments.

8. User Account Maintenance - Adding logins and users to databases, managing groups, and allocating permissions for object access is a core set of tasks typically managed by the administrator.

9. Installing and Configuring Servers - Including upgrades, EBFs, and patches, as well as tweaking the configuration values for a server, an administrator spends a lot of time with his or her head under the hood of the server itself.

10. Performing Integrity Checks - Using the DBCC commands, an administrator can find out whether a database has cross-linked pages and can fix any problems with the database. The most frequently used (read only) dbrepair command to fix a corrupted database is DROPDB, so for the part where the database gets fixed, see number 3.

In this chapter you'll have a look at specifically what is involved with each of these major responsibilities.

Sybase Technical Support

As any administrator can tell you, there are a finite number of solutions to Sybase application hiccups and an infinite number of problems. The number of solutions known by any given administrator is a subset of what the tech support people at Sybase could tell him or her. Whether operating in the role of internal tech support guru, or just being someone to coordinate the trouble call, a systems administrator should be appointed to note any repetitious or weird problems and get on the horn to Sybase technical support.

The kinds of things you should have before you call have already been addressed in Chapter 6.5, "Physical Database Implementation," as part of the troubleshooting methodology. At this point, all I want to register is the need to have someone in a position to speak knowledgeably about the server configuration and applications development environment. Typically, this person is your DBA.

Allocating Disk Space

The hunger for resources is not abated by ever-increasing hard disk sizes. As is true in the PC world, any SQL Server administrator will tell you that databases grow to fill the disk space available. There is no such thing as too much disk space.

At the same time, life is a competition for resources and, as is proven in our sample application, there are a great many worthy causes and only so much time, money, and disk space to go around. Someone needs to be in the unenviable position of determining who gets what. Most often, that is a management process by which two goats butt heads until one of them gives up, but the administrator is the individual who has to physically allocate the space according to the priority *du jour*.

The physical modeling process covered in Chapter 5.6, "Balancing the Workload," will allow you as an administrator to determine what's where and what's available.

One of the more frequent activities is either altering log space because it has proven insufficient or dumping the transaction log and restarting the Sybase process that filled it. This process has changed a great deal in Sybase System 10 with the introduction of a last-chance threshold for each database. More on that with the killing SPIDs commentary.

Restoring Databases

In production, systems people take it pretty seriously when you have to fall back on the restoration of a database from a database dump. Most often this is true because it means that a certain amount of work has been lost. However, in a development environment, this is the Sybase applications equivalent to an Undo button.

Databases can take quite a while to restore, depending on the size of your database and the speed of your server along with the medium from which you're performing the restore. As you can probably appreciate, if someone has to go back to tape to find a good dump to reload, not only is the entire process going to take more time, but it requires more operator intervention as well.

Certainly, bigger sites with tape jukeboxes and third-party backup utilities can expect to have this process pretty well organized. However, not everyone can afford the price of these toys regardless of how desirable.

Object-level restoration is not supported by Sybase, nor is restoration across server versions or types. This makes life very awkward for multiserver, multivendor, and multiversion sites. Later in this chapter I cover some of the features available with third-party backup products that augment Sybase native features.

A quick note here to reinforce the idea that restoring the master database is a drag. You want to have a recent dump on disk of your master database whenever you have made any changes to the systems tables. This includes any addition of logical devices, databases, systems procedures, as well as alteration of any databases, and so on. Obsessing about dumping the master database may seem like a nuisance, but it will save the day (and if you never need it, how can you complain?).

Backing Up Databases

This is the meat and potatoes of any administrator's life (and with all that work on his or her plate...). In any case, backups are integral to any environment and they need to be assigned, scheduled, and tested. Just as important, you need to have all of the procedures documented, and the skills necessary to complete the backups, as well as restoring databases from backup, should be invested in several individuals, just in case. Backup backup, as it were.

Depending on the size of your database and the amount of work it has to handle each day, you'll want to set up an appropriate backup strategy. Although backups in System 10 are much faster than they were, and you can stripe up to three backups concurrently, there is still a performance hit on the database being backed up. The best solution is still to schedule your backup in off hours, if possible.

That leaves transaction dumps. Of course, your administrator (or you, if you are the administrator) will need to carefully balance the amount of time the system can be down while a restoration is taking place. If you have to restore from backup, then you're limited to the amount of time required to reload the entire database. However, if your database dumps are infrequent, then you will also have to add the time it takes to replay the transaction logs that were dumped subsequent to the full database dump. Remember that a transaction log replays the transactions, meaning that it makes changes to the data in the order in which they were logged, whereas the full backup loads a binary image of what the database looked like at dump time.

I find that most people complain about performance when a dump is performed but they scream bloody blue murder while the system is reloading a database, even if the need for it is their fault. Most of the time they will try to find a way to blame you if the data is not one hundred percent recoverable. I would therefore err on the side of having frequent full backups, whether nabbed at noon or midnight. What works for you may be different.

Killing SPIDs

This is a favorite pastime of Sybase DBAs, young and old. For various reasons, a Sybase process may hang or just be blocking another process through acquired locks and look as if it should simply be eliminated. In Sybase versions prior to System 10, it was possible to issue a kill command, but if the process was sleeping (another symptom of it being hung), then the SQL Server would wait for it to wake up before killing it. Although that may be very gentlemanly, it certainly wasn't very effective, as it usually required a bounce (reboot) of the SQL Server to clear the SPID. System 10 is not subject to the same compunctions as its earlier brethren; it just kills the SPID and gets on with its work.

There is a related phenomenon that affects developers, though there is little you can do about it without having sa permission.

When a database transaction log reaches its last-chance threshold, it will suspend activity in that database until appropriate action is taken. In earlier versions this would have included rebooting the server, or dumping the transaction log with no_log (much more civilized), but in System 10 this alone will not get you back in business. You have to unsuspend the database.

This is done by issuing an lct_admin command. Specifically, you must enter:

```
select lct_admin ("unsuspend", 20) where 20 is the database id.
```

I include this here only because I think it's important to get a sense of what kind of support you will need from an administrator when it comes to developing or maintaining a production Sybase application.

Performance Diagnosis

Once your application starts to show its value by actually functioning, usually the first thing everyone wants is to make it faster. This is a key contribution to be made by the infrastructure or administration team, because performance problem diagnosis and tuning is generally looked after by this group.

In any client/server application there are three areas in which bottlenecks could occur: server side, client side, or in the network.

The biggest payback is usually generated by evaluating and tuning the server, though in some cases the bottleneck will be in how the application has been written or the length of time it takes to propagate the result set through the communications channel.

Sybase has a utility called RUNGEN, which can be used to generate a workload that simulates server activity. By issuing T-SQL commands in a continuous stream, RUNGEN allows you to fake a fully loaded server that can then be measured for performance. As you identify the areas where bottlenecks are occurring, you can rerun the suite of SQL statements to determine statistically whether improvements have been realized.

Of course, this implies that you have some means of monitoring SQL Server performance. There are some statistics that can be acquired using systems procedures, but to really get an idea of how hard your server is working, you will need something like SQL Monitor.

This product is sold separately by Sybase, which is about as annoying as having to pay for your gauges separately when you buy a car. There are third-party products as well, but SQL Monitor is the most frequently used.

Whereas operating system utilities will tell you what disks are being used and the percentage of utilization of CPU resources for the system as a whole, SQL Monitor is SQL Server specific. It tells you exactly what your Sybase database is doing as the jobs are being run. This is highly useful because it allows you to identify such things as whether your particular SQL jobs are CPU constrained or I/O bound. If the process is waiting for disk resources to complete, SQL Monitor will indicate what percentage of reads were refused, pending the completion of another operation.

Also, the product will give you continuing reports of how the data cache is being used. This is an important candidate for performance tweaking because it's much faster for SQL Server to retrieve data from memory than it is to read it each time from disk. Allocating more memory to cache can have a dramatic impact on application performance.

Of course, the tuning steps taken for your application will depend on how your queries actually work. In some cases, shared resources such as tempdb are oversubscribed and create a performance bottleneck. Your DBA would be the one responsible for determining how best to stripe tempdb across multiple disk devices, or whether to move to a solid state device (RAM disk) for tempdb.

One of the biggest drawbacks to the RUNGEN approach is that it does nothing to tell you whether the network or the client PC configuration has anything to contribute to good or bad performance. Sometimes the only way to determine this is by having a group of people step through the application with a stop watch, while back at the server, people monitor server load.

User Account Maintenance

The fastest way to create a mess in your SQL Server is to just allow everybody free range in all the databases. Soon, developers will be filling databases, blowing the log, dropping other people's database objects, and, in short, creating havoc with your application.

To avoid this, you channel all of your systems configuration and account management through a central point, typically the DBA. This is hardly news to anyone who has worked in a big iron shop, though some of you may wonder why the organization insists that you can't have the access privileges you need to get your work done. Well, the other kids have spoiled it for you. Not everyone can be trusted with the sa password, and your organization needs some guarantees when it comes to data security.

Generally, a DBA doesn't really care who belongs to what group, as long as they stay there. Depending on how your organization is structured, a project manager might be responsible for identifying who gets what access, and the DBA simply creates the account and issues the permissions. Or the DBA might be the one with the opinions on who should fit where. However these things are decided, login creation, adding users, and granting or revoking permissions are a necessary support requirement of any Sybase application.

Ensuring Data Integrity

There are a couple of ways that a DBA monitors SQL Server for data integrity. On backups, the DBA should issue DBCC (database consistency checker) commands before dumping the database. This ensures that the data being backed up is actually good and does not contain any cross-linked pages or other corruption.

On the applications side, usually the DBA gets involved in defining any triggers that would be maintained within a database. Certainly this is true if a trigger calls a remote stored procedure and initiates transactions on a remote server.

Another approach to ensuring data integrity is to set up and run the auditing database. As you might expect, there is a performance hit as all changes made by an individual or run against a particular database object are logged in the auditing database. However, this is one method of ensuring that you know exactly who did what to whom with which, and that you can trace data changes back to their source.

That's pretty much it for support required from a database administrator or administration group when it comes to developing Sybase applications.

Summary

In this chapter you saw the role of the DBA defined in terms of specific support to be provided to a development team or application users. On many development projects, the developers themselves have all the permissions needed to act as the DBA for their development server. However, this is not typically the case when an application goes into production.

In terms of a checklist, from this chapter you should have gained an appreciation for just what kinds of tasks and activities need to be assigned to and managed by the administrator. Better to do it in advance than scramble to get it done as implementation dates draw near.

The most appropriate choice for database administrator will depend on your particular organization. However, the most frequent candidate for the job is your server hardware or network administrator. These individuals bring a different set of priorities to the job than do developers, and you may find that they have a lot to offer when it comes to managing a shared, centralized resource such as a production SQL Server.

7.3

Project-Specific Training

Introduction

One of the key support activities is the development of training programs to support your Sybase applications. In this chapter I deal with the two kinds of training: third-party preparatory training for generic concepts and technology, as well as the development of customized training programs to prepare your end users for working with the new application.

As a consulting firm, one of the other frequently requested services my company is asked to provide is the development of client/server training programs tailored to an organization's unique needs or a particular project. In this chapter I share with you the tips and techniques that I use in providing this service.

Unquestionably, user training pays big dividends. For the most resistant users, training gives you an opportunity to get their hostility toward the technology out in the open and deal with it in a controlled environment. For those users with more open minds, it provides valuable assistance with the implementation stage by allowing them to realize what the technology will enable them to do using safe and predictable queries and application functions.

Even in the midst of war, countries provide their soldiers with basic training. The effectiveness of their training programs often helps swing the outcome towards victory. Implementing a client/server application is not usually a life or death proposition, but the need for training is no less keen.

By reading this chapter, you should be in a much better position to develop training materials based on your Sybase application.

Basic Training

I have probably mentioned already that, when implementing Sybase applications with GUI front ends to users with mainframe backgrounds, one of the most difficult skills to pick up is effectively using the mouse. If you get a chance to watch an experienced travel agent work with the arcane codes and antiquated terminal screens for many airline reservation systems, you can see just how good people can get at keyboard shortcuts. When you're replacing a long-term mainframe application in a business unit with low turnover rates, you can find that moving to a GUI-based front end is hardly the lifesaving improvement you anticipated.

Whatever you do, don't just throw your application into the unit and hope the users will gravitate to it like newborn calves. The way to successfully graft the new technology into an existing group is to give the group a structured approach to getting used to the technology. This means providing a continuing and intensive training program, beginning with basic application skills.

In-House or Out-of-House Training

There are several competing considerations when it comes to providing training. In-house training programs are customized, targeted, and flexibly scheduled, and they keep people on site. The downside is that they are expensive, and people are often distracted by phone calls, e-mail messages, and knocks on the door when they train in their own work environment.

Externally offered training programs share the cost across organizations, allow small groups or individuals to attend, and can offer instructors with higher (perceived or real) expertise. On the flip side, they can be canceled, they can be more expensive for larger numbers of students, and the examples are generic rather than specific to your application.

By and large, I believe that there are appropriate times to use both. Professional instructors familiar with Windows, for example, meet many resistant and difficult people and have tricks to overcome that resistance. Also, we all tend to be on our best behavior with strangers (New Yorkers excepted <g>), and this allows an outside instructor to sometimes have more luck in reaching people who are otherwise not with the client/server program. For these reasons, I recommend sending people out in small groups or as individuals at convenient times to learn basic GUI skills, if they don't have them already.

Customized internal training courses are best positioned for materials that are unique to your organization—say, familiarization with your particular application or in working with your development framework. Also, the best sources for expertise are likely to be internal. Last, you can gain advantages from having a group of people take training at the same time and providing them with the opportunity to share their impressions and experience as they go.

The saw-off, then, is that basic, generic training toward the beginning of the implementation process is most likely handled best by outside trainers, and as you gear up for implementation, you should develop and hold your own customized training offerings.

Technical Training Considerations

I often see third-party training organizations offering hands-on training with two or sometimes three people on the same workstation. This is mostly a matter of minimizing the investment in PCs or workstations required by the training provider rather than being a legitimate, value-added training device. People who don't have their own machine for training will frequently abdicate the keyboard to whoever is more interested than they are in doing the exercises. This means that, effectively, the lab and lecture format just became lecture-only for them. Make sure that each participant has his or her own machine, unless it's a concepts-only class.

Speaking of hands-on exercises, this should be your focus when reviewing training materials to determine which organization to use for any externally provided training sessions. Experience is the best teacher, and many of the technical training courses on the market today are not designed to reinforce a concept and build on the foregoing material toward a full understanding of the subject. Put in other terms, a lot of the training materials on the market today are really bad.

Remember that the critical success factor for technical training is retention of new approaches and techniques. The course itself must reinforce the material so that the key points are brought out early and repeated until the student knows them cold. Wherever possible, avoid training courses that use the fire hose approach—spraying the student with a vast volume of facts, TLAs (three-letter acronyms), and assertions until their heads spin. This is not quality training.

Developing Your Own Training

To get your users up to speed with your Sybase application, it's reasonable to expect that you will have to train them. For this reason, I recommend that you develop and hold structured training sessions that are specifically oriented toward your application.

When developing training courses, there is an approach to assist you in creating useful and practical training materials, the elements of which are described in the following paragraphs.

- ■ **Perform a Needs Analysis:** If this has not already been done, you must review all potential course attendees with a view to establishing their existing knowledge, levels of expertise, expectations, and requirements. Practically speaking, this means that you must identify whether they already understand the business, the technology involved, general procedures (customer service, order taking, product support, and so on), and ensure that the course focuses on specific "how to" skills that address the identified requirements.

- ■ **Develop a Course Syllabus:** This is the outline that breaks down the course into discrete modules, usually lasting a half hour to an hour. Each course component should have a specific focus and be placed in order to build on the material that has already been covered. Each heading should also have a detailed description of the scope and content of each module, usually in point form.

- ■ **Structure Reinforcement Exercises:** People learn only so much from listening and reading. Most real skills transfer is gained from reinforcing concepts with practical hands-on experience. As part of the course syllabus, you should identify what kind of exercises or labs the course will contain and at what point these exercises will be introduced into the material.

- ■ **Use Real-World Examples:** Even in the lecture material, if you can take examples, or reinforce statements with stories that revolve around the kinds of situations an attendee is likely to face, this will assist the student in grasping the material.

Remember that abstraction is a higher-order mental skill that does not come easily to everyone. Instead of expecting your course attendees to just "get it," it will no doubt work to all the participants' benefit if you lead them to understanding by using analogies that tell stories to which they can relate but also reinforce the right message.

■ **Use Multimedia:** This does not have to be any kind of fancy CD-ROM–based sights and sounds extravaganza. Any time you use more than two different media to build toward a point, you're using multimedia. Statistics show that retention from a speech is highest if people have hand-outs and something to view while listening to a speaker. The salient point here is that you should use slides, overheads, or projection screens, and make sure that your instructors do not just read the screens. Additionally, relevant but expanded hand-outs help people to reinforce and expand their understanding after the session is over when they review the take-away materials.

■ **Provide Quick-Reference Guides:** If you can reduce the key procedures or steps to a "cheat-sheet," then by all means do so. Many people will spend an extended period of time hacking their way through something (all the while getting increasingly frustrated) when they could just look up the correct syntax (or whatever it is). You can take advantage of the training session setting to make your users more productive when it comes to operating the application. Training is not just about drilling functions and features. It's also beneficial to use the structured training session to get your users on-side while they become more familiar with the reality of what the new application will mean to them.

Without knowing exactly what your application will consist of, it's difficult to make exact recommendations for how to structure your training sessions. At the same time, by committing to providing structured training in your application, you clearly demonstrate your willingness to provide a professional product backed up with a high level of support.

Other Training Approaches

Sometimes it's not feasible to hold a training session for an entire user group due to work constraints (such as, they have too much to do) or geographic considerations (such as, they live all over the country). In situations like this, you have to get creative in order to accomplish the objectives of training and support for your Sybase application. For example, you can try some of the following solutions.

■ **Train Trainers:** You might be able to get together a group of key individuals from each department or business unit and train them with the expectation that they, in turn, will train other members of their work unit. If you opt for this approach, I highly recommend that you provide little leeway in interpretation. Develop training kits that consist of slides (overheads), handouts, and a timed course outline with exercises. This will help ensure a consistency of training across the different trainers.

■ **Lunch-and-Learn Sessions:** If the company springs for finger sandwiches, maybe your users will be attracted to training like a mouse to cheese. Dedicating a demo room with available prototypes or mock-ups will help the users get familiar with the new software at their own speed. By holding it at lunch hour over a period of weeks, you allow everyone to see what the fuss is about without putting them into a formal student/teacher setting.

■ **Computer-Based Training:** If you look at the kind of screen capture demo disks sent out frequently by software vendors, you can see that there is no reason that CBT has to be elaborate or expensive. Remember that, by showing people screens and repeating the features and benefits of the new application, you give people the opportunity to get used to the idea. This is one of the primary reasons that training fails—it's too early. You can address this by distributing diskettes or mini-applications that give users a chance to launch the application and read more about it. Of course, you also can take this approach to the *n*th degree and develop full-blown applications that walk students through the technology and application at their own pace.

■ **Virtual Classrooms:** With conference calls and laptops, you can coordinate the review of your application during development across multiple sites where the students are interacting with you and each other over speakerphones while looking at the application running on their own PC. Granted, this has to be handled with a calm, cool, and collected coordinator, but it's one way to take advantage of the new technologies to bring a group of interested parties together. The biggest advantage to this approach is when your users or students are members of a group distributed geographically throughout the company. They need to learn and to deal with each other, because they have common concerns and problems, but this is difficult because they rarely spend time in physical proximity. Of course, this approach can be enhanced with video conferencing and other such niceties if you have the technology available, but conference calls are available to everyone with a speakerphone.

The idea is to get your message across clearly, and frequently, to ensure that your intended users are not shocked when they discover all the implications and ramifications of this wonderful new Sybase application you are delivering.

Summary

I wanted to take a few pages to explicitly address the need for training and explore some of the alternatives open to you for transferring skills to your users. If nothing else, this chapter should have given you some ideas on how to reach your audience and at what point in the project you would want to do so.

Unfortunately, training is one of the budget items cut first when economic times get tough for an organization. This generally leads to a wide range of skills and experience within any given job classification because people may have received spotty training or had to learn everything on the job.

When you really need a new application to succeed, you should look at how the training has been structured to address the prerequisites and ensure that people are encouraged towards an acceptance of the new tools and procedures.

In this chapter I covered a few practical techniques for sending people out, bringing trainers in, or developing and holding your own training sessions. Remember, developing the application is not enough; it has to be used. Your approach to training could be the key to making the acceptance of the application that you worked so hard to create a success.

7.4

Data Replication

Introduction

As part of the move toward systems integration across the enterprise, more Sybase applications are expected to maintain and synchronize replicated copies of data. In this chapter I discuss some of the issues involved in migrating data on a continuing basis, whether this data is taken from mainframes and stored on PCs or vice versa.

Architecturally, this is one of the greatest challenges of implementing client/server systems. In this chapter you'll be exposed to the issues surrounding integration of multiple vendors' platforms, techniques for creating "disconnectable" applications, and methods for successfully integrating your Sybase application within an infrastructure that crosses geographic boundaries.

Client/server technology is quickly changing and adapting to the business requirements that it's expected to satisfy, which themselves change rapidly. The incorporation of such technologies as WANs, gateways, and other middleware utilities makes even a straightforward business application such as a general ledger, accounts payable, accounts receivable system suddenly complex.

In this chapter you are taken on a tour of the options open to you when considering how best to keep and coordinate multiple copies of your data, within your Sybase application or without.

Migrating Data

As discussed in the implementation section, there comes a point in the life of any application when data needs to be converted from a traditional source (including paper files) to become the new primary source for the data.

This is the underlying concept of any data replication: determining the location where the primary data resides and allocating it for the use of others.

There are a number of reasons for creating copies of data as opposed to using communications to integrate systems with a centralized data store. These include:

- **Performance:** Applications that access local data can respond much more quickly than those limited to traditional WAN communications speeds. Also, balancing the load between read-intensive and write-intensive applications can dramatically affect user perceptions of performance regardless of the speed of the link between client and server.

- **Security:** Not only can replicated data be subsets of the data designated to be seen by a given unit or individual, but replicated data may form the basis for a backup server with up-to-date copies of the data kept off-site in a secure environment to allow recovery from a disaster.

■ **Reliability:** Data access can be guaranteed to be available if multiple servers are integrated into a replicated data environment. This relates to the security of a warm standby site, but also to the capability for a replicated environment to assure that data is synchronized at some point, regardless of system or network downtime.

■ **Mobility:** Applications users such as salespeople or executives may not be in a position to remain in one place while using their data. If a salesperson can take data to his or her clients, a significant competitive advantage can be gained. It looks cool, too.

Replicating data provides another tool to those of you in a position to architect solutions or propose options to address the kinds of requirements identified in this chapter.

SQL Server Utilities

Of course, the basic SQL Server product itself comes with utilities for moving data from text files held in the operating system up into Sybase tables, where you can then do whatever you like to it. The bulkcopy program (bcp) is a client program that functions as a utility for querying the database and creating text files or taking text files and populating database tables.

The bcp utility operates in two modes, slow and slower. The slowest mode of bulkcopy is invoked if you have any triggers, indexes, or rules defined on the target table. This is due to the need for SQL Server to log the operation because the rows handled by bulkcopy are in fact copied into the database. In the event that the connection is lost or the operation bombs for some other reason, the transaction is rolled back to the state it was in before beginning the bulkcopy.

On the other hand, if you don't have any of these database objects declared on the target table, the "fast" bulkcopy mode will be invoked automatically. In many cases, it's quicker to drop indexes, use fast bulkcopy to load the tables, and then reindex the tables. Of course, this is practical when the table volume is not absolutely huge and space is available for indexing. (To perform a clustered index, there must be 1.5 times as much space as the table to be indexed takes up.)

Many sites use bulkcopy in conjunction with communications utilities such as ftp or copying data across physical servers that have had disks made shareable through NFS.

On UNIX systems, CRON can be used to effectively schedule periodic transfers of files across platforms and run isql scripts to bulkcopy data into different servers. This is an inexpensive technique for replicating data using only operating systems and SQL Server default utilities to maintain and coordinate the replication process.

PowerBuilder Utilities

There is no necessity to approach data replication from the back end, even though this is the way it's most frequently done. PowerBuilder 4.0 provides a new utility, PIPELINE (discussed in a little more detail in Chapter 3.2, "PowerBuilder 4.0"), which moves data transparently between Watcom and SQL Server. One of the other uses for PowerBuilder application is to create connections to multiple data sources—for example, an Oracle Server and a SQL Server; by opening a datawindow from one and pasting the data into the other, voilà, she is replicated. This works well when the volume of data is not large and the data itself is to be used for read purposes on the target server.

For systems to which PowerBuilder does not connect directly, you can always use the Save As option to save a result set into a potentially compatible format. Tab, space, and comma delimited text files, as well as SQL statements, dif, sylk, and spreadsheet formats are all options that allow your data to be pulled out of the database with PowerBuilder and the resulting data saved for further processing.

The down side of this approach is that you would not want to have to do this repeatedly. It is intrinsically an operator-driven process. However, for applications for which an analyst is receiving or providing data to outside users and there is some value added in reviewing or messaging the data, this approach to replication may be highly effective.

Sybase Products

Of course, if you ask a Sybase sales rep for the best way to replicate data to and from SQL Server, you'll be told about Rep Server. For many applications, I would have to agree. I believe that you will find this product to provide powerful features and enable a degree of data integration previously unavailable.

The following should provide you with a helicopter-level overview of the Replication Server product, what it can do, and what I perceive are its drawbacks and limitations.

Replication Server

Originally released for UNIX platforms only, Rep Server is now also available for others, especially Windows NT. The Replication Server product integrates tightly with SQL Server and requires version 4.9.2 or higher to work. This means that the Rep Server product will not work with any 4.2 version of SQL Server, including Microsoft's.

Although Replication Server has its own executable code that runs in the same manner as the dataserver or backup server processes, it also must have its own database and disk resources on the primary SQL Server. This SQL Server is designated as primary because it has the data that will be replicated to other SQL Servers, which in turn will maintain replicated copies of the data.

This is an important data modeling concept because one of the key elements to be managed in a replicated data environment is the source server where updates, deletes, or inserts are to officially take place. This should become clear as you gain familiarity with some of the features of Replication Server, such as asynchronous stored procedures (but I am getting ahead of myself).

The major players when implementing a Replication Server include:

- **Primary Data Server (PDS):** This is the server that stores the master copies of the data to be replicated.
- **Primary Replication Server:** This is the rep server responsible for identifying and replicating qualified data from the PDS.
- **Log Transfer Manager:** The LTM polls the log of the database to be replicated in order to catch any changes to designated data for replication.
- **Remote Data Server:** This is (you guessed it!) the target data server to which the data will be replicated.
- **Remote Replication Server:** In many environments, you will want to have coordination between replication servers to ensure that changes are propagated as designed.
- **Connection:** Strictly speaking, this is not a SQL Server or Replication Server component, but it's a necessary part of the equation. The connection links the two PRSs and the RDS or RRS to allow replication to take place.

Figure 7.4.1 shows how each of these components is integrated.

FIGURE 7.4.1.

A typical Replication Server topology.

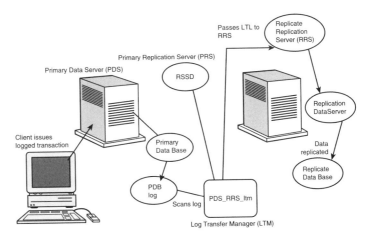

One of the key features of Replication Server is the LTM. Each database to be replicated must have its own LTM, and each table within the database has its log polled to determine whether any of the changes made to the data should be replicated. This is identified by the creation of replication definitions on the Primary Replication Server.

I should point out here that the syntax for installing and administering Replication Server is annoyingly different from anything you will be experienced with from using SQL Server. However, you do use isql or other client applications to connect to the Replication Servers and issue it commands. Create replication definition is one such command issued to Rep Server through isql.

Replication Definitions

The key to the power of Rep Server is in the facility to associate where clauses with the replication definition. Practically speaking, this means that you can create a replication definition that will monitor a log to determine whether a single column has been modified to a particular value and replicate that column (or row or table).

Simply defining a replication definition, however, gives you only half of the equation. The Remote Replication Server must subscribe to the definition. Once the subscription to a published replication definition is defined, it must be materialized. This is how Rep Server knows how to push the data out of the Primary Replication Server to the target data servers. Other facilities within Replication Server allow you to define routes for subsequent propagation of replicated data to other RRSs and, subsequently, other Remote Data Servers. By integrating many of these, you could conceivably create a global network of servers, all automatically replicating appropriate subsets of data as the connections allow.

Connections

I would like to build on that last point. One of the key distinctions of a product such as Replication Server is that it guarantees that data will be replicated *when* the link between the PRS and RRS or RDS is up. For integration of servers in locations with less than utterly reliable communications networks, it's just not practical to expect that your communications link will be up or even stable at any given time. Connections to subsidiaries or affiliates in third-world countries are especially prone to these kinds of problems.

For this reason, two-phase commit or remote-procedure calls simply won't do the trick. What is needed is a manager of the changed data to ensure that the transfer successfully takes place. That's the job that Replication Server was designed to do.

Replication Server is typically built on top of Wide Area Networking technology. By replicating only changes to data, the realities of constrained bandwidth are incorporated into the product's architecture. After the initial subscription has materialized, the two databases have identical copies of the data. The Log Transfer Manager constantly scans the log to determine whether qualified changes were made, and if so, the row images of the changed data are transferred to Replication Server. At that point, the Primary Replication Server and the remote server link, and the contents of the log are transferred. Once completed, the target server applies the changes to its database and the two are once more in synch.

Heterogeneous Environments

With the release of SQL Server 95 from Microsoft, people will be able to take advantage of the built-in replication services provided with this offering. I haven't seen much on the product at this point, but it's becoming apparent that the release of SQL Server 95 will be the first stage in the departure of the Microsoft product from its Sybase SQL Server origins. Certainly, Sybase System 10 is considerably different from the 4.2 offering on which the Microsoft product is based.

The reason you should be interested in this can be found in one of the key distinctions already emerging between the two products. Replication Server for SQL Server System 10 on the Windows NT platform is available as I write this in early 1995. From early indications, the key distinctions between the product offerings of the two companies will be found in the degree of openness and integration with third-party products.

This is not to imply that Microsoft will be strictly interested in connecting and replicating with other servers of a similar ilk, but to point out that the Sybase offerings already emphasize replication compatibility across multiple platforms, making it highly appropriate for heterogeneous environments.

Replicating Data to the Replicate Data Server

Specifically, the Replication Server from Sybase already provides for an LTM that runs against DB/2, allowing you to replicate logged changes to DB/2 data and communicate those changes to whichever SQL Servers subscribe to the Rep Server's replication definition.

Additionally, through the use of Open Server code, you can encapsulate a number of different vendors' database products and treat them as if they were SQL Servers. Additionally, you can integrate the OMNI SQL Gateway product from Sybase to provide this "virtual SQL Server" interface, connecting Replication Server to it and ensuring that all changes made to the designated primary database are in fact propagated across the enterprise.

Replicating Data from the Primary

On the output side, you have even more options. All logged changes scanned by the LTM and defined by Rep Server for replication allow you to translate the insert, update, and delete syntax into any operation you choose, including calling stored procedures. This is because the log entries that are replicated are not replicated using Transact-SQL. Instead, they are translated into Replication Command Language. One of the more powerful features of this RCL is the capability to define class libraries for the strings that apply the changes to the Remote Replication Server.

In a nutshell, this facility allows you to write update, insert, and delete operations in whatever language you choose, including that of third-party products.

The point here is that you can incorporate Replication Server into a wide range of products and requirements. Also, although the product may still be in its first couple of years on the market, it is sufficiently powerful to provide the glue to integrate not only Sybase applications, but multiplatform applications across the enterprise as a whole.

A new product announcement has been made concerning future support for replication between Watcom SQL databases and SQL Servers. I could not find anything more than a release bulletin, but the key attribute seems to be that it will be not only possible, but easy (whoa, do I sense a marketing hand in this) to propagate changes made in SQL Server out to Watcom databases for read purposes. This makes a great deal of sense in the use of disconnectable applications. Sales people and others who need to look up information will be able to pull it down from the more centralized source and keep it on the road. Of course, this is ostensibly possible now with SQL Server workgroup versions for OS/2 and Windows NT, but the Watcom product is designed for the vanilla-flavored Windows environment, and it is attractively priced. Just one more option when it comes to replicating data.

The Cost of Replication

The down side is the expense and the complexity. Of course, it would be unreasonable for anyone to expect that enterprise-wide integration for global companies would be either easy or cheap. Perhaps in the future, but not today. Replication Server is a powerful, but in some ways unnecessarily complex, product. The naming conventions and the interfaces are primitive, with rs_ prefixes indicating everything from a stored procedure in Rep Server to the tables that store user IDs. The interface is inconsistent with anything that you have already been exposed to in SQL Server (with the exception of isql, oh joy). However, once you get used to it, it's not so bad (kind of like vi in UNIX).

Asynchronous Stored Procedures

There is a feature in Replication Server that you may be interested in. It's a subtle but very powerful way to address a basic requirement in a replicated data environment. It addresses how you update locally a replicated data set and ensure that the data is propagated properly to the Primary Data Server.

This requirement can be found in any organization that wants to hold a master copy of all data on a centralized server, but still allow access, including insert, update, or delete capability to local offices.

Say that a corporation has its designated primary in New York, and it has a London office, among other locations. If, for business or architectural reasons, it's not feasible to distribute the data model so that London has its own primary data and New York a replicated copy of that data, then London must be able to update the Primary Data Server in New York. For bandwidth reasons and data volumes, this may not be a practical solution. Local data is then required.

Replication Server addresses this requirement through the provision of *asynchronous stored procedures*. These stored procedures reference data that is held on the local server—say, in London. An analyst might be using their Sybase application to review local London customer data and decide to update it. Because they have only replicated data, you would not want them to update the local copy. Instead, an asynchronous stored procedure passes the procedure name and the parameters down the communications link to New York and modifies the data on the primary server. As part of the regular replication definition and subscription process, the modified data is replicated from New York to London. Another retrieval of the local data in London will show the changes in the data as replicated from the primary data server.

Of course, you're right, there will be a propagation delay and the update will not be instantaneous. In many cases, however, the benefit of this feature—namely, not needing to manually synchronize updates to local and remote data—outweigh the disadvantages of the delay. If London and New York managed only their own data sets, and not each other's, this approach would make less sense. Certainly, it's possible to configure the replicated environment so that there are primary and replicated data at each site, and so that the replication works bidirectionally. Naturally, this adds yet another layer of complexity to the environment.

In any case, you should be gaining a sense that all sorts of replication possibilities are possible and the days of creating viable Sybase applications in a stand-alone mode are numbered.

Summary

In this chapter I wanted to simply introduce you to some of the issues and potential approaches to integrating your SQL Server with other data stores and applications across the network. Products such as Open Server, OMNI SQL Gateway, and Replication Server are highly complex and deserve books of their own to cover the material in any kind of depth.

For many of you, however, just beginning the process of understanding what can be done will be beneficial. Most Sybase applications are still departmental in scope. In leading shops, and over time, you will see this change to a more cohesive level of integration. The key requirement is to keep an eye on your data model and application architecture from the outset, to ensure that you can integrate when the time comes.

This integration may be as traditional as flat-file transfers or as complex as introducing Replication Server across a wide area network and integrating multiple vendors' environments. In any case, you must still know who owns the primary data, and ensure that there is no updating of replicated data that does not get incorporated into the primary copy. This is a fundamental of data integrity, and replication issues simply increase the complexity without altering any of the basic principles.

7.5

Using Object-Oriented Techniques

Introduction

I have to confess that I have been apprehensive about writing this particular chapter. My own feelings about object orientation fly in the face of some of the popular press and certainly the more trendy systems positions being taken in the industry today. So, I talked to a number of people about whether I should just axe this chapter from the book altogether, or stand up and say my piece. Overwhelmingly, the opinion was for me to put down in black and white the way I see the role of object orientation in developing Sybase applications.

In this chapter, I look at the Sybase SQL Server and, to an extent, PowerBuilder with an eye to object-oriented principles and how they can be applied. Before getting down to that, however, I attempt to dispel some of the pressure on systems architects today to incorporate object orientation into their projects. In short, I try to identify what I believe is practical and utterly dismiss a good deal of what people are focused on today when it comes to object-oriented approaches to developing systems. How applicable this advice or interpretation is to you will depend on your own requirements and beliefs. The validity of my position will emerge with time. For now, I will proceed to "call 'em the way I see 'em."

Object-Oriented Religion

While growing up, I was told that there are a number of topics guaranteed to start arguments: politics, religion, and sex. Somehow, object orientation has managed to encompass (dare I say encapsulate?) all three.

Certainly, the choice of tools in a technical organization such as an IS department involves some politics. And, increasingly, the extent to which a product incorporates object orientation is one of the political positions that various vendors jockey along with their internal adherents. Questions abound such as, is SQL Windows more object-oriented than PowerBuilder? Others maintain you should forget relational databases and wait for OODBMSs. Still others state that C++ is not a real language because it's too low level, and recommend that you do everything in small talk instead. On this basis, object orientation—both in products to buy and development techniques to use—has turned into a political football for many organizations.

At the same time, OO has all the trappings of a religion. It most certainly has dogma. And heretics. I have overheard conversations in which people who practiced systems development with different tools or approaches were treated to a virtual burning at the stake. The most telling attribute about a religion is that it requires belief. OO practitioners very quickly move conversations about systems development to the level of their belief, and typically are evangelical about their own epiphany on the road to Damascus. (My own beliefs outside of systems might be discerned from that observation.)

Now for sex. Object orientation has a set of benefits that is very, very attractive to IS managers and systems architects. Reusability, masking complexity, increased maintainability, and flexibility are more readily understood terms for polymorphism, encapsulation, and inheritance. In short, the benefits of OO have sex appeal.

Also, it's important to understand that even we technical types are not immune to fashion and trends. Everybody loves to get involved in hot topics and jump on bandwagons. In the past these have included CASE, DTP, Artificial Intelligence, and others. Some of them have been relegated to that special place in technical heaven where eight-tracks went. Others are living a more subdued but still valuable existence. Where object-oriented programming and products wind up remains to be seen.

Don't Get Me Wrong

Some of my best friends are object oriented. Really, I'm not against any particular orientation. I just think that the timing is wrong and the bigger point is being missed. More important, I think that there are other emerging trends of greater significance for organizations developing systems and a higher degree of potential for those of you developing Sybase applications.

To truly understand this, though, you have to look at history.

Distributed Computing

In the early 1970s there were a number of proponents of a concept called *distributed computing*. They saw the future and it was bright with MIPS distributed across networks with data sharing and all manner of organizational benefits. Many people tried to integrate this new systems thinking into products and applications, and there were a great many failures. Fifteen years later, we see the birth of an entirely new development architecture, namely client/server.

It Sure Looks Like Distributed Computing to Me

This is not to say that initiatives such as DCE are unnecessary, because we have made some strides with client/server. Far from it. Rather, I'm saying that while the concept was defined in the early 1970s, the reality was that a sufficient number of elements had to be combined before critical mass could be achieved. Client/server involves a great deal more than merely distributing cycles across a network. It involves, for example, the openness inherent in published APIs, the drive to the desktop fueled first by spreadsheets and then by GUIs, and the increasing bandwidth of networks and internetworks. Once major strides had been made in this larger community, then and only then did the migration start to take off. The key word here is *start*.

My position is that object-oriented computing is at the equivalent stage to client/server in the early 1970s.

Software Development Practices

When you look at how software is developed in organizations today, it should be clear that, for starters, most companies are just not organized enough to develop systems using an object-oriented approach. Reusability implies that you know what's out there to be used. Sure, projects have librarians for objects and individual developers have toolkits of reusable code, but how much of this is integrated across an entire department, let alone across the enterprise as a whole?

My point is that an entire generation of developers has grown up with the approach and tools that are in use today, and I don't see a wholesale migration to a new way of developing software until this generation of developers retires.

Now, don't freak. I'm not saying that you're dinosaurs, that you can't learn, that you're resistant to change, or any of those myriad obstacles that we see raised by users when implementing even new Sybase applications. Not at all.

I am saying that we are currently inundated with all of the technological change we can handle. The business cycle is such that management will be looking for decades of payback for their investment in the migration to client/server, and systems integration is more important at this time than any new software development approach.

Systems Integration

If you look at the amount of money spent on enterprise connectivity versus software development methodologies, I think you'll begin to see why I'm taking this position. Bandwidth is fundamentally more salable than developer training. Even now, most organizations I visit complain about the high cost of training but don't blink at expanding their communications and networking budgets by 100 percent. There is an underlying reason for this. Organizations want the benefits of coordination and they see how this can be realized by integrating computing and communications.

In fact, look at the relative merits of object orientation to Systems Integration. People have been integrating systems for a long time; there is a history there. Yes, I know it has been difficult to sell organizations on the need for systems integration. Somehow, people assume that these diverse multivendor technologies will just leap together into some kind of cohesive whole (sort of like a garbage dump). My teenage friends tell me that anarchy rules anyway. (Which it eventually does if you buy into the second law of Thermodynamics.) But this is changing as organizations realize that systems integration is not a trivial task, it needs doing, and it will pay back huge dividends in improving organizational response time.

Contrast this with object orientation. At a user and management level, who is going to see the benefits? No one. People may take advantage of the benefits, but they won't know, understand, or care how they were provided. Object orientation is a technical issue for software developers.

It's not a hot new technology, although I believe it will eventually form the model for all software development practices.

Organizational Reality

Globally, organizations have been reducing middle management left, right, and center. This means that the traditional sorting, filtering, and classification process has been removed from organizations just as they are increasing their scope across the globe. Talk about doing more with less. You all know how companies are dealing with this: by putting e-mail, fax, and increasingly sophisticated telecommunications solutions in place. Companies are investing in infrastructure to replace tasks previously performed by people. And rightly so, if the technology can do a better job.

One of the offshoots of this, however, is that the survivors of corporate restructuring are becoming much more sophisticated and certainly more adept at information management. They deal with a diverse number of systems everyday. It's the next natural stage of systems evolution for them to be integrated. The way I see it, for the rest of this decade and into the next there will be a market demand for systems integration that far outstrips any clamor for object-oriented applications. This means that the way your Sybase applications integrate with other data services and consumers will be more significant than whether or not you have built inheritance, encapsulation, or polymorphism into your apps.

Taking Advantage

Of course, it wouldn't be very bright to ignore the very real value that you can derive from taking an object-oriented approach even with relational databases, GUIs, PCs, and inter-networks. These may be the tools from which applications will be built for the foreseeable future, but you can still incorporate some measure of object orientation.

The question becomes more technical than philosophical. Relational databases and their resulting client/server applications don't lend themselves easily to a truly object-oriented approach. The pragmatic thing, then, is to compromise. (For anyone sympathetic to object-oriented principles, please excuse my lack of morality when it comes to applying technology. I really do believe that the most important thing is for the application to provide some benefit to the business, not adhere to esoteric albeit elegant development techniques. When these two things can be combined, it's a bonus.)

The following reviews the three major elements of object-oriented programming. As already stated, a development language must provide three things to be considered object oriented:

■ **Encapsulation:** Users of the object access services through messages to and from the object. It's not necessary (or even desirable) to understand what processing is performed by the object. The services provided are considered to be encapsulated in as much as they operate like a black box surrounding the code.

■ **Inheritance:** By declaring an ancestor object, all subsequent instances of that object inherit the characteristics of the ancestor if it is changed at any point. That is, if you make a change to an attribute of the ancestor object, that change is propagated through every use of the object elsewhere. The descendants inherit any continuing changes to their ancestor.

■ **Polymorphism:** The underlying principle of polymorphism is that the object can be used in many different ways and in very different applications. The services of the object are necessarily generic and may be adapted to purposes that had not necessarily been anticipated when the object was first created.

These are the primary tenets of object orientation, as you no doubt already know. Now I look at how these can be applied in a Sybase environment.

Inheritance within SQL Server

You just aren't going to get anything resembling inheritance with any System 10 or earlier version of SQL Server. The model database allows you to put users, groups, rules, defaults, user-defined datatypes, and other objects in any subsequently created database. This functions more as a copy feature than as a feature providing inheritance. Any changes made to the model after a database has been created do not automatically get propagated through to existing databases. Changes to rules and defaults also apply only to new rows added to the table, and they are not retroactive. So much for inheritance.

Encapsulation

Here we have a little more with which to work. Stored procedures essentially encapsulate logic from the user who calls the proc. Parameters are passed to the proc and results are returned that satisfy the qualifications defined within the proc. Systems procedures themselves are an excellent example of this feature. You may use systems procedures to add and delete users, for example, and have no idea which systems tables are being modified as a result of the operation. Especially when you are new to SQL Server, these procs are a godsend (small g). There is no reason why this feature can't be extended to include your applications, as I will illustrate later in this chapter.

Polymorphism

Maybe it's just me, but creating generic routines that accept parameters and can be applied to many different requirements just seems reasonable. What's the alternative? Hard code everything in your server? The biggest problem with any polymorphic entity is finding an existing piece of code (let's say object) to do what you want. Even if you can find it, it has to be sufficiently comprehensible or well documented to encourage reuse.

So I think you can see why I would say that with a stretch we can incorporate some measure of object orientation with SQL Server, but it's a bit of a force fit.

Object-Oriented Opportunities

Working with stored procedures provides the greatest opportunity for both polymorphism and encapsulation. However, SQL Server continues to demonstrate its UNIX command-line roots, and you have to seize these opportunities for yourself. There is nothing in the Sybase environment itself to encourage this approach.

One of the primary issues surrounding SQL Server development environments is the role of the DBA relative to the developers. As I discussed in Chapter 6.5, "Physical Database Implementation," there is a tendency for DBAs to want to reserve permission to create stored procedures for themselves, and developers generally want the keys to the car to take it where they want. This competition will have to be resolved in accordance with whatever culture prevails in your own shop.

There May Be a Middle Ground for Some of You

Generic procs can be developed and released that provide database access services. This may prove especially valuable when you have large database objects and want to ensure that a reasonable query plan is used for any given query.

Unfortunately, stored procedures cannot accept table names as parameters for the `create table` command. Until System 10, it wasn't even possible to incorporate create or drop table, index, or proc commands into stored procedures. However, you can generate database objects with generic names and use `sp_rename` to make them application or user specific.

Also, by developing a suite of generic procs and providing those to developers by way of the model database, you can encourage your developers to use stored procedures even if they are not in a position to create them for themselves. This can be especially attractive to PowerBuilder developers, for example, who may want to create datawindows based on stored procs without having the facility to write the procs themselves.

Object Orientation in PowerBuilder

Arguably, PowerBuilder is an object-oriented tool. Okay, at least it's more object oriented than SQL Server. The biggest problem with the object orientation in PowerBuilder is its inability to inherit datawindows. This is still true in PowerBuilder 4.0. However, all other objects within PowerBuilder can be inherited. To demonstrate this, we have created a GRANDPA.PBL for holding the ancestor or base objects that we used for CausesDB.

Managing Object Orientation

The real challenge to object orientation is not in creating languages, extensions, or defining principles. The real key is to understand how best to manage development efforts to take advantage of the technology as it evolves and matures.

As you have seen with client/server itself, there are frequently a number of techniques and approaches that become identified with a development paradigm (like a lot of people, I hate that word, but it works here). Host/slave, for example, integrated centralized services with structured development methodologies. As it happens, prototyping as a systems development technique was pioneered and proven in mainframe shops, yet it's more frequently identified with the client/server development methodology. Relational databases were developed for mainframes as well, yet these days you typically see rdbms products positioned on dedicated UNIX servers as more shops move their data off of DB/2, big iron combinations.

Repositories, check-in and check-out procedures, object reuse, and other techniques have been originated in non-object-oriented development shops, but it's most likely that these development techniques will become popularized with the advent of object-oriented programming as a widespread practice. I reiterate that I don't expect to see that take hold in corporate America any time soon.

This brings me to the real point of this dissertation. If you accept my premise that OO is such a departure from current practice that it will take a significant time for it to be adopted, then you must also accept that movement in this direction should occur now and will gain momentum over time. My recommendation is not to get swept up in the fad, but to adopt the principles that make sense now and watch as the practical aspects of the OO paradigm emerge.

Summary

Well, there you have it—one heretic's take on object-oriented programming. In this chapter I have set forth my argument as to why you should focus more on the integration of systems across the enterprise, developing expertise and experience in wide-area networking, distributed data, and replicated data as well as further solidifying your organization's experience in developing client/server applications.

From this discussion you should be able to see that object orientation is a bit of a technical red herring in the face of the larger issue, that being creating systems that bring together your organization as a whole. The political forces represented in attitudes such as the "Not Invented Here" syndrome weigh heavily against adaptation of applications across larger enterprises. Yet, these are the issues that must be addressed before getting all caught up in whether PowerBuilder is object oriented or merely object based. The entire argument is irrelevant.

Well, perhaps not. If you show me an organization that has integrated all of its operational units with distributed servers tied together over a high-speed network, with a published and consistently followed corporate data dictionary, developing applications with contributors across many geographic zones and with highly disciplined adherence to corporate standards for tools and development techniques, then I will agree that the shop is ready, willing, and able to address object-oriented programming as a high priority for the business.

If not, I'd say you have too much work to do.

7.6

Cross-Platform Development

Introduction

One of the key issues when developing Sybase applications is the management of applications that use and reuse the data across multiple platforms. As already indicated, I believe that the openness of SQL Server to any application incorporating DB or CT-Lib (or ODBC) has been primarily responsible for the fast growth and acceptance of the product in the marketplace.

Connecting shrink-wrapped applications is considerably easier than developing your own cross-platform applications. My intent with this chapter is twofold: to cover the underlying concepts and techniques for developing applications that are to be compiled across multiple platforms generally; and to look specifically at how PowerBuilder applications can be migrated across platforms.

This second part is a little tricky at the time that I wrote this, because PowerBuilder 4.0 has not yet been released, even in beta, with Mac and Motif support.

In this chapter I look at how PowerBuilder allows you to migrate your applications to Windows NT from the Windows 3.1 version, and from this you should be able to extrapolate the techniques applicable to Mac and Motif.

The Drive to Diversity

It must be obvious to everyone by now that the computer industry is quickly moving away from any model of highly-centralized, one-vendor computing. Even with a predictable back-lash against failed client/server projects and a return to fashion of the mainframe, integration of multiple client platforms within an organization is inevitable.

On one level there is no reason why we should not only encourage but be enthusiastic about this move. At the architectural level, it leverages investment in learning, allows for the application of the most suitable technology to the requirement (that is, Macs for graphic arts departments), and allows various regions to take advantage of the optimum pricing and technical support in their areas.

There is a serious disadvantage, however. Until this point, the only organizations taking on the challenge of offering multiple versions of their product have been vendors who are paid to offer these services. The internal IS organizations of companies have had tremendous backlogs of applications to be delivered, and increasing the complexity of any one of them poses the potential risk of reducing the number of applications that do get delivered.

At this point, those of us who design and develop applications for internal customers are facing a move to an entirely new level of complexity. Version management has been problematic in the past; now, we add the additional level of multiple versions for multiple platforms.

I guess we just didn't have enough challenge in our lives already.

Porting Documentation

One of the first jobs necessary in a heterogeneous shop is to share documents across multiple platforms and environments. Certainly, document publishing vendors such as FrameMaker have offered multiplatform solutions for years and have developed their own internal languages (MIF in the case of FrameMaker) to support cross-platform and version translation.

One of the key elements of success in providing a multiplatform product is to not only maintain compatibility of the feature set and documents across the various environments, but to be completely consistent with the norms and conventions of that environment. Windows, tool bars, and dialogue boxes must look absolutely normal to a user who never uses any other environment.

Another aspect to be addressed in cross-platform documentation is the importation of various graphics and external objects. It makes much more sense to pick up the location of an external document, say an ER diagram or a product design, and display the original than to replicate copies across the network of servers.

This has implications for cross-platform development, as well. It's not just a question of migrating (I actually mistyped that word as *migraining*, which I suppose is just as apt a description!) the application to another platform, but of looking for ways to create compound documents (and applications) that are constructed or access pieces from other environments when and as needed. Tools such as OLE 2.0 and format translators are beginning to make these techniques practical, though at this time reasonably difficult, to work.

Adobe Acrobat takes another approach to this kind of cross-platform document transferal. Because it allows you to translate documents to its format, you don't actually have to have a copy of MS Office, or whatever tool was used to create the document in order to view it. The basic assumption taken by Acrobat is that first you have to create the document, and then distribute it. People want read access who will never necessarily have to edit the document they wish to view.

This can be useful when you're considering applications to be developed and distributed across platforms as well. If possible, you should identify which components are the equivalent of read only, as it may be significantly easier to pull the data into a local store and use it for continuing reference.

Porting Applications

If you look at the techniques used by vendors when developing software for multiple platforms, you can see that they take advantage of a number of techniques already discussed in this (and other) books.

For example, the design of the product is modularized, and common naming and coding conventions are used. Every development group must be able to understand the detailed design specifications that come from the application architects. Certainly, no efficiency is to be gained from having multiple groups developing multiple specs for multiple platforms. Talk about a many-to-many relationship!

At the same time, there are a lot of good reasons to break your development team into discrete groups. Not only is it easier to develop and debug with people who understand your particular platform's idiosyncrasies and challenges, but most developers get truly good at only one or two platforms and prefer to work with people of like minds. This translates into the little daily efficiencies gained from comparing notes and work habits with people who spend most of their time on a PC, or with a Mac, or on a UNIX workstation.

Thus the design can be centralized, including the user interface guidelines, but the development effort is normally carried out by a group of people dedicated to working with the target platform.

This, of course, implies that you are planning to run discrete projects, each of which has its own audience and deadlines, even if the end result is a product that works the same way, independent of the platform it's on. For most vendor organizations, there is a primary platform for which the application is developed first, and then there are secondary or even tertiary platforms that have applications released later. With Sybase SQL Server itself, the primary development platforms are HP-UX, SunOS, and AIX. I have been told that Solaris is now a primary rather than a later port as well.

Cross Compiling

When it comes to developing applications for multiple platforms, there is another way to accomplish the same result as multiple concurrent project. By choosing a primary development environment for one platform, you can create an application that you then compile for a different platform and release it. No muss, no fuss, right? Well, as you might expect, the theory and the practice are a little different.

Cross-compiled applications have some of the same principles and attributes as a 4GL. That is, you're using one language to write the application, and it is responsible for translating the code into another language. Typically, this translation is to a lower-level language that is more complex than the 4GL developer wanted to learn or work with. As you know, the trade-off with this approach is performance. To be robust, the translation must have a great deal of overhead. In many cases, the generated code might be five or six times longer than code written by someone fluent with the lower language would write to accomplish the same result.

When you apply this approach to cross-platform development, you also have the requirement to restrict your code on the primary platform to features that can be translated into the target environment. If you're developing primarily for a feature-rich environment and expect to compile out to another, lesser-endowed platform, compromise will be required.

At this point, you might be interested in taking a look at some of the products and approaches that support this kind of cross-platform compilation.

Liant C++/Views

This product from Liant Software corporation is defined as a framework that encompasses the behavior of your entire application, as opposed to simply being a GUI development tool for multiple environments.

C++/Views provides a class browser as well as a class library. Through the browser, you have access to all of the source code elements used by your applications. However, the source code created by picking items from the GUI resource palette is kept separate from other source code, as are menu components. These are accessed through their respective editors, not the browser.

Like PowerBuilder and Visual Basic, it has a screen painter with drag-and-drop facilities to place objects on the interface under design. However, it also manages font and color selection along with memory management for you as the application developer. On the flip side, if you're a dyed-in-the-wool programmer, you may like Liant's approach because the product helps you manage your code rather than generate it for you.

Once you have built your interface and coded your application logic for the Windows 3.1 environment, you can compile the application into X/Motif, Mac System 7, OS/2, and Windows NT versions. Of course, the look and feel of the application is completely consistent with the target environment. Also, the code controlling the behavior of each window, such as field validations and input restrictions, translates into the environment on which the executable is to run.

As you might expect, there is some degree of tweaking required to port the application from the Windows environment to another.

zApp Developer's Suite

Unlike Liant's C++/Viewer, the zApp Developer's Suite allows you to create interfaces almost entirely through point-and-click operations with your mouse. You can use this interface to set restrictions on input fields, apply advanced windows controls, and provide for some level of error handling with the graphical interface editor.

Also, zApp handles the font and color selection within the application as well as its memory management across multiple platforms. zApp provides a consistent method of working with menus, interface controls, and source code. This helps you see your application in its entirety, rather than have to break out various components, depending on what aspect you want to work on next.

To generate an application for another platform under zApp, you first create the application under Windows 3.1, and then select the target platform and compiler. Once the source code, project, and resource files are regenerated, you must move them to the desired platform and run the application.

Tweaking is also required to get the application to run properly in its target environment. It should be noted that the environments supported by zApp include Windows NT, X/Motif, and OS/2 but not the Macintosh.

PowerBuilder Version 4.0

As you no doubt already know, PowerBuilder is more of a GUI application generator than a programming language supporting compilation across multiple platforms. With version 4.0, PowerBuilder allows the generation of executables for environments other than Windows 3.1.

The technique used by PowerBuilder is slightly different than that taken by Liant and zApp. Instead of allowing you to compile out to the target environment from Windows, you must transfer the pbl to a version of PowerBuilder running on that environment, and then compile your executable.

As I wrote this, the only other environment on which PowerBuilder 4.0 had been released was the Windows NT version. It was therefore a little difficult to forecast exactly how you should best transfer your executables into the Mac and X/Motif environments before generating an executable.

Incorporating Multiplatform Front Ends Into Sybase

From this brief treatment of how you can generate front end applications to work across multiple platforms, you should be able to make the jump to integrating these client applications into a Sybase SQL Server environment. First, like working with Sybase in a monolithic client environment, there remains the dilemma of exactly how best to split the processing and workload across the client and server systems.

When you know that you'll be generating applications to work in a heterogeneous client environment, however, this may help push you toward keeping more of the business logic and processing on the server side of the equation.

Consider for a second the impact of validations, rules, and error handling across Windows, OS/2, Mac, and Motif environments. To be absolutely sure that your applications provide the highest degree of data integrity and access security, you'll want to use stored procedures and triggers to handle access to data and its validation on input.

Although it may not be as operator friendly to pass through SQL Server error messages, this is the most appropriate place to begin for a version one application that is intended to be rolled out across multiple clients from the outset.

Certainly, you'll want to trap error messages, provide front-end validation, and prompt for correction before posting results to the database server, when it's feasible to do so. In the interests of developing and deploying your applications quickly, you should limit the complexity as much as possible and tackle multiplatform client/server applications with the integrity developed first on the common denominator: the SQL Server.

Summary

One of the most difficult aspects to deal with when designing and developing Sybase applications is the complexity of the systems solutions. Not only does Sybase SQL Server allow you to place it on multiple server environments and to scale the size of the database server according to your needs, but it is open to a large number of shrink-wrapped client applications running on an even greater number of platforms.

In the mid 1990s, we now see a new wrinkle emerging in development environments: that of multiplatform, internally developed applications, all of which can go up against SQL Server.

The promise of developing applications in one environment and then painlessly recompiling them for execution on other platforms is still in the far-off future. It is possible today, but it does require a great deal of time and attention.

The primary point which you should have taken from this chapter is simply this: regardless of the number of client environments you must deal with in your organization, whether third-party, shrink-wrapped or internally developed applications, Sybase can be an integral part of an enterprise-wide, cohesive client/server architecture.

Section

8

Auditing Your Sybase Applications

Introduction to the Section

Congratulations. You have made it through the concept, design, implementation, and support sections of the book. Now you'll find out how to determine whether in fact congratulations are in order, or whether the original aims of the application were met, and how well.

In the brief description of the audit process covered in Section 4, I said that a systems audit was like getting a report card. This is a useful construct when considering the benefits of formalizing a project audit process.

In this chapter you'll find out how the grading process works, what systems auditors look for, and how you can make this process more pleasant than a root canal. The audit marks the end of the first iteration of the project as a whole, providing a definite point at which you can focus on the start-to-finish process before determining where to go from here.

In this section you'll have the systems audit process defined and proceduralized with a checklist to ensure that you have covered all the necessary bases. Just as important, you'll learn how to turn the audit process into a benefits review, which is essential if you want senior management to reward you and your team for achieving your goals. Also, you'll be introduced to the methods that an organization can employ to ensure that the valuable implementation lessons are passed on throughout the company. Finally, you'll see how you can use an audit to solicit constructive criticism about the weaknesses and areas for improvement found in the application as built.

Because you are going to the bother of reading this book, it's a fair assumption that you're committed to developing the best Sybase application possible. The audit, although not a fun part of the job, is indeed a necessary evil and can provide a mechanism by which your application improves over time along with ensuring that your organization gains valuable insight into the client/server development process.

Stay with it, and use the material covered in this section to address the audit issue head on. At the very least, it will help you identify when it's all over and it's time to move on.

8.1

The Finishing Line

Introduction

I once saw a poster in a developer's office that contained a collection of old sayings modified to work in the systems world. One of the comments that caught my eye was "All's well that ends." Of course, Shakespeare thought that it had to end well, but with a client/server application, sometimes it's enough if the thing actually reaches some measure of completion. I believe from a developer's standpoint that this means it has worked out swell if there is no maintenance involved, but that is an unlikely expectation.

In any case, in this chapter you are introduced to the concept of completion when it comes to a client/server project. I use the term *project* advisedly, as the application itself should go on, although in some cases the audit may indicate that it's time to pull the plug.

As you read through this chapter you will no doubt come across my bias towards project thinking. Unlike other lifecycles and methodologies, where the maintenance or support phase is the longest portion of an application's life, I see all systems work organized into discrete projects. The audit should point to what was done right, and just as important, clearly identify those things that need to be incorporated into the next version. That version can be constituted as a new project, and if you're lucky, it will be assigned to someone else who can bring a fresh outlook and new enthusiasm to the task.

In this chapter I cover how to use the audit as a means of focusing your development efforts on quality, on completing the things that are most important to the success of the application as a whole and on using deadlines as a means of managing motivation and commitment. From this you should be able to see that a systems audit is indeed an important part of the applications development process.

The Light at the End of the Tunnel

When I introduced you to the concept of a tunnel chart, I indicated that part of the name came from the old saw about the light at the end of the tunnel being an oncoming train. Well, in the case of client/server projects, a most effective date for the yellow center of the chart is the arbitrary date selected for the audit. At some point, this will no doubt feel more like an onrushing train than any sort of date for celebration.

The cornerstone of using the impending audit to keep your project on track is in the immovablity of the date. It should be far enough out from the beginning of the project that it becomes a sort of "Ready or Not, Here it Comes" event. The idea is that the audit is going to occur on a fixed date, whether the system is built, implemented, in flames, or abandoned.

The audit is more than a progress report. Unless you work in some sort of autonomous Nirvana, you will have been involved in all kinds of such reports at each milestone and usually more frequently as the project goes on. An audit date should have been selected on the basis of allowing for enough time for the project to be pushed back, although not so far back that it moves into a completely new business cycle. Personally, I like to see an audit done in the same year that the project was originally scheduled for completion.

In any case, the audit should also contain with it some basis for allocating rewards for a job well done. This recognition for effort and achievement can range from time off with pay (which may simply be allowing people to take their vacation entitlement), to cash bonuses and new assignments. Continuing with the report card analogy, the big benefit to the end of the school year is getting the summer off. The difference between that and a systems audit is that unless you pass, you may have to go to summer school. In other words, back to the grindstone.

Define *Done*

There is no better example (that I can think of this second) for the problem in the employ of adjectives than when you order a steak in a restaurant (vegetarians, bear with me). If you order a steak medium rare in a dozen different restaurants, chances are that you will get at least a half dozen different results, from rare to well done. Some of the places that take the greatest pride in their beef have a legend or an explanation of what each of the terms means somewhere on the menu. This is equally applicable to performing an audit.

"This application is a world-class example of a tremendously talented team working with leading-edge technology to create a strong application that is of immeasurable benefit to the business." At first glance, this kind of assessment sounds pretty good, don't you think? The part that would bother me is the immeasurable benefit. If it can't be measured, the organization won't know how to reward you for your work. Concerning the adjectives *world-class*, *talented*, and *leading-edge*, you have to ask who is doing the assessment. Subjective appraisals won't help you determine what you did right, or what is left to be done. More important, everyone uses expressions such as *good* differently. People may be either too hard to please or too generous in their appraisal. To avoid this, you must define the criteria on which you expect to be measured well in advance.

Review the Business Case

If you really want to make your applications relevant to the business, you should be able to define the benefits that the organization can expect from the application as part of the business case that formed the original concept for the system. This doesn't mean that there won't be some unanticipated advantages uncovered. If you have been able to apply the technology effectively, there should be at least some measure of business reengineering. Few indeed are the business units that couldn't stand a little overhauling in how business is done.

The real key to success in any business endeavor is to identify what you want to achieve and then actually go out and do it. Businesses find all the time that what their shareholders and bankers want is not unexpectedly high returns, but consistency with the plan. People want to know what to expect and then get that. Management is certainly not an exception to this rule when it comes to their expectations for Sybase applications. They want you to identify what you are going to do and what benefit that is to them, and then they want you to give it to them. Consider the business case your promise to management as to what your application will provide, and for audit purposes, extract those commitments and measure your progress toward them.

The audit gives you an opportunity to evaluate more than just how well you did, however. In fact, one of the key questions to be addressed during the audit phase is how right were you. The initial concept for the system is one example that shows how you need to evaluate opportunity cost. Because hindsight is 20/20, take advantage of the opportunity to review whether or not the efforts spent on the system might have provided a better yield elsewhere.

Independent and Objective Audits

Self appraisal is pretty subjective stuff. Often, people say something is good when what they mean is that they like it. Their opinion becomes confused with objective fact. When you're looking at the audit role, this can become a very real problem; ultimately judgment will be passed in some way on the work that was done. To make this a fair process, it must be as objective as possible. This means that the audit must be performed by disinterested outsiders against established criteria using quantifiable measures wherever possible.

Objectivity is an interesting phenomenon. Perhaps the best practical example of how objectivity can be applied to human perception (and from there to evaluation) is found in the Robert A. Heinlein book, *Stranger in a Strange Land*. There he introduces the concept of a *fair witness*, a person trained to be fair and objective. The example he used was that most people would look at a house on a hill and point out that the there was a white house on the hill. A fair witness, on the other hand, would look at the same house and say that on the hill stood a house with white south and west sides. There is no need to make the assumption that the other sides are the same color when you can simply and clearly state what you see.

This is the sort of discipline required by a systems audit. It should be dry, unemotional, factual, complete, and fair. It should also be conducted by someone with nothing to gain by findings either favorable or not.

Auditors are often accused of being accountants without the personality. Yet from the requirements to be even handed, read nothing into a situation that isn't clearly established, and present findings in an unemotional and unbiased fashion, it's difficult to see how any amount of flamboyance would assist in doing the job.

Who you get to actually do the audit is up to you, but as long as they possess the characteristics covered here, they should be able to give you a fair and reasonable appraisal of how well you did against the plan. More important, the findings should be accepted by management and users alike, even those who have grown too close to the situation and can no longer be objective.

Focus on Quality

The audit gives you an opportunity to get more control over your client/server systems development and delivery process as well. As I have already established, one of the critical success factors for your application is to identify the value and contribution it will make during the business case or conceptual stage of the process. The audit will most definitely focus on bringing you back to the case to determine whether you have succeeded in meeting your commitments.

There is a more subtle use for the audit stage, however, and that is to help you refine and communicate the lessons learned about developing client/server applications.

To really be effective, you need to draw a line to indicate what point in time the audit will take place. This should already have been done and published as part of your tunnel chart. Then, have credible individuals walk through your development effort and give you feedback on the process as well as the result.

In other words, you audit each development stage as well as the ultimate outcome of the project. As mentioned previously, one of the key questions to be addressed by an audit is determining the continuing validity of the concept. Was it a short-term window of opportunity or a long-term strategy? The audit determines how circumstances affected the context for the decision to go ahead with your project.

The emphasis on quality comes as part of the process review. The design documentation is a quality indicator, for example. The audit should establish what was in place and the effect it had on the overall outcome. This is very much a warts-and-all assessment, in which the little glitches and big omissions alike should be noted, along with their effect on the quality of the product under construction.

The reason for doing this is twofold. First, most organizations are still getting their feet wet when it comes to client/server. This means that any investment in the new technology should be carefully monitored and mistakes and omissions should be expected, and, when found, they should be communicated throughout the organization's IS community to ensure that other groups don't make the same mistakes. If your client/server application is a learning experience, the greatest benefit to the organization accrues with the highest number of people who learn from it.

The second reason has to do with the commitment to quality. People tend to be motivated by such things as fear of personal embarrassment. Although I would hardly recommend threatening public humiliation as a means of motivating employees (hey wait, maybe it does have some potential?!), I am suggesting that when the process is highly visible, developers frequently do their best work. This includes making the effort to actually complete all of those "nice to have" aspects of a development, such as documentation, detailed design specifications, and incorporation of reusable objects.

The added pressure of setting a good example can help keep the members of the development team focused on more than just meeting the deadline with code that compiles.

Auditing Work in Progress

I may have made a mistake in implying that the audit phase is the last part of any client/server application development project. This is especially true when you take into account the objectives and effects of the previous segment. Because the audit can keep your group focused, and provide feedback to the organization as a whole on the strength and weaknesses of your approach, you should consider auditing each phase as you go.

By bringing in appropriate outside technical expertise as you go through each phase of the application development lifecycle, you will find that errors and omissions can be identified while there is still sufficient time to correct them. This is, after all, the real reason for doing this kind of review. Certainly, the last thing anyone wants to do is go on a witch hunt to find scapegoats for a failed project. And you definitely don't want to be the object of that particular game of hide and seek.

If instead you subject your project to professional scrutiny before completion or sign-off of each stage, you can ensure that everything is ready to move to the next level before actually getting started.

These are generally professional reviews, although they also may be set up on the basis of a peer review. That is, you may invite a number of other systems people within your organization to review what you have, ask questions, and make recommendations about anything that comes up from the peer review process. One advantage of peer review over external audits is the communication within your organization. If your peers are reviewing your work, they are also learning how you go about things. Depending on the differences between your approach and theirs, their review may give them tips and hints that can be applied to their own projects.

The biggest drawback of peer reviews is the complicated politics that frequently are an integral part of the process. Because there is a measure of judgment, or certainly the potential for judgment, as part of the review process, often there are people who use the opportunity to grind their particular axe. This means that if you are going to subject your work to peer review, you should have someone with sufficient political acumen and organizational clout manage the process to ensure that it stays professional and relevant.

Summary

The audit process is generally perceived as threatening by most people. You are subject to review and, potentially, criticism about work in which you have invested (I hope) a great deal of yourself and your abilities. This tends to make people shy away from it.

From the discussion in this chapter you should be able to see how your project and organization can benefit from a thorough review of the outcome of your project, as well as each stage of its development. When the stakes are high, you just can't risk not auditing the process. It's the only way to catch mistakes before it becomes too late.

Also, you should be able to see what kind of attributes are needed in a systems auditor; evenhandedness and a phlegmatically disinterested outlook are key characteristics. (I use *disinterested* in the precise sense of the word, not as a synonym for uninterested).

Just as important, you should be able to see why the audit process is as significant as the concept, design, implementation, and support phases of developing Sybase applications. Not only will committing to an audit help you keep focused on the task at hand, but it will ensure that at least some criteria for success are established at the outset. Identifying these elements of success and communicating that people will be evaluated against them is one sure way to guarantee that they are taken seriously by a project development team.

As with other aspects of the development process covered in this book, opening up your application for audit, especially if you do it voluntarily, takes a great deal of professional discipline. From reading this chapter you should have gained an appreciation for the benefits that you and your organization gain from subjecting yourself to this process. In the end, auditing your development process may sting at times, but it can only help ensure that your Sybase application is a success. And that is what this whole thing is about.

8.2

Identifying Enhancements Through Systems Audits

Introduction

As I have already said, the audit process is like getting your report card. In this chapter you'll see how to turn the outcome of the audit report into a set of constructive recommendations, not a trip to the woodshed.

You will see how to avoid turning the audit into an adversarial relationship where the deficiencies in your approach become the political capital of those who opposed your project. Just as important, you should gain a better sense of the role played by auditors in creating a uniform set of practices, which in turn create a structure to encourage the growth of client/server applications throughout your organization.

Us versus Them

The last thing you want to encourage in your development project is an attitude that the audit process is a case of us versus them. *They* are always looking to stifle creativity with rules and regulations. *They* are faceless, grey individuals who neither appreciate nor care about your trials and tribulations. *They* are organizational overhead and the accountants of systems developers.

Well, these are hard assertions to argue. Certainly, auditors don't get paid to be friendly, and there may be aspects of the job that encourage the less flamboyant members of the company. That doesn't change the value that they provide to the organization generally, or the contribution they can make to your project as a whole.

Okay, so I'm hectoring you and belaboring the point. But I've seen cases when a great deal of friction was created on a project because of audit-enforced guidelines—friction that could have been dispelled had anyone taken the position that, ultimately, like taking your vitamins, the audit was better for the organization and the project.

Application Architecture Audits

An auditor will look for a number of things when reviewing your application, some of which may seem positively at odds with an integrated application in an open systems environment.

Take, for example, the separation of processes. In a traditional audit, not only does the auditor look for compliance with development practices, but reviews the way the application itself is structured. Auditors hate to see the same person responsible for both submitting the invoices and preparing the checks to be cut. Even if this makes sense from the standpoint of the workflow of the business unit, it's a hole in security that should be addressed.

While you're busy trying to make the application as functional as possible, systems auditors want to ensure that the system can't be used to defraud the company.

The collapse of the Baring's Bank made international news headlines, and systems people everywhere had to consider whether it was a weakness in the system (meaning mismanagement) or the deliberate work of a determined individual. Systems audits should reveal whether an unscrupulous individual could take advantage of your systems features to bypass reasonable safeguards.

Voluntary Compliance

Very large firms have very large budgets and represent a great deal of money in the event of successful litigation. This is not something that most development teams ever consider. Software that is not approved or subsequently paid for by the organization could easily represent huge revenues to a company with a few underemployed lawyers. Of course, this is not much of a concern for smaller firms. But many systems people tend to identify themselves as a group within a unit within the organization as a whole. You may think there is just you and your team. But from the outside looking in, you could represent a pretty lucrative target. This is one of the things that auditors get paid to prevent. The Software Publisher's Association has brought in $14 million in judgments against software pirates since its inception in 1988. In 1995 the Association hired five software specialists to cruise the Internet and log into bulletin boards to see whether they can find copyright violators. This is the kind of activity that an organization simply cannot be aware of without effective software auditing.

Project Audits

The concept of systems audits as it relates to the Sybase application development lifecycle isn't really about systems audits as a practice or profession, however. Audits of a project don't have to be left to the very end, although there should always be some sort of review, whether it turns out the be the equivalent of the Academy Awards or an autopsy.

At this point I would like to introduce a checklist of practices that I look for as part of a complete or successful Sybase application. You may find it useful and instructive to review your own environment to determine how well it complies.

In no particular order, you should have the following:

■ **Documented Backup Procedures:** An audit of your shop should show a well-mapped schedule of full and incremental backups of Sybase databases, logs, and operating system files.

■ **Documented Server Maps:** These include up-to-date, hard-copy records of database devices, databases, segments, user IDs, server configuration, and the systems catalogs such as sysusages.

- **Documented Recovery Procedures:** You should have plans for how to rebuild the master database and load databases from disk and tape backups, including login names and who has necessary passwords for accounts such as sa, root, supervisor, and sybase.
- **Software Development Plans:** All enhancements, revisions, and new features identified in testing or through user walkthroughs that are not immediately incorporated must be recorded in some kind of development or enhancement plan. This plan should have targeted release dates associated with the enhancements and the team's track record for delivery monitored against the promises made.
- **Data Dictionary:** This should be an up-to-date and comprehensive data dictionary complete with assignment of accountability for maintenance of the dictionary.
- **Object Library:** A custodian should be readily identifiable who can in turn define and identify all application objects that are either in use or available for inheritance by application developers.
- **Down System Procedures:** You need a plan for who is to be notified before the server is bounced and what mechanisms (e-mail, phone, and so on) exist for contacting affected people.
- **Upgrade Procedures:** This involves identifying the test procedures for new upgrades and patches.

It may seem that the emphasis here is on documentation, policies, and procedures. Actually, audits do tend to focus on whether or not any given project has conformed to good management practices. The usual excuses of changing priorities, unexpected delays, or problems shouldn't affect whether an audit gets performed. The point is that it's easier to put off doing things that are supposedly good for you but for which there is little compulsion to actually complete.

Leverage Your Audit

Some of the most successful Sybase projects have been held up as exemplary to other units within their organizations. As you can imagine, this can be a double-edged sword. Say that you're charged with the responsibility of taking on a Sybase client/server application development effort. Then, based on your success, executives start touting your achievements as things for your colleagues to measure up to. Certainly, you can expect to be the subject of a certain amount of professional jealousy (it's not pretty, but it does happen).

By undergoing a warts-and-all audit, you accomplish two things. One, you identify where your particular project is weak and where it needs improvement prior to ultimate sign-off. But more important, the audit gives you a realistic case for using your project as a learning experience for the organization as a whole. It allows you to say things such as, "Yes, mistakes were made and here's what we learned from them." At the same time, you can to point to a project that was successful in large measure.

Think of the benefits that this can provide you in the context of a larger organization. By being willing to share not only your success but also the areas where your experience was hard won, you make yourself a more accessible resource to other project leaders and systems managers in your organization.

I have a client with subsidiaries around the globe who makes a point of flying his organization's IS managers and high-level team leaders to see each other's operations. By demonstrating your willingness to undergo an independent, objective, third-party audit without trying to sweep problems under the rug, you make your experience that much more valuable to your overall organization.

When you consider a technology as new as client/server, this is no small contribution.

Summary

The main point made in this short treatment of systems audits was that they should be taken as a necessary safeguard for any sensitive or important application.

The two main thoughts addressed were your willingness to undergo and support an audit, and how an audit can help prepare and protect you from either bad practice or oversight.

You should take the checklist of auditable practices and see how well your organization has done in establishing and documenting development and recovery procedures.

Last, I hope this chapter has given you a few ideas of how putting your project through an audit can benefit both you and your organization. You needn't get straight As to make it a worthwhile experience.

8.3

Auditing CausesDB

Introduction

In spite of the short treatment of the section on auditing, I hope that one key point is clear: the audit must be done. A discussion of technique, format, and procedure might be of value and interest to a systems auditor, but from the perspective of a developer, the emphasis is on one key question: How well did I accomplish what I set out to do?

It would be remiss of me not to apply the discipline of this question to our efforts in developing CausesDB, the sample application provided on the CD included with this book.

In this chapter I cover what was delivered as the deadline approached and discuss what contingency plans were taken when it became apparent that we would not be able to do everything we had hoped within the time available.

At the very least, by reading this chapter you'll gain a better idea of what is on the CD so that you can determine how you might be able to use it.

Promises, Promises

The first step to be addressed in any audit is identifying the expectations and commitments that were made as part of the original proposal. From the standpoint of CausesDB, there were a number of specific deliverables promised over the course of this book.

Audience

First, the sample application was to be relevant to you as a reader, in practically demonstrating how the techniques described and recommended in this book could be used. Second, the application was always intended to be a useful application in its own right, as something that could be used to review the financial background and objectives of a large number of charitable organizations. Finally, the charitable organizations themselves were identified as a user group that could circulate the application on its own in order to provide people with an opportunity to donate time and money to that organization's cause.

Process

I indicated throughout the book that the application would be built concurrently with the development of the material you have read. I also promised that you would be able to see samples of how the techniques described in the chapters would be applied within the context of the CausesDB application.

At the same time, I thought that this process would be extended to include alpha, beta, and finally a production version of the application. The development was always intended to include multiple iterations with input from our end user group—specifically, the charitable institutions themselves.

Content

One of the significant differences between this book and my earlier book on Sybase was the direction from Sams to minimize syntax. Understanding that the CD was to include actual source code and scripts that could be reviewed by developer/readers as they wanted, the real focus of this book was to be in descriptions of technique and methods.

CausesDB was to provide detailed and useful examples of how applications could take advantage of Sybase products and features.

Ready or Not, Here it is!

I think at one point early in the book, I identified that we would have to take the "ready or not, here it comes" approach. Certainly, any fixed and immovable deadline will mean that any compromise must be negotiated on the delivery side of the equation. This applies just as well to our development of the CausesDB application. However, lest you lose interest at this point, let me go on record as saying that I'm quite sure that you will find it an interesting and potentially valuable application in its current format.

Audience Experience

At this point I have gotten very little response from technical people who have seen the CausesDB application. Obviously, I expect to obtain a great deal more when this book has actually hit the bookstores. However, that is not to say that we didn't run through the process of demonstrating the application as a work in progress to other technical people. The feedback was that the application clearly demonstrates a number of Sybase-related applications development techniques, and because we were providing the source code, it should be of practical value to developers.

With the charities themselves we were not quite so fortunate. First, let me say that I appreciate the efforts that those organizations who agreed to participate contributed to the project. There can be no question that a great many of these people are overworked volunteers who had to make a special effort to help out with this project. At the same time, the reaction of many other organizations was, to put it plainly, underwhelming. Granted, this is a new idea and CD-ROM applications involve a new medium, but in some cases I was surprised by the degree of unwillingness and inaccessibility presented by some of these nonprofit organizations. I would like to think that much of this was rooted in the possibility that, without being able to see a prototype, they could not really imagine what we wanted to accomplish with this application.

The Actual Process

When it became obvious that we weren't going to be able to elicit the support of a sufficient number of charitable organizations to provide a useful database application, we had to look for an alternate means of coming up with the information. In this, the tax people have been quite helpful. Well, at least the Canadian tax authorities have delivered on their promises. The IRS, on the other hand, expressed a willingness to assist in the process which, over time, turned into a series of delays and miscommunications. No doubt some of this is due to the fact that the origin of the requests for information was, in fact, Canada. The North American Free Trade Agreement notwithstanding, I'm not sure that providing information to foreigners is something I would consider a priority, were I operating from their point of view.

In any case, we were told that the information on U.S. charities would be made available, but the timing didn't work out to be consistent with the deadline for publication of this book. You can look on the Macmillan forum on CompuServe to see whether the data has been posted, as I will put the data on CompuServe as soon as we have it available.

You might find a review of the data entry module of particular interest if you work with a number of nonprogramming, but somewhat sophisticated, end users. The original PowerBuilder Enterprise CD didn't actually include the .PBL necessary to utilize datawindows created in PB4.0 as forms in InfoMaker. As a result, the InfoMaker application included on this CD shows only what you can do with the bare bones InfoMaker product. However, keep in mind that you can acquire IMSTYLE4.0 .PBL from the PowerMaker/View sections within the Powersoft forum on CompuServe. This allows you to create complex windows, with scripts and logic, which can then be picked up and used by end users who want to assemble applications but who are not in a position to write any code.

I think that the volunteer developers deserve an acknowledgment. All of the people involved in this project gave up a considerable number of hours in the evening and on weekends in order to create a useful application to provide background and to support any decision you might make to support a worthy cause.

Considerable discussion took place about the objectives of the application, as well as dissection of the techniques recommended for analysis and specification of CausesDB. From this I took the opportunity to refine and revise the process I have recommended here for designing and developing successful Sybase applications.

Content Provided

The proof, as always, is in the pudding. You'll be the judge and ultimate auditor of how well the application supports good Sybase application development practices. At this point, I would simply like to explain what you will and won't find on the CD.

You'll find a stand-alone Watcom runtime database, populated with data from 78 Canadian charitable institutions. Along with this, there is about a dozen multimedia advertisements or promotional clips that have been provided by participating groups.

The decision support and data retrieval application comes in three flavors: one version in PowerBuilder 4.0 for Windows, one for Windows NT, and another in Visual Basic 3.0. The source code, in the form of libraries and catalogs, has been included. You may find that the application provides a feature that you would like to use. Feel free to browse the application to determine the exact syntax and procedure used to perform the function.

I regret that you won't find much in the way of stored procedures. Given the stage of development that we reached in this process, the development team was just not ready to move the logic out of the application and into stored procedures.

Where to Go Next

Interestingly, it looks as if this application is beginning to have a life of its own. This was, of course, one of the things that I had hoped to accomplish at the outset, but it is never possible to predict for certain. I encourage anyone who would like an up-to-date version of the application to call my company, Word N Systems, at (416) 597-9257, and we'll be delighted to give you an update.

The intent at this point is to take the CD that you have as part of this book and use that as the beta version of the application. This will be demonstrated to the participants, and we'll work on building up a much more complete version of the application, with more sound bites and promos to give each charity the opportunity to state their case.

If anyone has comments or would like to throw in any piece of functionality, enhancements, or what-have-you, by all means post a note on the Macmillan forum on CompuServe. I check for messages periodically and would be happy to respond to whatever comments, questions, or criticisms you have to offer.

Summary

CausesDB clearly demonstrates the key functional areas of a Decision Support System (DSS), albeit a small one. Those of you interested in reverse engineering the product might be particularly interested in the performance of the large .AVI files retrieved from the SQL Server versus the CD or hard disk.

Additionally, to provide a fair and reasonable demonstration of why you might choose to use a third-party tool, in this case Visual Basic specifically, over a database development environment such as PowerBuilder, we threw in a demonstration of a third-party multimedia package as part of CausesDB.

Even if you're a dyed-in-the-wool PB developer, you might want to bring up the videos for the Calgary Zoo, where we've stashed a sample of the Zoo's attractions for your viewing pleasure. Under PowerBuilder, we could call only the Microsoft Media Player, which on some systems leaves a little something to be desired for presentation quality.

In any case, I hope you'll agree that the application deserves a passing grade for its delivery considering the objectives stated in this book.

I

Index

Add to Your Sams Library Today with the Best Books for Programming, Operating Systems, and New Technologies

The easiest way to order is to pick up the phone and call

1-800-428-5331

between 9:00 a.m. and 5:00 p.m. EST.

For faster service please have your credit card available.

ISBN	Quantity	Description of Item	Unit Cost	Total Cost
0-672-30467-8		Sybase Developer's Guide (book/disk)	$40.00	
0-672-30695-6		Developing PowerBuilder 4 Applications, Third Edition (book/disk)	$45.00	
0-672-30564-X		PowerBuilder Developer's Guide (book/CD)	$49.99	
0-672-30453-8		Access 2 Developer's Guide (book/disk)	$44.95	
0-672-30512-7		DB2 Developer's Guide, Second Edition	$59.99	
0-672-30565-8		FoxPro 2.6 for Windows Developer's Guide, Second Edition (book/disk)	$45.00	
0-672-30496-1		Paradox 5 for Windows Developer's Guide, Second Edition (book/disk)	$49.99	
0-672-30473-2		Client/Server Computing, Second Edition	$40.00	
0-672-30486-4		Rightsizing Information Systems, Second Edition	$40.00	
0-672-30715-4		Teach Yourself Visual Basic in 21 Days, Bestseller Edition	$35.00	
0-672-30173-3		Enterprise Wide Networking	$39.95	
0-672-30440-6		Database Developer's Guide with Visual Basic 3 (book/disk)	$44.95	
0-672-30596-8		Develop A Professional Visual Basic Application in 21 Days (book/CD)	$35.00	
❏ 3 ½" Disk		Shipping and Handling: See information below.		
❏ 5 ¼" Disk		TOTAL		

Shipping and Handling: $4.00 for the first book, and $1.75 for each additional book. Floppy disk: add $1.75 for shipping and handling. If you need to have it NOW, we can ship product to you in 24 hours for an additional charge of approximately $18.00, and you will receive your item overnight or in two days. Overseas shipping and handling adds $2.00 per book and $8.00 for up to three disks. Prices subject to change. Call for availability and pricing information on latest editions.

201 W. 103rd Street, Indianapolis, Indiana 46290

1-800-428-5331 — Orders   1-800-835-3202 — FAX   1-800-858-7674 — Customer Service

Book ISBN 0-672-30700-6

PLUG YOURSELF INTO...

THE MACMILLAN INFORMATION SUPERLIBRARY™

Free information and vast computer resources from the world's leading computer book publisher—online!

FIND THE BOOKS THAT ARE RIGHT FOR YOU!

A complete online catalog, plus sample chapters and tables of contents give you an in-depth look at *all* of our books, including hard-to-find titles. It's the best way to find the books you need!

- ● STAY INFORMED with the latest computer industry news through our online newsletter, press releases, and customized Information SuperLibrary Reports.

- ● GET FAST ANSWERS to your questions about MCP books and software.

- ● VISIT our online bookstore for the latest information and editions!

- ● COMMUNICATE with our expert authors through e-mail and conferences.

- ● DOWNLOAD SOFTWARE from the immense MCP library:
    - Source code and files from MCP books
    - The best shareware, freeware, and demos

- ● DISCOVER HOT SPOTS on other parts of the Internet.

- ● WIN BOOKS in ongoing contests and giveaways!

TO PLUG INTO MCP: →

GOPHER: gopher.mcp.com

FTP: ftp.mcp.com

WORLD WIDE WEB: **http://www.mcp.com**

Using the
Companion Disc

What's on the CD-ROM

The companion CD-ROM contains the author's sample applications, multimedia files, and demos of third-party tools.

Software Installation Instructions

1. Insert the CD-ROM into your CD-ROM drive.
2. From File Manager or Program Manager, choose Run from the File menu.
3. Type **<drive> INSTALL** and press Enter, where **<drive>** corresponds to the drive letter of your CD-ROM. For example, if your CD-ROM is drive D, type **D:INSTALL** and press Enter.
4. Follow the on-screen instructions in the installation program. Files will be installed to a directory named \DEVSYBAS, unless you choose a different directory during installation.

INSTALL creates a Windows Program Manager group named Developing Sybase Applications. This group contains icons for installing and running applications from the CD-ROM. INSTALL also creates a directory on your hard drive named \DEVSYBAS.

Most files are accessed directly from the CD-ROM. This means that you should insert the CD-ROM into your drive before double-clicking on icons in the Program Manager group.